Marketing Planning:
A Global Perspective

Marketing Planning:
A Global Perspective

Svend Hollensen

The *McGraw·Hill* Companies

London   Boston   Burr Ridge, IL   Dubuque, IA   Madison, WI   New York   San Francisco
St. Louis   Bangkok   Bogotá   Caracas   Kuala Lumpur   Lisbon   Madrid   Mexico City
Milan   Montreal   New Delhi   Santiago   Seoul   Singapore   Sydney   Taipei   Toronto

Marketing Planning: A Global Perspective
Svend Hollensen
ISBN-13 9780077104184
ISBN-10 0-07-710418-8

 **Education**

Published by McGraw-Hill Education
Shoppenhangers Road
Maidenhead
Berkshire SL6 2QL
Telephone: 44 (0) 1628 502 500
Fax: 44 (0) 1628 770 224
Website: www.mcgraw-hill.co.uk

British Library Cataloguing in Publication Data
A catalogue record for this book is available from the British Library

Library of Congress Cataloging in Publication Data
The Library of Congress data for this book has been applied for from the Library of Congress

Acquisitions Editor: Mark Kavanagh
Editorial Assistant: Natalie Jacobs/Jane Ashford
Marketing Manager: Marca Wosoba

Text design by Fakenham Photosetting Limited
Cover design by Ego Creative
Printed and bound in the UK by Bell & Bain Ltd.

Brief table of contents

Detailed table of contents

Part 2 Developing the marketing strategy and programme

5 Strategic market planning *88*

6 The segmentation process *119*

7 Marketing mix decisions I: product *153*

Part 3 **Implementing and managing the marketing plan**

Preface

The main purpose of this book is to take the reader through the process of marketing planning, while also providing a detailed explanation of all the concepts and methodologies used in that process.

In addition, a primary aim of this book is to introduce a *modern* and *well-structured* introduction to marketing planning from an academic/student viewpoint. The book's subtitle, 'A Global Perspective', is one example of this more 'modern' approach. All firms (even the smallest) are feeling the influence of the increasing globalization of the industries in which they are operating: their customers are getting bigger (via consolidation in the industry) and more globally oriented. These customers increasingly want to deal with suppliers that can work with customers on a global basis (Global Account Management). At the same time, however, customers also want their suppliers to adapt their marketing plans to the different markets (countries) in which they operate.

Audience for this book

This book aims to target the academic market.

Primary audience

Undergraduate students: second and third year. Such groups could use this book as:

- the main textbook in short specialized courses like 'Marketing', 'Marketing Planning', 'International Marketing Planning' and 'Developing Global Marketing Plans'
- supplementary text in general marketing/marketing management/international marketing courses.

Secondary audience

This audience is likely to comprise:

- marketing practitioners
- others who wish to learn 'how to prepare a marketing plan'.

Key features of this book

Focus on a 'global perspective'

'International/global marketing planning' is treated more extensively in the present volume than in competitor books. Many of the students using this book are likely to go on to have marketing jobs in SMEs (small and medium-sized enterprises), which previously were not concerned with internationalization. However, these SMEs are now facing competition in their home markets from multinational companies, so they are not only competing locally and nationally, but globally as well. This 'global perspective' is also likely to result in cases where a firm's product is sold to several markets at the same time.

Case studies from real companies

Unlike some other marketing planning books, this one contains case studies of real companies. This book (and its accompanying website) also includes references to web resources (market information in certain industries), which students can use as the basis for developing marketing plans. Furthermore, this book deals with the development of the marketing plan in co-operation with other actors (e.g. customers).

Implementing a resource perspective

This book analyses internal competencies as the basis for developing a marketing plan. The resource perspective (inside-out view) is gaining popularity in the marketing literature, but is overlooked by some competitor textbooks (although they all include details of SWOT analysis). The input for the 'SW' part of this analysis, however, comes from this resource perspective. In students' later jobs as marketing planners and co-ordinators it would be a disaster for their firms to consider only external opportunities, without taking any internal restraints into consideration.

Financial consequences

This book offers extensive coverage of the marketing plan's financial consequences, in the form of budgets, financial metrics, and so on.

Academic market

In other books, developing a marketing plan is based on a sort of 'recipe', with few references to other books and articles. This book differs in that it makes many references to books, journal articles, websites, web databases, and so on.

Additional features on companion website

Visit www.mcgraw-hill.com/textbooks/hollensen to access the following valuable supplementary material.

- For students: students can link to any of the online resources listed in the text, and there are also further opportunities to 'click' on to market information from different parts of the world.

- For lecturers: lecturers can access the 'Instructor's Manual' and PowerPoint slides on the password-protected section of the website.

Outline of the book

The three parts into which this book is divided follow the three main steps involved in the marketing planning process:

1 analysis of the internal and external situation

2 developing the marketing strategy

3 implementing and managing the marketing plan.

Figure 1 shows a schematic outline of the book.

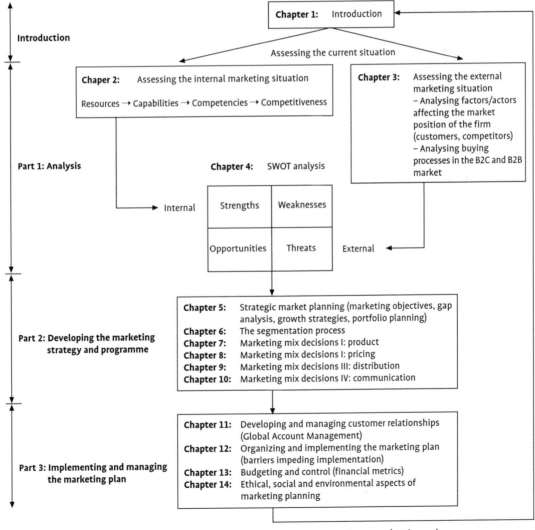

Figure 1

Case studies

A relevant case study appears at the end of each chapter. Table 1 lists these.

Table 1	Overview of case studies		
Chapter	**Case titles/subtitles**	**Company headquarters in following country/ area**	**Geographical target area in the case; target market (B2B/B2C or both)**
1	**Sauer-Danfoss** Marketing planning in the hydraulic OEM business	Germany, Denmark, USA	World B2B
2	**Häagen-Dazs** Revitalizing the brand	USA	World B2C
3	**Toto** Is the American market ready for the Japanese high-tech toilet brand?	Japan	World/USA B2C & B2B
4	**Red Bull** The superstar of energy drinks is seeking new markets	Austria	World B2C
5	**Th!nk Neighbor** Ford's entry into the electric car market	USA	World B2C & B2B
6	**Carlsberg/BBH** Planning for further market share in Eastern Europe and Russia	Baltic region, Denmark	Europe B2C
7	**Vitakraft** Transforming a 'small' German pet food brand into a global player	Germany	World B2C
8	**Braun electric toothbrushes** Is it wise to offer a low-priced battery version of Oral-B?	USA	World B2C
9	**Quicksilver** Choosing distribution channels reprenting a casual lifestyle-driven and board-riding heritage	USA	World B2C
10	**Playtex** The US conglomerate is seeking a foothold in the European lingerie market	USA	Europe B2C
11	**Enercon** Are buyer–seller relationships relevant in the wind turbine (WT) industry?	Germany	World B2B
12	**Bob Martin Company** The UK's leading brand name for pet healthcare is seeking a foothold in Japan	UK	Europe/world B2C
13	**Jordan Toothbrushes** Developing an international marketing control and budget system	Norway	World B2C
14	**Body Shop** Is it an 'ethical' company?	USA	Europe/world B2C & B2B

Guided tour

Learning Objectives

Each chapter opens with a set of learning objectives, summarizing what readers should learn from each chapter.

Figures and tables

Each chapter provides figures and/or tables to help you to visualize the various marketing models, and to illustrate and summarize important concepts.

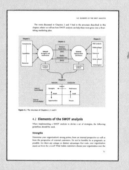

Exhibit boxes

Exhibit boxes, distributed throughout the chapters, contain real-life examples designed to put the material covered into context.

Chapter summary

This briefly reviews and reinforces the main topics you will have covered in each chapter to ensure you have acquired a solid understanding of the key themes.

Questions for discussion

These questions are designed to provoke interesting debates and discussions on the theories and concepts covered in each chapter. They are designed to promote understanding and conceptualization.

References

At the end of each chapter is a references section, which offers sources of alternative and more in-depth information on the topics covered.

Case studies

Each chapter includes its own case study to highlight and clarify the material covered. Each case is accompanied by a set of questions to test understanding.

Technology to enhance learning and teaching

Visit **www.mcgraw-hill.co.uk/textbooks/hollensen** today

Online Learning Centre (OLC)

After completing each chapter, log on to the supporting Online Learning Centre website. Take advantage of the study tools offered to reinforce the material you have read in the text, and to develop your knowledge of marketing in a fun and effective way.

Resources for students include:

- weblinks to market/company information
- marketing planning template
- financial planning template
- MCQ self-test questions
- three additional case studies
- suggested answers to discussion questions.

Also available for lecturers:

- PowerPoint slides
- suggested answers to case study questions
- guidance on teaching using case studies.

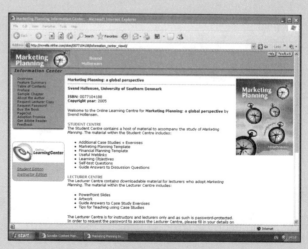

For lecturers: Primis Content Centre

If you need to supplement your course with additional cases or content, create a personalized e-book for your students. Visit www.primis-contentcenter.com or e-mail primis_euro@mcgraw-hill.com for more information.

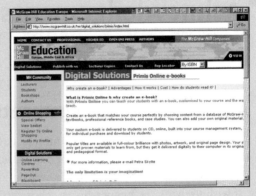

Study Skills

We publish guides to help you study, research, pass exams and write essays, all the way through your university studies.

Visit **www.openup.co.uk/ss/** to see the full selection and get a £2 discount by entering promotional code study when buying online!

Computing Skills

If you'd like to brush up your computing skills, we have a range of titles covering MS Office applications such as Word, Excel, PowerPoint, Access and more.

Get £2 off these titles by entering the promotional code **app** when ordering online at www.mcgraw-hill.co.uk/app.

Acknowledgements

Author's acknowledgements

Writing any book is a long-term commitment and involves time-consuming effort. Its successful completion depends on the support and generosity of many people. The realization of this book is certainly no exception.

I wish to thank the many scholars whose articles, books and other materials I have cited or quoted. It is not, I'm afraid, possible to acknowledge everyone by name.

I also wish to acknowledge the help I have received from the firms highlighted in the case studies, whose managers provided the valuable material that enabled me to write up the cases. I have been in direct personal contact with some of the companies and I thank the managers involved for their very useful comments.

A number of reviewers have been involved in the development of this text, and I would like to thank them for their important and valuable contribution.

I am grateful to my publisher, McGraw-Hill. Throughout the revision of this text, I had the pleasure of working with the editors who have seen this project through to its completion. I would therefore like to thank Acquisitions Editor Mark Kavanagh and Editorial Assistant Natalie Jacobs, and the team behind them, for their encouragement and professionalism in transforming my manuscript into the final book.

I also extend my greatest gratitude to my colleagues at the University of Southern Denmark for their constant help and inspiration.

Finally, I thank my family for their support throughout the writing process. I am pleased to dedicate this edition to Jonna, Nanna and Julie.

Svend Hollensen
Sønderborg, Denmark
May 2005
svend@sam.sdu.dk

Publisher's acknowledgements

Our thanks go to the following reviewers for their comments at various stages in the text's development: Charles Dennis; Johan Janssen; Ray McDowell; Cariona Neary; Kristine Pole; Susan Rennie.

About the author

Svend Hollensen (svend@sam.sdu.dk) is an Associate Professor in Marketing at the University of Southern Denmark (Mads Clausen Institute). He gained practical experience during his job as a marketing co-ordinator in a large Danish multinational enterprise, as well as in his capacity as international marketing manager in a company producing agricultural machinery. In both jobs, he was involved in the development of international marketing plans. Having spent this time in industry he received his PhD in 1992 from Copenhagen Business School.

Part 1

Analysis

Part contents

Introduction

Learning Objectives

After studying this chapter you should be able to:

- understand why marketing planning is so important

- explain the difference between marketing planning and a marketing plan

- explain the difference between goals and objectives

- explore and explain the different stages in developing a marketing plan.

1.1 **Why prepare a marketing plan?**

The purpose of this book is to provide an overview of the structured marketing planning process that contributes to the development of a viable marketing plan. There are some key reasons why marketing planning has become so important. Recent years have witnessed an intensifying of competition in many markets. Many factors have contributed to this, but among some of the more significant are:

- a growth in global competition, as barriers to trade have been lowered and global communications improved

- linked to the above, the role of the multinational conglomerate has expanded; this now disregards geographical and other boundaries and seeks profit opportunities on a global scale

- in some economies, prevailing legislation and political ideologies have served to foster entrepreneurial and 'free market' values

- continual technological innovation, giving rise to new sources of competition for established products and markets.

The importance of competition, and hence competitor analysis, in contemporary strategic marketing cannot be overemphasized. For this reason we shall be looking at this aspect in more depth in later chapters. This importance is now widely accepted among both marketing academics and practitioners. Successful marketing in a competitive economy is about competitive success and that, in addition to a customer focus (a true marketing orientation), also includes competitive positioning.

The marketing concept holds that the key to achieving organizational goals lies in determining the needs and wants of target markets, and delivering the desired 'satisfaction' more effectively and efficiently than competitors (here again the competition aspect comes in).

Marketing planning is an approach adopted by many successful, market-focused businesses. While it is by no means a new tool, the degree of objectivity and thoroughness with which it is applied varies considerably. This book presents a straightforward format for conducting comprehensive marketing analyses, making the most of the resulting marketing intelligence to determine marketing strategies, and for ensuring detailed, actionable marketing programmes are put in place that implement the recommended strategies and achieve the desired marketing results: the ultimate objective of a marketing planning initiative.

Marketing planning can be defined as the structured process of researching and analysing marketing situations, developing and documenting marketing objectives, strategies and programmes, and implementing, evaluating and controlling activities to achieve the objectives. This systematic process enables companies to identify and evaluate any number of marketing opportunities that can serve as paths to the organization's goals, as well as potential threats that might block these paths. In practice, the marketing environment is so changeable that paths to new opportunities can open in an instant, even as others become obscured or completely blocked. Thus, marketing planning must be approached as an adaptable, ongoing process rather than a rigid, annual event designed only to produce a written report.

The outcome of this structured process is the marketing plan, a document that summarizes what the marketer has learned about the marketplace and indicates how the firm plans to achieve its marketing objectives. The marketing plan not only documents the organization's marketing strategies and lists the activities employees will need to implement in order to achieve the marketing objectives, but also shows the mechanisms that will measure progress towards the objectives and allows for adjustment if actual results take the organization off course.

A marketing plan is one of several official planning documents created by a company. These include the business plan, which outlines the organization's overall financial and operational objectives and strategies, and the strategic plan, which discusses the organization's general long-term strategic direction.

Marketing plans generally cover a one-year period, although some (especially those dealing with new products or markets) may project activities and financial performance further into the future. Marketers must start the marketing planning process at least several months before the marketing plan is scheduled to go into operation; this allows sufficient time for thorough research and analysis, management review and revision, and co-ordination of resources among departments and business units.

Like all types of planning, marketing planning concerns the future. It is the approach to the future that is important. The future involves a time dimension, which needs to be clearly specified, and depends on a clear understanding of organizational and market needs.

The avoidance strategy of 'do nothing' achieves little; therefore a planned approach to the future depends on the ability to predict, anticipate, prepare and adapt. Marketing planning means change. It is a process that involves deciding *now* what to do in the *future*, with a full appreciation of the resource position, the need to set clear, communicable, measurable objectives, the development of alternative courses of action, and a means of assessing the best route towards the achievement of specified objectives. Marketing planning is designed to assist the process of marketing decision-making under prevailing conditions of risk and uncertainty.

Above all, the process of marketing planning has a number of benefits, as detailed below.

- **Consistency**: the individual marketing action plan will be consistent with the overall corporate plan and with other departmental or functional plans. It should also be consistent with those of previous years, minimizing the risk of management 'fire-fighting' – that is, incoherent, case-by-case action plans. In this way marketing planning prevents the short-sighted tendency to concentrate all effort on the 'here and now'.

- **Responsibility**: those who have responsibility for implementing the individual parts of the marketing plan will know what their responsibilities are and should

5

have their performance monitored against the plan. Marketing planning requires management staff, collectively, to make clear judgemental statements about assumptions, and it enables a control system to be designed and established whereby performance can be assessed against predetermined criteria.

- **Communication**: those implementing the marketing plan will also know what the overall objectives are, the assumptions that lie behind them and the context for each of the detailed activities.

- **Commitment**: assuming that the plan is agreed upon by those involved in its implementation, as well as by those who will provide the resources, it should stimulate a group commitment to its implementation and ultimately lead to better decision-making.

Plans must be specific to an organization and its current situation. There is not one system of planning but many systems, not one style but many styles, and a planning process must be tailor-made for a particular firm in a specific set of circumstances.

Marketing planning as a functional activity can only work within a corporate planning framework. The marketing planner must not lose sight of the need to achieve corporate-level objectives by means of exploiting product and market combinations. There is an underlying requirement for any organization adopting marketing planning systems to set a clearly defined business mission as the basis from which the organizational direction can develop.

Without marketing planning, it is more difficult to guide research and development (R&D) and new product development (NPD), set required standards for suppliers, guide the sales force in terms of what to emphasize, to whom and what/whom to avoid, set realistic, achievable sales targets, and avoid competitor actions or changes in the marketplace. Above all, businesses that fail to incorporate marketing planning in their marketing activities may not be in a position to develop a sustainable competitive edge in their markets.

1.2 The main stages in developing a marketing plan

Marketing planning is a systematic process involving the assessment of marketing opportunities and resources, the determination of marketing objectives, and the development of a plan for implementation and control.

Marketing planning is an ongoing analysis/planning/control process, or cycle (see Fig. 1.1). Many organizations update their marketing plans annually as new information becomes available. Some companies operate three- or five-yearly planning cycles, some six-monthly. Most common perhaps is an annual revision with a three-year focus. In this way, the marketing plan can include detailed recommendations for the next two years, with extrapolations for the third.

Once incorporated, the key recommendations can then be presented to senior managers within the organization. Companies that are developing marketing plans for the first time are usually relieved to find that the workload reduces year on year, as updating requires less input. Much of the hard work comes in the initiation of marketing planning.

The final task of marketing planning is to summarize the salient findings from the marketing analyses, the strategic recommendations and the required marketing programmes in a short report: the written marketing plan. This document needs to be concise yet complete in terms of presenting a summary of the marketplace and the business's position, explaining thoroughly the recommended strategy and containing the detail of the required marketing mix actions. For many managers, the written plan will be all they glean from the marketing planning activity. It must therefore be informative and to the point, while mapping out a clear set of marketing activities designed to satisfactorily implement the desired target market strategy.

Figure 1.1 illustrates the several stages that have to be proceeded through in order to arrive at a finished marketing plan. Each of the stages illustrated will be discussed in more detail later in this chapter.

As illustrated in Fig. 1.1, the development of a marketing plan is a process, and each step in that process has a structure that enables the marketing plan to evolve from abstract information and ideas into a tangible document that can easily be understood, evaluated and implemented. The following section is devoted to an in-depth discussion of each step in this process (Gilmore *et al.*, 2001; Day, 2002).

Step 1: **mission, corporate goals and objectives**

An organization's mission is an expression of its purpose; it states what the organization hopes to accomplish and how it plans to achieve this goal. This expression of purpose provides management with a clear sense of direction.

The corporate mission statement requires detailed consideration by top management to establish the business the company is really in and to relate this to future business intentions. It is a general statement that provides an integrating function for the business, from which a clear sense of business definition and direction can be achieved. This stage is often overlooked in marketing planning and yet, without it, the plan will lack a sense of contribution to the development of the total business. By deriving a clear mission statement, boundaries for the 'corporate entity' can be conceived in the context of the environmental trends that influence the business.

It is helpful to establish the distinctive competencies of the organization and, in so doing, to focus on what customers are buying rather than on what the company is selling. This will assist in the development of a more marketing-orientated mission statement. A clear mission statement should include the customer groups to be served, the customer needs to be served, and the technologies to be utilized.

The general purpose expressed in the organization's mission statement must be translated into more specific guidelines as to how these universal intentions will operate. Organizations and the people who manage them tend to be more productive when they have established standards to motivate them, specific directions to guide

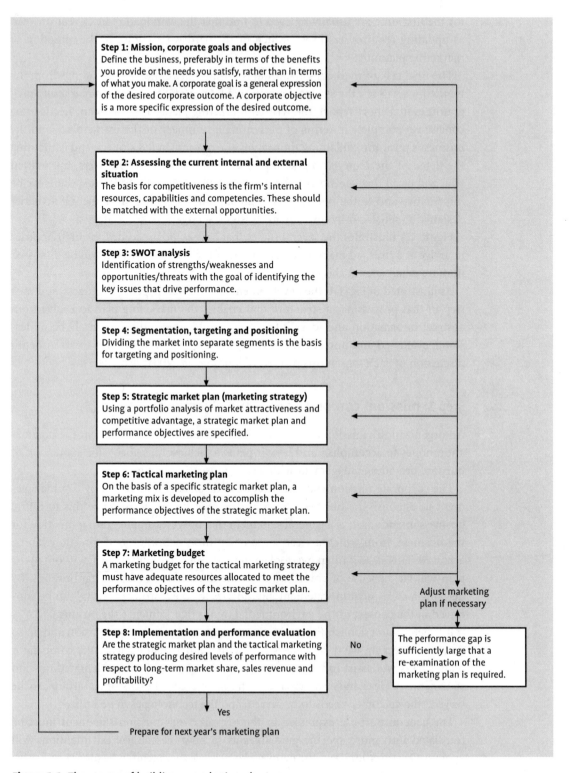

Step 1: Mission, corporate goals and objectives
Define the business, preferably in terms of the benefits you provide or the needs you satisfy, rather than in terms of what you make. A corporate goal is a general expression of the desired corporate outcome. A corporate objective is a more specific expression of the desired outcome.

Step 2: Assessing the current internal and external situation
The basis for competitiveness is the firm's internal resources, capabilities and competencies. These should be matched with the external opportunities.

Step 3: SWOT analysis
Identification of strengths/weaknesses and opportunities/threats with the goal of identifying the key issues that drive performance.

Step 4: Segmentation, targeting and positioning
Dividing the market into separate segments is the basis for targeting and positioning.

Step 5: Strategic market plan (marketing strategy)
Using a portfolio analysis of market attractiveness and competitive advantage, a strategic market plan and performance objectives are specified.

Step 6: Tactical marketing plan
On the basis of a specific strategic market plan, a marketing mix is developed to accomplish the performance objectives of the strategic market plan.

Step 7: Marketing budget
A marketing budget for the tactical marketing strategy must have adequate resources allocated to meet the performance objectives of the strategic market plan.

Adjust marketing plan if necessary

Step 8: Implementation and performance evaluation
Are the strategic market plan and the tactical marketing strategy producing desired levels of performance with respect to long-term market share, sales revenue and profitability?

No

The performance gap is sufficiently large that a re-examination of the marketing plan is required.

Yes

Prepare for next year's marketing plan

Figure 1.1 The stages of building a marketing plan

them and stated achievement levels against which to compare their performance. The terms 'goals' and 'objectives' are defined and used in a variety of ways and often treated as interchangeable concepts. For our purposes, however, the terms 'goals' and 'objectives' have different meanings and uses.

A *goal* is a general and qualitative expression of a desired outcome that provides general guidelines by which management can direct its actions. Goals help identify, clarify and prioritize intended accomplishments, and help bridge the gap between the organization's mission and its objectives by focusing the efforts of the strategic business unit (SBU) management team. By refining and illuminating the mission statement, goals provide more specific direction as to which business opportunities the organization intends to pursue. Marketing goals are the general result the organization hopes to achieve through its marketing efforts. These goals also identify the general focus through which marketing resources will be directed and allocated. Marketing goals, then, are the benchmarks that establish direction for a strategic marketing plan.

In contrast, an *objective* is a specific and quantitative expression of a desired outcome. The corporate objectives of the organization are time dependent and determined to achieve shareholder expectations. These should be derived from the mission statement to ensure integration within a corporate and marketing planning system. Strategy is the means by which objectives are achieved. If objectives specify *what* is to be done, then strategy lays down *how* it is to be done.

In step 5 (see below) we will specify and explain the marketing objectives used in the strategic market plan.

Step 2: **assessing the current internal and external situation**

This situation analysis attempts to address the question 'Where is the organization now?' It encompasses external and internal forces that shape market attractiveness, competitive position and current performance. At the lower level of the planning process, the annual marketing planner has the advantage of the availability of the vast amount of information generated by previous strategic marketing plans. For the marketing planner the issue often becomes one of determining which previously generated information is relevant and applicable to the particular business unit or product line and what new information is needed.

The basis for competitiveness is the firm's internal resources, capabilities and competencies (see Chapter 2); these should be matched with the external opportunities (see Chapter 3). All together, this adds up to step 3: SWOT analysis.

Step 3: **SWOT analysis**

SWOT analysis is critical in summarizing key strengths (S) and weaknesses (W), as well as opportunities (O) and threats (T). The steps that follow will be only as good as the situation analysis and key performance issues that are uncovered in the situation and SWOT analyses.

Perhaps the most difficult and elusive part of a marketing plan is the identification of key performance issues. A key performance issue is a problem or unaddressed opportunity that is an underlying cause, and that limits market or profit performance, or both.

In assessing current situations, SWOT analysis attempts to identify one or more strategic relationships or match-ups between the SBU's current strengths or weaknesses and its present or future opportunities and threats. Organizations must seek out 'strategic windows' in which the key requirements of a market and the particular competencies of the organization best fit together. Identifying these limited time periods is one reason to use SWOT analysis.

Strengths are the bases for building company competencies and, ultimately, competitiveness. An internal organizational scan attempts to ascertain the type and degree of each SBU's strengths and weaknesses. By recognizing their special capabilities and serious limitations, firms are better able to adjust to the external environmental conditions of the marketplace.

'Know yourself and your competence' is the basic tenet that guides this assessment of the abilities and deficiencies of an organization's internal operations. It is also the basic tenet in the so-called Resource Based View (RBV), which will be discussed in Chapter 2.

All businesses have *weaknesses*. Successful businesses try to minimize or conquer their shortcomings. A weakness can be any business function or operation that is not able to resist external forces or withstand attack. A weak business function or operation is one that is deficient or inferior in its ability to reap the benefits presented by an external opportunity. Weaknesses are mostly viewed in comparative terms: a company has a weakness when it is unable to perform a business function or conduct a business operation as effectively and efficiently as its competitors.

The internal factors that may be viewed as strengths or weaknesses, depending upon their impact on the organization's position (they may represent a strength for one organization but a weakness, in relative terms, for another), may include all of the 4Ps (product, price, place (distribution), promotion), as well as personnel, finance, and so on.

The second part of a SWOT analysis involves the organization's external environments. This environmental scanning process represents the opportunities and threats that are part of a SWOT analysis. The external factors, which again may be threats to one organization while offering opportunities to another, may include such matters as technological change, legislation and socio-cultural change, as well as changes in the marketplace or competitive position.

Opportunities are unsatisfied customer needs that the organization has a good chance of meeting successfully. For an environmental occurrence to be considered an opportunity by a particular business, a favourable combination of circumstances must exist. A unique business strength must fit an attractive environmental need in order to create a high probability of a successful match, as when a low-cost producer identifies an unserved market of low-income consumers. Good opportunities are needs that the firm can satisfy in a more complete fashion than can existing competitors. A sustainable competitive advantage is a key determinant in establishing what is and what is not a good opportunity for a particular business.

Threats are hostile aspects of the external environment that could potentially injure the organization.

The following actions suggested by the SWOT matrix are those that might be expected, and provide the strategic marketing manager with some options:

- match strengths and opportunities
- convert weaknesses to strengths
- convert threats to opportunities
- minimize, if not avoid, weaknesses and threats.

SWOT analysis is just one aid to assessing the current situation – it is not the only technique available. It has its weaknesses in that it tends to persuade companies to compile lists rather than to think about what is really important to their business. It also presents the resulting lists uncritically, without clear prioritization, so that, for example, weak opportunities may appear to balance strong threats.

The aim of any SWOT analysis should be to isolate what will be important to the future of the organization and what subsequent marketing planning needs to address.

Step 4: **segmentation, targeting and positioning**

In addition to analysing the overall environment, marketers need to analyse their markets and their customers, whether consumers or businesses. This means looking closely at market share trends, changing customer demographics, product demand and future projections, buying habits, needs and wants, customer attitudes and customer satisfaction. Marketers have to apply their knowledge of the market and customers – acquired through research – to determine which parts of the market, known as segments, should be targeted for marketing activities. This means dividing the overall market into separate groupings of customers, based on characteristics such as age, gender, geography, needs, behaviour or other variables. With today's technology, some companies even build segments that consist of only one customer (at a time). The purpose of segmentation is to group customers with similar needs, wants, behaviour, or other characteristics that affect their demand for or usage of the good or service being marketed.

Once the market has been segmented, the next set of decisions centres on targeting, including whether to market to one segment, to several segments, or to the entire market, and how to cover these segments. The company also needs to formulate a suitable positioning, which means using marketing to create a competitively distinctive place (position) for the brand or product in the mind of targeted customers. This positioning must effectively set the product apart from competing products in a way that is meaningful to customers.

Step 5: **strategic market plan (marketing strategy)**

At this point in the marketing planning process, the company has examined its current situation, looked at markets and customers, set objectives, and identified targeted segments and an appropriate positioning. Now management can create the marketing strategies and tactics that will take the firm down the path towards its customers, working with the basic marketing mix tools of product, place (or distribution), price and promotion, enhanced by service strategies to build stronger customer relationships.

Marketing strategies and programmes must be consistent with the organization's overall corporate goals and objectives. Marketing objectives are essentially about the match between products and markets – what products and services will be in what position in what markets – so they must be based on realistic customer behaviour in those markets. Objectives for pricing, distribution, advertising, and so on, are at a lower level and should not be confused with marketing objectives, although they are part of the marketing strategy needed to achieve marketing objectives.

To be most effective, objectives should be measurable. This measurement may be in terms of sales volume, money volume, money value, market share or percentage penetration of distribution outlets. As it is measured, it can, within limits, be monitored and corrective action taken if necessary. Usually marketing objectives must be based, above all, on the organization's financial objectives; financial measurements are converted into the related marketing measurements. An example of a measurable marketing objective might be 'to enter market X with product Y and capture 15 per cent of the market by value within the first three years'.

In principle, the strategic market plan describes how the firm's marketing objectives will be achieved. It is essentially a pattern or plan that integrates an organization's major goals, policies and action sequences into a cohesive whole. Marketing strategies are generally concerned with the 4Ps:

1 product strategies

    - developing new products, repositioning or relaunching existing ones and phasing out old ones

    - adding new features and benefits

    - balancing product portfolios

    - changing the design or packaging

2 pricing strategies

    - setting the price to skim or to penetrate

    - pricing for different products and market segments

    - deciding how to match competitive pricing

3 promotional strategies

    - specifying the communication platform and media

- deciding the public relations brief
- organizing the sales force to cover new products and services or markets

4 placement (distribution) strategies

- choosing the channels
- deciding levels of customer service.

One aspect of the marketing strategy that is often overlooked is timing. Choosing the best time for each element of the strategy to come into play is often critical. Sometimes, taking the right action at the wrong time can be almost as bad as taking the wrong action at the right time. Timing is, therefore, an essential part of any plan and should normally appear as a schedule of planned activities.

Exhibit 1.1 Global marketing of Masterfoods M&M's

It all started with Frank Mars back in 1911 when he and his wife Ethel started making and selling a variety of buttercream candies from the kitchen of their home in Tacoma, Washington. Working in Europe during the 1930s, it occurred to Forrest Mars (son of Frank) to give chocolate a protective candy coating to stop it from melting. This idea gave birth to M&M's candies, and their success was assured when they were adopted as a staple ration for US forces. Today, Mars is a $14 bn business operating in over 100 countries. Mars, Inc. now operates its three core businesses – snackfood, petcare and main meal food – under the Masterfoods name in most parts of the world. It is one of the world's largest fmcg businesses. Among its brands are M&M's, Mars, Snickers, Bounty, Starburst, Milky Way and Twix.

Forrest Mars Senior had developed his recipe for M&M's chocolate candies having seen soldiers eating pellets of chocolate encased in a sugary coating during the Spanish Civil War. M&M's became widely available to the American public during the 1940s. In 1948, the brown pouch we are familiar with today replaced the original cardboard tube.

As America entered the 1950s, M&M's Chocolate was becoming a household name, particularly with the growth of television. In 1954, M&M's Peanut was introduced to the brand's portfolio, and the sales of both varieties continued to grow. That same year, the universally loved M&M's brand characters and the famous slogan, 'The milk chocolate melts in your mouth, not in your hand', debuted in the brand's initial TV advertising.

In 1960, M&M's Peanut added three new colours to the mix: red, green and yellow joined the original brown. In 1972, the first appearance of the M&M's brand characters on packaging reinforced brand awareness, as they became increasingly well known through print and TV advertising. In 1976, the colour orange was added to the M&M's Peanut mix.

The global characters

As a front runner, Red feels distinctly superior to Yellow and is proud to be a 'Spokescandy' for M&M's. He feels the need to continually remind consumers why he is so special and in his relationship with the other M&M's characters has a tendency to be scheming, attention-seeking and cunning. Red is the undoubted 'leader of the M&M's pack'. The slightly more hapless Yellow feels that, as a peanut, it is his right to be loved for being just what he is. Yellow relies on Red to tell him exactly what to do, and trusts him implicitly. This allows Red to take advantage of Yellow unmercifully, a situation that has existed since Yellow was introduced in late 1954. Despite his hard shell and peanut and chocolate centre, Yellow is at heart a softie.

The characters became a hit with consumers, surpassing the popularity of Mickey Mouse and Bart Simpson (Source: Marketing Evaluation, Inc.). In 1995, over half a century after the candies were introduced, consumers in America helped write a new chapter in the history of the brand with a huge marketing drive. They were asked to vote for a new colour to appear in the M&M's pack. The options available to them included blue, pink, purple or no change – 'no change' won by 54 per cent with over ten million votes cast.

In 1996, the brand introduced M&M's MINIs in re-closable plastic tubes in six different colours. The historic moment of 1997 was the debut of Green, the first female M&M's character. This multifaceted '90s woman and author starred in a number of popular commercials. Green toured the USA promoting her autobiography, *I Melt For No One*, and quickly matched the celebrity status of her male colleagues, Red, Yellow and Blue.

M&M's globalization strategy

Today M&M's is a $3 bn global brand that has secured and retained its dominant market position as number one confectionery brand, through extensive use of global marketing strategies. This strategy has been underpinned with new product developments and strong advertising 'personalities' introduced to the M&M's family.

A global business identifies world markets for its products. Global companies plan and co-ordinate activities on a global basis. By operating in more than one country, benefits from savings or economies on activities such as R&D, marketing, operations and finance are achieved, which may not be available to purely domestic operators. M&M's is an example of a successful global business endeavour.

M&M's global branding has hinged on the deliberate development of distinct personalities or characters for each M&M's colour. Globally recognizable packaging, the 'melts in your mouth, not in your hand' slogan and the distinctive 'M' on each candy all play an important role in the global branding process.

Localization of M&M's global strategy

Localizing the product: it is important to conduct research on the customer's reaction to a new product. Research and development (R&D) is essential in order to adapt to changing market situations and customer needs. Masterfoods Ltd addressed this by refining the M&M's recipe, revamping packaging and introducing a new 'character' for the Irish market. Masterfoods Ltd found that Europeans preferred milk chocolate and this was a factor in the 1998 relaunch of M&M's in Ireland.

Localizing the packaging design: the strategy at relaunch included conducting local research to establish how best to build the M&M's brand to suit the Irish temperament. Packaging was revamped to include the characters of Red and Yellow on the packs. This was a key tool in increasing brand awareness. Using the M&M's characters in everyday situations allowed Irish consumers to relate to both Red and Yellow.

Localizing advertising and promotions: advertising is essential to inform customers that a product is available, to persuade or remind the customer to purchase the product by constantly bringing the product to their attention. To work effectively, a global brand must communicate a cohesive image and message about core brand values to all its consumers. It must stand on an easily recognizable transnational platform but also operate efficiently in a distinctly local environment. M&M's started out as a uniquely American phenomenon; its expansion on to a global stage and into different national markets has been characterized by impactful marketing and advertising, innovative product expansion and highly interactive promotions.

Source: adapted from www.mars.com, www.masterfoods.com, www.business2000.ie

Step 6: **tactical marketing plan**

The next step in the marketing planning process is the development of a tactical marketing plan to put the strategic market plan into effect. Although the overall marketing strategy to protect, grow, reduce focus, harvest, enter or exit a market position is set by the strategic market plan, more specific tactical marketing strategies need to be developed for each of the key performance issues. Each element of a tactical marketing strategy is a specific response to a key performance issue that exists within the context of the market situation.

Therefore, the firm's overall marketing strategies need to be developed into detailed plans and programmes. Although these detailed plans may cover each of the 4Ps, the focus will vary, depending on the organization's specific strategies. A product-orientated company will focus its plans for the 4Ps around each of its products. A market or geographically orientated company will concentrate on each market or geographical area. Each will base its plans on the detailed needs of its customers and on the strategies chosen to satisfy these needs.

The most important element is the detailed plans, which explain exactly what programmes and individual activities will take place over the period of the plan (usually over the next year). Without these specified – and preferably quantified – activities the plan cannot be monitored, even in terms of success in meeting its objectives.

Step 7: **marketing budget**

The classic quantification of a marketing plan appears in the form of budgets. The purpose of a marketing budget is to pull all the revenues and costs involved in marketing together into one comprehensive document. It is a managerial tool that balances what needs to be spent against what can be afforded, and helps in making choices about priorities; it is then used in monitoring the performance in practice. The marketing budget is usually the most powerful tool with which the relationship between desired results and available means can be 'thought through'.

Resources need to be allocated in a marketing budget based on the strategic and tactical market plans. Without adequate resources, the tactical marketing strategies cannot succeed and, as a consequence, performance objectives cannot be achieved.

Specifying a marketing budget is perhaps the most difficult part of the market planning process. Although specifying the budget is not a precise process, there must be a logical connection between the strategy and performance objectives and the marketing budget. Each area of marketing activity should be allocated to centres of responsibility. Indeed, as a key functional area of business the marketing budget is one of the key budgets used to manage the total budgetary control system of the organization. In many organizations, budgeting is the transitional step between planning and implementation, because the budget, and allocated centres within it, will project the cost of each activity over a specified period of time, and also act as a guide for implementation and control.

Step 8: **implementation and performance evaluation**

The best marketing plan is useless without effective implementation. Once strategies and plans are implemented, the company needs to formulate ways to determine effectiveness by identifying mechanisms and metrics that can be used to measure progress towards objectives. Most companies use sales forecasts, budgets, schedules and other tools to set and record standards against which progress can be measured. By comparing actual results against daily, weekly, monthly, quarterly and yearly projections, management can see where the firm is ahead, where it is behind and where it needs to make adjustments to get back on the right path. In the course of reviewing progress, marketers also should look at what competitors are doing, as well as what the markets are doing, so that they can put their own results into context.

To control implementation, marketers should start with the objectives they have set, establish standards for measuring progress towards those targets, measure the performance of the marketing programmes, diagnose the results, and then take corrective action if results fail to measure up. This is the marketing control process. This process is iterative: managers should expect to retrace their steps as they systematically implement strategies, assess results and take action to bring performance in line with expectations. Companies use this control process to analyse their marketing implementation on the basis of measures such as market share, sales, profitability and productivity.

There are three main marketing planning approaches, in terms of involvement of the organization as a whole.

1 **Top-down planning**: here top management sets both the goals and the plan for lower-level management. While decision-making may be quick at the top level, implementation of the plans may not be as speedy because it takes time for various units (division, groups, departments) to learn about the plans and to reorganize their tasks accordingly to accomplish the new goals.

2 **Bottom-up planning**: in this approach, the various organizational units create their own goals and plans, which are then approved (or not) by higher-level management. This can lead to more creative approaches, but it can also pose problems for co-ordination. More pragmatically, strategy all too frequently emerges from a consolidation of tactics.

3 **Goals-down-plans-up planning**: this is the most common approach, at least among the organizations that invest in such sophisticated planning processes. Top management set the goals, but the various units create their own plans to meet these goals. These plans are then typically approved as part of the annual planning and budgetary process.

Summary

Marketing planning is the structured process companies use to research and analyse their marketing situation, develop and document marketing objectives, strategies and programmes, and then implement, evaluate and control marketing activities to achieve their marketing objectives. The marketing plan, which documents the results of the marketing planning process, serves an important co-ordination function by helping to develop internal consensus, providing internal direction, encouraging internal collaboration, co-ordinating resource allocation, and outlining the tasks, timetable and responsibilities needed to achieve the marketing objectives.

There are many benefits to a good marketing plan. The process of market planning can lead a business to the discovery of new market opportunities, to better utilization of assets and capabilities, to a well-defined market focus, to improved marketing productivity and to a baseline from which to evaluate progress towards goals.

The eight broad steps in developing a marketing plan are:

1 mission, corporate goals and objectives

2 assessing the current internal and external situation

3 SWOT analysis

4 segmentation, targeting and positioning

5 strategic market plan (marketing strategy)

6 tactical marketing plan

7 marketing budget

8 implementation and performance evaluation.

The development of a marketing plan involves process and structure, creativity and form. The process begins with a broad view of market opportunities that encourages a wider consideration of many market opportunities. For each market opportunity, a strategic market objective is set, based on market attractiveness and competitive advantage attained or attainable in the market. For each market to be pursued, a separate situation analysis and marketing plan is required. The situation analysis enables the business to uncover key issues that limit performance. These key performance issues are the basic guidelines from which marketing strategies are developed.

With the marketing strategy and budget set, an estimate of market and financial performance metrics must be projected over a specified time frame. If the marketing plan fails to produce desired levels of performance, the marketing strategy needs to be re-examined.

Questions for discussion

1 How could businesses engaged in no market planning or in highly formalized market planning both miss meaningful market insights?

2 What are the differences between marketing objectives and marketing strategies? What should marketing strategies cover?

3 What is the relationship between the mission statement and SWOT analysis? What is the relationship between the mission statement and the firm's objectives?

4 What is the role of SWOT analysis in the marketing planning process? What is the role of key issues in SWOT analysis?

5 Why is the development of a marketing budget so important to the success of the marketing plan?

6 What is the purpose of the performance evaluation? What role should it play in the successful implementation of a marketing plan?

7 In which ways may the whole organization be involved in marketing planning?

References

Day, G.S. (2002) Managing the market learning process. *Journal of Business & Industrial Marketing* 17(4), pp. 240–52.

Gilmore, A., Carson, D. and Grant, K. (2001) SME marketing in practice. *Marketing Intelligence & Planning* 19(1), pp. 6–11.

Case 1 Sauer-Danfoss: marketing planning in the hydraulic OEM business

Sauer-Danfoss, Inc. (www.sauer-danfoss.com) is one of the leading companies worldwide in developing and manufacturing components and integrated hydraulic systems that generate, transmit and control fluid power for mobile equipment. Sauer-Danfoss provides hydraulic systems exclusively for original equipment manufacturers (OEMs) in the fields of agriculture, construction (including road building), lawn and turf, material handling, and speciality vehicles.

Sauer-Danfoss operates in the $12 bn world mobile hydraulics market, which is growing at an annual rate of 4–5 per cent. Today Sauer-Danfoss is number three in the world market after Bosch Rexroth (10 per cent) and Parker (10 per cent). The current worldwide market share of Sauer-Danfoss is around 8 per cent.

Sauer-Danfoss tries to capitalize on four current macro market trends:

1 increased outsourcing of design and production of complex component systems by OEMs

2 rapid replacement and enhancement of mechanical systems by electronics

3 expansion of global presence of OEMs who require global suppliers

4 growing focus of OEMs on reducing their number of suppliers.

The firm's biggest customers include Caterpillar, Case New Holland and Deere & Company. Besides these large global accounts, Sauer-Danfoss also has to take care of minor OEM customers, whose focus is on a specific country or region.

The total product solution Sauer-Danfoss offers its customers can vary, but typically consists of:

- work function pump and motor
- control valves
- propel pump and motor
- power steering
- micro controller
- control joystick and graphic display (in cabin).

Questions

1 How is marketing planning in this business different from a typical B2C marketing situation?

2 Discuss the relevance of Sauer-Danfoss developing relationships with large OEM customers.

Source: adapted from different sources, including www.sauer-danfoss.com

Assessing the internal marketing situation

Learning Objectives

After studying this chapter you should be able to:

- describe the difference between the Market Orientation View (MOV) and the Resource Based View (RBV)

- discuss the connection between MOV/RBV and market driven/market driving

- explain the 'competitive triangle'

- describe and discuss the drivers for customers' 'perceived value' and 'relative costs'.

2.1 Introduction

The foundation of any marketing plan is the firm's mission and vision statement, which answers the question, 'What business are we in and where should we go?' Business mission definition profoundly affects the firm's long-run resource allocation, profitability and survival. The mission statement is based on a careful analysis of benefits sought by present and potential customers, and analysis of existing and anticipated environmental conditions.

When examining internal *strengths* and *weaknesses*, the marketing manager should focus on organizational resources, company or brand image, employee capabilities and available technology.

When examining external *opportunities* and *threats*, the marketing manager must analyse aspects of the marketing environment. This process is called environmental scanning – the collection and interpretation of information about forces, events and relationships in the external environment that may affect the future of the organization or the implementation of the marketing plan. Environmental scanning helps identify market opportunities and threats, and provides guidelines for the design of marketing strategy. The six macro-environmental forces studied most often are social, demographic, economic, technological, political and legal, and competitive. These forces are examined in Chapter 3.

The matching of internal strengths and weaknesses with external opportunities and threats automatically leads us to the two important views we will discuss in this chapter:

1 the Market Orientation View (MOV) – outside-in perspective (see Section 2.2)

2 the Resource Based View (RBV) – inside-out perspective (see Section 2.3).

2.2 Market Orientation View (MOV)

The term market (or marketing) orientation generally refers to the implementation of the marketing concept. Kohli and Jaworski (1990) define market orientation in the following terms:

> A market orientation entails (1) one or more departments engaging in activities geared toward developing an understanding of customers' current and future needs and the factors affecting them, (2) sharing of this understanding across departments, and (3) the various departments engaging in activities designed to meet select customer needs. In other words, a market orientation refers to the organization-wide generation, dissemination, and responsiveness to market intelligence.

One key is achieving understanding of the market and the customer throughout the company, and building the capability for responsiveness to market changes. The real customer focus and responsiveness of the company is the context in which marketing strategy is built and implemented.

Another issue is that the marketing process should be seen as interfunctional and cross-disciplinary, and not simply the responsibility of the marketing department. This is the real value of adopting the process perspective on marketing, which is becoming more widely adopted by large organizations.

In MOV it is also clear that a deep understanding of the competition in the market from the customer's perspective is critical. Viewing the product or service from the customer's viewpoint is often difficult, but without such a perspective a marketing strategy is highly vulnerable to attack from unsuspected sources of competition.

In essence, market orientation refers to the way a firm implements the marketing concept. In principle, this three-component view of market orientation (generation of, dissemination of and responsiveness to market intelligence) makes it possible to diagnose an organization's level of market orientation, pinpoint specific deficiencies and design interventions tailored to the particular needs of an organization. It should be emphasized that a market orientation is not the exclusive responsibility of a marketing department but, rather, is a company-wide mode of operation.

Research suggests that market orientation is related positively to business performance (Narver and Slater, 1990). Further, it is likely to be strongly related to performance under conditions of high market turbulence, technological stability, strong competition and a weak economic environment. A market orientation yields higher customer satisfaction and repeat business, and appears to increase employees' commitment to their organizations. In seeking to implement a market orientation, these authors suggest that the commitment of top management to the idea is key, particularly in reminding employees that it is critical for them to be sensitive and responsive to market developments. In addition, market orientation seems to require a certain level of risk tolerance on the part of senior managers and a willingness to accept an occasional failure as a normal part of transacting business. The nature of interdepartmental dynamics also plays a very important role: interdepartmental conflict reduces market orientation, while interdepartmental connectedness facilitates it. Moreover, the role of market-based reward systems and decentralized decision-making in engendering market orientation is strong, suggesting that reward systems should take into account an individual's ability to sense and respond to market needs. A market orientation flourishes in corporate environments in which continuous learning and improvement are encouraged. Thus the concept of market orientation is likely come to full fruition only when it is enveloped in the learning organization (O'Driscoll *et al.*, 2001).

2.3 **Resource Based View (RBV)**

The traditional market orientation literature emphasizes the superior performance of companies with high-quality, organization-wide generation and sharing of market intelligence leading to responsiveness to market needs; the RBV suggests that high performance strategy is dependent primarily on historically developed resource endowments.

Resource-based marketing essentially seeks a long-term fit between the requirements of the market and the abilities of the organization to compete in it. This does not mean that the resources of the organization are seen as fixed and static. Far from it: market requirements evolve over time and the resource profile of the organization must be continuously developed to enable it to continue to compete, and indeed to enable it to take advantage of new opportunities. The essential factor, however, is that opportunities are seized where the organization has an existing or potential advantage through its resource base, rather than just pursued ad hoc.

Why do organizations exist? The simple answer for commercial organizations may be 'to earn returns on their investments for the shareholders and owners of those organizations'. For non-commercial organizations, such as charities, faith-based organizations, public services, and so on, the answer may lie in the desire to serve specific communities. However, organizations, both commercial and non-profit, are rarely driven by such simple goals. Often there are many demands, sometimes complementary, sometimes competing, that drive decisions.

In the context of commercial organizations a number of primary stakeholders can be identified. These include shareholders and owners, managers, employees, customers and suppliers. While the market-orientated culture (MOV) discussed above serves to place customers high in the priority ranking, the reality for most organizations will be a complex blend of considerations of all relevant stakeholders.

The RBV of the firm discussed above implies that the first stage in assessing strengths and weaknesses should be to conduct an audit of the resources available to the company, including both the tangible and intangible (see Fig. 2.1). The types of resources and capabilities listed earlier can be simplified as follows.

- **Technical resources**: a key resource in many organizations, and one becoming increasingly important in a world of rapidly changing technology, is technical skill. This involves the ability of the organization to develop new processes and products, through research and development, which can be utilized in the marketplace.

- **Financial standing**: a second important resource is the organization's financial standing. This will dictate, to a large extent, its scope for action and ability to put its strategies into operation. An organization of sound financial standing can raise capital from outside to finance ventures. In deciding marketing strategy a major consideration is often what financial resources can or cannot be put into the programme.

- **Managerial skills**: managerial skills in the widest possible sense are a further resource of the organization. The experience of managers and the way in which they discharge their duties and motivate their staff have a major impact on corporate performance.

- **Organization**: the very structure of the organization can be a valuable asset or resource. Some structures, such as the matrix organization, are designed to facilitate wide use of skills throughout the organization. This system has proved useful in focusing control at the brand level, encouraging a co-ordinated marketing mix

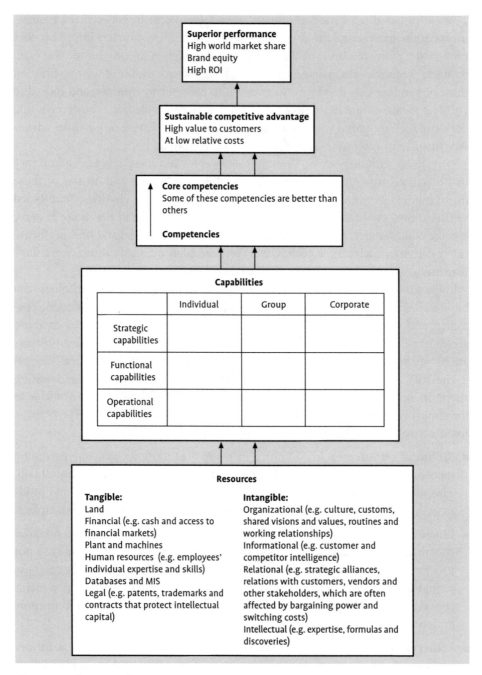

Figure 2.1 The roots of competition

and facilitating a flexible, rapid response to changing circumstances. It is not without its drawbacks, however. The product management system can lead to responsibility without authority, conflicts between product managers within the same organization, and the syndrome where managers move on to their next product management job having maximized short-term returns at the expense of longer-term market position.

■ **Information systems**: the information and planning systems in operation also provide a valuable resource. For example, those organizations such as banks dealing in foreign currency speculation rely heavily on up-to-the-minute and accurate information systems. New technological developments, such as electronic point-of-sale scanning, allow data to be collected and processed in a much shorter time than was the case a few years ago. Those companies with the systems in place to cope with the massive increases in data that such newer collection procedures are creating will be in a stronger position to take advantage of the opportunities afforded.

A resource-based model for sustainable competitive advantage in a global environment is presented in Fig. 2.1. It adopts the basic logic of earlier models that link resources, competitive advantage and performance (Day and Wensley, 1988) but extends this earlier work by demonstrating the richness of the resource pool that is potentially available to a firm operating in a global environment. In the literature generally, resources have been categorized on the basis of barriers to duplication, and a broad distinction is made between assets and capabilities. Assets, in turn, can be thought of as being either tangible or intangible. Tangible assets refer to the fixed or current assets of an organization, which have a relatively long fixed-run capacity and include plant, equipment, land, other capital goods and stocks, debtors, and bank deposits. Intangible assets include a firm's intellectual property, its corporate reputation and its brand equity; these have relatively unlimited capacity and can be used in-house, rented or sold. Capabilities have been described using a variety of terms, including skills, invisible assets and intermediate goods.

Resources are broken down into two fundamental categories:

1 tangible resources

2 intangible resources.

Tangible resources include those factors containing financial or physical value as measured by the firm's balance sheet. Intangible resources, on the other hand, include those factors that are non-physical (or non-financial) in nature and are rarely, if at all, included in the firm's balance sheet.

Intangible resources essentially fall into two categories: assets and skills (or capabilities). If the intangible resource is something that the firm 'has', it is an asset. If the intangible resource is something that the firm 'does', it is a skill and it is being turned into a capability. However, the distinction between assets and capabilities may not be so easy to make.

Intangible assets such as copyrights, patents, registered designs and trademarks are all afforded legal protection through property rights. Such legal protection can create barriers to competitive duplication. Other forms of intellectual property include held-in-secret technology. Held-in-secret technology – technology developed specifically to fit the firm's unique strategy and particular business model – can lead to unique, socially complex and context-specific assets that it may be difficult for competitors to understand let alone duplicate. Given their legally enforceable protection or held-in-secret standing, intellectual property assets are argued to be more difficult to duplicate than tangible resources.

According to Fig. 2.1 capabilities can be seen as strategic, functional or operational.

- **Strategic capabilities** underpin the definition of direction for the firm. They include issues such as the dominant logic or orientation guiding management (which will strongly influence strategic direction), the ability of the organization to learn (to acquire, assimilate and act on information), and the ability of senior managers to manage the implementation of strategy.

- **Functional capabilities** lie in the execution of functional tasks. These include marketing capabilities, financial management capabilities and operations management capabilities.

- **Operational capabilities** are concerned with undertaking individual line tasks, such as operating machinery, the application of information systems and completion of order processing.

Second, capabilities may lie with individuals, with groups or at the corporate level.

- **Individual competencies** are the skills and abilities of individuals within the organization. They include the ability of the individual to analyse critically and assess a given situation (whether this is a CEO assessing a strategic problem or the shop floor worker assessing the impact of a machine failure).

- **Group competencies** are where individual abilities come together in teams or ad hoc, informal, task-related teams. While the abilities of individuals are important, so too is their ability to work together constructively.

- **Corporate-level competencies** relate to the abilities of the firm as a whole to undertake strategic, functional or operational tasks. This could include the ability of the firm to internalize learning, so that critical information is not held just by individuals but is shared throughout the firm.

There is always a risk that such lists are arbitrary and simplistic when we come to study a real organization, but perhaps the most fundamental importance of the RBV of the firm is that it underlines the fact that many important resources and capabilities are created through company history; they are the result of enduring accumulation and learning processes. Often they cannot be changed easily or rapidly. This approach should enrich our understanding of a company's potential in the marketplace, and can be linked to the issue of market orientation through the competitive positioning of the firm (i.e. choice of market targets and pursuit of competitive advantage).

The RBV can also be linked to the core competencies issue considered below. They are different approaches to a similar issue – understanding what a company is capable of achieving by exploiting its capabilities in the marketplace. In recent years much attention has been devoted to identifying and understanding the 'core competencies' of organizations. The need to identify the 'distinctive competency' of a company is underlined by a very influential analysis of successful international businesses by Prahalad and Hamel (1990), who argue that a company is likely to be genuinely world class at perhaps five or six activities, and superior performance will come from focusing on those to the exclusion of others. The late 1990s saw much effort to refocus major organizations on to their core activities.

Prahalad and Hamel (1990) define core competencies as the underlying skills, technologies and competencies that can be combined in different ways to create the next generation of products and services:

- at 3M a core competency in sticky tape has led the company into markets as diverse as Post-it notes, magnetic tape, photographic film, pressure-sensitive tapes and coated abrasives
- Black & Decker's competency is in small electrical motors, which can be used to power many tools and appliances
- for Canon the core competencies are its skills and technologies in optics, imaging and microprocessor controls, which have enabled it to survive and thrive in markets as diverse as copiers, laser printers, cameras and image scanners.

Three tests are suggested by Prahalad and Hamel for identifying core competencies.

1 A core competency should be *difficult for competitors to copy*. Clearly a competency that can be defended against competitors has greater value than a competency that other companies can share.

2 A core competency provides *potential access* to a wide variety of markets. Competencies in display systems are needed, for example, to enable a company to compete in a number of different markets, including flat-screen TVs, calculators, laptop or notebook computers, mobile phones, and so on.

3 A core competency should make a *significant contribution* to the benefits the customer derives from using the ultimate product or service. In other words, the competency is important where it is a significant determinant of customer satisfaction and benefit.

Note that these requirements are essentially the same as those emerging from the earlier RBV literature to define resources capable of creating sustainable competitive advantage. Added to these three characteristics a further useful test is whether the competency can be combined with other skills and capabilities to create unique value for customers – the grouping of competencies discussed earlier. It could be, for example, that a competency does not fulfil the above criteria, but when combined with other competencies is an essential ingredient in defining the firm's uniqueness. Put another way: what would happen if we did not have that competency?

Prahalad and Hamel (1990) argue that the critical management ability for the future will be to identify, cultivate and exploit the core competencies that make growth possible. The argument about core competencies is compelling, and (according to Prahalad and Hamel) it is certainly driving major corporate changes, such as:

- the emergence of a network of strategic alliances, where each partner brings its core competency into play to build a market offering
- the demerger and sale of non-core activities and brands
- organizational changes away from SBUs and towards a new 'strategic architecture'.

However, we should bear in mind that strategy is about more than simply choosing to focus on a few core competencies (Porter, 1985).

It is very easy to be impressed with excellence in the way a company performs an activity or produces a product or service, and to believe this to be a core competency. This must be tested against the market before we accept it as a foundation for our competitive positioning. It may be helpful to identify core competencies but then to see which of them are 'differentiating capabilities' (i.e. which produce competitive advantage).

Activities are not the same as competencies: 'quality products' and 'marketing strength' are not competencies, they are attributes emerging from core competencies. In the 1980s General Electric focused on marketing to build a strong brand image but lost out to Panasonic (Matsushita), which understood that excellence in components and assembly had a greater impact on value added for the customer. Honda's core competency is in small engine manufacture. It has moved from an initial position in motorcycles and transferred its small engine expertise into small cars, pumps, lawnmowers and other products where engines are the significant value-added element.

Avoid lists: by definition, core competencies should be no more than a handful of activities. Most successful companies have targeted one or two key activities – their identification is a major management issue.

Achieve management consensus: if competencies are to be nurtured and shared widely in the organization as the basis for strategy, then management must agree what they are and act accordingly. It was noted earlier that this might not be straightforward.

Leverage core competencies: it is not enough to identify core competencies and agree what they are. This is pointless unless they underpin all strategic decision-making.

Share core competencies outside the organization: focusing on core competencies may well favour the use of collaboration to link to the value-adding competencies of other companies. Indeed it may be logical for companies to share their specialist expertise with others, a good example being the automotive sector. A similar approach is seen in the intra-firm transfer of best practices.

As shown in the upper part of Fig. 2.1, sustainable competitive advantage is one thing that cannot be copied by the competition. Dell Computer is a good example of a company that has a sustainable competitive advantage. Others include Rolex (high-quality watches), Nordstrom department stores (service) and Ryanair (low price).

2.4 Market driven versus market driving

The market-driven approach is derived from the construct and principles of 'market orientation' that are in many ways synonymous with 'market driven'. However, instead of *following* the requests of the customer and adapting offerings, organizations sometimes need to undertake a more proactive approach in order to reshape, educate and lead the customer or, more generally, the market. Academicians define this kind of orientation as 'driving market' or 'market driving'.

The primary differences between a market-driving philosophy and the existing paradigms of market-driven behaviour, customer leading and product pioneering are summarized in Table 2.1.

Table 2.1 Market-driven versus market-driving perspectives

	Market driven	Market driving
General	Firm responds to acts within the framework and constraints of existing market structure and characteristics	Firm can and will act to induce changes in the market structure and changes in the behaviours of the players (customers and competitors)
Customer orientation	Adaptation	Be at the cutting edge of new customer needs
Identifying, analysing and answering to the customer	■ Predict which technologies are likely to be successful given consumer needs and preferences ■ Respond to market structure	■ Shape customers' behaviour proactively ■ Pioneer ■ Predict how customer needs and market boundaries evolve with various technological futures
Competitor orientation	■ Continuous benchmarking ■ Imitating	■ Shape the market structure proactively ■ Identify and develop difficult-to-imitate internal and external competencies ■ Discontinuous disruption

As previously suggested, market-driven behaviour relies heavily on exploitative learning, which occurs within *existing* market boundaries, and hence is primarily regarded as a reactive rather than a proactive stance. The customer-leading philosophy, also known as proactive market orientation, is essentially an extension of market-driven activity. Customer leading makes use of the untapped market space uncovered by exploratory learning. Firms utilizing this approach are more likely to introduce innovations that radically change customer behaviours and preferences.

Two contributions have recently been put forward that focus on internal and external market-driving issues. First, Jaworski *et al.* (2000) discuss how market driving may be achieved through influencing the fundamental structure of a market and/or the behaviours of key players. Second, Kumar *et al.* (2000) advance an analysis of intra-firm behaviours that facilitate market driving. These two contributions require further discussion.

Jaworski *et al.* (2000) were among the first to initiate the market-driving approach based on the consideration that the current literature has an unbalanced focus on preserving the status quo (that is, on existing customer attribute preferences and current market structure). Jaworski *et al.* (2000) focus their analysis on the strategic business unit level and construct a conceptual framework through plotting the market orientation approach against two dimensions of market structure and market behaviour.

Figure 2.2 Market driven vs. market driving strategy

A market-driven approach occurs where market behaviour and structure are 'given' (that is, where existing market structures and behaviours are accepted by the firm). However, market driving is possible when firms 'shape' market structure through altering the composition of market players and/or when organizations 'shape' market behaviour through varying the behaviour of market players – for example, shaping customer behaviour by identifying, advancing and exploiting customer-valued product attributes previously overlooked by other players (see Fig. 2.2).

A market-driven approach is defined as 'the activities of learning, understanding, and responding to stakeholder perceptions and behaviours within a given market structure', while a market-driving approach is defined as 'changing the composition and/or roles of players in a market and/or the behaviour(s) of players in the market' (Jaworski *et al.*, 2000: 45). Market driving is argued to be a 'multiplicative function', with those firms that influence more players or affect market structure more significantly being viewed as *more* market driven. In this respect, market-driving approaches are similar to market-driven approaches in that they are presented as a continuous variable.

Exhibit 2.1 **Reuters' core competency is eroded**

Reuters is a 151-year-old British institution which is experiencing some difficulties. The group, best known as the world's biggest international news and television agency, makes more than 90 per cent of its revenue from the financial services business, to which it provides its trademark data-packed screens. The 2002–2003 downturn in banking and finance hit Reuters hard. Meanwhile, US rival Bloomberg and Canadian player Thomson Financial have both eaten into Reuters' 'core competency' as the most authoritative source of information for business. Consequently, in February 2003 Reuters announced that it planned to cut 3000 jobs over the next three years.

Suddenly, Reuters' brand value, which most companies would kill for – a 151-year heritage, a voice of authority, a solid Britishness – has begun to appear detrimental. Tradition seems like stuffiness, authority like inertia and Britishness like a colonial hangover.

How, then, should Reuters go about redefining its business and its own competencies?

Source: adapted from Chandiramani (2003)

2.5 **Major sources of competitive advantage: value and costs**

Companies producing offerings with a higher perceived value and/or lower relative costs (compared to competitors) are said to have a competitive advantage and thus win the competitive game. The 'high perceived value' advantage can be considered as differentiation, but the elements of this must be evaluated from a comparative customer perspective. The word 'perceived' is used to emphasize the fact that value is a subjective evaluation rather than a direct measure of utility. This involves an element of judgement and is sometimes seen as irrational: it is how customers themselves rate the offering in relation to other competitive products or services that is critical in a purchase decision.

The prime consideration of the value of any resource to an organization lies in the answer to the question 'Does this resource contribute to creating value for customers?' Value creation may be direct, such as through the benefits conveyed by superior technology, better service, meaningful brand differentiation and ready availability. The resources that contribute to these benefits (technology deployed, skilled and motivated personnel, brand name and reputation, and distribution coverage) create value for customers as soon as they are employed. Other resources may, however, have an indirect impact on value for customers. Effective cost control systems, for example, are not valuable to customers in and of themselves. They add value for customers only when they translate into lower prices charged, or via the ability of the organization to offer additional customer benefits through the cost savings achieved.

The value of a resource in creating customer value must be assessed relative to the resources of competitors. For example, a strong brand name such as Nike on sportswear may convey more value than a less well-known brand. In other words, for the resource to contribute to sustainable competitive advantage it must serve to distinguish the organization's offerings from those of competitors (Hooley *et al.*, 2004). The 'value' of a product or service should be seen in relation to the customer's cost of obtaining the product/service and the cost of ownership.

These costs will include such issues as the buying price of an offering compared to the price of a competitive offering. These elements might be modified by the perceived cost of obtaining and cost of ownership. The way components are assessed and compared could vary from one customer to another. It is possible to 'delight' customers by exceeding their expectations.

The 'perceived value' (compared to price), together with the relative cost, is illustrated in Fig. 2.3. The underlying drivers for 'perceived value' (value drivers) are also listed in this figure. These drivers are discussed in more detail below.

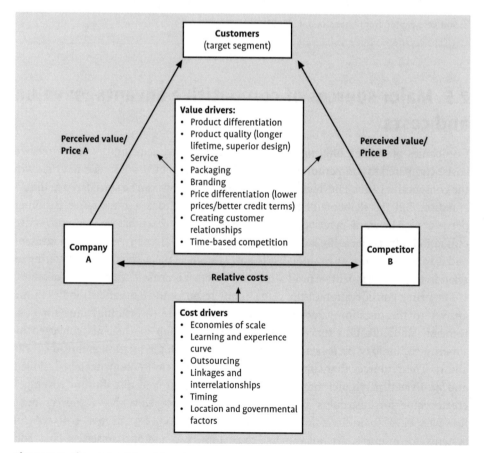

Figure 2.3 The competitive triangle

Cost drivers

Economies of scale

Economies of scale are perhaps the single most effective cost driver in many industries. Scale economies stem from doing things more efficiently or differently in volume. In addition, sheer size can help in creating purchasing leverage to secure cheaper and/or better-quality (i.e. less waste) raw materials and securing them in times of limited availability.

There are, however, limits to scale economies. Size can bring with it an added complexity that can lead to diseconomies. For most operations there is an optimum size above and below which inefficiencies occur.

The effects of economies of scale are often more pronounced in the manufacturing sector than in services. While manufacturing operations such as assembly lines can benefit through scale, the advantages to service firms such as advertising agencies are less obvious.

Capacity utilization has been shown to have a major impact on unit costs. The PIMS (profit impacts of marketing strategies) study has demonstrated a clear positive association between utilization and return on investment.

Learning and experience curves

Further cost reductions may be achieved through learning and experience effects. *Learning* refers to increases in efficiency that are possible at a given level of scale through an employee having performed the necessary tasks many times before.

Experience curves tell us that costs decline at a predictable rate as experience with a product increases. The experience curve effect encompasses a broad range of manufacturing, marketing and administrative costs. Experience curves reflect learning by doing, technological advances and economies of scale. Firms like Airbus and Texas Instruments use historical experience curves as a basis for prediction and setting prices. Experience curves allow management to forecast costs and set prices based on anticipated costs as opposed to current costs.

The Boston Consulting Group (BCG) extended the experience curve beyond manufacturing and looked at the increased efficiency that was possible in all aspects of the business (e.g. in marketing, advertising and selling) through experience. BCG estimated empirically that, in many industries, costs reduced by approximately 15–20 per cent each time cumulative production (a measure of experience) doubled. This finding suggests that companies with larger market share will, by definition, have a cost advantage through experience, assuming that all companies are operating on the same experience curve. This is, incidentally, why relative market share is used as a proxy for cash generation in the BCG matrix.

Experience can be brought into the company by hiring experienced staff, and be enhanced through training. Conversely, competitors may poach experience by luring away skilled staff.

Outsourcing

Labour cost can be an important component of total costs in low-skill, labour-intensive industries such as product assembly and apparel manufacturing. Many US and European manufacturers outsource production activities to Mexico, eastern Europe and China in order to achieve cheaper manufacturing costs. Increasing numbers of companies are also outsourcing activities such as software programming and other labour-intensive jobs to India.

Linkages and interrelationships

External linkages with suppliers of factor inputs or distributors of the firm's final products can also result in lower costs. Recent developments in just-in-time (JIT) manufacturing and delivery can have a significant impact on stockholding costs and work in progress. Beyond the cost equation, however, the establishment of closer working links has far wider marketing implications. For JIT to work effectively requires a very close working relationship between buyer and supplier. This often means an interchange of information, a meshing of forecasting and scheduling, and the building of a long-term relationship. This in turn helps to create high switching costs (the costs of seeking supply elsewhere) and hence barriers to competitive entry.

Interrelationships with other SBUs in the overall corporate portfolio can help to share experience and gain economies of scale in functional activities (such as marketing research, R&D, quality control, ordering and purchasing).

Timing

Timing, though not always controllable, can lead to cost advantages. Often the first mover in an industry can gain cost advantages by securing prime locations, cheap or good-quality raw materials and/or technological leadership. Second movers can often benefit from exploiting newer technology to leapfrog first-mover positions.

Location and governmental factors

The final cost drivers are location (geographic location to take advantage of lower distribution, assembly, raw materials or energy costs) and institutional factors such as government regulations (e.g. larger lorries on the roads can reduce distribution costs but at other environmental and social costs). The sensitivity of governments to lobbyists and pressure groups will dictate the ability of the company to exercise institutional cost drivers.

Sometimes, governments may provide assistance to target industries with grants and interest-free loans. Government assistance enabled Japanese semiconductor manufacturers to become global leaders.

Value drivers

Product differentiation

Product differentiation seeks to increase the value of the product or service to the customer. Levitt (1986) suggested four levels of a product: core offer, expected offer, augmented offer and potential offer. Differentiation is possible at all four levels.

Core offer (basic offering)

A different way of satisfying the same basic want or need. It is typically created by a change in the technology, the application of innovation.

Expected offer

Additional benefits normally provided with the core offer. This often involves improvements on expected features such as warranties, packaging quality or service (e.g. it could mean offering a lifetime guarantee on audiotape, as Scotch did).

Augmented offer

Additional benefits not normally provided, but serving to differentiate from competitors' offers. These could be credit facilities, additional features, branding, delivery, and so on.

Potential offer

Anything else that could (in future) be used to differentiate from existing competitors' offerings. These features can, potentially, attract and hold customers.

In most highly competitive markets, any breakthrough or development is soon spotted and often copied quickly, and many skill-based augmentations are easy for competitors to imitate. For this reason, many advantages last for only a very short period of time. If an advantage is offset by a competitor, what was once an augmentation by one supplier can become an expected feature demanded from all suppliers. This illustrates one aspect of migration between the levels of a total product. Thus, a continuing migration might take place, with features moving in from the outer to the inner ring of Fig. 2.4.

Product quality and service

For manufactured products, quality can include durability, product features and superior design. For services it often comes down to the tangible elements of the service, the reliability and responsiveness of the service provider, promptness, assurance provided, and the empathy and caring attention (willingness to help) demonstrated.

For a marketer it will be obvious that quality (satisfying customer needs) is a *necessary* objective, but it may not be *sufficient* to gain a sale or ensure repeat business. There will be certain levels of quality that are expected as 'order qualifying'. These have to be met in order to be considered in the marketplace, but this is the minimum acceptable level and does nothing to contribute towards achieving a competitive advantage. As discussed in previous chapters, customers will assess the comparative value of competitive offerings and will decide based on their own perceptions and personal frames of reference.

Quality programmes that lead towards the delivery of 'superior' customer value are the only ones that really count. These could be the result of including real tangible and intangible features that enhance the benefits of the offering. The ultimate test,

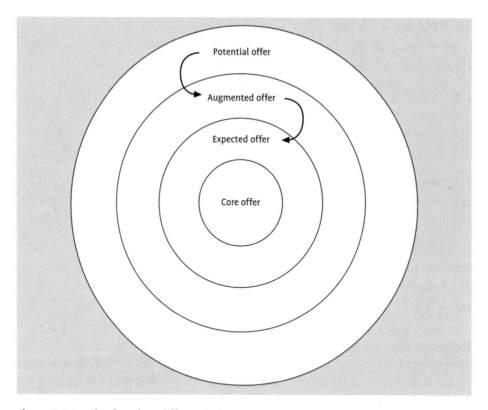

Figure 2.4 Levels of product differentiation

however, is the perception by a customer that an offering not only meets their needs, but also does so in a way that offers the greatest *added* value to them.

It is important, too, to remember that a quality programme of service delivery cannot save a poor product. While the activities that surround the promotion of an offering can sometimes dominate at the point of sale, the true test is whether the product/service meets the customer's basic needs, both current and over the life of the product. This will be the ultimate test and will be remembered long after the clever advertising of the low price is forgotten (Adcock, 2000).

Packaging

Packaging can also be used to differentiate a product. Packaging has five main functions, each of which can be used as a basis for differentiation (Adcock, 2000).

1 Packaging *protects* the product during transit and prior to consumption to ensure consistent quality (e.g. the use of foil packs for potato crisps to ensure freshness).

2 Packaging *stores* the product, and hence can be used to extend shelf life or facilitate physical storage (e.g. tetra packs for fruit juice and other beverages).

3 Packaging *facilitates use* of the product (e.g. applicator packs for floor cleaners, wine boxes, domestic liquid soap dispensers).

4 Packaging helps *create an image* for the product through its visual impact, quality of design, illustration of uses, etc.

5 Packaging helps *promote* the product through eye-catching, unusual colours and shapes, etc.

Branding

A brand name is an indication of what to expect from a product – a quality statement of a value-for-money signal. It is often the feeling among managers that the ability of most companies to copy the tangible aspects of competitors' actions, such as production method or application of technology, and to replicate service levels will mean that these offer little in the way of sustainable competitive advantage.

A brand, however, is an intangible, which develops out of exchanges with customers, and is impossible for competitors to copy. Therefore, it is able to distinguish a specific offer, separating it from others in the same product class. If branding is considered from the perspective of a potential customer it can be seen as a way of helping buyers to choose between different offerings and to determine those that best meet given needs. The ability to identify a particular brand thus makes the purchase decision quicker and easier, and offers some reassurance by reducing the risk of unfamiliar selection.

A sustainable competitive advantage is a function of the speed with which competitors can imitate a leading company's strategy and plans.

The rate of technological and market change is now so fast and products so transient that customers find security and continuity in the least tangible of the company's assets: the reputation of its brands and company name.

Price differentiation

Lower price as a means of differentiation can be a successful basis for strategy only when the company enjoys a cost advantage or where there are barriers to competing firms with a lower cost structure competing at a lower price. Without a cost advantage a price war can be a disastrous course to follow. Premium pricing is generally only possible where the product or service has actual or perceived advantages to the customer and therefore is often used in conjunction with or to reinforce a differentiated product. In general, the greater the degree of product or service differentiation the more scope there is for premium pricing. Where there is little other ground for differentiation, price competition becomes stronger and cost advantages assume greater importance.

Creating customer relationships

Creating closer bonds with customers through enhanced service can help establish a position in the market that is easier to defend. As suggested above, a major advantage of JIT manufacturing systems is that they require closer links between supplier and buyer. As buyers and suppliers become more enmeshed so it becomes more difficult for newcomers to enter.

Creating switching costs (the costs associated with moving from one supplier to another) is a further way in which customer linkages can be enhanced. This enhancement of linkages with customers makes it less likely they will shop around for other sources of supply.

Time-based competition

Competitive advantage and how one gains it have changed much over the years. In less-developed markets advantage can be gained through simple market mechanisms such as achieving distribution where none existed before. As markets mature, competitive advantage becomes increasingly difficult to attain. Many factors contribute to this, including increases in the sophistication of competitors and consumers, consumer mobility, distribution intensity, and flow of product and market information. At a macro level, such things as the structural nature of industries, networking, alliances and governmental interventions contribute to difficulties in achieving competitive advantage in a mature market.

In essence, time-based competition focuses on gaining advantage by being faster than competitors – faster in responding to market changes, faster with new product development and introductions, faster in integrating new technology into products, and faster in distribution and customer service. Success stories of time-based competitors are numerous; for example, the Japanese used time-based competition as a fundamental component of their automobile manufacturing strategy, which caught US firms off guard. Japanese auto manufacturers reduced new car design time to two and a half to three years as compared to Detroit's four to over six years. Being twice as fast resulted in the Japanese having fresher designs that embodied more current and sophisticated technology.

The fundamental ingredients of time-based competition are low-cost variety and fast response time. Companies using this strategy concentrate on compressing the time required to manufacture and distribute their products and cutting the time required to develop and introduce new products. By doing this companies can offer a broader product line, cover more market segments and rapidly increase the technological sophistication of their products. The benefits of these practices can be generically expressed as gains in faster *response time*.

In essence, time-based competition is a customer-focused strategy. Speed and variety are the means by which a company can do more for its clients. However, succeeding at this requires a co-ordinated company effort. A time-based competitor develops the high degree of internal responsiveness and co-ordination among different parts of the company that allows it to discern differences among key customers and customize the products and services delivered to each. Thus, the ultimate purpose of the time-based competitor is not maximizing speed and variety, but owning the customer (Stalk and Hout, 1990; Johnson *et al.*, 2000).

Summary

The essence of Chapter 2's internal analysis is competitive advantage. Over time, as markets have developed and evolved, achieving competitive advantage has required an increasingly sophisticated response. Decades ago competitive advantage could be achieved through one product or market variable such as price or distribution control. Today, competitive advantage has taken on a multidimensional character – effective competitive advantage requires a co-ordinated combination of several product and market variables. Further, potential ingredients in competitive advantage have broadened to include such intangibles as time and information.

Companies need to build their own competitive advantages rather than copy those of a competitor. The sources of tomorrow's competitive advantages are the skills and assets of the organization. Assets include patents, copyrights, locations, and equipment and technology that are superior to those of the competition. Skills are functions such as customer service and promotion that the firm performs better than its competitors.

Each of the activities within the value chain, the primary activities and the support functions, can be used to add value to the ultimate product or service.

The traditional Market Orientation View (MOV), or the outside-in perspective, emphasizes the customers and places their needs and wants high in the priority ranking.

Termed the Resource Based View (RBV), or the inside-out perspective, of the firm or the focus on 'core competencies', this new approach suggests that performance is essentially driven by the resource profile of the organization and that the source of superior performance lies in the possession and deployment of distinctive, hard-to-imitate or protected resources.

Compared to its competitors the company that is producing offerings with a higher perceived value (compared to the price) and/or lower relative costs is said to win the 'competitive game'.

The drivers for a better relative cost position are:

- economies of scale (high volume)

- learning and experience curve

- outsourcing

- linkages and interrelationships

- timing

- location and governmental factors.

The drivers for a better 'perceived value' position are:

- product differentiation (more features)

- product quality (longer lifetime, superior design)

- service
- packaging
- branding
- price differentiation (lower prices/better credit terms)
- creating customer relationships
- time-based competition.

Questions for discussion

1 Explain the difference between the RBV and the MOV.

2 What does it mean to be 'market driven' or 'market driving'?

3 List the major sources for creating organizational competitiveness.

4 Explain the idea behind the 'competitive triangle'.

5 Which are the main value and cost drivers in the 'competitive triangle'?

References

Adcock, A. (2000) *Marketing Strategies for Competitive Advantage*. Chichester: Wiley.

Chandiramani, R. (2003) What must Reuters do to battle leaner rivals? *Marketing*, 27 February, p. 13.

Day, G. and Wensley, R. (1988) Assessing advantage: a framework for diagnosing competitive superiority. *Journal of Marketing* 52, April, pp. 1–20.

Hooley, G., Saunders, J. and Piercy, N. (2004) *Marketing Strategy and Competitive Positioning*, 3rd edn. Financial Times/Prentice Hall.

Jaworski, B., Kohli, A. and Sahay, A. (2000) Market-driven versus driving markets. *Journal of Academy of Marketing Science* 28(1), pp. 45–54.

Johnson, J., Busbin, J. and Bertsch, T. (2000) Uses and repercussions of the Internet on global market entry strategies. *Journal of Global Competitiveness*, American Society for Competitiveness, Spring, pp. 5–15.

Kohli, A.K. and Jaworski, B.J. (1990) Market orientation: the construct, research propositions, and managerial implications. *Journal of Marketing* 54, April, pp. 1–18.

Kumar, N., Scheer, S. and Kotler, P. (2000) From market driven to market driving. *European Management Journal* 18(2), pp. 129–41.

Levitt, T. (1986) *The Marketing Imagination*. New York, NY: Free Press.

Narver, J.C. and Slater, S.F. (1990) The effect of market orientation on business profitability. *Journal of Marketing* 54, October, pp. 20–35.

O'Driscoll, A., Carson, D. and Gilmore, A. (2001) The competence trap: exploring issues in winning and sustaining core competence. *Irish Journal of Management* 22(1), pp. 73–90.

Porter, M.E. (1985) *Competitive Advantage.* New York, NY: Free Press.

Prahalad, C.K. and Hamel, G. (1990) The core competence of the corporation. *Harvard Business Review*, May–June, pp. 79–91.

Stalk, G. Jr and Hout, T.M. (1990) *Competing against Time: How Time-based Competition is Reshaping Global Markets.* New York, NY: Free Press.

Case 2 Häagen-Dazs: revitalizing the brand

The idea for Häagen-Dazs dates back to the early 1920s. Reuben Mattus, a young entrepreneur with a passion for quality and a vision for creating the finest ice cream, worked in his mother's ice cream business selling fruit ice and ice cream pops from a horse-drawn wagon in the bustling streets of the Bronx, New York. To produce the finest ice cream available, he insisted on using only the finest, purest ingredients.

The family business grew and prospered throughout the 1930s, 1940s and 1950s, and, by 1961, Mattus had decided to form a new company dedicated to his ice cream vision. He called his new brand Häagen-Dazs, to convey an aura of the old-world traditions and craftsmanship to which he remained dedicated.

Häagen-Dazs started out with only three flavours: vanilla, chocolate and coffee. But Mattus's passion for quality soon took him to the four corners of the globe. His unique ice cream recipes included dark chocolate from Belgium and hand-picked vanilla beans from Madagascar, creating distinctive and indulgent taste experiences.

The Häagen-Dazs brand quickly developed a loyal consumer base. Its early success was created by word of mouth and praise. Without the benefit of advertising the story of this incredibly rich and creamy confection spread rapidly. At first, it was only available at gourmet shops in New York City, but soon distribution expanded throughout the east coast of the USA, and by 1973 Häagen-Dazs products were enjoyed by discerning customers throughout the United States. Then, in 1976, Mattus's daughter Doris opened the first Häagen-Dazs café. It was an immediate success, and its popularity led to a rapid expansion of Häagen-Dazs shops across the USA.

In 1983, Mattus agreed to sell Häagen-Dazs to The Pillsbury Company, which remained committed to the tradition of superior quality and innovation on which Häagen-Dazs had been founded. Since then, it has become a global phenomenon, available in 760 franchise-based cafés in 54 countries.

Since the beginning, Häagen-Dazs has sought to innovate and bring new frozen dessert experiences to its customers, including distinctive flavours such as Vanilla Swiss Almond, Butter Pecan and Dulce de Leche, to name just a few. Häagen-Dazs was also the first to introduce the world to ice cream bars for a grown-up palate, with the introduction of the Häagen-Dazs ice cream bar line in 1986. Other super-premium innovations followed, with Frozen Yoghurt in 1991, Sorbet in 1993 and the Italian-inspired Gelato line in 2000.

In 1999 the Swiss food company Nestlé formed a 50–50 joint venture with US-based Pillsbury, linking Nestlé's novelty ice cream unit and Pillsbury's Häagen-Dazs frozen dessert business in a bid to snatch a bigger slice of the $11 bn American market.

The two units are of similar size and had combined sales of about $600 mn in 1998. The move will lead to cost savings in operational costs, especially distribution. Nestlé's strong distribution system as the world's biggest food company would help put Häagen-Dazs products on more shelves in US grocery stores, while its own products, such as Nestlé Crunch and Drumsticks, would also get a boost.

Häagen-Dazs was for many years the darling of the ice cream world. Everybody wanted to be associated with it, devoured it in vast quantities and defended it when upstarts such as Ben & Jerry's came on the scene. It was only available at gourmet shops and commanded a loyal and committed following. This was helped by its first TV advertising, from ad agency Bartle Bogle Hegarty, which broke in 1995. The work was controversial, presenting the brand as a seduction tool, featuring entwined couples indulgently feeding the ice cream to each other.

Häagen-Dazs revolutionized ice cream in the late 1980s. It forced the ice cream industry to reconsider what indulgence meant. It introduced the concept of premium, quality ice cream as an indulgent treat and communicated its values clearly. The fact that the original flavours contained ingredients such as Belgian dark chocolate and hand-picked vanilla beans from Madagascar created a distinctive brand and fostered indulgent taste experiences. The brand has been synonymous with super-premium ice cream. Innovation has been key for the brand.

Häagen-Dazs today

Today, however, the excitement around the brand has all but melted away. High-quality ingredients, premium packaging and great product delivery are all now standard fare. An explosion of brands and the unstoppable march of own-label have eroded its appeal. Building and maintaining a brand that is susceptible to factors outside of normal market forces – the weather – is a challenge. To allow it to fall out of favour with discerning ice cream fans is less forgivable and the brand's worldwide sales fell by 16.5 per cent between April 2003 and April 2004 as the competition caught up.

Although Häagen-Dazs introduced more flavours, variants and ad campaigns, none has captured the imagination in the way the competition has. For example, Wall's Magnum made great inroads into the concept of personal indulgence and has found different ways of delivering it.

Consumers have not lost faith in the quality of the Häagen-Dazs product, they are just being offered more exciting recipes and packaging elsewhere.

Maybe it's time for Häagen-Dazs to take a deep breath and plunge itself into uncharted territory once again.

Questions

1 What are the values and resources contained in the Häagen-Dazs brand?

2 What should Häagen-Dazs do to revitalize its brand?

3 Appendix 2.1 shows the costs connected with establishing a Häagen-Dazs ice cream café as a franchisee. Try to produce a break-even analysis based on the costs listed in Appendix 2.1 and supplemented with your own assumptions.

Source: different public sources

Appendix 2.1

New franchisee

	Range
Initial franchise fee	$20,000
Travel and living expenses to attend application interview	$1,500
New store marketing fee	$3,500
Travel and living expenses during training	$3,100
Leasehold improvements	$8,000–$195,000
Deposits and licences	$7,500–$17,500
Equipment, fixtures and furnishings	$20,000–$75,000
Opening inventory	$5,000–$9,000
Insurance	$1,500–$2,500
Additional funds – 3 months	$10,250–$63,500
TOTALS:	**$80,000–$400,000**
Other fees	
Royalty fees	3% of gross sales
General marketing contribution	$3,800 paid annually (traditional shop)
Local marketing contribution	1% of gross sales

Note: the amount of initial investment will vary dependent upon a number of factors, including the type of shop that is planned.

Source: different estimates

Assessing the external marketing situation

Chapter contents

Learning Objectives

After studying this chapter you should be able to:

- explain the elements in the PEST analysis

- discuss the focal company's relationships to the different actors in the value net

- understand how the company can establish relationships to competitors

- discuss how B2B customers make purchase decisions.

3.1 **Introduction**

Of central importance in developing a robust marketing plan is awareness of how the environment in which the marketing takes place is changing. At its simplest, the whole marketing system can be divided into three levels, as follows (see Fig. 3.1).

1 **The focal company**: understanding and analysing the internal situation was dealt with in Chapter 2.

2 **Industry level/value net**: the focal company's most important actors/stakeholders at this level are suppliers, partners/complementors, competitors and, of course, the customers.

3 **Macro level**: the most important changes taking place in the macro environment can be summarized in the so-called PEST analysis:

P   Political and legal factors

E   Economic factors

S   Socio-cultural factors

T   Technological factors.

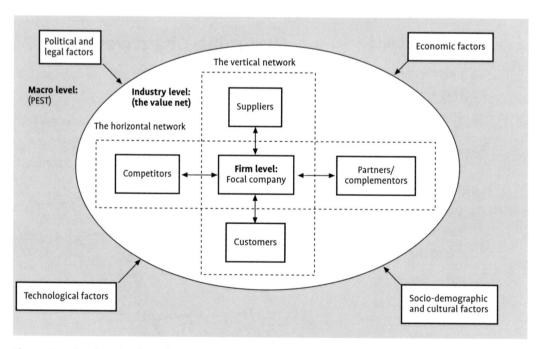

Figure 3.1 The three levels in the marketing system/value net: firm level, industry level, macro level

The following section examines each of the four elements of the PEST analysis.

3.2 **PEST analysis**

Political, legal and economic factors

During the past 20 years, a new and fundamentally different form of international commercial activity has developed, greatly increasing worldwide economic and political interdependence. Very few countries remain isolated in the world of business; rather than merely buying resources from and selling goods to foreign nations, multinational companies (MNCs) now make direct investment in fully integrated operations that cover the spectrum of goods and services. Today, MNC networks control a large and growing share of the world's technology, marketing and productive resources.

Rates of economic growth fluctuate over time and across the globe. While growth is undoubtedly cyclical, the indications are that the developed economies are unlikely to see again the rate of growth experienced in the first decades after the Second World War.

The state of national and international economies affects businesses directly in a number of ways; for example, it affects interest rates and hence the cost of borrowing. In times of slow economic growth governments, or their central banks, tend to reduce interest rates to make borrowing cheaper and hence stimulate spending. When economic growth is rapid, concerns for growing inflation, or economic 'overheating', lead to increased interest rates to dampen demand.

Interest rates have a number of effects in addition to directly raising or lowering the cost of borrowing. In particular they have a psychological effect on the confidence of consumers and businesses, affecting purchasing decisions beyond purely rational, or economic, judgement.

Company investment decisions are often delayed in times of relatively high interest rates and that can then have an obvious knock-on effect on suppliers further down the supply chain. Consumers too may delay purchases, especially where they are to be made using loans that are increasingly expensive. The housing market, for example, is particularly vulnerable to interest rate changes.

Perhaps one of the most obvious ways in which the political and economic environment affects demand is through the fiscal, or taxation, policy of the regime that is in power. Where taxation rates are high they result in low disposable incomes, which can depress demand. Low taxation tends to be a spur to growth. But there are two main types of taxes and their effects may be different. Direct taxation taxes income and hence affects the overall disposable income available for purchases. Indirect taxation, on the other hand, taxes purchases and may, through its selective application, shift demand from one area to another.

Employment and unemployment rates also follow economic and business cycles. In times of economic slowdown firms may find their order books less full and hence be forced to pursue efficiency gains through 'downsizing'.

National governments, through their economic and fiscal policies, set the economic climate in which organizations operate. The political hue, or leaning, of a government can affect the policies it pursues in a number of ways. Crudely, the position of a government on the political spectrum from left to right, from centrally planned (as in the communist era in the Soviet Union) to market-led free-for-all (as most exemplified in the United States), indicates the broad manner in which decisions are likely to be made.

The extent to which fiscal policy will have a direct effect on the strategy pursued by an individual organization will clearly vary significantly. What is important here is to recognize the impact and, as importantly, predict how this may change with changes in government or changes in local or international legislation.

The EU: the euro and the enlargement

January 1992 saw the realization of the dream of many Europeans with the creation of the European single market. This single market of over 320 million consumers was created to allow the free flow of products and services, people and capital between the member states. By January 2002 a single European currency, the euro (€), had been introduced into all but a handful of the EU member states, further facilitating trade and exchange across the old political borders. On 1 May 2004, ten new states became members of the EU: the three Baltic States, Hungary, Poland, the Czech Republic, Slovakia, Cyprus, Malta and Slovenia. This enlargement will have significant implications for many organizations, both commercial and non-commercial, as Europe expands. The population of the European Union will rise by around 20 per cent, while GDP will rise by only 5 per cent. Significant differences in labour costs, for example, are likely to raise questions of location for many firms.

Socio-demographic and cultural environment

Demographic factors

The western 'demographic time bomb' has started to have an impact on diverse businesses. With generally better standards of living, life expectancy has increased. In the developed West the over-sixties age group currently makes up around 20 per cent of the population, and this figure is predicted to rise to nearer one-third by 2050. These 'grey' consumers are relatively rich. The over-fifties own around three-quarters of the world's financial assets and control half of the discretionary budget. Perhaps surprisingly, however, around 95 per cent of consumer advertising is aimed at the under-fifties. It is likely that marketers will increasingly come to recognize the potential value of this market and target more offerings and promotions towards it. At the other end of the spectrum the youth market has also become more affluent and poses new opportunities for marketers. The fashion and music industries have been quick to recognize this new-found affluence. Related to this youth market has been the emergence of the enigmatic 'Generation X' consumer, who is hostile to business values and traditional advertising and branding, and rejects many conventional product offers. The pay-off in understanding the values and preferences of this type of consumer has been substantial for companies such as Nike in clothing.

Many western societies are becoming increasingly multi-ethnic. In the United

Kingdom, for example, by the late 1990s ethnic minorities comprised 5.5 per cent of the population and forecasts predicted the number would double in the next 50 years.

Social factors

A number of significant pressures on organizations can be identified. First and foremost, customers are becoming increasingly demanding of the products and services they buy. Customers demand, and expect, reliable products with quick, efficient service at reasonable prices. Furthermore there is little long-term stability in customer demand.

A further social change has been in attitudes to, and concern for, the physical environment. Environmental pressure groups impact on businesses, so much so that major oil multinationals and others spend large amounts of money on corporate advertising each year to demonstrate their concern and care for the environment. The activities of Greenpeace have begun to have a major impact on public opinion and now affect policy-making at national and international levels. It is to be expected that concern for the environment will increase and hence will be a major factor in managing that prime marketing asset – company reputation.

Cultural factors

Before an American can be a successful leader among different cultures, he must clearly understand his own culture and be aware of imposing his culture or traditions on those of other cultures; Edward T. Hall (1976) has suggested the concept of high- and low-context communication as a way of understanding different cultural orientations. The American communicates in a low-context nature, which means that messages are explicit. Words carry most of the information in communication. In a low-context culture one gets down to business quickly. In a high-context culture it takes considerably longer to conduct business because of the need to know more about a business person before a relationship develops. In Asia, if you are not willing to take the time to sit down and have a cup of green tea with people, you have a problem. In a high-context culture, such as France, Japan and most of the Middle East, less information is contained in the verbal part of the message. Much more information resides in the context of communication, including the background, associations, and basic values of the communicators (Hall, 1976).

In the 1970s, Geert Hofstede developed methods to detect and measure elements of national cultural systems that affect behaviour in work situations. Hofstede's 'research' was extracted from an existing bank of paper-and-pencil survey results collected within subsidiaries of one large multinational business organization in 40 countries and covering, among others, many questions about values. The survey was held twice, around 1968 and around 1972, producing a total of over 116,000 questionnaires. Theoretical reasoning and statistical analysis revealed the four main dimensions on which country cultures differ. These were labelled Power Distance, Uncertainty Avoidance, Individualism and Masculinity. Each of the 40 countries could be given a score on these four dimensions (Hofstede, 1980). Later research, which dealt with

Asians as the subject, added the dimension 'Long-term Orientation'. By learning how each country scored on these dimensions, a human resource (HR) professional can understand the culture of a country and then implement practices that are appropriate for that culture. Descriptions of Hofstede's five dimensions follow.

Power distance

Power distance is the extent to which the less powerful members of society accept that power is, and should be, distributed *unequally.* Inequality can occur in areas such as prestige, wealth and power, or in teacher–student and parent–child relationships. Different societies place different weights on status. In corporations, inequality in power is inevitable because it serves an important function and is usually formalized in hierarchical boss–subordinate relationships.

Uncertainty avoidance

This is the extent to which people try to avoid situations where expectations and outcomes are not clear. These are situations where people feel threatened by poorly defined or ambiguous conditions, and vary considerably among people in different countries. Employees with high uncertainty avoidance would tend not to break company rules even when they think it is in the company's best interest to do so, and tend to remain within the same company for long periods of time. They prefer to work with long-term acquaintances and friends rather than with strangers (Gannon, 2001).

Individualism

Individualism describes the relationship between an individual and the groups to which he/she belongs. Individualism is described by Griffin and Pustay (1998) as a cultural belief that the person comes first. People with high individualism put their own interests and those of their immediate families ahead of those of others.

Masculinity (goal orientation)

This is aggressive and materialistic behaviour. Hofstede described this dimension as masculinity vs femininity, however authors referring to Hofstede's study tend to call this dimension goal orientation, due to the misunderstandings that using the word 'masculinity' can give rise to.

Long-term orientation

The time horizon of long-term orientation is the extent to which people within a culture have a long-term vs a short-term outlook on work, life and other aspects of society. Asian cultures have long-term future orientations that value hard work, perseverance and dedication. Other cultures tend to focus on the past and present, with respect for tradition and the fulfilment of social obligations.

Last but not least, religions and religious institutions affect markets in a variety of ways. Religion is one of the foundations of moral teaching in most civilizations, and as such it defines and informs the kinds of problems faced in the market by buyers (consumers) and sellers (marketers). Marketers need to understand the effects of religion on the kinds of issues they face in business and, more important, how these issues are defined, informed and regulated by religion. Understanding the relationships between religions and markets should be important to macro marketing since religions affect the foundations of people's understanding of the world, and thus their understanding and acceptance of markets and marketing institutions. Religion affects perceptions of development, quality of life, appropriate standards of exchange, and competition.

Exhibit 3.1 McDonald's France: a faster penetration of the French market than expected

At first glance McDonald's fast food and French gastronomy don't go together very well. Indeed, from the beginning, McDonald's was afraid of entering the French market. The French traditionally have a very complex relationship with America because they like the American people, but not American politics. When McDonald's launched its first restaurant in Paris in 1979 it tried to combat these perceptions by positioning itself as a family restaurant brand, rather than a burger bar or a US-themed restaurant. McDonald's recognized the increasing importance of kids influencing family decisions. Furthermore the company has tried hard to adapt to French habits. It has put regional specialities and recipes on its menu, including well-known French brands such as Danone yoghurt and Kronenbourg beer.

The result

Surprisingly, McDonald's France grew from zero restaurants to over 1000 in 24 years. The same progress took more than 30 years in the UK and German markets.

Source: adapted from Jones (2004)

Technological factors

The latter part of the twentieth century saw technological change and development impact on virtually every industry. The microprocessor, for instance, has been attributed with heralding the post-industrial age and it is probably this invention above all others that has had the most profound effect on our lives today. Microprocessors have revolutionized data collection, processing and dissemination. They have caused major changes in production technology and have served to increase the rate of technological change. This shortening of commercialization times has, in turn, led to a shortening of product life cycles, with products becoming obsolete much more quickly than before. Computer integration of manufacturing and design is helping to shorten product development times.

Newer technology has had a major impact on particular aspects of marketing. Computers, and their wide availability to management, have led to increased interest in sophisticated market modelling and decision support systems. Increased amounts of information can now be stored, analysed and retrieved much more quickly than in the past. In 1965 Gordon Moore of Intel predicted exponential growth in the numbers of transistors that would be possible on integrated circuits. Moore's Law, as it became known, holds that 'the processing power of the silicon chip will double every 18 months'. This prediction has proved remarkably accurate. Of course, the Internet – the global electronic communications network – is also fast emerging, not only as a new marketing communications vehicle, but as potentially a whole new way of going to market, which may significantly change the competitive structure of industries.

Time and distance are shrinking rapidly as firms use the Internet to aim their offerings at truly global markets. One result is that cross-national segments are now emerging for products and services from fast foods, through books and toys, to computers and automobiles.

Exhibit 3.2 Cross-cultural 'gift giving' behaviour and Masterfoods' introduction of the Celebrations brand

The whole concept of exchanging gifts is a very important part of consumer behaviour. Marketers study it with great interest, because it presents opportunities to create products that meet the particular gift-giving needs of the consumer at a specific time. The way we give presents reflects both how we feel about ourselves and the recipient. Gift giving in many societies is ritualized, connected to calendar events and intertwined with aspects of culture.

The exchange of gifts is also important in older societies and in other cultures with a number of different types of gift. Some are given freely as a token of love and affection; others are ritualized, where it is expected that there will be a return. This is known as *reciprocity*.

In Japan, gift giving is of great social importance and when the Japanese go on holiday they often spend a lot of time and money on buying gifts for people back home. In most societies giving gifts is socially important, indicating the status of the receiver and the giver, and also marking occasions such as paying a visit, making a romantic gesture or saying thanks. Chocolate is very often the gift of choice. It provides a feeling of caring, yet is sufficiently neutral to be acceptable to most people.

In western societies we exchange gifts at certain times of the year. Big events include Christmas, Easter, birthdays and occasions like Mother's Day.

'Self-gifting' has recently emerged as a new market segment. Self-gifting is the idea of giving presents to ourselves rather than waiting for a special occasion or for someone to give us a gift. Sometimes we need to comfort or reward ourselves. We may have had a bad day and we need something to make us feel better. On the other hand we may feel that we need to reward ourselves for something we have achieved. Motivation theorists have pointed out that we all have a need for recognition. Sometimes the company we work for, our colleagues or our family will give us recognition but occasionally we have to provide it for ourselves. Confectionery is a favourite option, with the Masterfoods' product Celebrations often being chosen, because it gives a sense of marking an occasion and a reward but is not too formal. We can use it to provide an emotional benefit to make ourselves and those around us feel better. Using theories of motivation we can also see that Celebrations can satisfy both social and self-esteem needs.

Masterfoods looked at its main competitors (like Nestlé) and saw that it needed a range of chocolates to compete in the gift category. It launched Celebrations in 1997 and filled a gap in its portfolio of products and the market. Masterfoods approached this in an innovative way by using, or leveraging, its well-known chocolate brands. It turned these (like Bounty, Snickers and Mars) into twist-wrapped bite-size sweets and created a distinctive, easily recognizable brand identity known as 'Celebrations'.

From an early age we are taught the value of sharing, the need to let others have a taste of what we enjoy. Celebrations also recognizes that there are occasions where we buy confectionery not so much as a gift, but more as something that is to be shared around. This is often true at informal gatherings, when going to the cinema, to parties or when staying at home. Celebrations provides bite-sized, twist-wrapped, miniature versions of familiar chocolate bars. This means that people can choose the one they like, which reinforces the concept of sharing.

Source: adapted from www.masterfoods.com, www.business2000.ie; Pereira, T., Ennew, C. and Tynan, C. (2004) Consumer self gift behaviour: an explanatory analysis. European Marketing Academy Conference, May, Murcia, Spain; Tynan, C. and McKechnie, S. (2004) Celebrating Christmas: a review and research agenda. Academy of Marketing Conference, University of Gloucestershire, UK, July.

3.3 Relations to actors in the industry value net

This task environment refers to the immediate external market where interactions which have a direct effect on our company take place. Since the firm has relationships with different types of interdependencies, with different objectives for the development of the relationship, and so on, it is important organizationally to differentiate between how different relationships are handled. In particular, relationships and interactions are typically established with the following actors (see Fig. 3.1):

- suppliers
- customers

- complementors/partners
- competitors.

These relationships are discussed in more detail below.

Relationships with suppliers

There seem to be three major strategic issues related to purchasing management:

1 the decision of whether to make an item in-house or to buy from external suppliers

2 the development of appropriate relationships with suppliers

3 the managing of the supplier base in terms of size and relationships between suppliers.

The first strategic issue is to decide what items to procure. This is defined by the scope of the operations that are undertaken in-house by the buying company. This determines the degree of vertical integration, which in purchasing terms has been addressed as the 'make-or-buy issue'.

What to produce internally and what to buy from external suppliers has been an issue in manufacturing firms for a very long time, despite the fact that it was apparently not identified as a matter of strategic importance until the 1980s. It is evident that buying firms over time have come to rely more on 'buy' than 'make'. Consequently, outsourcing to external suppliers has increased dramatically over time.

Having suppliers that compete with one another is one way of increasing efficiency in purchasing operations. A buying company can switch from one supplier to another and thus encourage the vendors to improve their efforts. The opportunity to play off suppliers against each other in terms of price conditions has, in particular, been a recommended purchasing strategy. The secret of this strategy is to avoid becoming too integrated with suppliers, because integration leads to dependency. Customer relationships based on this logic are characterized by low involvement from both parties.

The tendency in the overall industrial system towards increasing specialization has called for more co-ordination between individual companies. This in turn leads to more adaptation between buyer and seller in terms of activities and resources. These adaptations are made because they improve efficiency and effectiveness. They also create interdependencies between customer and supplier. Such relationships are characterized by a high-involvement approach.

High-involvement relationships typically provide different types of benefit from low-involvement ones, since it is not the individual transaction that is optimized. On the contrary, customers are eager to improve long-term efficiency and effectiveness. Instead of focusing on price in each transaction, efforts are concentrated on affecting long-term total costs. The purchasing behaviour of buying companies affects a number of costs, of which price is sometimes only a minor consideration in comparison with other costs. For example, product development has become increasingly common. Integrating resources with suppliers can reduce lead times in product development and decrease total R&D spending. Furthermore, the revenues of the buying company might increase owing to enhanced product quality.

The widely recognized lean and agile supply practices in such relationships have demonstrated that buyers and suppliers can work together to improve supply relationship, or even supply network, performance and consequently allow the supply chain to deliver better value to the ultimate customer. Lean supply techniques aim to eliminate waste in all areas of the business, from the shop floor to manufacturing processes, and from new product development to supply chain management. Agile supply techniques, on the other hand, are directed towards reducing the time it takes for a supply chain to deliver a good or service to the end customer, and are aimed at supply chains that have to respond to volatile demand patterns. Both the 'lean' and 'agile' supply schools have provided a great deal of case evidence that demonstrates that collaboration, in the cause of lean or agile goals, can be effective in bringing down costs and/or increasing product functionality. For example, the lean school has often referred to the Japanese automobile industry, especially the Toyota Motor Corporation, as a good example of lean practice. The agile school, in turn, has pointed to the production of the Smart Car, a car that offers total customization, backed up by a service that offers responsiveness to customer demands.

However, the idea that collaboration constitutes 'best practice' ignores two key factors. First, not all transactions will justify the resources required for a collaborative relationship. Entering a collaborative relationship will only make economic sense if the expected financial and strategic rewards are deemed to be higher than the costs associated with the establishment of such a relationship. Second, not all the suppliers that buyers deal with will wish to allocate the resources required for a collaborative relationship to be developed. A buyer may have both the resources and the inclination to develop a collaborative relationship in a given situation. However, the supplier in question may have other priorities. The supplier may prefer to allocate its resources to other customers – those that it deems more relevant to the achievement of its business goals.

Furthermore, even where collaborative relationships are developed, there is by no means just one form of collaboration. For example, in some power situations getting suppliers to collaborate will not be possible. In particular, such relationships will differ in both their conduct and outcome depending on the power–dependency relationships concerned. As has long been argued in the social science literature, there are four generic buyer–supplier power structures: buyer dominance, interdependence, independence and supplier dominance (Hollensen, 2003: 229).

There are two generic ways of working in the context of supplier relationship management: *arm's length* and *collaborative*. An arm's length way of working involves a low level of contact between buyer and supplier. Low contact means the absence of initiatives that are aimed at cost reduction or functionality enhancement. In arm's length exchanges, the buyer and supplier simply exchange the contractual information that is required for the transaction to take place; for example, information about the placing of the order, the recording of the fulfilment and the payment of the invoice.

A collaborative way of working is much more proactive. It involves high contact and close communication, and is aimed at the creation of surplus value in a relationship. With this approach, buyers work jointly with suppliers either to reduce suppliers' costs or to increase the functionality of the product. The buyer will often closely monitor and measure the performance of suppliers, but will also take on board suggestions about performance improvement that come from suppliers. The buyer will also often get involved in developing suppliers' skills and capabilities through joint development activities.

The bond between buyers and suppliers can also increase through investing in relationship-specific adaptations to processes, products or procedures. Relationship-specific adaptations are those adaptations that are non-transferable to relationships with other buyers or suppliers. These could be adaptations of the following kind: adaptations of the product specification, adaptations to the product design, adaptations to the manufacturing process, adaptations to delivery procedures, adaptations to stockholding, adaptations to planning procedures, adaptations to administrative procedures and adaptations to financial procedures.

To understand the power relationship, the power resources of both sides need to be looked at together: when the buyer has high power resources and the supplier has low power resources, the buyer will be dominant; when the buyer has low power resources and the supplier has high power resources, the supplier will be dominant; when the power resources are high for both buyer and supplier, then they will be interdependent; when both parties have low power resources, they will be independent from each other.

Exhibit 3.3 **Dell faces different buying behaviour in different countries**

Dell's experience shows that different nationalities do indeed have different preferences when it comes to buying computers. Customers in France and Germany tend to use their credit cards less than others; therefore, they may be less likely to buy online. People in the Nordic countries are very willing to buy online. A German customer is more likely to be interested in all the technical and pricing details. On the other hand, a Swedish customer likes to make a more spontaneous decision when talking to the sales person. Customers in the UK and France are very sensitive to price.

These cultural differences are important because all advertisements and other promotional material must be designed to suit each country. Dell has an advertising manager in each country who is consulted about the details of any local campaign. National differences also influence the type of media used for an advertisement. For example, in the UK and Spain, there are TV channels with very large audiences. Accordingly, TV advertising is used more frequently in these countries.

Source: adapted from www.dell.com, www.business2000.ie

Relationships with customers

In the relationship approach a specific transaction between the focal company and a customer is not an isolated event but takes place within an exchange relationship characterized by mutual dependency and interaction over time between the two parties. An analysis could stop at the individual relationship. However, in the network approach such relationships are seen as interconnected. Thus, the various actors in a market are connected to each other, directly or indirectly. A specific market can then be described and analysed as one or more networks.

An exchange relationship implies that there is an individual specific dependency between the seller and the customer. The relationship develops through interaction over time and signifies a mutual orientation of the two parties towards each other. In the interaction the buyer is equally as active as the seller. The interaction consists of social, business and information exchange, and an adaptation of products, processes and routines to better achieve the economic objectives of the parties involved.

Suppose we regard the environment of the individual relationship as consisting of other relationships. Suppose, further, that the relationships are connected, directly or indirectly, to each other. Then we can envision the market as a network. Following a sociological definition, networks are sets of interconnected exchange relationships between actors. Exchange in one relationship is conditioned by exchange in other relationships. Instead of the concept 'markets-as-networks', the ideas of 'industrial networks' and 'business networks' are used, signifying a somewhat different emphasis of the analyses. A relationship between two actors is 'embedded' in a network.

Marketing planning should start at the relationship level. Interaction with the buyers and potential buyers is an important aspect of the planning process. The planning should include objectives and activities concerning the development of the relationships. The objectives should not only be formulated for the business exchange, such as sales volume and type of product, but also for social and information exchange, and for adaptation processes for products, processes and routines. The development of individual relationships should not be restricted to aggregated data on sales, market shares, customer satisfaction, and so on.

Relationships with partners/complementors

This kind of relationship is based on collaboration between manufacturers of complementary functions and/or products/services. In such a collaboration, each partner has a strategic resource that the other needs and, in this way, each partner is motivated to develop some kind of exchange process between supplier and customer.

For example, partners divide value chain activities between themselves. One partner develops and manufactures a product while letting the other partner market it. The focal company (see Fig. 3.1), A, may want to enter a foreign market, but lacks local market knowledge and does not know how to get access to foreign distribution channels for its products. Therefore, A seeks and finds a partner, B, which has its core competencies in the downstream functions, but is weak in the upstream function. In this way A and B can form a coalition whereby B can help A with distribution and selling in a foreign market, and A can help B with R&D or production. Another example is a joint marketing agreement where the complementary product lines of two firms are sold together through existing or new distribution channels, thus broadening the market coverage of both firms.

Relationships with competitors

Before entering any relationship with competitors, it is important to analyse the competition in so far as it will affect ease of market entry and potential profitability. The domination of a market by a few large companies may suggest difficulties in market entry and subsequent distribution. A more fragmented structure may pose fewer problems. In analysing the competition, a number of factors need to be considered. These range from the number and size of competitors, their capabilities (strengths and weaknesses), their international marketing strategies, and their sales volume and relative market share, to the type of competitor (i.e. multinational versus local and their relative resources). The major multinational competitors, such as Microsoft and Unilever, have access to extensive financial and other resources, but local competitors should not be ignored as they have fewer administrative overheads, lower operating costs and greater flexibility.

Generally, the relationships between competitors (horizontal network) have not been analysed to the same extent as vertical relationships. Co-operative relationships in the vertical network (see Fig. 3.1) are easier to grasp as they are built on a distribution of activities and resources among players in a supply chain. Horizontal networks, on the other hand, are more informal and invisible, and based more on social exchanges.

When competitors are involved in resource exchange alliances, competition introduces some problems. The dilemma is that in creating an alliance with a competitor, an organization is, in fact, making them more competitive.

For collaboration to succeed, each competitor must contribute something distinctive: basic research, product development skills, manufacturing capacity, access to distribution. In the network approach, the market includes both complementarities and substitutes, both co-operating and competing firms. Competitors also strive to develop their own networks. Such competitive activity is a major force for change in these networks. Competitors are predominantly negatively connected to each other; they might compete for customers, suppliers or other partners. Competing firms also often have customers, distributors or suppliers in common. Sometimes this implies a negative connection, but sometimes competing firms do not have conflicting objectives *vis-à-vis* a common counterpart.

Interaction among competitors has traditionally been treated within economic theory, and has been explained in terms of the structure of an industry within which it operates. It is further argued that intensity in competition is dependent on the degree of symmetry between companies, while the degree of concentration determines whether competitors act in collusion or competition with each other. Variations in patterns of interaction are also viewed via a relational approach to competitive interaction.

Based on the motives for interaction and the intensity of the relationship concerned, five types of interaction are distinguished: conflict, competition, co-existence, co-operation and collusion. Conflict and competition are described as active *vis-à-vis* competitors, although they differ in terms of the motives for specific interaction. Conflict represents object-orientated competition, geared to destroying the opposing counterpart. Competition is goal-orientated, directed towards achieving one's own goals even though this may have a negative effect on other competitors. Co-existent competition occurs when actors do not see one another as competitors, and therefore act independently of each other. Tacit collusion arises from implicit agreements among the actors to avoid active competition. Finally, in co-operation, the companies involved strive towards the same goals; for example, by working together in strategic alliances or projects. The interaction between competitors is variable and can involve both co-operative and competitive interaction.

Exhibit 3.4 **The nature of fashion markets**

Fashion is a broad term that typically encompasses any product or market where there is an element of style that is likely to be short-lived. Fashion markets typically exhibit the following characteristics.

- **Short life cycles**: the product is often ephemeral, designed to capture the mood of the moment; consequently the period in which it will be saleable is likely to be very short and seasonal, measured in months or even weeks.

- **High volatility**: demand for these products is rarely stable or linear. It may be influenced by the vagaries of the weather, films, or even by pop stars and footballers.

- **Low predictability**: because of the volatility of demand it is extremely difficult to forecast with any accuracy even total demand within a period, let alone week-by-week or item-by-item demand.

- **High-impulse purchasing**: many buying decisions by consumers for these products are made at the point of purchase. In other words, the shopper when confronted with the product is stimulated to buy it, hence the critical need for 'availability'.

Today's fashion marketplace is highly competitive and the constant need to 'refresh' product ranges means that there has been an inevitable move by many retailers to extend the number of 'seasons' (i.e. the frequency with which the entire merchandise within a store is changed). In extreme cases, typified by the successful fashion retailer Zara, there might be 20 seasons in a year.

Source: adapted from www.fashion.com; Christopher, M., Lowson, R. and Peck, H. (2004) Creating agile supply chains in the fashion industry. *International Journal of Retail & Distribution Management* 32(8), pp. 367–76.

3.4 **Analysing buying processes in the B2B market**

It could be relevant to look at buying processes in both the B2B and B2C markets. However, in this book's context the focus is on the B2B buying process as this reflects the views of the direct business customer. Organizational purchasing decisions are made to meet the objectives of an organization rather than the needs of an individual buyer.

Consumer behaviour relates to the buying behaviour of individuals (or families) when purchasing products for their own use. Organizations buy to enable them to provide goods and services to the final customer. This has implications for marketing management, as we shall see later. Organizational buying behaviour has many similarities to consumer behaviour; both encompass the behaviour of human beings, whether individually or in groups. Organizational buyers do not necessarily, though, act in a more rational manner than individual consumers. Organizational buyers are affected by environmental and individual factors, as outlined in the previous section. One of the main differences from consumer buying is that organizational buying usually involves group decision-making (known as the 'decision-making unit' (DMU) and sometimes referred to as the buying centre). In such a group individuals may have different roles in the purchase process. These can be categorized as follows.

- **Initiator**: the person who first suggests making a purchase.

- **Influencers/evaluators**: people who influence the buying decision. They often help define specifications and provide information for evaluating options. Technical personnel are especially important as influencers.

- **Gatekeepers**: group members who regulate the flow of information. Frequently, the purchasing agent views the gatekeeping role as a source of his or her power. A secretary may also act as a gatekeeper by determining which vendors get an appointment with a buyer.

- **Decider**: the person who has the formal or informal power to choose or approve the selection of the supplier or brand. In complex situations, it is often difficult to determine who makes the final decision.

- **Purchaser**: the person who actually negotiates the purchase. This could be anyone from the president of the company to a purchasing agent, depending on the importance of the decision.

- **Users**: members of the organization who will actually use the product. Users often initiate the buying process and help define product specifications.

One person may play all the above roles in the purchase decision or each role may be represented by a number of personnel. The sales person trying to sell to an organization should be aware of the roles people assume in the buying centre.

Another difference in organizational buying is that some products are more complex than others and it requires specialist knowledge to purchase them. As many products are changed according to the specifications of the buyer there is more communication and negotiation between buyer and seller. After-sales service is also very important in organizational buying, and suppliers are often evaluated quite rigorously after purchase. In general, organizational markets have fewer, larger, buyers who are geographically concentrated. Another aspect of organizational buying is the nature of derived demand – that is, demand for organizational (especially industrial) goods is derived from consumer markets. If demand for the end-product consumer good falls then this has an effect along the production line to all the inputs. So, in organizational marketing the end consumers should not be ignored and trends should be monitored.

Organizational buying decisions can be categorized into 'buy classes' in terms of how complex they are (similar to the low-/high-involvement decision-making in consumer markets). These classes are described below.

1 **Straight re-buys**: these occur often, are relatively cheap and are usually a matter of routine. If the supplier is an 'in supplier' – that is, they are on the company's approved list of suppliers – then they have to perform in a way that ensures they do not get taken off the list. If they are 'out suppliers' they have to try to get on to the approved list.

2 **Modified re-buy**: this situation requires some additional information about, or evaluation of, suppliers. It is usually the case that specifications and so on have been modified since the last purchase.

3 **New task**: a new task, or new buy, situation (i.e. when the company has not bought the product before) is the most complex purchase decision. Search and evaluation procedures are extensive.

Summary

In this chapter, the influences of the environment are divided into three levels, as follows.

1 **Macro level**: the most important changes taking place in the macro environment can be summarized using the so-called PEST analysis:

    P Political and legal factors

    E Economic factors

    S Socio-cultural factors

    T Technological factors.

2 **Industry level/value net**: the focal company's most important actors/stakeholders at this level are suppliers, partners/complementors, competitors and, of course, the customers.

3 **The focal company**: understanding and analysing the internal situation was dealt with in Chapter 2.

This chapter states that it is not enough to discuss the activities that a single firm performs: it is essential to *understand* how these activities are linked to the activities in the firm's value net (i.e. to the firm's customers, suppliers, partners/complementors and competitors). Hence, companies are dependent for their success on their relationships with others. Many of the strategic choices a company makes will be in response to the actions of these other companies. In this way, a firm's strategy may be thought of as a kind of game, because there is nothing predetermined about the various choices a firm might make.

Relationships in the value net perspective enable firms to develop competitive advantage by leveraging the skills and capabilities of their partners to improve the performance of the total value chain. Firms not only compete as individual companies, they also compete as groups of companies that co-operate to bring value to the ultimate customer.

The last part of the chapter focused on the buying decision process of the most important and direct customer: the B2B customer. In B2B decision-making, two additional influences are included. These are group influences and organizational factors. The actual decision-making process will depend on whether the purchase is a new task, a modified re-buy or a straight re-buy for the organization. The process involved is similar to the consumer decision-making process.

Questions for discussion

1 Explain the importance of a common European currency (the euro) to firms selling goods to the European market.

2 Why is the international marketer interested in the age distribution of the population in a market?

3 Why is political stability so important for international marketers? Find some recent examples from the press to underline your points.

4 How can the change of major political goals in a country have an impact on the potential for success of an international marketer?

5 Explain why a country's balance of trade may be of interest to an international marketer.

6 Do you think that cultural differences between nations are more or less important than cultural variations within nations? Under what circumstances is each important?

7 What layers of culture have the strongest influence on business people's behaviour?

8 Identify some constraints in marketing to a traditional Muslim society.

9 What are the major differences in buying behaviour in the two main markets, B2C and B2B?

10 What is the buying centre in a company? Describe its functions and the implications for the selling organization.

11 Explain the idea behind the value net model.

12 Why is it sometimes necessary to establish relationships with competitors?

References

Gannon, M. (2001) *Understanding Global Cultures: Metaphorical Journeys through 23 Nations*, 2nd edn. Thousand Oaks, CA: Sage Publications, Inc.

Griffin, R.W. and Pustay, M.W. (1998) *International Business: A Management Perspective*. Addison Wesley.

Hall, E. T. (1976) *Beyond Culture*. Garden City, NY: Anchor.

Hofstede, G. (1980) *Culture's Consequences: International Differences in Work-related Values*. Beverly Hills, CA, and London: Sage.

Hollensen, S. (2003) *Marketing Management*. London: Financial Times/Prentice Hall, an imprint of Pearson Education.

Jones, M.C. (2004) Special size French fries. *Brand Strategy*, April, pp. 28–9.

Case 3 Toto: is the American market ready for the Japanese high-tech toilet brand?

The Japanese corporation Toto (www.toto.co.jp) was founded in 1917 as a manufacturer of ceramic sanitary equipment and plumbing hardware. Toto has grown to become one of the industry leaders. Today Toto is the largest toilet manufacturer in the world, producing more than seven million toilets annually. Toto's net sales in the financial year 2004 (ending 31 March 2004) were JP¥467,925 mn (US$4427 mn). The net profits were JP¥11,732 mn (US$111 mn). By 31 March 2004 there were 16,800 employees at the corporation.

Toto dominates the Japanese toilet market with a market share of 65 per cent, way ahead of its rival, Japanese Inax Corporation, which has about 25 per cent market share.

Only 10 per cent of Toto's total turnover comes from abroad. However, new-build housing in Japan is 30 per cent lower than at its height and companies such as Toto can no longer rely on a frenzy of construction to propel sales of toilets. Toto is having to forge a new strategy both at home and abroad, especially in China and the United States. Toto's top management would like the foreign share of total turnover to increase. In particular, they would like to increase the export of toilets to the United States where Toto's share of the total toilet market is around 6 per cent.

Japanese toilet culture

Japan is renowned in Asia, perhaps even the world, for its clean toilets and outstanding standards of hygiene. Two different types of toilet are found in Japan. The first type is known as the 'Asian toilet' by some, and the 'squat toilet' by others. It is basically a porcelain base with a hole in it. This sort of toilet can be found all over Asia and is the traditional form of toilet favoured by that region's people. However, this is slowly changing as the newer Asian cities now offer sit-down western-style toilets (including the public toilets). These are perceived to be much cleaner than squat toilets. The Japanese toilet that attracts the most attention, though, is perhaps the electronic sit-down toilet, of which Toto is the most prolific manufacturer. This toilet's seat has its own heater, a welcome feature during the cold Asian winter. It also has hydraulic jets that can be used to spray water and thus clean the 'private parts'. In Japan 55 per cent of homes now possess combined toilets/bidets (such as the Toto Washlet). Toto hopes to repeat this success by increasing market share in the high end of the US toilet market.

Competition in the US toilet market

Westerners just aren't used to paying hundreds or even thousands of dollars for high-tech versions of toilets. The relatively long history of flush toilets in the United States and Europe (around 100 years) has resulted in many competitors and cheap toilets.

Among the competitors in the American market are American Standard, Kohler, Mansfield, Gerber, Crane and Eljer.

As indicated above, Toto's market share is very low in a US market where (on average over the past few years) *ten million toilets* are sold annually. Table 3.1 shows the market share of the different manufacturers.

Table 3.1 **Market share in the US toilet market**	
Manufacturer	**Market share (%)**
Kohler	24
American Standard	23
Crane	12
Mansfield	9
Eljer	8
Toto	6
Briggs	6
Others	12
Total	100

Source: based on author estimates from different sources

As explained in Appendix 3.1 toilets can be divided into two types: the traditional two-piece type and the one-piece type, where Toto holds a stronger position (a market share of approximately 10 per cent).

The following section takes a closer look at the two most important competitors in the USA.

American Standard (www.americanstandard.com)

This group's principal activities are carried out via three divisions: Air Conditioning Systems, Bath and Kitchen and Vehicle Control Systems. The Bath and Kitchen division, previously known as Plumbing Products, was renamed in 2002 to reflect the company's new strategic approach of focusing on total customer needs rather than on specific product sales.

Before American Standard, there was the Standard Sanitary Manufacturing Company. It was founded in 1875 and merged with several other small plumbing manufacturers in 1899 to form the Standard Sanitary Manufacturing Company. Standard Sanitary pioneered many of the plumbing product improvements introduced in the early part of this century, including the one-piece toilet (see Appendix 3.1), built-in tubs, mixer taps (which mix hot and cold water to deliver water at the desired temperature) and tarnish-proof, corrosion-proof chrome finishes for brass fittings. By 1929, Standard had become the world's largest producer of bathroom fixtures.

Today, American Standard is among the world's largest producers of bathroom and kitchen fixtures and fittings. Around the world, its products are sold under brand names such as Ideal Standard, Standard, Porcher, Jado, Absolute, Trevi and Sottini. American Standard is the brand that is best known to home owners across the USA. With the company tracing its roots back to the nineteenth century, many Americans remember growing up with American Standard and Standard logos in their child-hood homes. It is estimated that three out of every five bathrooms in the USA today include an American Standard product.

The Bath and Kitchen division employs about 6900 people, and has its headquarters in Piscataway, NJ, as well as 14 facilities throughout the USA, Canada and Mexico. A research and development centre was recently opened in Piscataway with state-of-the-art computer design and product modelling equipment, as well as an extensive product-testing laboratory.

Bath and Kitchen enjoys global design and innovation resources from American Standard's Global Bath and Kitchen operation, with manufacturing and product development facilities throughout North America, Europe, South America and Asia. Worldwide, American Standard's Bath and Kitchen business racked up $1.9 bn in sales in 2002.

Kohler (www.kohlerco.com)

Kohler Co. was founded in 1873 and celebrated its 125th anniversary in 1998. It is a privately held company with 20,000 employees worldwide. Kohler operates 44 manufacturing plants, 26 subsidiaries and affiliates, and sales offices worldwide. Its estimated sales in 2002 were US$3.0 bn.

Kohler makes bathroom products under the names Hytec, Kohler and Sterling (plumbing products); Ann Sacks (ceramic tile, marble, stone products); and Kallista (bathroom fixtures). Brands in Europe include Jacob Delafon and Neomediam plumbing products and Sanijura bath cabinetry. Kohler also makes small engines, generators, electrical switchgear and high-end furniture. Additionally, Kohler owns The American Club resort, golf courses and other real estate; it also breeds Morgan horses at Kohler Stables in Kentucky. Chairman Herbert Kohler Jr and his sister Ruth Kohler, grandchildren of the founder, control the company.

Herbert Kohler has reorganized the company and has vowed that it will never go public. Kohler is building a new manufacturing facility in Mexico and is expanding some of its US factories.

Washlet infomercial for the Americans

Toto introduced its Washlet to the US market in 1980. The Washlet is a combination of a bidet and toilet in one unit – using electronics to bring warm water to the user's nether regions. Generally, American homes are not equipped with bidets, but where these are present, they are usually stand-alone fixtures used in conjunction with toilets. Until now, American homes have more or less rejected the idea of combining the bidet and toilet in one unit.

In order to increase acceptance of the Washlet, Toto's American subsidiary, Toto USA, Inc., in September 2003 announced the national launch of its Washlet infomercial. This was part of an unprecedented $1.5 mn national marketing campaign that included print ads in high-end consumer and design publications, and public relations. The one- and two-minute educational spots focused consumers' attention on a cultural evolution in toilet hygiene. The theme of the infomercial was three simple words: 'Are You Clean?'

Using a light, humorous touch, the infomercial encouraged viewers to recognize a cultural conundrum: they would not consider dry toilet paper as an appropriate means to clean dishes after a meal or dirt from their bodies when showering but, oddly, they would rely on it to cleanse their most crucial of intimate areas. Having brought the efficacy of this cultural practice into question, the infomercial quickly segued to the unique benefits and features of the Toto Washlet, the high-tech personal hygiene system inspired by water.

As the infomercial pointed out, Toto's Washlet is a special seat that transforms any ordinary toilet into a warm-water cleansing unit. Operated by wireless remote, the Washlet seat's multitask functions provide gentle front- and back-aerated warm-water spray, which can be regulated for preferred water pressure and temperature. Other features include oscillating or pulsating spray massage, heated seat, automatic catalytic air deodorizer and warm air dryer – all of which are governed by its 'fuzzy logic' energy-saving mode.

The Washlet infomercial provided consumers with an 800 number for immediate purchase or information requests. Consumers were also given the address of the authorized Washlet dealer nearest them, where they could go and see and, in some cases, experience the Washlet first hand. Internet users were directed to http://www.washletoffer.com, an interactive website for direct consumer purchases of the complete Washlet line. The website gives consumers the full Washlet story, including streaming video product demonstrations and testimonials from both consumers and medical professionals. This highly user-friendly and secure site offers all four Washlet products – the top-of-the-line Washlet S300, intermediate E200, entry-level C100 and the popular Travel Washlet.

Toto's Washlet infomercial ran for three months, until the end of 2003, on a mix of national cable networks including Fox, Discovery, Bravo, TechTV, Style, Life, Oxygen and Ovation. The time slots selected, which were primarily late night and early morning, were designed to maximize feedback about the programme's effectiveness with a wide range of viewers based on repeat viewership at a manageable cost.

Questions

1 Explain the buying behaviour of the main decision-makers in the US toilet market.

2 Evaluate the threats and opportunities for Toto when entering the US toilet market with a much higher level of marketing resources.

3 Was the infomercial the right way to promote the Washlet toilet in the USA or are there better ways?

Sources: adapted from Helms, T. (2003) The toilet marketplace. *Supply House Times*, September 2003, pp. 72–8; Pilling, D. (2004) Toto flushes old ways down the pan: toilet maker sells to remodellers and China's super rich. *Financial Times*, 2 March, Edition 1, p. 30; www.ceramicindustry.com; www.toto.co.jp; www.worldtoilet.org.

Appendix 3.1 Toilet terms explained

One-piece toilet

As its name suggests, this toilet is one complete unit. This allows for easy cleaning by eliminating those nooks and crannies that bacteria like to hide in. Toto is one of the market leaders in this segment.

Two-piece toilet

With this toilet, the tank and bowl come separately and are then coupled together on site. These toilets are generally less expensive than the one-piece design. This toilet is also known as a close-coupled toilet.

Flush valve

Located at the centre of the tank, this valve is activated by the toilet's flush handle and releases the water held in the tank. A larger flush valve increases the water flow rate through the toilet. Mostly used in Europe.

Gravity flush system

This system uses nothing more than water weight to generate flushing pressure. It's quiet, simple and requires less maintenance than other more complex flushing systems. Mostly used in North America.

Pressure-assisted flush system

A pressurized air tank assists the toilet's flushing process. This system can be very noisy, quite expensive and can require regular, costly maintenance. This system is used in the new Toto toilets.

SWOT analysis

Chapter contents

Learning Objectives

After studying this chapter you should be able to:

- explain how a SWOT analysis can capitalize on a company's internal and external issues

- understand the reasons for matching strengths and opportunities, and converting weaknesses and threats

- discuss the importance of doing some research as the basis for SWOT analysis

- discuss the barriers to and benefits of conducting SWOT analyses

- explain the reasons for preparing multilevel SWOT analyses.

4.1 **Introduction**

Successful SWOT analysis is fundamentally a process of finding the optimum fit between the firm's controllable strengths and weaknesses and the uncontrollable opportunities and threats posed by the environment in which the firm operates (not just the current environment, but also that of the foreseeable future). This explains why drawing up a SWOT (strengths, weaknesses, opportunities and threats) profile is by far the most popular of all marketing planning approaches. It provides a means by which all the key internal (company-related) and external (environment-related) issues can be summarized at a glance. A good SWOT profile facilitates the development of a strategy that capitalizes on a company's strengths, minimizes any weaknesses, exploits emerging opportunities and avoids, as far as possible, any threats.

By carefully matching environmental trends to the firm's own distinctive competencies the strategic market planner is able to devise strategies that build on the firm's strengths, while at the same time minimizing its weaknesses. By doing this, the marketer aims to achieve what is termed a 'strategic fit'.

Among the many fads and fashions in strategic management, the SWOT framework has enjoyed consistent popularity among both researchers and practitioners during the past few decades. SWOT analysis originated from efforts at Harvard Business School (HBS) to analyse case studies (Panagiotou, 2003). In the early 1950s, two Harvard business policy professors, George Albert Smith Jr and C. Roland Christensen, started to investigate organizational strategies in relation to their environment. In the late 1950s, another HBS business policy professor, Kenneth Andrews, expanded on this thinking by stating that all organizations must have clearly defined objectives and keep abreast of them. In the early 1960s, classroom discussions in business schools were focusing on organizational strengths and weaknesses in relation to the opportunities and threats (or risks) in their business environments. In 1963, a business policy conference was held at Harvard, where SWOT analysis was widely discussed and seen as a major advance in strategic thinking.

The SWOT framework became popular during the 1970s because of its inherent assumption that managers can plan the alignment of a firm's resources with its environment. Subsequently, during the 1980s, Porter's (1980) introduction of the industrial organization paradigm, with his five forces/diamond models, gave primacy to a firm's external environment, overshadowing the popularity of SWOT analysis. In the 1990s, Barney reinvented SWOT as the foundation framework linking the firm's resources to sustained competitive advantage (Barney, 1991).

Looking back to Chapters 2 and 3, Fig. 4.1 illustrates the 'roots' of the marketing planning approach. In Chapter 2 in particular, there was comprehensive discussion of the roots of the Resource Based View (RBV, inside-out), based on the firm's strengths and weaknesses, and the Market Orientation View (MOV, outside-in), based on opportunities and threats in the environment.

The roots discussed in Chapters 2 and 3 lead to the processes described in this chapter, where we will see how SWOT analysis can help these roots grow into a flourishing marketing plan.

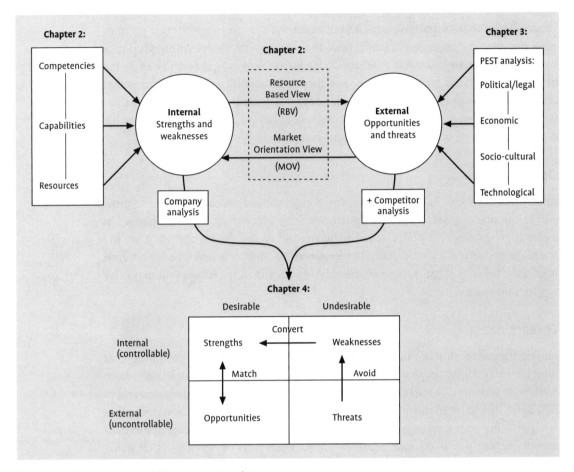

Figure 4.1 The structure of Chapters 2, 3 and 4

4.2 **Elements of the SWOT analysis**

When implementing a SWOT analysis to devise a set of strategies, the following guidelines should be used.

Strengths

Determine your organization's strong points, from an internal perspective as well as from the perspective of external customers. Do not be humble; be as pragmatic as possible. Are there any unique or distinct advantages that make your organization stand out from the crowd? What makes customers choose your organization over the competition? Are there any products or services your competition cannot imitate (both currently and in the future)?

Weaknesses

Determine your organization's weaknesses, again not only from an internal point of view, but also, and more importantly, from that of your customers. Although it may be difficult for an organization to acknowledge its weaknesses, it is best to handle the bitter reality without procrastination. Are there any operations or procedures that can be streamlined? How and why do competitors operate better than your organization? Is there any way that your organization could avoid its weaknesses? Does the competition have a certain market segment conquered?

Opportunities

Another major factor is to determine how your organization can continue to grow within the marketplace. After all, opportunities are everywhere, such as changes in technology, government policy, social patterns, and so on. Where and what are the attractive opportunities within your marketplace? Are there any new emerging trends within the market? What does your organization predict in the future that may offer new opportunities?

Threats

No one likes to think about threats, but they still have to be faced, despite the fact that they are external factors that are out of the firm's control (for example, the major worldwide economic slump after 11 September 2001). It is vital to be prepared and to face up to threats, even during turbulent times. What is your competition doing that is suppressing your own organizational development? Are there any changes in consumer demand that make new demands on your products or services? Is changing technology damaging your organization's position within the marketplace?

4.3 **Matching and converging in the SWOT matrix**

SWOT analysis should not just be an academic exercise used to classify information correctly. Rather, it should serve as a catalyst to facilitate and guide the creation of marketing strategies that will produce the desired results. The process of organizing information within the SWOT analysis can help the firm see the difference between where it thinks it is, where others see it as being and where it hopes to be.

To address these issues properly, the marketing manager should appraise every strength, weakness, opportunity and threat in order to determine its total impact on the firm's marketing efforts. This assessment will also give the manager an idea of the basic strategic options he has (see also Fig. 4.1). The following actions are those suggested by the SWOT matrix:

1 make a match between strengths and opportunities

2 convert weaknesses to strengths

3 convert threats to opportunities

4 minimize, if not avoid, weaknesses and threats.

4.4 **The application of the SWOT analysis**

The application of SWOT analysis is the matching of specific internal and external factors, which creates a strategic matrix that makes sense. It is essential to note that the internal factors are within the control of your organization (these include operations, finance, marketing and other areas). The external factors are outside your organization's control (these include political and economic factors, technology, competition and other areas). The four combinations that could result from SWOT analysis are called the Maxi-Maxi (strengths/opportunities), Maxi-Mini (strengths/threats), Mini-Maxi (weaknesses/opportunities) and Mini-Mini (weaknesses/threats), as illustrated in Fig. 4.2.

	Strengths (S)	Weaknesses (W)
Opportunities (O)	Maxi-Maxi (S/O)	Maxi-Mini (S/T)
Threats (T)	Mini-Maxi (W/O)	Mini-Mini (W/T)

Figure 4.2 The application of the SWOT matrix

Maxi-Maxi (S/O): this combination shows the organization's strengths and opportunities. In essence, an organization should strive to maximize its strengths to capitalize on new opportunities.

Maxi-Mini (S/T): this combination shows the organization's strengths in consideration of threats (e.g. from competitors). In essence, an organization should strive to use its strengths to parry or minimize threats.

Mini-Maxi (W/O): this combination shows the organization's weaknesses in tandem with opportunities. It encourages the organization to conquer its weaknesses by making the most of any new opportunities.

Mini-Mini (W/T): this combination shows the organization's weaknesses in comparison with current external threats. This is most definitely a defensive strategy: to minimize an organization's internal weaknesses and avoid external threats.

As mentioned above, the SWOT analysis is the matching of specific internal and external factors. However, what about matching items within internal factors and items within external factors? The primary reason this is not done is that matching these factors will create strategies that do not make sense. Let's take the example of a combination of strength and weakness (both internal factors): let's say one of your organization's strengths is 'plenty of financial resources' and one of its weaknesses is 'lack of sales training'. Mixing these two factors together, your management team might simply decide to plan more training for the sales force. The obvious riposte to this purposeless strategy is 'So what!' This is because there's no point in sales training just for the sake of it. A successful sales training programme must have a specific target in response to external changes; the specific needs of the sales force for training must be determined in line with external and internal factors. In other words, the strategy must have an external factor as a trigger in order for it to be feasible (this could, for example, be the customer's need for advice and service from the sales people before buying any products (Lee *et al.*, 2000)).

4.5 **Necessary analyses**

A well-conceived SWOT analysis depends on an extensive analysis of the company itself, its competitors and its environment (market and industry). An internal (company) analysis involves a comprehensive appraisal of company strengths and weaknesses, and every aspect of the business should be assessed. For example, coverage should include financial capabilities, technical abilities, location, plant and equipment, personnel, distributor relationships, customer relationships, and so on. In particular, the firm should try to identify its core competencies (Hamel and Prahalad, 1994). This concept is useful because it emphasizes the need to consider market opportunities in the light of a company's particular skills relative to its actual or potential competitors. When analysing actual or potential competitors, not only should their numbers be taken into consideration but also key competitors should be examined individually (see Fig. 4.1) in an effort to identify the firm's potential for creating a sustainable competitive advantage in the market. The main questions to ask about competitors are as follows.

- What is their (marketing mix) offer?
- What is their competitive advantage?
- How well are they performing?
- What does their SWOT profile look like?
- How are they likely to compete in future?

In conducting a market analysis there are two types of 'market' that should be considered: the 'immediate market' and the 'wider world'. The immediate market refers to the specific market(s) in which the firm actually/potentially operates, with customers and other, more general, market characteristics comprising the most important aspects of this analysis. A customer analysis revolves around asking questions such as why customers buy and what benefits they seek, when and where they buy, and who is involved in the purchase decision. Central to a customer analysis is the concept of *market segmentation*. This is the process of subdividing a market into smaller groups of customers with similar needs and wants/responsiveness to market offerings, which are, or may become, significant for planning a separate target marketing strategy. Having defined candidate market segments, a more general market analysis then involves the assessment of the relative 'attractiveness' of each segment. This necessitates estimating their size, growth rates, competitive structure and potential for profitability. Ideally, a profile of each market should gradually be built up so that each segment can be evaluated in light of the company's particular strengths and weaknesses, and its ability to compete. Finally, the 'wider world' comprises all those factors relating to the political, economic, social and technological environments surrounding a company that, albeit over the longer term, continually act to reshape both buyer and competitor behaviour. It is therefore important to analyse these factors so that any new opportunities or threats emanating from the wider world can be anticipated and acted upon (Brooksbank, 1996).

4.6 Benefits of and barriers to conducting a SWOT analysis

To its credit, SWOT analysis is supremely simple; possibly its greatest advantage is that its use allows management to focus its attention on key issues that affect business development and growth. The benefits of the SWOT analysis are not only seen in its outputs (which may be used in the development of sound strategic business plans) but also in the very *process* of carrying it out. SWOT is not only a static analytical tool that helps generate an understanding of business activity, but also a dynamic part of the management process, which can actually facilitate management development and can be harnessed to the advantage of all involved. It can be seen as a valuable management tool, which may easily be absorbed to good effect into the realities and practicalities of an organization's existing planning and strategy formulation processes.

On the other hand, the reasons why so many organizations take the 'ask the manager' approach and not a more analytical path in form of a SWOT analysis are numerous. They include the following (Jenster and Hussey, 2001; Hussey, 2002).

- **Lack of guidance on how to do it.** There are very few books that attempt to explain how to undertake an integrated company analysis. It is also true to say that many MBA programmes spend very little time on this. Being told that something is important but not the detail of how to do it certainly makes it harder to do the job well.

- **Better management information systems.** Managers today have access to better, more comprehensive and more up-to-date management information systems than was the case in the past. This can greatly facilitate the corporate appraisal, provided the right information has been collected in the first place, which does not always happen. Regular access to information can mean that managers really are informed about every important aspect of their business and therefore do not need special exercises. It can also lead to complacency and a situation where critical factors are not related to each other or thoroughly understood, and the view taken of the organization is fragmented and purely functional.

- **Pressure on managers**. The pressure on managers for immediate results has always been high but is currently greater than ever. It is certainly much quicker to ask them to define corporate strengths and weaknesses than to spend precious time on special analyses. Therefore managers have to be convinced that this extra time is justified. The pressure for a quick fix means that managers will often be tempted to reach for a faddy technique instead of going back to basic principles, and this is rarely the most effective way to deal with a strategic problem.

- **The complexity of many companies**. Many companies are very large and complex, which can make the task of carrying out a comprehensive appraisal seem rather daunting, and with the decline of large strategic staff departments the task of organizing such a study is devolved to busy line managers. However, it is a task that lies within the competence of most managers and if approached in a sensible way need not be overwhelming.

Those who still doubt that an analytical approach can yield additional and important strategic information should ponder the following three points.

1 Why is it that a change of chief executive so often leads to a more careful company analysis and a completely different insight into the appropriate vision and strategy for the organization?

2 Similarly, why are management consultants so often able to give an organization clarity of thinking about itself after they have been called in to undertake a general review of it?

3 Why does it sometimes take the implementation turmoil after a major acquisition to reveal things about both the buying and the acquired organization that were not known before?

Exhibit 4.1 **SWOT analysis of Honda Motor Company corporate level***

Honda Motor Company, based in Tokyo, Japan, is the world's largest motorcycle manufacturer and also the third largest auto manufacturer in Japan. The company produces and develops a broad spectrum of products, such as passenger cars, motorcycles and general-purpose engines for speciality sports cars. Besides being the manufacturer of the end product (cars, motorcycles, etc.), Honda is also a major OEM supplier of small engines to manufacturers of, for example, motorcycles, pleasure boats, snowmobiles and golf cars.

Strengths	Weaknesses
Globalization strategy: Honda meets the requirements of local markets by not only establishing regional sales networks, but also developing and manufacturing products locally. As a result, it has over 120 manufacturing facilities in 29 countries that pool resources to serve local needs. **Asian operations**: rapid economic growth in the region has expanded the market for motorcycles and automobiles significantly. However, the low ratio of vehicle ownership also creates a latent demand. Between 1998 and 2004, overall demand for motorcyles in India, Indonesia, Thailand, China, Malaysia, the Philippines and Vietnam expanded by about 75 per cent. Honda has successfully tapped into this opportunity by launching new products at affordable prices, which are a result of cost-setting efforts.	**Weakening financials**: a key worrying factor for the company is its mounting debt levels. **Poor presence in pick-ups**: in the North American market, which provides Honda with more than half of its global sales and profits, the company has kept away from the lucrative full-size pick-ups segment. The company has been so . focused on passenger cars that it has not built the necessary infrastructure for the pick-ups segment. **Mixing OEM and end-product market**: in the motorcycle market in particular, Honda is both a supplier of small engines (OEM supplier) and, at the same time, offers the end product itself: the motorcycle. Consequently, Honda can be in a situation where it is competing with its own customers.
Opportunities	**Threats**
Expanding Asian market: the company stands to benefit from the expanding motorcycle market in Asia. Honda has been making aggressive sales and marketing efforts in the region, which resulted in significant sales increases in Asia during fiscal 2004, with unit sales up 18 per cent. **Environment-friendly products**: Honda has always maintained a focus on safety and environmental aspects. It has actively explored alternative fuels and developed hybrid vehicles with gasoline-electric engines. Also helping the company are electric vehicles and others powered by compressed natural gas and fuel cells.	**Exposure to currency risks**: the high degree of foreign sales exposes the company to a high degree of currency risk, especially in the dollar–yen relationship, as over 50 per cent of Honda's sales are in the USA. **Volatile pricing environment**: prices for automobiles, motorcycles and power products in certain markets have, at times, experienced sharp changes over short periods of time. **Counterfeit products**: though China offers the company the largest potential, the market there is flooded with counterfeit products. **Competitive price pressure**: overcapacity within the industry has increased and will probably continue to increase if the economic downturn continues in Honda's major markets or worldwide, leading, potentially, to further increased price pressure.

* It does not claim to be complete.

4.7 **Multilevel SWOT analyses**

SWOT analysis may be undertaken on different organizational levels. When we talk about SWOT analysis we actually mean a *series of analyses*, each focusing on a specific organizational level or product/market combination. Of course, we can talk about a corporate SWOT analysis (as described in Exhibit 4.1 or SBU SWOT analysis), but in Fig. 4.3 we can also see that the following four combinations are possible on a product/market level:

1 Product 1 and Market 1

2 Product 1 and Market 2

3 Product 2 and Market 1

4 Product 2 and Market 2.

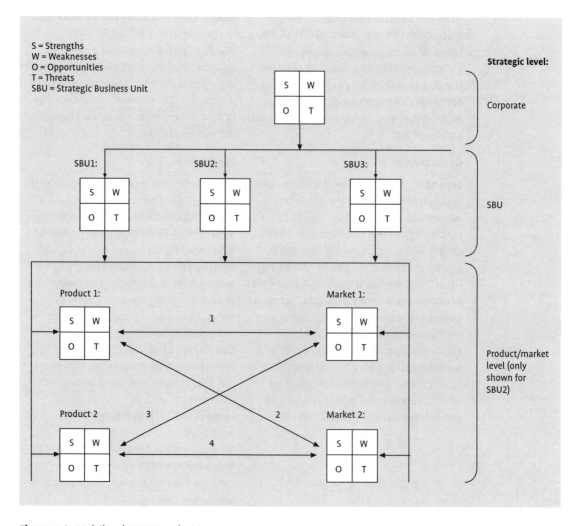

Figure 4.3 Multilevel SWOT analysis

In Fig. 4.3 the different combinations are shown only for SBU2. There would be similar combinations for the other SBUs.

The result of a SWOT analysis

No matter how subjective or objective SWOT analysis becomes, it may be significantly enhanced by considering it as a management process in which the very activity of carrying out the analysis is as important as the final result.

Summary

The SWOT profile (strengths, weaknesses, opportunities and threats) is by far the most popular of all marketing planning tools. It provides a means by which all the key internal (company-related) and external (environment-related) issues can be summarized at a glance. A good SWOT profile facilitates the development of a strategy that capitalizes on a company's strengths, minimizes any weaknesses, exploits emerging opportunities and avoids, as far as possible, any threats.

The *internal* (company) analysis involves a comprehensive appraisal of company *strengths* and *weaknesses*, and every aspect of the business should be assessed. For example, coverage should include financial capabilities, technical abilities, location, plant and equipment, personnel, distributor relationships, customer relationships, and so on.

The *external* analysis helps identify market *opportunities* and *threats*, and provides guidelines for the design of the marketing strategy.

Those macro environmental forces most studied are the so-called PEST factors: political/legal, economic, socio-cultural and technological. Furthermore, there is, of course, 'competition', which is often a threat, but as we saw in Chapter 3's value net, it can also be an opportunity where those involved can supplement each other's competencies. The firm, then, should try to identify its core competencies. This concept is useful because it emphasizes the need to consider market opportunities in the light of a company's particular skills relative to its actual or potential competitors.

Questions for discussion

1 What are the purposes of carrying out a SWOT analysis?

2 What are the major steps in a SWOT analysis?

3 What is the idea of matching a firm's strengths with opportunities in the market?

4 Why is the final result less important than the process involved in the SWOT analysis?

References

Barney, J.B. (1991) Firm resources and sustained competitive advantage. *Journal of Management* 17(1), pp. 99–120.

Brooksbank, R. (1996) The BASIC marketing planning process: a practical framework for the smaller business. *Marketing Intelligence & Planning* 14(4), pp. 16–23.

Hamel, G. and Prahalad, C.K. (1994) *Competing for the Future.* Boston: Harvard Business School Press.

Hussey, D. (2002) Determining strategic capability. *Strategic Change,* Jan–Feb, Vol. 11, pp. 43–52.

Jenster P. and Hussey D. (2001) *Company Analysis: Assessing Strategic Capability.* Chichester: Wiley.

Lee, S.F., Lo, K.K., Leung, R.F. and Ko, A.S.O. (2000) Strategy formulation framework for vocational education: integrating SWOT analysis, balanced scorecard, QFD methodology and MBNQA education criteria. *Managerial Auditing Journal* 15(8), pp. 407–23.

Panagiotou, G. (2003) Bringing SWOT into focus. *Business Strategy Review* 14(2), pp. 8–10.

Porter, M. (1980) *Competitive Strategy.* New York, NY: The Free Press.

Case 4 Red Bull: the superstar of energy drinks is seeking new markets

Red Bull was founded by Dietrich Mateschitz, a former Unilever employee, who often travelled in Asia. It was during his travels in the region that he was inspired by the local energy tonics available and worked with Bangkok-based TC Pharmaceuticals to create his own non-carbonated energy drink, Red Bull Kratingdaeng, which was initially sold only in Asia. (The Kratingdaeng brand is still used in Indonesia.)

Wanting to bring the product to the West, Mateschitz formed Red Bull GmbH in 1994, with the actual launch of the Red Bull energy drink occurring in 1987. Mateschitz's partner in the venture is Thai businessman Chaleo Yovidhya. Both men own a 49 per cent stake; the remaining 2 per cent belongs to Chaleo Yovidhya's son, Chalerm. Red Bull's headquarters are located in central Austria in the town of Fuschl am See.

Now marketed in over 70 countries, the niche energy drink has shown its global appeal and proved quite profitable, and Mateschitz was welcomed into the *Forbes* magazine Billionaires' Club in early 2003.

Employees at the firm totalled 1452 in 2002 worldwide, up from 1127 in 2001. Sales reportedly increased almost 11 per cent in 2002, and 1.3 billion cans of the drink were sold in 2002, up from 1.2 billion in 2001. It is estimated that 40 per cent of this turnover increase was generated in the USA. The positive results spurred founder and managing partner Dietrich Mateschitz to claim that Red Bull now accounted for 70 per cent of the worldwide energy drinks market. The growing company, with three production sites in Austria, hoped to increase output from 1.3 billion cans per year to 1.5 billion in 2003.

As a private company Red Bull does not publish financial information. However, company press releases and estimates show that sales have increased steadily, and the indication from press reports is that the company has been enjoying a consistent rise in its sales over many years. In 2002 it is estimated that total revenues of Red Bull were about €1.1 bn.

Product strategy

The company is strictly focused on the production and selling of its Red Bull energy drink. Though 2003 saw the release of Red Bull Sugarfree, this marked the extent of the firm's diversification. The company's tight focus allows it to put all of its forces into the production and marketing of this relatively new type of soft drink.

The many materials used to produce the drink, such as the amino acid taurine and the carbohydrate glucuronolactone, are manufactured by pharmaceutical companies. As a result, a can of Red Bull is essentially the same in any international market, with minor variations in vitamin content due to the national standards in any given market. Still something of a novelty and niche product, Red Bull highlights what is at times an unusual ingredient list. Red Bull's primary ingredient is taurine, an amino acid that is found naturally in the body, particularly muscle tissue. Each can contains 1000 milligrams of taurine, or about 70 times the amount found in a person weighing 70 kilograms. According to the company, taurine is integral to the beverage as it is a key substance used by the body at times of physical exertion and stress, which must be replenished.

Not surprisingly the drink contains caffeine; one can has 80 milligrams, an amount that company literature equates to a cup of filtered coffee. The drink also contains glucuronolactone (600 milligrams per can), a carbohydrate that can be produced by the human body through the presence of glucose. Glucuronolactone can also be consumed by eating certain grains and drinking red wine.

Last of Red Bull's main ingredients are sugar and glucose. Each can contains 27 grams of these, though not in the sugar-free version, of course.

The combination of these ingredients creates a drink that the company says will increase physical endurance, mental alertness and concentration. It is meant to be drunk prior to or during times of physical or emotional strain.

The brand did, however, run into some negative press in 1999 when the Red Bull name was linked to the death of an 18-year-old Irish student. The brand was also implicated in an Irish murder case and then reported to have played a role in the death of three teenagers in Sweden. However, the company has managed to navigate through these difficulties, though it is now required in certain regions, namely the EU, to carry a warning label regarding the product's high caffeine content.

Promotion strategy

The international slogan for Red Bull energy drink, a product that claims not only to augment physical strength and reaction speed, but also improve concentration and alertness, is 'Red Bull gives you wings'. It is a popular drink, particularly with young men; Red Bull's biggest consumers include athletes, students, and nightclubbers in need of a late-night lift. However, the company's website claims that the brand is marketed to 'opinion-leaders and hard-working people with active lifestyles'.

A great many of the drink's promotional activities revolve around sporting events, particularly more cutting-edge or extreme sports stemming from founder Dietrich Mateschitz's own keen interest in snowboarding and skateboarding. This is very evident on the company website, which includes lists of athletes who use Red Bull (many of them involved in so-called extreme sports such as paragliding and surfing).

Popular among the sporting events sponsored by Red Bull is Flugtag, or 'flying day' in German, an event that originated in Austria in 1992, but has since sprouted up in over 20 cities such as Berlin, Barcelona, San Francisco and London (as of August 2003). Entry is open to any participant with a man-powered flying machine. This free event is judged by a celebrity panel (previous panel members include Formula One driver Eddie Irvine and pop-group manager Louis Walsh).

Red Bull has other associations with Formula One racing through its former sponsorship of the Sauber and Arrows teams, and via its takeover of the Jaguar Formula

One team to launch its own car in the 2005 season. Mateschitz also sponsors a driver search initiative in the USA.

However, Red Bull activities are not limited to sporting events. It markets on school campuses, often finding student brand managers to actively push the product on site. One such campaign in Australia included the distribution of literature claiming that the drink stimulates brain cells, thus improving study capabilities.

To promote Red Bull's popularity on the club scene, the company sponsors Red Bull Music Academy. This annual, two-week event provides a forum for well-known and aspiring DJs to exchange information and meet music industry executives.

Distribution strategies

Since inception, a key growth strategy at Red Bull has been to increase international distribution. It has consistently worked on growing international sales, first making moves outside its domestic market in 1992, just five years after the first cans of Red Bull appeared on the Austrian market. Now available in over 70 countries worldwide, Red Bull has a well-developed network of local subsidiaries set up in key markets to oversee distribution in any given region.

However, in newer and less-developed markets the company often relies on local partnerships, as is the case in India where the company has forged an alliance with local distributor Narang Hospitality Services Ltd. The deal, signed in 2002, gives Red Bull the chance to establish a foothold in what is still a relatively untapped market for energy drinks. Immediate plans for distribution will target the resident western community through pubs, upscale shopping areas and corporate canteens.

Outlet channels differ widely for Red Bull. In its larger markets, like the UK, the drink is available through major retailers like Sainsbury's as well as through convenience stores and an assortment of on-trade venues like bars and nightclubs. The British military was also a customer in 2003, providing the drink to its troops during the Iraq conflict. Similarly, police administrators are looking into joining forces with Red Bull because of the drink's ability to combat fatigue.

In some western European markets Red Bull has had its distribution opportunities curtailed by government regulation. Due to the product's high caffeine content, distribution in Norway, Denmark and France has been limited to pharmacies, where it has been classified as a medicine. In addition, EU regulators ruled in early 2002 that all cans must contain a warning label regarding the drink's caffeine content.

International expansion

Given that all production occurs in Austria, one of Red Bull's largest tasks is the expansion of the drink throughout the international arena. International expansion has been key to the Red Bull business plan and began in 1992 when the drink became available in Hungary, just five years after the drink's initial domestic release.

Major western European expansion occurred in 1994 with releases in key markets like the UK and Germany, not to mention the Netherlands and Switzerland. This was followed in 1995 by further introduction of the product in eastern Europe, Australia and Brazil. Another important new launch for company occurred in 1997 thanks to Red Bull's release in the USA.

At the time of writing, the drink is sold in over 70 countries. The company now also has offices in many of its distribution regions, such as South America, where it has offices scattered throughout the continent from Mexico to Argentina. As mentioned above, recent expansion included a move into the Indian market in 2002.

International competition

In 2001 Red Bull enjoyed a successful year; the company pulled itself ahead one place in the international functional drinks market, increasing its share by nearly half of one point. Its ranking of seventh put the brand behind Kirin Brewing and ahead of GlaxoSmithKline in functional drinks. In terms of global brand rankings, Red Bull is eighth behind Dakara by Suntory but ahead of GlaxoSmithKline's Lucozade.

Red Bull's increased world market share resulted from the cumulative growth experienced by many of its individual markets. Both the UK and Ireland performed extremely well in 2001, increasing share by about 1 percentage point each. Similarly, the North American market share increased by 0.3 of a percentage point as the drink's popularity continued to increase in that key market.

In the functional drinks market, Red Bull faces competition from major players like PepsiCo and the Coca-Cola Company, both of which have leading brands in that sector. In fact, PepsiCo owns the brand leader Gatorade, while the Coca-Cola Company has the Powerade and Aquarius brands, which rank third and fourth respectively. Other major western brands include GlaxoSmithKline's Lucozade and Cadbury Schweppes's Snapple.

New competitors have sprung up in a number of markets, posing a threat to Red Bull. In the UK, two such brands, Bull Ring and Red Devil, currently produce energy drinks, and in South Africa the Mad Bull and Red Eagle brands also threaten to take market share. In Germany and Austria there are Flying Horse, Cult and Mad Bat. All of them are (like Red Bull) from Austrian manufacturers.

In some cases, Red Bull has pursued these copycat producers, as in the case of Live Wire. In 2002 Red Bull won its case against this lookalike brand; however, the company was unable to recuperate any of the damages and only a small portion of its legal fees because Live Wire went out of business two months prior to the court's ruling. Similarly, Red Bull has battled the Mad Bull brand in South Africa. However, the costly litigation and loss of sales resulting from copycat makers continues to eat into Red Bull's profits.

Red Bull's market shares

Red Bull has a broad global reach, with key markets in western Europe and North America. In western Europe the company's breadth is extensive and it claims a significant place in important markets such as the UK, Germany, Austria and

Switzerland. Though not quite as well developed the brand is also available in Mediterranean regions such as Spain and Italy. Exceptions to this are France, Norway and Denmark, where the drink is considered a medicine and is therefore available only in pharmacies.

In North America, Red Bull is banned in Canada due to its high caffeine content. Thus the company's growing position relies on sales in the USA, which have been increasing since the brand was launched in 1997.

While the company's market share continues to grow in eastern Europe, Australasia, and Africa and the Middle East, Red Bull's Latin American presence is more negligible. Its distribution in the region, though geographically far reaching (including markets as far north as Mexico and Venezuela, and down to Argentina), is less well developed.

Table 4.1 Red Bull regional market shares in functional drinks by geographical sector (2002)

Region	Market share in region (2002) % retail volume
Western Europe	17%
Eastern Europe	38%
North America	1.0%
Latin America	0.3%
Far East	1.8%
Australia/New Zealand	5.8%
Africa/Middle East	8.8%
Total world	**app. 15%**

Source: adapted from Euromonitor

Future opportunities

The drink remains very much a niche product as, as noted above, its high caffeine content immediately disqualifies it from large consumer segments. First, it is considered unsuitable for children under 16; it is also to be avoided by the elderly, those sensitive to caffeine and pregnant women. Though its target audience, young adults (particularly men), has some earning power, the brand is inherently limited by its ingredient list. If Red Bull wants to move beyond its niche placement and reach the entire functional drinks spectrum or even the larger realm of soft drinks, it will have to purchase or develop another brand. One option would be a complementary functional drink.

Given that Red Bull is frequently consumed before participation in sport, the company could perhaps create an 'après-sport', hydrating drink that also replenishes vitamins and minerals lost during physical exertion. This type of drink would also be suitable for the entire population. It is true that the marketing of such a drink would be expensive, and would require Red Bull to broaden its image, moving away from its current strictly youthful and distinctly masculine image. However, moving into broader functional and soft drink avenues would at once protect it against any fluctuation in demand and simultaneously give it access to larger streams of revenue.

Besides these future opportunities there is of course the opportunity for Red Bull to try and expand its international coverage to additional international markets. Alternatively, it could try to win greater market share in the markets in which it is already represented.

Questions

1 What are the explanations for the international success of Red Bull?

2 Which of the above future opportunities should Red Bull pursue? Use SWOT analysis as a starting point.

Developing the marketing strategy and programme

Strategic market planning

Chapter contents

Learning Objectives

After studying this chapter you should be able to:

- understand the importance of strategic marketing planning

- identify the main steps in strategic marketing planning

- develop an appropriate business mission statement

- describe the criteria for stating good strategic marketing objectives

- understand how portfolio models are used to select alternatives

- explain the advantages and disadvantages of using strategic models like Ansoff's growth matrix, and the BCG and GE models.

5.1 **Introduction**

The word 'strategy' is derived from a Greek term, translated roughly as the 'art of the general (or commander-in-chief)'. It should be borne in mind, though, that military strategy, and relatively traditional perspectives at that, is only one source of insight into the nature of marketing strategy. Useful analogies can also be found in both sports and evolutionary ecology, as well as in more formal game theory. Strategy, then, originally referred to the *skills and decision-making processes* of the general (executive), while 'stratagem', translated as 'an operation or act of generalship', referred to a *specific decision* made by the executive.

To complicate matters even further, some writers suggest that a 'strategy' implies a formal and explicitly stated logic, while others have argued that a strategy can emerge from a set of decisions and need not be stated explicitly. Mintzberg and Walters (1985) even distinguished specifically between 'deliberate' and 'emergent' strategies.

Planning is a complex process and in explaining it to anyone there must be consideration of communication. Presenting a model of a number of stages is a common way to attempt to effect communication. All the stages are interrelated, but this approach, like the final plan itself at a particular point in time, is like a freeze-frame photograph. With time there is change, hence planning is a continuous process where each stage needs to be considered and reconsidered for relevancy and in relation to the other stages. The plan is the stages 'frozen' in time; the process is a continuous assessment of the relevancy of each of these stages with changes in time.

In planning we look ahead to decide what to do. The planning process itself is a systematic way of approaching the following questions, and they will be used as a framework for the rest of this chapter.

- What business are we in? (vision and mission statement – Section 5.2)

- Where are we today? (situation analysis – Chapter 4)

- Where do we want to go? (strategic objectives – Section 5.3)

- How do we get there?

  - Estimation of the planning gap, and problem diagnosis (Section 5.4)

  - The search for strategic alternatives (Ansoff's growth matrix, Porter's three generic strategies, the BCG and GE models – Section 5.5)

  - Strategy evaluation and selection (Section 5.6)

  - Estimating financial consequences/How can progress be measured? (marketing metrics – Section 5.7)

Although there is never any certainty about the future, every business or organization will sensibly lean towards a proactive rather than a reactive stance. A proactive stance is one where the organization tries to forecast the future in order to influence it – that is, plan to adapt to it rather than just surrender to it. This contrasts with a more reactive stance, where action mainly takes place in response to events with no plan to anticipate them or seek to influence them. This is similar to the two concepts explained in Chapter 2: market driving (Resource Based View) versus market driven (Market Orientation View).

5.2 **Vision and mission statement**

The vision and mission concepts are often intertlinked, but generally there is a difference:

- a business *mission* statement describes 'who we are and what is the overall purpose of our business'

- a business *vision* statement describes 'where we wish to go', 'what we wish to become'; it provides a mental image of the successful accomplishment of the mission; it is typically:
  - short
  - idealistic and imaginative
  - enthusiasm-inspiring
  - ambitious.

The rest of this section will primarily be about the mission:

The mission reflects the unique qualities of the programme.

Whether the organization is a large corporation or a small non-profit agency, its mission statement articulates its strategic scope clearly. The mission statement should answer fundamental questions such as 'What is our business?', 'Who are our constituencies?', 'What value do we provide to customers, employees, suppliers and other constituent groups?' and 'What should our business be in the future?' Senior management staff in all businesses need to answer such questions. The responsibility for developing and articulating a mission statement is at the corporate level.

Mission statements should be driven by three factors: heritage, resources and environment.

The organization's *heritage* is its history – where it has been, what it has done well and what it has done poorly. A good mission statement cannot ignore previous events and how they have shaped the organization. It also must be sensitive to the organization's image in the minds of its constituencies. Past successes should be extended, past failures avoided, and the organization's current image must be addressed realistically. For example, for a food company to adopt a mission statement such as 'to be a world leader in information technology in five years' will be perceived as unrealistic by customers, employees and shareholders. Such a mission statement is likely to elicit more scepticism than support.

Resources refers to everything the organization can manage, such as cash reserves, recognized brands, unique technologies and talented employees. Resources can also include borrowing power, existing relationships with distributors and excess plant capacity. A good mission statement notes the organization's resources and sets paths that are compatible with what the organization has at its disposal. As in the case of heritage, mission statements that are out of touch with the organization's resources elicit scepticism and can do more harm than good. If a minor regional brand were to include 'penetrating Asian markets' in its mission statement, this would be met with substantial scepticism.

The *environment* is everything happening currently that affects the company's ability to achieve objectives or implement strategies, both inside and outside the organization. Some environmental factors are temporary, such as a hurricane. Most temporary factors are too short-lived to be considered in a mission statement. Other factors, however, such as changes in the political system of the Russian Republic, the rise of Islamic fundamentalism, terrorist acts, and the rise or fall of oil prices, may have a longer life and should be considered in the mission statement *if* they affect the organization's ability to survive and prosper.

At the corporate level, the mission statement defines the organization's business and reflects fundamental beliefs about its strengths and weaknesses, as well as its environment. Corporate mission statements can vary in length, but should always communicate a clear sense of the organization's purpose, and be specific enough to be useful in developing goals and objectives. Typically, mission statements focus on meeting customer needs and providing value to shareholders. In addition, they often include judgements about the most promising directions for organizations, implying that those directions not listed are not as promising and should be given lower priority or ignored altogether.

Not all organizations have mission statements, and not all mission statements meet the ideal standards described here. Developing a company mission statement that provides long-term vision and guidance in developing goals and objectives can be difficult. Writing an effective mission statement requires senior managers to struggle with the questions listed earlier – questions that sound simple but can be tough issues for an organization to address. The increasing visibility and importance of marketing as a philosophy for doing business, however, forces many organizations to tackle the task of defining their corporate mission. At the same time, an emphasis on marketing also helps organizations ensure that meeting customer needs profitably lies at the centre of any mission statement.

5.3 **Strategic objectives**

Strategic management also requires that firms set *strategic objectives*: specific and measurable performance standards for strategically important areas. Whereas a mission statement may set broad goals, such as 'being the best company in the world', strategic objectives must specify what it means to be 'best'. Management must define the criteria it will use to assess performance and then specify a desired level of achievement for each criterion.

An organization cannot set realistic, realizable objectives until it has the requisite information but, on the basis of experience, marketing management will none the less have tentative views on sales volume, market share or whatever indicators represent progress towards accomplishing the firm's vision. What exactly these tentative views are will be influenced by subjective estimates of what is considered reasonable at the time in relation to what resources are likely to be available.

For a manager to be able to direct an activity towards the achievement of some objectives it must be possible to imagine the goal in a way that is meaningful for guiding the activity. This is why objectives purely concerned with profit are inadequate: they offer too little guidance.

Strategic objectives can be stated in terms of different criteria, such as euro sales, market share or return on investment, or they can be stated in absolute or relative terms. To be effective, objectives must be specific in terms of:

- the performance dimension being measured

- the measures most appropriate for the performance dimension

- the target value for each measure

- the time by which the target should be achieved.

The emphasis given to each component of the organization's objectives, and the level at which measures and the time horizon are set, can vary according to position in the organizational hierarchy. At the corporate level, profit and growth objectives might be most important and the time horizon might be set in five-year increments. At a business-unit level, however, cash flow and cost reductions may be most important in declining markets, and market share gains in emerging markets. Likewise, the time horizon might be shorter than five years for business units because a new technology will render current operations obsolete, or it might be longer because market acceptance is slow. The characteristics of business units and their immediate environment should primarily determine strategic objectives, provided that the objectives do not violate the organization's mission. The objectives should also be compatible with the culture unless the business unit is soon to be divested.

Strategic objectives at different organizational levels can sometimes conflict. Conflict can also arise between the different levels of organizational thinking. An organization might set objectives pertaining to a desired culture that conflict with its more specific objectives for staff development. Consider, for example, a mission statement that lists as a goal 'providing opportunities for employees' personal development' at the same time as the company claims to value teamwork. Maximizing individual employee development can undermine teamwork if the primary means of development is to promote high performers quickly. Such a company has conflicting objectives, even if they are implicit and not easily recognized.

Managers must establish strategic objectives with great care. These must be articulated at every level of the organization at which it makes sense to have objectives. They must be expressed in terms that are easily understood by the people who are required to achieve them, they must be measurable and specific, and they must be set at achievable levels. Setting objectives at attainable, yet challenging, levels is important.

It should be clear that strategic objectives must be compatible with the organization's mission; at the same time they may conflict over what are relevant evaluation criteria, performance measures and time horizons. Conflict between strategic objectives must be resolved through compromise, and it is senior management's job to reconcile these differences within the broad framework of having a market-orientated philosophy of doing business.

5.4 Estimation of the planning gap, and problem diagnosis

What do the 'facts' suggest will be the future if the firm takes no action to change current strategies? Such a prediction is known as a 'reference projection'. A reference projection is the future that can be expected in the absence of planned change. The reference projection is compared with 'target projection', or the setting of tentative goals, which the firm sets for itself. The planning (performance) gap is the difference between the target and the reference projections (see Fig. 5.1).

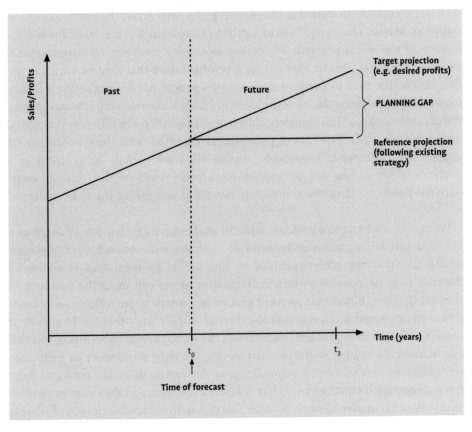

Figure 5.1 Illustration of the 'planning gap'
Source: *Marketing Management*, Hollensen, Pearson Education Limited (2003)

The gap may stem from the difference between future desired profit objectives and a forecast of projected profit based on past performance and following existing strategy.

In the face of such a planning gap, a number of options are available; the intention, however, is to close the gap. This could be achieved by revising objectives in a downward direction; such a step might be taken where the initial objectives are unrealistic. Alternatively, or in addition, the gap could be closed by actions designed to move the company off the projection curve and towards the desired curve.

The planning gaps identified will depend on which performances are of interest. At the highest level, this could be cash flow projections, economic value added, cash flow return on investment, earnings per share, sales and market share or various financial indices like return on investment (ROI). At the marketing level, this could be in terms of sales, market share, costs, market penetration or various behavioural indices like buyer attitudes.

Problem diagnosis

If a firm has a large planning gap, we would be likely to pinpoint this as a problem; or, more accurately, to state that the planning gap itself is not the problem but the symptom of one. The recognition of a problem situation is not in itself the identification of the actual problem. We do not discover a problem, we diagnose one. Problem diagnosis aims to identify the *type* of solution that applies, which is the first step on the road to developing an actual solution, just as diagnosing a failure to start the car as being due to some electrical fault is the first step towards getting the car started again. Unfortunately, different people will make different diagnoses, depending on their experience, professional expertise and their concerns. Of course, some companies may evade responsibility and define the problem as a problem of persuading the government to increase tariffs on their foreign competitors' products. Here the solution is viewed as increasing the firm's political muscle.

We cannot understand a problem without understanding what would count as a solution, just as we cannot understand an objective without understanding what would count as the achievement of it. The actual problem that is addressed depends to some extent on which individual or group can make the problem, as they see it, count. But all management groups in a company are influenced by credible arguments and so true technical expertise usually wins the day. Hopefully it must, for if the wrong problem is addressed, the wrong decisions are made and this can be more wasteful of resources than solving the right problem in an inefficient way. Although we hesitate to acknowledge it, the fact is that once we move away from some pure deductive system like mathematics, we are in the realm of persuasion, where persuasive rhetoric is crucial so that a dramatic description of what is considered to be the problem can emotionally compel attention and, often, our assent.

Exhibit 5.1 Starbucks considers India as a new market

Today, Starbucks operates 8000 cafés worldwide, including over 100 locations in China. Its long-term expansion goal is to have 30,000 cafés worldwide.

India, on target to become the most populous country in the world after China, produces and consumes the most tea in the world. Strangely enough, though, it could be next on Starbucks' list of hot new markets for gourmet coffee outside of the United States.

Both India and China are still small players in terms of domestic coffee consumption. China has one of the world's smallest coffee markets, whereas India ranks 36th out of 53 nations with the biggest sales of packaged coffee, according to market research firm ACNielsen. The United States tops the list, followed by Germany, France, Japan and Italy.

India is a tea-based culture. Starbucks and other coffee bars are substitutes, but these cafés offer an opportunity for younger people to socialize outside of the home. 'With the liberalization of the economy, there are a large number of young Indians with good jobs and attractive incomes,' says Brotin Banerjee, vice president of marketing at New Delhi-based Barista Coffee Company. 'Many still live with their parents. So their income is largely disposable and they need to spend it on something. Why not on gourmet coffee?'

Competition

Industry reports suggest that India's nascent gourmet coffee market holds the potential for 5000 cafés over the next five years.

Barista opened its first 'coffee bar' in India four years ago. Today it operates 130 cafés around the country, which bear a resemblance to Starbucks. Barista already has a brand identity and customer loyalty. It also has prime locations in big metropolitan cities. Barista's menu features everything from latte to cappuccino, caramel caffé, caffé mocha, flavoured coffee and desserts like brownies and cakes.

Strategy opportunities for Starbucks

Starbucks is keen to tap in to India's burgeoning middle-class market of 200 million people. However, unlike its domestic US approach, where its stores are largely company owned, government regulations in India will require it either to form joint ventures with local players or create franchise operations. Apparently that's not an issue, since the company faced a similar hurdle in China and opted for the joint-venture route.

Source: adapted from Bhatnagar (2004)

5.5 The search for strategic alternatives for closing the 'planning gap'

The strategic options for closing the planning gap should not only fit the problematic situation and take account of trends and competition, but should also exploit the firm's core competencies and strengths. Where the solution is other than a crisis one, there is time for more reflective planning, guided by:

- the situation as revealed by the performance gap

- the perceived problem

- the strengths, weaknesses, opportunities and threats identified in the historical review/situation analysis

- current strategies and policies

- existing capabilities or competencies.

The strategy search process should always allow for the possibility of inspiration, which may beat anything arrived at by methodical analysis. It is not uncommon for someone to come up with an idea that is instantly recognizable as being the right answer: genius sometimes lies in what appears, once stated, as a truism. The inspired solution is thus accepted, not because it saves time (this would just be to accept a faster way of producing unsatisfactory end results) but because it is perceived to be superior and effective. This said, the identification of appropriate strategies rests on having the requisite experience, and the content of the strategy, not the procedure, is all-important. Where the requisite experience is lacking, the search for strategies is likely to be hampered by obstacles.

The mental screening and evaluation of strategies can be demanding. In effect we are mentally rehearsing hypotheses about the relationship between strategies and their likely benefits – but not *just* benefits, since strategies can have side-effects that can constitute dysfunctional consequences.

Ansoff's generic strategies for growth

One aspect of strategic management is the development of specific strategies for achieving company objectives. Strategies must respond to the environment and provide specific guidelines for decision-making. Because organizations face unique combinations of internal and external factors, the strategies developed by any one organization are unlikely to be entirely adaptable to any other organization. At a more general level, however, it is possible to discern recurring patterns in the strategies adopted by organizations. These recurring patterns are called *generic strategies*.

If we elaborate on the 'planning gap' depicted in Fig. 5.1 we get what is illustrated in Fig. 5.2, where the 'gap' is filled up with Ansoff's expansion strategies (Ansoff, 1965).

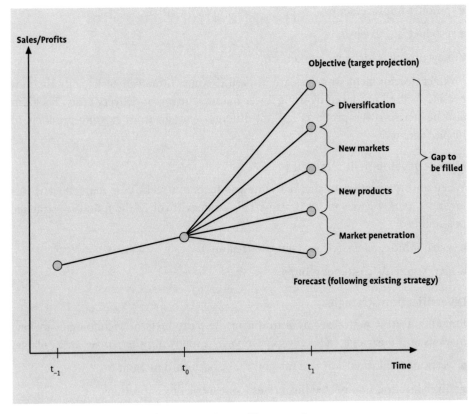

Figure 5.2 Filling the 'planning gap' with Ansoff's strategies

Market penetration

Organizations seeking to grow by gaining a larger market share in their current industry or market follow a *penetration* strategy. The following alternatives are available:

- increase market share on current markets with current products
- increase product share (increase frequency of use, increase quantity used, new applications).

Penetration strategies can be very successful when the company has a technological or production advantage that allows it to take market share away from competitors while still operating profitably. However, such strategies can also be very costly if they rely primarily on setting prices below those of competing products.

Product development strategies

Organizations can also remain within their established industries or markets and seek expansion by introducing new products or services in current markets. This is also called a *technology development strategy*. This strategy may take the following forms:

- product improvements
- product line extensions
- new products for same market.

Product development strategies are in peril if competitors can easily copy the new product being introduced by using lower manufacturing or delivery costs. They can also be at risk if the products are not different enough from existing products to inspire demand.

Market development strategies

When an organization retains the same products but seeks new markets, it is following a *market development* strategy. This strategy involves the following strategic possibilities:

- geographic expansion (new countries/regions)
- new segments/customer groups.

Diversification strategies

Pursuing a growth strategy by introducing new products or technologies in new markets or industries is called *diversification*. The following alternatives are available:

- vertical integration (forward integration or backward integration)
- diversification into related businesses (concentric diversification)
- diversification into unrelated businesses (conglomerate diversification).

This term 'diversification' is frequently associated with expansion into areas unrelated to the company's current operations in order to offset cyclical downturns in one area with cyclical growth in other areas. Diversification was popular with many large companies in the 1970s and gave rise to legendary conglomerates.

Another way of illustrating the 'planning gap' and moving the company towards the desired curve (or position in the market) is to look at existing sales and compare these with total served market and the market potential (Fig. 5.3). The single firm is mainly able to increase market share by filling the '4Ps gaps', by using one or more Ps in combination. However, unless the firm is a major player in the industry it will not be able to influence the size of the unserved market or the degree of market penetration. (We will look at the 4Ps in more detail in later chapters.)

Market potential

The most difficult estimate to make is probably that of 'market potential' in the whole market, including all segments. In the B2C market it is often achieved by determining the maximum potential individual usage and then extrapolating this by the maximum number of potential consumers (in the B2B market it would be the maximum number of firms). The maximum potential individual usage, or at least the maximum attainable average usage, will usually be determined from market research figures. For

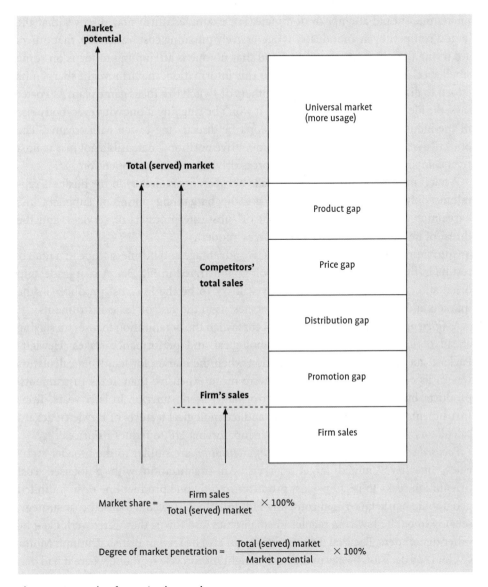

Figure 5.3 Levels of gaps in the market

guidance one can look at the numbers using similar products. Alternatively, a marketer can look at what has happened in other countries. It has often been suggested that Europe follows patterns set in the United States, but with a certain time lag.

Porter's three generic strategies

Strategies based on distinctive advantage and business scope

According to Porter (1985), forging successful strategy begins with understanding of what is happening in one's industry and deciding which of the available competitive

99

niches one should attempt to dominate. For example, a firm may discover that the largest competitor in an industry is aggressively pursuing cost leadership, that others are trying the differentiation route, and that no one is attempting to focus on some small speciality market. On the basis of this information, the firm might sharpen its efforts to distinguish its product from others or switch to a focus game plan. As Porter says, the idea is to position the firm 'so it won't be slugging it out with everybody else in the industry; if it does it right, it won't be directly toe-to-toe with anyone'. The objective is to mark out a defensible competitive position – defensible not just against rival companies, but also against the forces driving industry competition.

What it means is that the give-and-take between firms already in the business represents only one such force. Others are the bargaining power of suppliers, the bargaining power of buyers, the threat of substitute products or services, and the threat of new entrants (Porter's 'five forces' model).

Combining the dimensions of distinctive advantage and business scope in a matrix results in the strategic orientation typology illustrated in Fig. 5.4. A cost leadership orientation suggests that the company will try to be the low-cost producer in the markets and industries in which it competes, as in the case of Texas Instruments.

A *differential advantage* orientation occurs when the organization focuses on staying ahead of its competitors in the technological and performance stakes. Hewlett-Packard adopted this strategic orientation when the market for handheld calculators was in its early stages. Its calculators were more expensive than Texas Instruments' products, but HP's technology and performance were superior. In later years, Texas Instruments matched the performance and technological features of Hewlett-Packard calculators while retaining its cost leadership, forcing HP to reduce its prices.

Focused cost advantage and *focused differentiation* are similar to the broader strategies, but have limited target markets. An organization with a focused cost orientation seeks to be a low-cost producer in only one product line or in a limited geographic market. German company Lidl initially followed a focused cost strategy, seeking to be the low-cost retailer in small cities and towns that were overlooked by other discounters. Focused differentiation can also be seen in British Triumph Motor Cycles Ltd's decision to stay in the heavyweight motorcycle segment, where it had distinctive features.

The BCG portfolio matrix model

A good planning system must guide the development of strategic alternatives for each of the company's current businesses and new business possibilities. It must also provide for management's review of these strategic alternatives and for corresponding resource-allocation decisions. The result is a set of approved business plans that, taken as a whole, represent the direction of the firm. This process starts with, and its success is largely determined by, the creation of sound strategic alternatives.

The top management of a multi-business firm cannot generate these strategic alternatives. It must rely on the managers of its business ventures and on its corporate

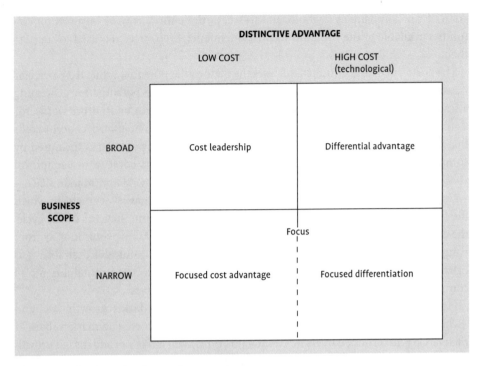

Figure 5.4 The three (four) generic strategies
Source: adapted from Porter (1985)

development personnel. However, top management can and should establish a conceptual framework within which these alternatives can be developed. One such framework is the portfolio matrix associated with the Boston Consulting Group (BCG). Briefly, the portfolio matrix is used to establish the best mix of businesses in order to maximize the long-term earnings growth of the firm. The portfolio matrix represents a real advance in strategic planning in several ways:

- it encourages top management to evaluate the prospects of each of the company's businesses individually and to set tailored objectives for each business based on the contribution it can realistically make to corporate goals

- it stimulates the use of externally focused empirical data to supplement managerial judgement in evaluating the potential of a particular business

- it explicitly raises the issue of cash-flow balancing as management plans for expansion and growth

- it gives managers a potent new tool for analysing competitors and for predicting competitive responses to strategic moves

- it provides not just a financial but also a strategic context for evaluating acquisitions and divestitures.

The portfolio matrix approach has given top management the tools to evaluate each business in the context of both its environment and its unique contribution to the goals of the company as a whole, and to weigh the entire array of business opportunities available to the company against the financial resources required to support them.

The portfolio matrix concept addresses the issue of the potential value of a particular business for the firm. This value has two variables: first, the potential for generating attractive earnings levels now; second, the potential for growth or, in other words, for significantly increased earnings levels in the future. The portfolio matrix concept holds that these two variables can be quantified. Current earning potential is measured by comparing the market position of the business to that of its competitors. Empirical studies have shown that profitability is directly determined by relative market share.

Growth potential is measured by the growth rate of the market segment in which the business competes. Clearly, if the segment is in the decline stage of its life cycle, the only way the business can increase its market share is by taking volume away from competitors. Although this is sometimes possible and economically desirable, it is usually expensive, leads to destructive pricing and the erosion of profitability for all competitors, and ultimately results in a market that is ill served.

Figure 5.5 shows a matrix with its two sides labelled 'Market growth rate' and 'Relative market share'. The area of each circle represents sales. The market share of each circle is determined by its horizontal position. Each circle's product sales growth rate (corrected for inflation) in the market in which it competes is shown by its vertical position.

With regard to the two axes of the matrix, relative market share is plotted on a logarithmic scale in order to be consistent with the experience curve effect, which implies that profit margin or rate of cash generation differences between two competitors tends to be proportionate to the ratio of their competitive positions. A linear axis is used for growth, for which the most generally useful measure is volume growth of the business concerned; in general, rates of cash use should be directly proportional to growth.

Classification of the BCG Boxes

Using the two dimensions illustrated in Fig. 5.5, one can classify businesses and products into four categories. Businesses in each category exhibit different financial characteristics and offer different strategic choices, as described below.

Stars

High-growth market leaders are called *stars*. They generate large amounts of cash, but the cash they generate from earnings and depreciation is more than offset by the cash that must be put back in the form of capital expenditure and increased working capital. Such heavy reinvestment is necessary to fund the capacity increases and inventory and receivable investment that go along with market share gains. Thus, star products represent probably the best profit opportunity available to a company, and their competitive position must be maintained. If a star's share is allowed to slip because the star has been used to provide large amounts of cash in the short run or

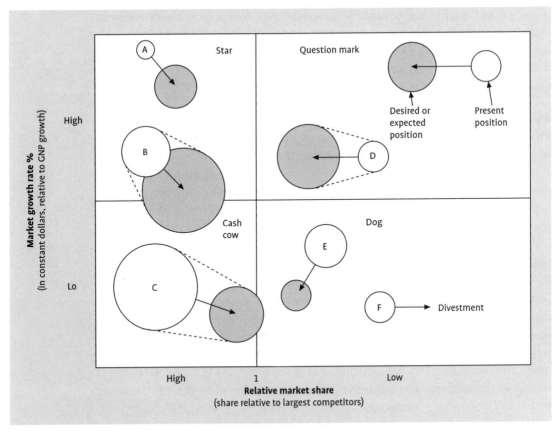

Figure 5.5 The BCG model
Source: *Marketing Management*, Hollensen, Pearson Education Limited (2003)

because of cutbacks in investment and rising prices (creating an umbrella for competitors), the star will ultimately become a dog (see below).

The ultimate value of any product or service is reflected in the stream of cash it generates net of its own reinvestment. For a star, this stream of cash lies in the future – sometimes in the distant future. To obtain real value, the stream of cash must be discounted back to the present at a rate equal to the return on alternative opportunities. It is the future pay-off of the star that counts, not the present reported profit. For General Electric (GE), the plastics business is a star in which it keeps investing. As a matter of fact, the company even acquired French company Thomson's plastics operations to further strengthen its position in the business.

Cash cows

Cash cows are characterized by low growth and high market share. They are net providers of cash. Their high earnings, coupled with their depreciation, represent high cash inflows and they need very little in the way of reinvestment. Thus, these businesses generate large cash surpluses that help to pay dividends and interest, provide debt capacity, supply funds for research and development, meet overheads, and also make cash available for investment in other products. Thus, cash cows are the foundation on which everything else depends. These products must be protected. Technically speaking, a cash cow has a return on assets that exceeds its growth rate. Only if this is true will the cash cow generate more cash than it uses.

Question marks

Products in a growth market with a low share are categorized as *question marks*. Because of growth, these products require more cash than they are able to generate on their own. If nothing is done to increase market share, a question mark will simply absorb large amounts of cash in the short run and later, as the growth slows down, become a dog (see below). Thus, unless something is done to change its perspective, a question mark remains a cash loser throughout its existence and ultimately becomes a cash trap.

What can be done to make a question mark more viable? One alternative is to gain share increases for it. Because the business is growing, it can be funded to dominance. It may then become a star and later, when growth slows down, a cash cow. This strategy is a costly one in the short run. An abundance of cash must be poured into a question mark in order for it to win a major share of the market, but in the long run this strategy is the only way to develop a sound business from the question mark stage. Another strategy is to divest the business. Outright sale is the most desirable alternative. But if this does not work out, a firm decision must be made not to invest further in the business. The business must simply be allowed to generate whatever cash it can while none is reinvested.

Dogs

Products with low market share positioned in low-growth situations are called *dogs*. Their poor competitive position condemns them to poor profits. Because growth is low, dogs have little potential for gaining sufficient share to achieve viable cost positions. Usually they are net users of cash. Their earnings are low, and the reinvestment required just to keep the business together eats cash inflow. The business, therefore, becomes a cash trap that is likely to regularly absorb cash unless further investment is rigorously avoided. An alternative is to convert dogs into cash, if there is an opportunity to do so. GE's consumer electronics business had been in the dog category, maintaining only a small percentage of the available market in a period of slow growth, when the company decided to unload the business (including the RCA brand acquired in late 1985) to Thomson, France's state-owned, leading electronics manufacturer.

Table 5.1 summarizes the investment, earning and cash flow characteristics of stars, cash cows, question marks and dogs. Also shown are viable strategy alternatives for products in each category.

Strategy implications

In a typical company, products could be scattered in all four quadrants of the portfolio matrix. The appropriate strategy for products in each cell is given briefly in Table 5.1.

Table 5.1 **Characteristics and strategy implications of products in the strategy quadrants**				
Quadrant	**Investment characteristics**	**Earning characteristics**	**Cash-flow characteristics**	**Strategy implication**
Stars	Continual expenditures for capacity expansion	Low	Negative cash flow (net cash user)	Continue to increase market share, if necessary at the expense of short-term earnings
Cash cows	Capacity maintenance expenditures	High	Positive cash flow (net cash contributor)	Maintain share and leadership until further investment becomes marginal
Question marks	Heavy initial capacity expenditures High research and development costs	Negative to low	Negative cash flow (net cash user)	Assess chances of dominating segment: if good, go after share; if bad, redefine business or withdraw
Dogs	Gradually deplete capacity		Positive cash flow (net cash contributor)	Plan an orderly withdrawal so as to maximize cash flow

In summary, the portfolio matrix approach provides for the simultaneous comparison of different products. It also underlines the importance of cash flow as a strategic variable. Thus, when continuous long-term growth in earnings is the objective, it is necessary to identify high-growth product/market segments early, develop businesses and pre-empt the growth in these segments. If necessary, short-term profitability in these segments may be forgone to ensure achievement of the dominant share. Costs must be managed to meet scale-effect standards. The appropriate point at which to shift from an earnings focus to a cash-flow focus must be determined and a liquidation plan for cash-flow maximization established. A cash-balanced mix of businesses should be maintained.

The portfolio matrix approach is not, however, a panacea for strategy development. In reality, many difficulties limit the workability of this approach. Some potential mistakes associated with the portfolio matrix concept are:

- overinvesting in low-growth segments (lack of objectivity and 'hard' analysis)

- underinvesting in high-growth segments (lack of guts)

- misjudging the segment growth rate (poor market research).

The GE (General Electric) multifactor portfolio matrix

The BCG model discussed above provides a useful approach for reviewing the roles of different products in a company. However, the growth rate–relative market share matrix approach leads to many difficulties. At times, factors other than market share and growth rate bear heavily on cash flow, the mainstay of this approach. Some managers may consider return on investment a more suitable criterion than cash flow for making investment decisions. Further, the two-factor portfolio matrix approach does not address major investment decisions between dissimilar businesses. These difficulties can lead a company into too many traps and errors. For this reason, many companies (such as GE and the Shell Group) have developed the multifactor portfolio approach.

Unit of analysis

The framework discussed here may be applied to either a product/market or an SBU. As a matter of fact, it may be equally applicable to a much higher level of aggregation in the organization, such as a division or a group.

For an individual business, there can be four strategy options: (i) investing to maintain or (ii) investing to grow (the dark area of Fig. 5.6); (iii) investing to maintain or regain; (iv) investing to exit (the light area of Fig. 5.6). The choice of a strategy depends on the current position of the business in the matrix (i.e. towards the high side, along the diagonal or towards the low side) and its future direction, assuming the current strategic perspective continues to be followed. If the future appears unpromising, a new strategy for the business is called for.

Analysis of present position on the matrix may not pose any problem. At GE, for example, there was little disagreement on the position of the business. The mapping of future direction, however, may not be easy. A rigorous analysis must be performed, taking into account environmental shifts, competitors' perspectives, and internal strengths and weaknesses.

A new product portfolio approach

As discussed earlier, Porter identified three generic strategies: (i) overall cost leadership (i.e. making units of a fairly standardized product and underpricing everybody else); (ii) differentiation (i.e. turning out something customers perceive as unique – an item whose quality, design, brand name or reputation for service commands higher-than-average prices); and (iii) focus (i.e. concentrating on a particular group of customers, geographic market, channel of distribution or distinct segment of the product line).

Porter's choice of strategy is based on two factors: the strategic target at which the business aims and the strategic advantage the business has in aiming at that target.

In summary, Porter's framework emphasizes not only that certain characteristics of the industry must be considered in choosing a generic strategy, but that they in fact dictate the proper choice.

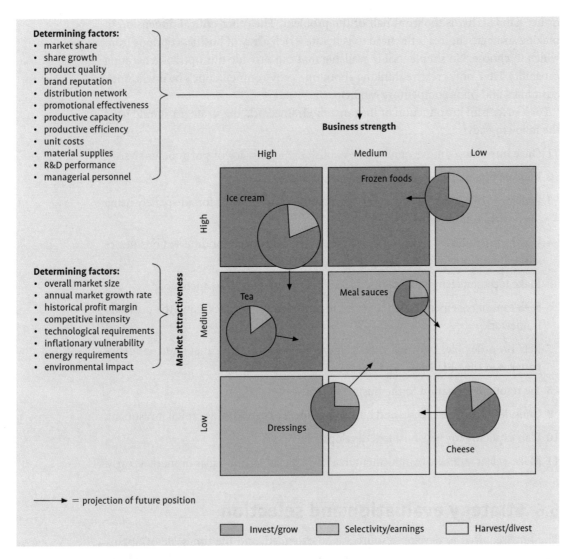

Figure 5.6 Illustration of the GE matrix of Unilever (estimate of SBU positions and prescriptive strategies for business units in Unilever's foods division – note that the graphic illustration of the business units does not necessarily reflect the real position of Unilever in these markets).
Note: The total area of business units (circles) represents the total market and the 'slice' represents the Unilever share of that market.

Portfolio approaches provide a useful tool for strategists. Granted, these approaches have limitations, but all these limitations can be overcome with a little imagination and foresight. The real concern about the portfolio approach is that its elegant simplicity often tempts managers to believe that it can solve all problems of corporate choice and resource allocation. The truth is that it addresses only half of the problem: the back half. The portfolio approach is a powerful tool for helping the strategist to select from a menu of available opportunities, but it does not put the menu into his or her hands. That is the front half of the problem. The other critical dimension in making strategic choices is the need to generate a rich array of business options from which to choose. No simple tool is available that can provide this option-generating capability. Here only creative thinking about one's environment, one's business, one's customers and one's competitors can help.

For a successful introduction of the portfolio framework, the strategist should heed the following advice.

1 Once introduced, move quickly to establish the legitimacy of portfolio analysis.

2 Educate line managers in its relevance and use.

3 Redefine SBUs explicitly because their definition is the 'basis for adequately using the portfolio framework.

4 Use the portfolio framework to seek the strategic direction for different businesses without haggling over the fancy labels by which to call them.

5 Make top management acknowledge SBUs as portfolios to be managed.

6 Seek top management time for reviewing different businesses using the portfolio framework.

7 Rely on a flexible, informal management process to differentiate and influence patterns at the SBU level.

8 Tie resource allocation to the business plan.

9 Consider strategic expenses and human resources as explicitly as capital investment.

10 Plan explicitly for new business development.

11 Make a clear strategic commitment to a few selected technologies or markets early.

5.6 Strategy evaluation and selection

The time required to develop resources is so extended, and the timescale of opportunities so brief and fleeting, that a company that has not carefully delineated and appraised its strategy is in trouble. This underlines the importance of strategy evaluation. The adequacy of a strategy may be evaluated using the following criteria.

- **Suitability** – Is there a sustainable advantage?

- **Validity** – Are the assumptions about the external environment realistic?

- **Feasibility** – Do we have the skills, resources and commitment?

- **Internal consistency** – Does the strategy hang together?

- **Vulnerability** – What are the risks and contingencies?

- **Workability** – Can we retain our flexibility?

- **Appropriate time horizon** – Do we allow enough time for implementation?

We will now look at each of these in turn.

Suitability

Strategy should offer some sort of competitive advantage. In other words, strategy should lead to a future advantage or an adaptation to forces eroding current competitive advantage. The following steps may be followed to judge the competitive advantage a strategy may provide: (i) review the potential threats and opportunities to the business; (ii) assess each option in light of the capabilities of the business; (iii) anticipate the likely competitive response to each option; (iv) modify or eliminate unsuitable options.

Validity

Strategy should be consistent with the assumptions about the external product/market environment. At a time when more and more women are seeking jobs, say, a strategy assuming traditional roles for women (e.g. raising children and staying home) would be inconsistent with the environment.

Feasibility

Money, competency and physical facilities are the critical resources a manager should be aware of in finalizing strategy. A resource may be examined in two different ways: as a constraint limiting the achievement of goals and as an opportunity to be exploited as the basis for strategy. It is desirable for a strategist to make correct estimates of resources available without being excessively optimistic about them. Further, even if resources *are* available in the corporation, a particular product/market group may not be able to lay claim to them. Alternatively, resources currently available to a product/market group may be transferred to another group if the SBU strategy deems it necessary.

Internal consistency

Strategy should be in tune with the different policies of the corporation, the SBU and the product/market arena. For example, if the corporation decided to limit the top five customers' business of any unit to 40 per cent of total sales, a product/market strategy emphasizing greater than 40 per cent reliance on the top five customers would be internally inconsistent.

Vulnerability

The degree of risk may be determined on the basis of the perspectives of the strategy and available resources. A pertinent question here is 'Will the resources be available as planned in appropriate quantities and for as long as it is necessary to implement the strategy?' The overall proportion of resources committed to a venture becomes a factor to be reckoned with: the greater the quantities of resources, the greater the degree of risk.

Workability

The workability of a strategy should be realistically evaluated with quantitative data.

Sometimes, however, it may be difficult to undertake such objective analysis. In such a case, other indications may be used to assess the contributions of a strategy. One such indication could be the degree of consensus among key executives about the viability of the strategy. Identifying ahead of time alternative strategies for achieving the goal is another indication of the workability of a strategy. Finally, establishing resource requirements in advance, which eliminates the need to institute crash programmes of cost reduction or to seek reduction in planned programmes, also substantiates the workability of the strategy.

Appropriate time horizon

A viable strategy has a time frame for its realization. The time horizon of a strategy should allow implementation without creating havoc in the organization or missing market availability. For example, in introducing a new product to the market, enough time should be allotted for market testing, training of sales people, and so on. However, the time frame should not be so long that a competitor could enter the market first and skim the cream off the top.

Strategy selection

After information on trade-offs between alternative strategies has been gathered as discussed above, a preferred strategy should be chosen for recommendation to management. Usually, there are three core marketing strategies that a company may use: (i) operational excellence; (ii) product leadership; (iii) customer intimacy. Operational excellence strategy amounts to offering middle-of-the-market products at the best price with the least inconvenience. Under this strategy, the proposition to the customer is simple: low price or hassle-free service or both. Wal-Mart, Price/Costco and Dell Computer epitomize this kind of strategy. The product leadership strategy concentrates on offering products that push performance boundaries. In other words, the basic premise of this strategy is that customers receive the best product. Moreover, product leaders don't build their propositions with just one innovation: they continue to innovate year after year.

For product leaders, competition is not about price or customer service, it is about product performance. The customer intimacy strategy focuses not on what the market wants but on what specific customers want. Businesses following this strategy do not pursue one-time transactions, they cultivate relationships. They specialize in satisfying unique needs, which often only they recognize, through a close relationship with and intimate knowledge of the customer. The underlying proposition of this strategy is: we have the best solution for you, and provide all the support you need to achieve optimum results.

The core strategy combines one or more areas of the marketing mix. For example, the preferred strategy may be product leadership. Here the emphasis of the strategy is on product, the area of primary concern. However, in order to make an integrated marketing decision, appropriate changes may have to be made in price, promotion and distribution areas. The strategic perspectives in these areas may be called *supporting strategies*. Thus, once the core strategy has been selected, supporting strategies should be delineated. Core and supporting strategies should fit the needs of the marketplace, the skills of the company and the vagaries of the competition.

Reformulation of current strategy may range from making slight modifications in existing perspectives to coming out with an entirely different strategy. How much examination and review a product/market strategy requires depends on the nature of the strategy (in terms of the change it seeks from existing perspectives) and the resource commitment required. Another point to remember in developing a core strategy is that the emphasis should always be placed on searching for new ways to compete. The marketing strategist should develop strategy around those key factors in which the business has more freedom than its competitors.

Exhibit 5.2 **International service strategies**

Service businesses tend to be more diverse than manufacturing firms. Manufacturing companies generally are less exposed to cultural differences overseas, whereas services more directly affect the behaviour of customers and service employees. Customers enter service outlets; they do not generally enter manufacturing plants. Service expectations often vary from country to country. Because the firms tend to be more deeply embedded in the culture of each country, differences in social customs, behaviour and manners must be built into the design and delivery of the service. Cultural norms governing time and the centrality of work in people's lives influence employee behaviour and commitment. In many emerging markets, public transport rarely runs on time, businesses rarely open on time and employees usually show up for work late.

Both service products and their delivery systems often require adaptation in international markets. Manufactured products may need to be modified overseas, but the process generally remains much the same. Service firms, in contrast, have to develop appropriate systems to serve the different needs of customers overseas. When they do not fit the needs of the local market, they will likely fail. In 1996, Wal-Mart began opening its superstores in Indonesia. The stores were large, clean and clearly laid out, but Indonesians rejected the layout: they preferred to shop at Matahari, a chain of small, shabby local stores that resembled traditional street vendors where customers could haggle over prices. After two years of rejection of its retail model, Wal-Mart closed its stores and withdrew completely from the Indonesian market.

Unlike most dotcoms, bricks-and-mortar service firms and stores need to achieve service density. They benefit from focusing sales in defined areas rather than spreading them broadly across a country or region. Most developing countries exhibit substantial differences in per capita income between rural and urban inhabitants. Most international consumer service businesses locate first in the major urban centres, seeking to take advantage of the purchasing power and critical mass of city dwellers. Urban centres help maximize the sales of each store or outlet. They create the potential for service density, which offers the fastest path to returns on invested capital. With the largest number of outlets of any chain store in the world, 7-Eleven is an example of an international retailer that has focused on building service density as it expands. Locating stores in Japan in clusters of 30 shops delayed the achievement of full national distribution but made 7-Eleven the most profitable chain in Japan during the 1990s.

Source: adapted from www.wal-mart.com; www.7-eleven.com; Davis, T.R.V. (2004) Different service firms, different international strategies. *Business Horizons* 47(6), pp. 51–9.

5.7 **Estimating financial consequences**

Most forms of corporate strategic analysis have to include not only a financial evaluation of the current position but also an assessment of the financial impact of future strategic choices. Such a financial evaluation often relies on the management and financial accounting information systems within the firm, but more recently a number of key conceptual issues have been raised. Most important has been the development of so-called ABC (Activity Based Costing) which, broadly, attempts to shift the focus of cost analysis towards individual elements in the various business activities or processes involved in the development and delivery of products and services. This follows on from earlier developments in management accounting, which looked at ways of constructing management accounts so that financial performance could be measured along various dimensions (such as product groups, sales territories and key customers) as a form of strategic diagnosis.

In interpreting financial data for strategic purposes it is inevitable that two fundamental conceptual issues almost always occur at some stage: the nature of opportunity cost, and the distinction between fixed and variable costs. For financial accounting purposes, it is a well-established principle that the 'cost' of a particular activity should be based on adjusted, 'real', historic costs. It is also clear that for strategic management accounting purposes, the costs should be an 'opportunity' cost based on alternative possible uses of the assets concerned. This inevitably leads to the difficult position that the cost of any specified activity depends on the cost of other alternatives. Indeed strong advocates of developments in strategic management accounting would argue that even this cost should be compared with one's competitors' costs rather than treated as an absolute figure.

In terms of the variability of costs, the simple principle is that while in the short run almost all costs are fixed, strategic analysis with its focus on the longer term tends towards a situation in which, to paraphrase the famous Keynesian dictum, 'In the long run, all costs are variable.'

The task for much strategic financial analysis is therefore to ensure that the assumptions about what is fixed and what is variable, which are built into the financial analysis, are consistent with the actual resource choices that the firm or organization faces.

Summary

In the process of selecting the right marketing strategies we need to examine past errors and recognize that learning is impeded when the chief concern is to defend past decisions. Of course, nothing can guarantee that a decision, however well made, will turn out right. It is wrong to assume that a bad outcome implies the decision was badly made since it may have been the most rationally defensible answer at the time. In any case, past strategies are seldom absolutely wrong or right, but have different degrees of imperfection.

A diversified organization needs to examine its widely different businesses at the corporate level to see how each fits within the overall corporate purpose and to come to grips with the resource allocation problem. The portfolio approaches described in this chapter help management determine the role that each business plays in the corporation and allocate resources accordingly.

The various portfolio techniques, like the Boston Consulting Group's (BCG's) growth market share matrix, General Electric's (GE's) business screen and Porter's work, plus various quantitative techniques, all help to order and bring out the implications of the data collected. These techniques can be useful in offering frameworks, analogies and models that help structure a problem situation and reduce mental overload, as well as protecting firms from a complete degeneration into ad hoc analysis.

Various portfolio approaches were critically examined in this chapter. The criticisms relate mainly to operational definitions of dimensions used, weighting of variables, and product/market boundary determination.

The Ansoff growth matrix suggests that if a company lacks new products with which to generate growth in coming years, investments may be made in new products. If growth is hurt by the early maturity of promising products, the strategic effort may be directed towards extension of their life cycles.

The BCG model suggests locating products or businesses on a matrix with relative market share and growth rate as its dimensions. The four cells in the matrix, whose positions are based on whether growth is high or low and whether relative market share is high or low, are labelled stars, cash cows, question marks and dogs. The strategy for a product or business in each cell, which is primarily based on the business's cash flow implications, was outlined.

The third approach, the GE model, again uses two variables (industry attractiveness and business strengths), but these two variables are based on a variety of factors. Here, again, a desired strategy for a product/business in each cell was recommended. The focus of the multifactor matrix approach is on the return-on-investment implications of strategy alternatives rather than on cash flow, as in the growth rate–relative market share matrix approach.

Portfolio techniques also tend to ignore interaction or synergy between the different business opportunities being evaluated. Further, these techniques are limited because they rely on imperfect measures and estimates. Even with comparatively simple dimensions such as relative market share and market growth, the actual estimation of these factors for each alternative being evaluated must rely on incomplete, and sometimes incorrect, historical information, and on estimates by experts whose 'crystal balls' may be cloudy. Pessimistic projections can cause companies to ignore high-potential products, and overly optimistic projections can lead companies to make large investments in ventures that are doomed to fail.

However, portfolio techniques are attractive to managers for several reasons. First, they make it possible to compare widely diverse alternatives by using the same factors in a relatively consistent manner. They also allow managers to simplify very complex problems to more manageable levels by eliminating hundreds of details. Reducing the information-processing load of decision-makers enables them to understand problems better and to project into the future with more confidence and accuracy. In short, portfolio techniques make the evaluation of strategic alternatives simpler and more manageable, and for these reasons alone they are valuable.

Questions for discussion

1 What is the main difference between a vision and a mission?

2 How may corporate objectives be derived from the corporate mission?

3 What is the difference between the mission statement and the firm objective?

4 What purpose may a product portfolio serve in the context of marketing strategy?

5 What are the advantages and disadvantages of using portfolio models in strategic market planning?

6 What is the meaning of relative market share in the BCG model?

7 What are the most important advantages and disadvantages of using the GE matrix compared to the BCG matrix?

References

Ansoff, H.I. (1965) *Corporate Strategy: An Analytical Approach to Business Policy for Growth and Expansion.* New York: McGraw-Hill.

Bhatnagar, P. (2004) Starbucks: a passage to India. CNNMoney (Money.cnn.com), 1 November.

Hollensen, S. (2003) *Marketing Management.* London: Financial Times/Prentice Hall, an imprint of Pearson Education.

Mintzberg, H. and Walters, J.A. (1985) Of strategies, deliberate and emergent. *Strategic Management Journal* 6, pp. 257–72.

Porter, M. (1985) *Competition Advantage: Creating and Sustaining Superior Performance.* New York: The Free Press.

Case 5 'Th!nk Neighbor': Ford's entry into the electric car market

Ford unveiled its plans for the environmentally friendly Th!nk brand at Detroit Automotive Show in 2000. It had developed the Th!nk 'environmental mobility brand' with two primary goals in mind: to sell environmentally friendly vehicles and to develop new technologies to power those vehicles.

Th!nk Group would consist of two organizations: Th!nk Mobility and Th!nk Technologies. Th!nk Mobility would sell vehicles such as the Th!nk City, the former Norwegian electric car that went into production at a factory in Aurskog, near Oslo.

Th!nk Mobility introduced three other vehicles at the 2000 Detroit show, geared primarily for the North American market. The Th!nk Neighbor is a low-speed vehicle resembling a golf cart, designed for travelling around closed residential communities or industrial sites. The Th!nk Bike Fun and Th!nk Bike Traveler are electric bicycles.

Th!nk Technologies, meanwhile, would be responsible for developing and commercializing Ford's fuel-cell vehicles.

The Th!nk Neighbor was introduced in November 2000. The retail price for this vehicle is around $6000.

Ford Motor's position in the global automotive industry

The world car industry is dominated by multinational companies, with five major groups: General Motors (GM), Ford, DaimlerChrysler, Toyota and Volkswagen. All these companies have car production plants in all parts of the world. The industry is under pressure to consolidate, and M&A (mergers and acquisitions) is part of the daily business. The accompanying table gives the different manufacturers' production figures in different parts of the world.

Ford, the main US rival to GM, is the world's second largest car company, and the most profitable. Unlike GM, it has tended to market cars under its own label – until recently. In recent years, it has gone on a buying spree abroad, acquiring luxury car makers Jaguar and Aston Martin in the UK, and a big stake in Japan's number three car company, Mazda. Ford has been highly profitable in recent years and, even after its purchase of Volvo, still has a large war chest from which to fund further acquisitions. Ford acquired Land Rover from BMW in 2000. In general, the growth of the world automotive manufacture industry is relatively low, at approximately 2 per cent per year.

Questions (part 1)

1 Prepare a 'rough' (not detailed) BCG matrix for Ford's main business areas.

2 What could be the strategic motives for Ford's entry into electric cars?

Table 5.2 **Total light vehicle production, 2003 (estimate) (1000 units)**

Manufacturer	HQ in:	Europe (western and eastern)	North America	Japan/ Korea	South America	Rest of world*	Total worldwide
General Motors	USA	1989	4895	53	606	498	8041
Ford Motor Company	USA	2203	4047	844	303	377	7775
DaimlerChrysler	D/USA	1664	2775	1100	56	808	6404
Toyota	Japan	342	1287	4035	69	1066	6800
Volkswagen	D	3571	382	–	619	528	5099
Renault/Nissan	F/Japan	2524	625	1359	186	172	4866
Honda	Japan	188	1223	1307	56	184	2957
PSA (Citroën and Peugeot)	F	2627	–	–	117	99	2844
Fiat	Italy	1845	–	–	522	77	2445
Hyundai	S Korea	10	–	2105	14	49	2178
Suzuki	Japan	211	48	916	11	950	2135
Daewoo	S Korea	87	–	530	–	48	665
Fuji Heavy	Japan	–	116	445	–	–	561
BMW	D	768	115	–	–	48	932
Other manufacturers		1527	–	–	–	818	2345
Total light vehicle production		19559	15513	12693	2560	5722	56047

Source: estimates made by the author, based on different public sources, trade magazines, manufacturer websites, etc.

* Includes Australia, China, India, Indonesia, Malaysia, Philippines, South Africa, Taiwan and Thailand

General information about the global golf industry and the golf cart market

Some market facts about golf:

- there are about 32,000 golf courses around the world; 59 per cent are in the USA, 19 per cent in Europe, 12 per cent in Asia and 10 per cent in other countries
- 56 million people around the world play golf
- the number of golf courses opening has decreased from over 900 in 1991 to a current figure of below 500 per year.

The following text concentrates on the golf cart market in the two most important golfing regions of the world: the USA and Europe.

Worldwide there are currently (beginning of 2005) 923,000 golf carts in use on golf courses. In the USA, 54 per cent of golf carts are electric, in Europe 31 per cent are

117

electric. In North America there are 47 carts per course; the rest of the world averages nine carts per course. The average age of carts in use at golf courses is three and a half years.

Augusta, Georgia, is the home of the three biggest golf cart producers in the world: Club Car, E-Z-Go and Yamaha (the latter is owned by the Yamaha Motor Company of Japan, but has a US production site near the two others, in Newman, Georgia). These three golf cart makers are market leaders, both in the United States and in Europe. Together they dominate approximately 90 per cent of the golf cart market in the USA, and 80 per cent of the golf cart market in Europe. The total market for new golf carts in 2004 was 125,000 units in the United States and 75,000 units in Europe. In both regions all three aforementioned golf cart makers are fairly equal in terms of market share, but the market leader in the United States is E-Z-Go, whereas it is Club Car in Europe.

Questions (part 2)

3 Evaluate the threats and opportunities for Ford entering the golf cart market.

4 Propose a marketing strategy for entering golf courses in Europe and United States with Th!nk Neighbor.

Source: adapted from Banks, C. (2000) Another brand to Th!nk about. *Ward's Auto World* 36(8), August, pp. 73–4; car statistics from *Ward's AutoWorld* (http://waw.wardsauto.com); Diem, W. (2000) Second Th!nks are best. *Automotive Engineer* 25(9), October pp. 49–50; Fanning, S.F. (2003) Segmentation of golf course markets. *Appraisal Journal* 71(1), pp. 62–8; golf statistics (www.golf-research.com); *Golf Week* magazine (www.golfweek.com); Gritzinger, B. (2001) Ford introduces 'front porch on wheels'. *AutoWeek* 51, p. 8; Kaufmann, S. (2000) Ford introduces new golf car. *Golf Week*, 1 October, p. 10 (http://www.golfweek.com); Miel, R. (2002) Ford cuts electric car program. *Plastics News* 14(28), pp. 3–5; Shmanske, S. (2004) Market preemption and entry deterrence: evidence from the golf course industry. *International Journal of the Economics of Business* 11(1), Feb, pp. 55–69; Wernle, B. (2000) New global Ford group Th!nks green. *Automotive News Europe* 5(2), 17 Jan, pp. 6–7.

The segmentation process

Chapter contents

Learning Objectives

After studying this chapter you should be able to:

- understand the advantages of segmentation
- describe the steps involved in segmentation
- explain the STP process
- discuss criteria for successful segmentation in B2C and B2B markets
- discuss ways of segmenting global markets
- discuss possible barriers to implementing segmentation in the organization.

6.1 **Introduction**

Segmentation sounds like a process of breaking large markets into smaller ones. In the extreme, it involves designing a unique product and marketing programme for each buyer; examples would include designing office buildings and insurance plans to meet the needs of individual corporations. However, segmentation is really a process of aggregation. The idea is to pull together groups of customers who resemble each other on some meaningful dimensions.

Segmentation is the strategy of developing different marketing programmes for different customer groups or segments. It recognizes heterogeneity in the market. Each customer segment has its own unique demand function based on price, physical product characteristics, and non-physical attributes reflecting image and perform-ance. You build volume by appealing to group preferences.

First, you need to identify the best ways to segment a market and then pin down the characteristics of each group (this second step is called *profiling*). Next, you must evaluate the attractiveness of the segments and select the most appropriate target markets. Finally, you need to position your product or service relative to competitive offerings within the chosen market segments.

6.2 **The benefits and underlying premises of market segmentation**

There are a number of important benefits that can be derived from segmenting a market, which can be summarized in the following terms.

- Segmentation is a particularly useful approach to marketing for the smaller company. It allows target markets to be matched to company competencies (see also Chapter 2) and makes it more likely that the smaller company can create a defensible niche in the market.

- It helps to identify gaps in the market, i.e. unserved or underserved segments. These can act as targets for new product development or the extension of the existing product or service range.

- In mature or declining markets it may be possible to identify specific segments that are still in growth. Concentrating on growth segments when the overall market is declining is a major strategy in the later stages of the product life cycle.

- Segmentation enables the marketer to match the product or service more closely to the needs of the target market. In this way a stronger competitive position can be built.

- The dangers of not segmenting the market when competitors do so should also be emphasized. The competitive advantages noted above can be lost to competitors if the company fails to take advantage of them. A company practising a mass-marketing strategy in a clearly segmented market against competitors operating a focused strategy can find itself falling between many stools.

Let us first consider the underlying requirements for market segmentation and take an overview of segmentation issues (Hooley *et al.*, 2004).

It is possible to describe three basic propositions that underpin market segmentation as a component of marketing strategy.

1 For segmentation to be useful customers must *differ from one another* in some important respect, and this can be used to divide the total market. If they were not different in some significant way, if they were totally homogeneous, then there would be no need or basis on which to segment the market. However, in reality, all customers differ in some respect. The key to whether a particular difference is useful for segmentation purposes lies in the extent to which the differences are related to different behaviour patterns (e.g. different levels of demand for the product or service, or different use/benefit requirements) or susceptibility to different marketing mix combinations (e.g. different product/service offerings, different media, messages, prices or distribution channels) – that is, whether the differences are important to how we develop a marketing strategy.

2 The operational use of segmentation usually requires that segment targets can be *identified by measurable characteristics* to enable their potential value as a target market to be estimated and for the segment to be identified. Crucial to utilizing a segmentation scheme to make better marketing decisions is the ability of the marketing strategist to evaluate segment attractiveness and the current or potential strengths the company has in serving a particular segment. Depending on the level of segmentation analysis, this may require internal company analysis or external market appraisal.

3 The effective application of segmentation strategy also requires that selected segments be *isolated* from the remainder of the market, enabling them to be targeted with a distinct market offering. Where segments are not distinct they do not form a clear target for the company's marketing efforts.

For any segmentation scheme to be useful it must possess those three characteristics.

6.3 The STP (segmentation, targeting and positioning) approach

Most marketers recognize the three stages of market segmentation: segmentation, targeting and positioning (STP). According to this model (illustrated in Fig. 6.1), the process begins with the aggregation of customers into groups, to maximize homogeneity within, and heterogeneity between, segments.

Managers attempt to *segment* the market – that is, to identify groups of consumers that are internally homogeneous, but distinct from each other. Very small groups of customers identified through the segmentation process are called *niche* markets. Managers then select one or more market segments and niches to *target* with their marketing programmes. For each target market, they need to make decisions on how

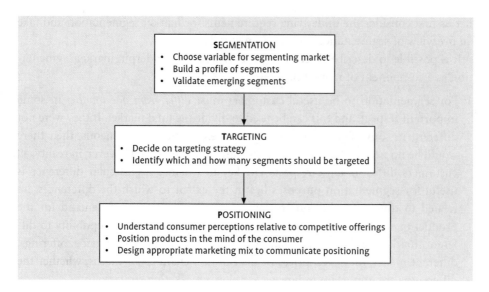

Figure 6.1 The STP of market segmentation

to *position* their products in order to differentiate themselves from the competition and to create a unique spot in customers' minds. Figure 6.1 illustrates the process of segmentation, targeting and positioning (STP).

The implicit goal of all STP is to improve marketing performance over what it would be without this process. Thus, an organization may aim to use STP to increase customer satisfaction, competitive differentiation and/or profitability. The STP process offers additional benefits when used properly. It greatly increases marketers' ability to develop a thorough understanding of the needs of their well-defined customer segments, and it improves their ability to respond to changing segment needs. Marketing efficiency is improved as resources are targeted at segments that offer the most potential for the organization. Because the marketing programme is better matched with segment requirements, its effectiveness is enhanced. Specifically, STP analyses help marketing managers design a product line to meet market demand, determine the advertising messages that will have most appeal, select media that will have maximum impact for each segment, and time product and advertising launches to capitalize on market responsiveness.

Prior to conducting STP analyses, managers should define the purpose and scope of segmentation, including their marketing objectives, whether the purpose is to explore new segments or better serve existing ones, whether existing data will be used or money invested in market research, and the level of detail they need from the STP exercise. These choices help focus the segmentation effort on the most important issues for the organization. For example, when the purpose is to better serve current segments, researchers need to pay greater attention to profiling these segments. On the other hand, if the purpose is to identify new segments, researchers will pay greater attention to grouping customers, identifying the number of segments, and profiling new segments. Evidence of how this process works in practice raises two fundamental concerns:

1 businesses that believe they are applying a market segmentation approach may not necessarily be doing so, and

2 marketers who are following the prescribed steps may not be achieving results that can be implemented.

The first problem arises in part from the imprecise use of segmentation language. The intrinsic attractiveness of the process and the pleasing nature of the benefits on offer have resulted in the label of 'segment' being applied to almost any grouping of customers. In many cases these groupings do not consist of customers with homogeneous needs and buying behaviour.

The second problem concerns the fact that marketers who follow the prescribed segmentation sometimes fail to generate a usable segmentation solution. In this respect the apparent simplicity of the three-stage STP process belies some of the underlying difficulties.

Bases for segmenting markets

Some of the major issues in market segmentation centre on the bases on which the segmentation should be conducted and the number of segments identifiable as targets in a particular market. The selection of the base for segmentation is crucial to gaining a clear picture of the nature of the market – the use of different bases can result in very different outcomes. In fact the process of segmentation and the creative selection of different segmentation bases can often help the firm to gain new insights into old market structures that in turn may offer new opportunities – this is not merely a mechanical piece of statistical analysis.

In addition to choosing the relevant bases for segmentation, to make the segments more accessible to marketing strategy, the segments are typically described further on common characteristics. Segments formed on the basis of brand preference, for example, may be further described in terms of customer demographic and attitudinal characteristics to enable relevant media to be selected for promotional purposes and a fuller picture of the chosen segments to be built up.

The next section examines the major bases used in B2C markets, and the section after that looks at B2B markets.

6.4 **Segmenting consumer markets (B2C)**

As mentioned already, a market may be segmented using a number of different bases. At the end of the day, the bases selected – for, as we shall see later, they are often used in combination to segment markets – must fulfil the criteria outlined earlier for effective segmentation. Having said that, there are a number of bases in consumer markets that, in the past, have been widely used in segmenting these markets. What this section will do, then, is discuss some of the most frequently used bases. It starts with some of the more traditional and conventional bases of segmentation in consumer markets, such as geographic and demographic bases. It then looks at some of the more recent developments in segmentation, and in particular the use of geo-demographic, lifestyle and combination bases. Finally, this section on consumer market segmentation will examine what are often referred to as *behavioural segmentation bases*, which use the behaviour of consumers themselves as the basis for identifying market segments.

Let's start with two of the more conventional, and still widely used, bases for segmenting consumer markets: geographic and demographic bases for segmentation.

Socio-demographic segmentation

This approach comprises a wide variety of bases for subdividing markets; some of the more common bases used include the following.

Geographic segmentation

This consists of dividing a market on the basis of different geographical units. In international marketing, different countries may be deemed to constitute different market segments. Similarly, within a country a market may be segmented regionally into, for example, northern versus southern segments.

Geographic segmentation is still widely used, at least as one element in a combination of segmentation bases. Clearly, geographic segmentation is potentially at its most powerful and useful when considering international markets, and therefore is considered in more detail on page 137.

Gender

A basic approach to segmentation of the market for household consumables and for food purchases is to identify 'housewives' as a specific market segment. For marketing purposes, 'housewives' can include both females and males who have primary responsibility for grocery purchase and household clothes. This segmentation of the total potential market of, say, all adults will result in a smaller (around half the size) identified target. Many segmentation schemes use gender as a first step in the segmentation process, but then further refine their targets within the chosen gender category (e.g. by social class). In some markets the most relevant variable is gender preference (e.g. the 'gay' market for certain products and services).

Age

Age has been used as a basic segmentation variable in many markets. The market for holidays is a classic example, with holiday companies tailoring their products to specific age groups such as 'under-30s' or 'senior citizens'. In these segmentation schemes it is reasoned that there are significant differences in behaviour and product/service requirements between the demographic segments identified.

Family life cycle

This basis for *life cycle/stage segmentation* centres on the idea that consumers pass through a series of quite distinct phases in their lives, with each phase being associated with different purchasing patterns and needs. The unmarried person living in their parents' home, say, may have very different purchasing patterns from a chronological counterpart who has left home and recently married. It is also recognized that the purchasing pattern of adults often changes as they approach and move into retirement.

Producers of baby products, for example, build mailing lists of households with newborn babies on the basis of free gifts given to mothers in maternity hospitals. These lists are dated and used to direct advertising messages for further baby, toddler and child products to the family at the appropriate time as the child grows.

The basic life cycle stages are presented in Table 6.1.

Table 6.1 Stages of the family life cycle

Stage	Financial circumstances and purchasing characteristics
Bachelor Young, single, not living at parental home	Few financial burdens, recreation orientated; holidays, entertainments outside home
Newlywed Young couples, no children	Better off financially, two incomes; purchase home, some consumer durables
Full nest I Youngest child under 6	Home purchasing peak; increasing financial pressures, may have only one income earner; purchase of household 'necessities'
Full nest II Youngest child over 6	Financial position improving; some working spouses
Full nest III Older married couples with dependent children	Financial position better still; update household products and furnishings
Empty nest I Older married couple, no children at home	Home ownership peak; renewed interest in travel and leisure activities; buy luxuries
Empty nest II Older couples, no children at home, retired	Drastic cut in income; medical services bought
Solitary survivor Still in labour force	Income good, but likely to sell home
Solitary survivor Retired	Special needs for medical care, affection and security

In some instances segmentation by life cycle can help directly with product design, as is the case with package holidays. In addition to using age as a segmentation variable, holiday firms target different stages of the life cycle very specifically, from the Club Med emphasis on young singles, to Centre Parcs family holidays, to coach operators' holidays for senior citizens.

Occupation/social class

These are linked together because, in many developed economies, official socio-economic group (social class) categorizations are based upon occupation. In the UK, this occupation is that of the 'head of the household', because this is what is regarded as being the criterion that determines the social class of the household. One way of doing it is shown in Table 6.2.

Table 6.2 **Social class/occupation**	
Social class grading	**Occupation**
A	Higher managerial
B	Intermediate management
C1	Supervisory/lower management
C2	Skilled manual
D	Semi-skilled/unskilled
E	Lowest levels of subsistence, e.g. pensioners (with no supplementary income)

As occupation is the only factor in this system that is used to ascribe social class, it is obviously important that the codes used to classify occupations into the different social categories – six in this case – are valid. Of greatest importance in this validity aspect is that the different occupations used to designate social class actually discriminate and distinguish between different customer groups, and their purchasing habits and needs.

Quite simply, although this long-established system of assigning social class is widely used in marketing, there is increasing doubt as to the extent to which social class is nowadays a meaningful basis for segmenting some markets; in part this arises from the fact that it is no longer so strongly related to income groups. For example, it is often the case that those in the skilled manual group (C2) earn higher incomes than their lower- or even intermediate-management counterparts (C1 or B) in industry. Such groups are often in a position to purchase products and services that were once 'traditionally' the prerogative of the upper social grades.

This increasing concern regarding the poor predictive power of many of these more conventional demographic bases for segmenting consumer markets, coupled with improvements in data collection and analysis methods, has led to the development in recent years of newer, and some would suggest more powerful, bases for segmenting consumer markets, such as personality or so-called lifestyle/psychographics segmentation.

Subculture

Besides belonging to a workplace environment individuals are members of a variety of subcultures. These subcultures are groups within the overall society that have peculiarities of attitude or behaviour. For a subculture to be of importance for segmentation purposes it is likely that membership of it has to be relatively enduring and not transient, and that membership of the subculture is of central importance in affecting the individual's attitudes and/or ultimate behaviour.

The major subcultures used for segmentation purposes are typically based on racial, ethnic, religious or geographic similarities. In addition, subcultures existing within specific age groupings may be treated as distinct market segments. For example, targeting members of the youth hip-hop culture has certain implications for the marketing of, say, clothing.

Personality characteristics

Personality characteristics are more difficult to measure than demographics or socio-economics. They are generally inferred from large sets of questions, often involving detailed computational (multivariate) analysis techniques. Perhaps the main value of personality measures lies in creating the background atmosphere for advertisements and, in some instances, package design and branding.

Lifestyle characteristics

This research attempts to isolate market segments on the basis of the style of life adopted by their members. At one stage these approaches were seen as alternatives to the social class categories discussed above.

Lifestyle segmentation is often referred to as *psychographics*. It is based on the fact that individuals have characteristic modes and patterns of living that may influence their motives to purchase selected products and brands. For example, some individuals may prefer a 'homely' lifestyle, whereas others may see themselves as living a 'sophisticated' lifestyle. Although there is much evidence to support the idea of this form of segmentation, in its earliest applications it proved to be disappointing in practice. However, more recent applications are proving that it now has much to commend it.

Lifestyle segmentation is concerned with three main elements: activities (such as leisure activities, sports, hobbies, entertainment, home activities, work activities, professional work, shopping behaviour, housework and repairs, travel and miscellaneous activities, daily travel, holidays, education and charitable work); interaction with others (such as self-perception, personality and self-ideal, role perceptions – as mother, wife, husband, father, son, daughter, etc. – and social interaction, communication with others, opinion leadership); and opinions (on topics such as politics, social and moral issues, economic and business–industry issues, and technological and environmental issues).

The approaches to consumer market segmentation that have been described so far have all been *associative*; that is to say, they are used where we feel that differences in purchasing behaviour/customer needs may be associated with them. If, say, we use social class or lifestyle to segment a market we are assuming that purchasing behaviour is a function of social class or lifestyle. Most of the problems with using such associative bases tend to be related to the issue of the extent to which they are truly associated with, or are a reflection of, actual purchasing behaviour. Because of this, many marketers believe that it is more sensible to use *direct* bases for segmenting markets. As mentioned, such bases take actual consumer behaviour as the starting point for identifying different segments and are often referred to as *behavioural* segmentation bases.

Examples of some of the more frequently used behavioural bases in consumer markets include those described below.

Occasions for purchase

Attitudinal characteristics attempt to draw a causal link between customer characteristics and marketing behaviour. Here, segments are identified on the basis of differences in the occasions for purchasing the product.

Usage segmentation

Here, a distinction may be made between 'heavy', 'light' and 'non-user' segments. The usage segmentation concept is more useful in some markets than in others. In the soap market, for instance, it is noted that heavy users of soap account for 75 per cent of purchases. However, heavy users account for nearly half the population and constitute a very diverse group. By contrast, bourbon whiskey is consumed by around 20 per cent of adults only, and heavy users account for 95 per cent of consumption, making this a much tighter target market.

Benefit segmentation

Benefit segmentation takes the basis of segmentation right back to the underlying reasons why customers are attracted to various product offerings. As such it is perhaps the closest means yet to identifying segments on bases directly relevant to marketing decisions. Developments in techniques such as conjoint analysis make them particularly suitable for identifying benefit segments.

This is a very meaningful way to segment a market. The total market for a product or service is broken down into segments distinguished by the principal benefits sought by each segment. For example, the market for shampoo includes the following benefit segments, which can be clearly observed from manufacturers' advertisements:

- cleanliness

- protection from dandruff, greasiness, dryness, etc.

- reasons of scalp medication

- reasons of well-being.

A 'benefits sought' basis for segmentation can provide useful insights into the nature and extent of competition, and the possible existence of gaps in the market.

Behavioural segmentation

The most direct method of segmenting markets is on the basis of the behaviour of the consumers in those markets. Behavioural segmentation covers purchases, consumption, communication and response to elements of the marketing mix. The study of purchasing behaviour has centred on such issues as time of purchase (early or late in the product's overall life cycle) and patterns of purchase (the identification of brand-loyal customers).

Innovators

Because of their importance when new products are launched, innovators (those who purchase a product when it is still new) have received much attention from marketers. Clearly, during the launch of new products, isolation of innovators as the initial target segment could significantly improve the product's or service's chances of acceptance in the market. Innovative behaviour, however, is not necessarily generalizable to many different product fields. Attempts to seek out generalized innovators have been less successful than looking for individual innovators in a specific field. Generalizations seem most relevant when the fields of study are of similar interest.

Opinion leaders can be particularly influential in the early stages of the product life cycle. Recording companies, for example, recognize the influence that DJs have on the record-buying public and attempt to influence them with free records and other inducements to play their recordings.

While innovators are concerned with initial purchase, loyalty patterns are concerned with repeat purchase; as such they are more applicable to repeat purchase goods than to consumer durables, though they have been used in durables markets (see the example of Volkswagen, below).

This direct approach is based on the extent to which different customers are loyal to certain brands (brand loyalty) or possibly to certain retail outlets (store loyalty). Identifying segments with different degrees of loyalty enables a company to determine which of its customers or prospective customers may be brand- or store-loyal prone. Such a market segment is a very attractive one on which to concentrate future marketing efforts. Once they are convinced of the relative merits of a brand or supplier, such customers are unlikely to transfer their allegiance.

Where existing brand loyalty is already strong in a market, the would-be new entrant is faced with a particularly difficult marketing problem. In such a situation, it may be necessary to identify and target the non-brand-loyal segment.

Volkswagen, the German automobile manufacturer, has used loyalty as a major method for segmenting its customer markets. It divided its customers into the following categories:

- First Time Buyers, and

- Replacement Buyers:
    - (a) Model-loyal Replacers
    - (b) Company-loyal Replacers
    - (c) Switch Replacers.

These segments were used to analyse performance and market trends, and for forecasting purposes.

In the context of e-marketing, companies such as Site Intelligence have devised methods of segmenting website visitors and purchasers using combinations of behavioural (visits) and demographic characteristics.

Exhibit 6.1 **The use of occasion-based segmentation at Coca-Cola**

Typical segmentation approaches fall short of what is needed to grow sales and profits because they segment on what customers *currently do*, instead of what customers *will do*. Occasion-based segmentation identifies opportunities for growth based on the occasion when the product or service is used. In many categories, like beverages, the same consumer can experience a wide variety of needs, based on the situation. For example, you get up in the morning and you drink coffee and orange juice; at lunch you drink iced tea or a soft drink; in the afternoon maybe diet soda or perhaps a coffee from Starbucks; for dinner you may drink water and, later that night, perhaps juice again. Throughout the day the same person experiences many different needs and then makes beverage choices based on those needs. Coca-Cola has identified the psychological needs that drive those choices, and has positioned its brand to be the preferred choice, because this allowed it to segment the opportunity in a way that was consistent with how consumers use the category.

Source: adapted from Zyman and Singleton (2004)

6.5 **Segmenting business markets (B2B)**

The imperative to divide the market into different segments in order to offer products that match differing needs is at the very heart of both B2B and B2C marketing and is called market segmentation. The strength, width and depth of the segmentation demands will vary from industry to industry and from country to country depending on factors that often change and which will be discussed later in this chapter. Only if the varying and diverse benefits demanded by different industries and organizations are known can products and services be offered with benefits that will satisfy these many disparate needs.

The basic approach to segmentation, targeting and positioning does not differ greatly between consumer and organizational markets. As one might expect, segmenting industrial product markets introduces a number of additional bases for segmentation, while precluding some of the more frequently used ones in consumer product markets.

The hierarchical approach to B2B segmentation

This approach was developed by Wind and Cardozo (1974) and is illustrated in Fig. 6.2. Basically, the approach calls for industrial markets to be segmented in two stages. The first stage includes formation of macro segments, based on the characteristics of the organization. The second stage involves dividing these macro segments into micro segments, based on the characteristics of the decision-making units (DMUs).

This hierarchical approach enables an initial screening of organizations and selection of these macro segments, which on the basis of organizational characteristics provide potentially attractive market opportunities. Organizations that may have no use for the given product or service can be eliminated. Starting with the grouping of organizations into homogeneous macro segments also provides a reduction in total research effort and cost. Instead of examining detailed buying patterns and attempting to identify the characteristics of the DMU in each organization individually, such analysis is limited only to those macro segments that passed the initial screening.

Once a set of acceptable macro segments has been formed, the marketer may divide each of them into micro segments, or small groups of firms, on the basis of similarities and differences among DMUs within each macro segment. Information for this second stage will come primarily from the sales force, based on sales people's analysis of situations in particular firms or from specially designed market segmentation studies.

This concept of successively combining industrial market segmentation bases giving, hopefully, more and more precise and hence meaningful segments is taken even further in the model developed by Shapiro and Bonoma (1984). Their 'nested' approach is shown in Fig. 6.3.

This approach identifies five general segmentation bases, which are arranged in the nested hierarchy shown, moving from the outer nests towards the inner. The segmentation bases (criteria) also move from macro to micro criteria. The bases are: demographics, operating variables, purchasing approach, situational factors and personal characteristics of the buyer. We will now examine each of these in turn.

Demographics

This category represents the outermost nest, which contains the most general segmentation criteria. These variables give a broad description of the segments in the

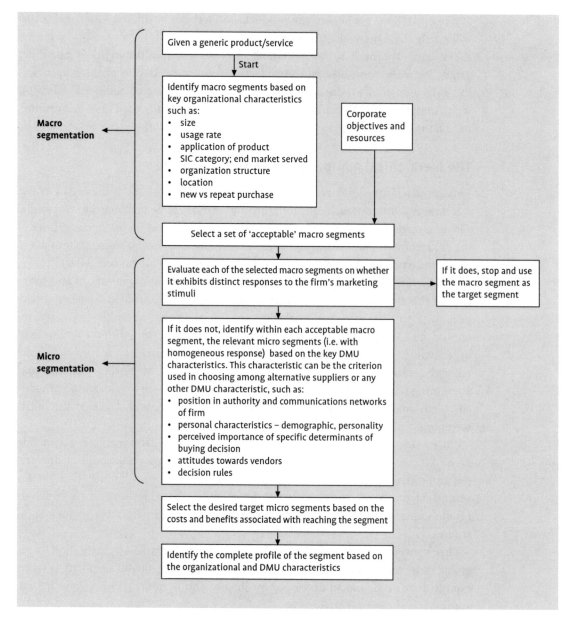

Figure 6.2 The hierarchical approach to the segmentation of B2B markets
Source: adapted from Wind and Cardozo (1974: 456); and Dibb (1998: 401)

market, and relate to general customer needs and usage patterns. They can be determined without visiting the customer, and include industry and company size, and customer location.

Demographic characteristics of companies can be a useful starting point for business segmentation; indeed they characterize the approaches most commonly used by business marketing companies. Factors that can be considered here include demo-

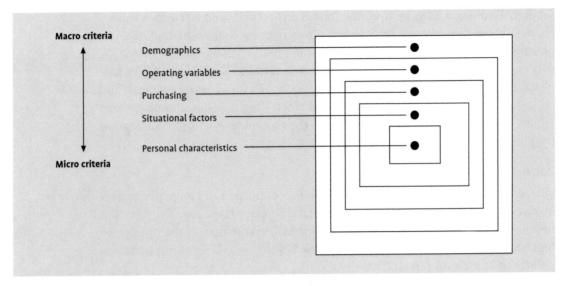

Figure 6.3 The 'nested' approach to B2B market segmentation
Source: adapted from Shapiro and Bonoma (1984)

graphics such as industry type, customer size and location, but also operating variables such as customer technology and capabilities, different purchasing policies and situational factors including product application.

Factors such as the Standard Industry Classification (SIC) provide a first stage of analysis, both for identifying target industries and subdividing them into groups of companies with different needs or different approaches to buying. This may be the basis for vertical marketing to industry sectors. Retailers and hospitals, for example, both buy computers, but they will have different applications and different buying strategies.

Size may also be highly significant if, for instance, small companies have needs or buying preferences that are distinctly different from those of larger companies. Typical measures would be variables such as number of employees and sales turnover. Size may be very significant because it impacts on issues such as volume requirements, average order size, sales and distribution coverage costs and customer bargaining power, which may alter the attractiveness of different segments as targets. Company size may be analysed alongside other demographics.

Operating variables

The second segmentation nest contains a variety of segmentation criteria called 'operating variables'. These enable more precise identification of existing and potential customers within demographic categories. Operating variables are generally stable and include technology, user/non-user status (by product and brand), and customer capabilities (operating, technical and financial).

The customer's stage of technology development will impact directly on its manufacturing and product technology, and hence on its demand for different types of product. Traditional factories operating mixed technologies and assembly methods require different product and subassembly inputs (e.g. test equipment, tooling, components) compared to the automated production unit. High-technology businesses may require very different distribution methods (e.g. Marks & Spencer requires suppliers to have the capability to co-operate in electronic stock control and cross-docking to avoid retail stockholding). Increasingly, high-technology firms require that their suppliers are integrated into their computer systems for all stages of the purchase process.

Purchasing approaches

One of the most neglected but valuable methods of segmenting an industrial market involves customers' purchasing approaches and company philosophy. The factors in this middle segmentation nest include the formal organization of the purchasing function, the power structure, the nature of the buyer/seller relationship, purchasing policies and purchasing criteria.

How customers organize purchasing may also identify important differences between customers. For example, centralized purchasing may require suppliers to have the capability to operate national or international account management, while decentralized purchasing may require more extensive field sales operations. Depending on a supplier's own strengths and weaknesses, the purchasing organization type may be a significant way of segmenting the market.

Situational factors

Up to this point the model has focused on the grouping of customer firms. Now it moves to consider the tactical role of the purchasing situation. Situational factors resemble operating variables, but are temporary and require a more detailed knowledge of the customer. They include the urgency of order fulfilment, product application and size of order.

Customers might divide, for example, into: those who want single supply sources versus those who want to dual-source important supplies; public-sector and similar organizations where bidding is obligatory versus those preferring to negotiate price; those actively pursuing reductions in their supplier base compared to others. Indeed the model proposed above of the customer's relationship requirements as a basis for segmenting may be even more useful in the business market, where the demand for partnership between suppliers and customers characterizes many large companies' approaches to purchasing.

The product application can have a major influence on the purchase process and criteria, and hence supplier choices. The requirements for a small motor used in intermittent service for a minor application in an oil refinery will differ from the requirements for a small motor in continuous use for a critical process.

An added complication in business markets, however, is the decision-making unit (DMU). Many business purchase decisions are made or influenced by a group of individuals rather than a single purchaser. Different members of the DMU will often have different perceptions of what the benefits are, both to their organization and to themselves.

In the purchase of hoists, for example, the important benefit to a user may be lightness and ease of use, whereas the purchasing manager may be looking for a cheaper product to make his purchasing budget go further. Architects specifying installations for new plant may perceive greater benefit in aesthetically designed hoists, and maintenance personnel may look for easy maintenance as a prime benefit.

Buyers' personal characteristics

People, not companies, make purchase decisions, although the organizational framework in which they work, and company policies and needs may constrain their choices. Marketers for industrial goods, like those for consumer products, can segment markets according to the individuals involved in a purchase in terms of buyer/seller similarity, buyer motivation, individual perceptions and risk-management strategies.

Business goods markets can be segmented by issues such as:

- **buyer/seller similarity** – compatibility in technology, corporate culture or even company size may be a useful way of distinguishing between customers

- **buyer motivation** – purchasing officers may differ in the degree to which they shop around and look at numerous alternative suppliers, and dual-source important products and services, as opposed to relying on informal contacts for information and remaining loyal to existing personal contracts

- **buyer risk perceptions** – the personal style of the individual, intolerance of ambiguity, self-confidence and status within the company may also provide significant leverage.

The notion of segments and of 'good' segmentation

Technically speaking, segmentation means grouping together similar customers. The results of segmentation performed by a given company depend on the quality of the information available and on the company's own characteristics (in particular, technological and organizational abilities), and the types of decision it wishes to make. Thus, market segmentation can vary according to how the company sees the market, and whether it is for the present or a future offer. Indeed, it may be the case that two competitors in the same market can produce two different market segmentations. Above all, segmentation helps to identify closely related (similar) customer groups. Statistically speaking, the aim is to minimize intragroup variance (to create sufficiently 'homogeneous' groups) and to maximize intergroup variance (to create groups that are different from each other). This means it is also an intellectual process (and/or statistical, if statistical data analysis techniques are used), which aims to give the company a simplified representation of its market, by incorporating the aspects of customer behaviour and the market dynamics that can affect it. Such a representation is always a simplification. This is necessary to make the market understandable and the segmentation usable. Therefore, the process must lead to a well-thought-out and controlled summary of the initial information.

Thus, the segment is by convention a group of 'customer units', although a market – a population – can be divided into an almost infinite number of segments. Each segment must have an operational 'reality' for the company, meaning that the company can define a suitable, autonomous and coherent marketing strategy for each group. The process depends on the market in question. The complexity of the segmentation is proportional to market volume, value and heterogeneity, which command the number of variables taken into consideration by the process. In other words, the quality depends on the work performed and how this complexity was managed and 'summarized'.

Thus, we can talk of 'good segmentation' as having led to the creation of homogeneous segments, all different between themselves, with a specific and identified competition, large enough to be profitable and operational. It thus justifies a differentiation in the offers, and/or in access to the market, and/or in the marketing process. It therefore affects both the supply strategy and customer approach, making it the key to the marketing process.

Exhibit 6.2 Cadbury's segmentation strategy in chocolate confectionery

The Cadbury brand name has been in existence since 1824 when John Cadbury opened his first shop in Birmingham, England. Cadbury's market share grew in 2003 to 7.2 per cent of the world chocolate market, making it the fourth largest global chocolate brand after Mars, Nestlé and Hershey Foods. Cadbury's core markets are currently the UK, Ireland, Australia and New Zealand. The Cadbury brand is very well known in these markets and consumers have established patterns of chocolate consumption.

Market research shows that women purchase almost two-thirds of all confectionery, but eat just over half of what they buy themselves as they are the gatekeepers when making purchasing decisions for the rest of the family. By targeting the gatekeeper with a new product the chances of a successful launch are increased.

Cadbury has identified three key segments in chocolate confectionery.

1 *Take home* confectionery is generally purchased in a supermarket for later consumption in and out of the home. Here consumers make more rational decisions and consider the price of the product, the value they place on the brand and the quantity purchased.

2 The *gift* segment of the market contains products that are purchased for everyday gift occasions such as Valentine's Day, birthdays and Christmas. The

core drivers in making a purchasing decision in this segment are 'need a token of appreciation', 'need a romantic gesture' and 'need to celebrate a special occasion'.

3 *Impulse* purchases are typically products bought for immediate consumption. The core drivers for this type of purchase are indulgent and immediate consumer needs such as 'need filling up', 'need a light snack', 'feel like indulging' and 'need some energy'.

In general the impulse market accounts for 50 per cent of total chocolate sales; 80 per cent of these sales are made on an impulse basis. Research has found that growth in the impulse market is driven by changes in lifestyle that are affecting the way we eat and an increasing demand for convenience. Snacking has become a part of everyday life and chocolate has become a unique impulse category because it is eaten throughout the day rather than specifically at mealtimes. The peak times for confectionery eating are late morning, late afternoon, after school and during the evening.

Changing lifestyle patterns, eating on the go and impulse snacking do already and continue to play a pivotal role in the confectionery market. Continual snacking, or 'grazing', has replaced traditional mealtimes for many people. The Cadbury product range addresses the needs of each and every consumer, from childhood to maturity, from impulse purchase to family treats. For example, an analysis of the 'gift' sector highlights the importance of developing innovative products to address specific markets. Cadbury designs products to coincide with Christmas, Easter, Valentine's Day, Mother's Day and Father's Day, and other calendar landmarks. Cadbury uses marketing strategies such as the 'Choose Cadbury' strategy to encourage a link between chocolate and these events, ensuring there is a Cadbury chocolate product suitable and available for every occasion.

Source: adapted from www.cadbury.com; www.business2000.ie; www.cadburyworld.co.uk; Mortimer, R. (2004) Cadbury's purple reign. *Brand Strategy* 186, October, pp. 28–30; Jardine, A. and Wentz, L. (2004) Cadbury adopts umbrella strategy. *Advertising Age* 75(34), 23 August; Parry, C. (2004) Cadbury leads the way with Dairy Milk. *Marketing Week (UK)* 27(30), 22 July, pp. 24–6.

6.6 Segmenting (screening) international markets and countries

Selecting target countries

The assessment of international marketing opportunities usually begins with a screening process that involves gathering relevant information on each country and filtering out the less desirable countries. A 'top-down' model for selecting foreign markets is shown in Hollensen (2004: 232). This model includes a series of four filters to screen out countries. The overwhelming number of market opportunities makes it necessary to break the process down into a series of steps. Although a firm does not want to miss a potential opportunity, it cannot conduct extensive market research studies in every country of the world.

The screening process is used to identify good prospects. Two common errors of country screening are (i) ignoring countries that offer good potential for the company's products, and (ii) spending too much time investigating countries that are poor prospects. Thus, the screening process allows an international company to focus efforts quickly on a few of the most promising market opportunities by using the published secondary sources available.

The first stage of the selection process uses macro variables to discriminate between regions and countries that represent basic opportunities, and countries with little or no opportunity or with excessive risk. Macro variables describe the total market in terms of economic, social, geographic and political information. Often macroeconomic statistics indicate that the country is too small, as demonstrated by its gross national (or domestic) product. It may be that the gross national product seems large enough, but the personal disposable income per household may be too low. Political instability can also be used to remove a country from the set of possible opportunities.

In the second stage of the selection process, variables are used that indicate the potential market size and acceptance of the product or similar products. Often, proxy variables are used in this screening process. A *proxy variable* is a similar or related product that indicates a demand for your product.

The third stage of the screening process focuses on micro-level considerations such as competitors, ease of entry, cost of entry and profit potential. Micro-level factors influence the success or failure of a specific product in a specific market. At this stage of the process, marketers may be considering only a small number of countries, so it is feasible to get more detailed, up-to-date information via primary data-collection methods like specific potential customers. During the screening process the focus switches from potential market to actual market and, finally, to company profitability.

The market screening process requires a significant amount of effort. Once the target country has been selected, there is a tendency to focus on the selected markets and ignore the rejected countries. However, the world market is continually changing, and countries that were rejected last year may provide significant opportunities next year.

Selecting global segments

Increasing numbers of industries are global. To succeed in this environment firms have to shift from a domestic perspective to considering the world as the arena of operations both with respect to consumer markets for products and services and resources markets for raw materials, R&D, manufacturing, and human and capital resources.

The globalization of industries is also accompanied by trends towards regional economic integration: the European Union, NAFTA and the various other efforts towards regional integration in Asia and Latin America. The implication for segmentation of these developments is that management has to consider portfolios of segments that include:

- global segments
- regional segments
- segments within specific countries.

Added to this complexity is the need to consider as the unit of analysis not just countries but countries by mode of entry, since both the risk and attractiveness of a country depend on the mode of entry. The selection and implementation of a portfolio of segments, which includes global segments, regional segments and segments within countries (by mode of entry), requires a significant amount of information on all relevant markets around the world. The creation and maintenance of such a data/knowledge base is not a trivial undertaking and is one of the major obstacles to the development of global segmentation strategies. The creation of processes for the development and maintenance of country, regional and world databases is a high-priority undertaking for all global firms, yet the development of effective segmentation can take place even without such databases if the firm will proceed in an iterative bottom-up and top-down segmentation. This process involves three bottom-up steps (contrary to the previous top-down model of country selection):

1 segmentation of the market in each country (by mode of entry)

2 examination of the resulting segments in all the selected countries to identify common segments across countries – clustering of country segments

3 creation of a global portfolio based on various clusters of segments.

The resulting portfolio of segments should be compared to a desired (top-down) conceptual portfolio of segments. The comparison and contrast of the two portfolios should be driven by the concept of global operation, which balances the need to develop strategies that best meet the needs of the local markets (given the idiosyncratic market, competitive and environmental conditions), while at the same time trying to achieve economies of scale and scope by focusing on cross-country segments in a number of markets.

Governmental buying and segmenting

A large number of international business transactions involve governments. For example, governments handle 80 per cent of all international trade of all agricultural products. The US government buys more goods and services than any other government, business, industry or organization in the world. Selling to governments can be both time-consuming and frustrating. Governmental buying processes tend to be highly bureaucratic.

Governments make it harder for a foreign firm to sell to them; many place their own domestic firms ahead of foreign operations. Also, negotiating with foreign governments can be a very formal process. Understanding cultural differences is essential in order not to overstep boundaries.

Government procurement processes vary very much from country to country.

Targeting strategies

Having evaluated the relative attractiveness of different market segments we are now in a position to select a targeting strategy. A company can select from three broad strategies with respect to targeting. These are *undifferentiated* target marketing, *differentiated* target marketing and *concentrated* target marketing (see Hollensen, 2003: 331).

Positioning strategy

The final stages of the STP process involve the development of positioning strategies, together with a supporting marketing mix. In their seminal work in this area, Ries and Trout (1981) suggested that positioning is essentially 'a battle for the mind'. In other words, positioning takes place in the mind of the customer. For example, let us assume that a company seeks to enter the market for 'instant coffee', in which there are already competitors producing brands A, B, C, D, E, F and G. The company must establish what the customers believe to be the appropriate attributes when choosing between brands in this market, and the perceived position of existing competitors with respect to these attributes. If we imagine that the important attributes have been found to be 'price' and 'flavour', a possible positioning map (also called a brand map) might be drawn up, like the one shown in Fig. 6.4.

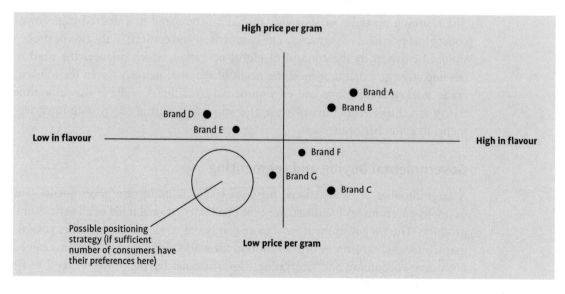

Figure 6.4 Hypothetical positioning map: instant coffee market
Source: adapted from Lancaster and Massingham (2001: 163)

With this information, the company must decide where to position its product within the market segment. Possibilities are contained within the box, the parameters of which, in the example shown in Fig. 6.4, are low to medium price per gram and low to medium flavour. Perhaps a caffeine-free product could also be considered? Such a product would give the new brand distinctiveness, as opposed to positioning it next to another and fighting head on for market share.

The most appropriate position for the new coffee brand depends on a number of factors. For example, as outlined earlier, we must assess the relative attractiveness of a particular position in a market for the new brand compared to our resources and competencies in the company. Of course it is also important to consider whether the number of customers in the chosen position is large enough to generate sufficient profit. Similarly, and related to this, we must assess the relative strengths of existing competitive brands in the market and whether we want to tackle this competition head on or not. Finally, we must consider what our objectives for the new product are, particularly with regard to brand image.

Once we have assessed brand positioning in the market and determined where we wish to position our products and brands, the final step in the process of segmentation, targeting and positioning involves the design of marketing programmes, which will support the positional strategy in selected target markets. In our instant coffee example, the company must therefore determine what price, flavour (product), distribution and promotional strategy will be necessary to achieve the selected position in the market.

Although positioning is particularly crucial when developing and launching a new product for a market, it is also relevant to the management of existing products and brands. Because markets evolve and change over time – including, for example, changes in customer tastes, competition, etc. – the marketer must continuously assess the effectiveness of existing positioning strategies for products and brands. Often, existing brands will need to be repositioned to reflect changing market dynamics.

6.7 Difficulties of implementing segmentation in the organization

It is important to preface this review of implementation difficulties by explaining what is meant by segmentation implementation. For the purposes of this discussion, implementation difficulties arise when the segmentation process has failed to generate a solution that can be put into practice. This means that, for whatever reason, it has not been possible for the business concerned to use the segmentation scheme to develop suitable and distinct marketing mixes for different customer groups: the developed segmentation scheme has not been actioned effectively.

141

The main problems

According to Dibb and Simkin (2001) the main problems are those described below.

Infrastructure barriers

All aspects of segmentation can suffer when an organization's infrastructure is inappropriate or too inflexible to deal with the process. These difficulties encompass anything to do with the corporation's culture, structure or resources acting as a segmentation barrier. For example, the marketing function in a business with a particularly entrenched organizational structure may fail in its attempts to implement segmentation if it has not secured the commitment of senior managers. Similarly, a business lacking the financial resources to collect appropriate market data will also have problems adopting a segmentation approach.

Many infrastructure difficulties relate to people issues. They arise because the business is devoting insufficient human resources to the segmentation process or because the individuals involved lack the required skills and experience to carry it out. Poor communication between functions and inadequate commitment from senior management also can cause problems.

Segmentation process issues

Despite an extensive segmentation literature, there is surprisingly little practical help available to those wishing to apply a market segmentation approach. Whereas many managers are familiar with the STP (segmentation, targeting and positioning) notion of marketing segmentation, they often express surprise about the lack of simple, practical advice available to them on how to proceed.

Implementation barriers

The underlying assumption of academic segmentation is that new solutions can simply be substituted for existing segmentation schemes. In practice, it is rarely simple for a business to make wholesale changes to its segmentation. Even assuming that the necessary resources are available to carry out a segmentation project, the planning and implementation of the process are constrained by a number of practical and operational concerns.

What should be done about the problems?

The requirement for appropriate marketing skills does not end with the identification of a segmentation solution. Businesses must continue to allocate appropriate personnel and resources if suitable marketing programmes are to be developed. Care must be taken to ensure that these programmes closely match the segments identified.

Dibb and Simkin (2001) show the benefits of a good fit between a segment solution and the marketing programme designed to implement it. This view should then be used to build a more appropriate and simpler segmentation structure, allowing the business to develop marketing programmes that match customer requirements more closely.

Summary

Segmentation is an operation of classification. It aims to provide management with a representation of the markets that is designed to help them make choices. This representation is the result of a process founded on a simplification of the initial data. The result depends on the variety and quality of data available.

In segmentation, targeting and positioning, we are seeking to identify distinct subsets of customers in the total market for a product. Any subset might eventually be selected as a market target, and on that basis a distinctive marketing mix will be developed:

- a better understanding of customers, their needs and wants

- a better understanding of competition and the kind of competitive advantage to pursue

- a more effective use of company resources

- the development of more effective marketing plans.

In order to secure these advantages, the base(s) used for segmentation should fulfil the following criteria.

- **Measurability/identifiability**: the base(s) used to segment a market should ideally lead to ease of identification (who is in each segment) and measurability (how large is each segment).

- **Accessibility**: the base(s) used to segment a market should ideally lead to marketers being able to reach selected market targets with their marketing efforts.

- **Substantiality**: the base(s) used to segment markets should ideally lead to segments that are sufficiently large for it to be worthwhile serving them as distinct market targets.

- **Meaningfulness**: the base(s) used to segment markets must lead to segments that have different preferences/needs and show clear variations in market behaviour/response to marketing efforts.

The overall differences between segmentation in B2B and B2C markets were identified and highlighted.

Many variables exist as bases for *consumer segmentation* (B2C), ranging from behaviour to attitudes to background characteristics. The most commonly used characteristics are product and brand usage, and demographics/socio-economics, primarily because of the ease of obtaining this sort of data from secondary sources. Ultimately, however, for a segmentation scheme to be useful to marketing management it should seek not only to describe differences in consumers but also to explain them. In this respect attitudinal segmentation can offer better prospects.

Many ways to segment *business markets* (B2B) can be identified at both the macro and micro level, including by geographical location, industry sector, type of industry, organization size, products and services sold, the buying situation, and the culture of the company. Group and individual differences were identified and reasons given for when and how this information should be used in the segmentation process. It is highly probable that more than one way to segment a market will be used, perhaps using geographical location, industry sector, organizational size and types of product marketed.

Finally, segmentation is the first part of the so-called STP process, which consists of:

- **segmentation** – identifying the most productive bases for dividing a market, identifying the customers *in different segments and developing segment descriptions*

- **targeting markets** – evaluating the attractiveness of different market segments, parts of segments (niches) or groups of segments, and choosing which should be targets for marketing

- **positioning** – identifying the positioning of competitors (in the market and the target segments or niches), to develop the firm's own positioning strategy.

Questions for discussion

1 What stages are involved in market segmentation?

2 Under which conditions, if any, might segmentation be unnecessary and unwise?

3 Why should marketers go beyond demographic variables when segmenting consumer and business markets?

4 Can market segmentation be taken too far? What are the potential disadvantages of over-segmenting a market? What strategy might a firm pursue when it believes that the market has been broken into too many small segments?

5 Which variables or descriptors might be most appropriate for segmenting the market for the following products and services? Explain your reasoning.

   (a)   DVD players

   (b)   portable computers

   (c)   games for PCs and consoles

   (d)   holidays

   (e)   wind turbines

6 Segmentation leads to differentiated marketing. How might a company avoid producing too many varieties of a product?

7 Under what circumstances would a marketer want to change a product's positioning?

References

Dibb, S. (1998) Market segmentation: strategies for success. *Marketing Intelligence & Planning* 16(7), pp. 394–406.

Dibb, S. and Simkin, L. (2001) Market segmentation – diagnosing and treating the barriers. *Industrial Marketing Management* 30, pp. 609–25.

Hollensen, S. (2003) *Marketing Management.* London: Financial Times/Prentice Hall, an imprint of Pearson Education.

Hollensen, S. (2004) *Global Marketing – A Decision-oriented Approach*, 3rd edn. London: Financial Times/Prentice Hall.

Hooley, G., Saunders, J. and Piercy, N. (2004) *Marketing Strategy and Competitive Positioning*, 3rd edn. London: Financial Times/Prentice Hall.

Lancaster, G. and Massingham, L. (2001) *Marketing Management*, 3rd edn. McGraw-Hill.

Ries, A. and Trout, J. (1981) *Positioning: The Battle for your Mind.* New York: McGraw-Hill.

Shapiro, B.P. and Bonoma, T.V. (1984) How to segment industrial markets. *Harvard Business Review,* May–June, pp. 104–10.

Wind, Y. and Cardozo R. (1974) Industrial market segmentation. *Industrial Marketing Management* 3, March.

Zyman, S. and Singleton, D. (2004) Segmenting opportunity. *Brand Strategy*, June, pp. 52–3.

Case 6 Carlsberg/BBH: planning for further market share in eastern Europe and Russia

The global beer industry

Despite a clear trend towards consolidation, the global beer market remained highly fragmented in 2002, with the top 10 producers accounting for 43 per cent of total volume sales. Anheuser-Busch remained unchallenged as the world's largest brewing operation, with a volume share of 9 per cent. The company owes much of its strength to its lead in the massive US market, although its Budweiser brand is marketed on an international scale.

Anheuser-Busch's primary foreign markets are China, the UK, Canada and Ireland. In October 2002, the company entered into an agreement with leading Chinese brewer Tsingtao, with the former pledging to raise its stake in Tsingtao from 4.5 to 27 per cent over seven years. This is likely to give the brewer's international business a significant boost given China's status as the largest beer market in the world in volume terms.

Despite its efforts to expand its brewing operations, the aggressive expansion activities of key rivals such as Interbrew and SABMiller are likely to impact on Anheuser-Busch's revenues and market share over the forecast period. In March 2004, for example, fourth-ranked Interbrew announced that it had agreed to merge with Latin American brewing giant AmBev. The combined entity will be the largest brewing company in the world by volume, displacing Anheuser-Busch.

Carlsberg

As a European company, Carlsberg sells particularly strongly in western Europe, especially in its domestic market of Denmark, where it claimed a volume share of more than 62 per cent in 2002. In recent years, however, the brewer has been building up its operations in the key emerging markets of eastern Europe and Asia-Pacific, through its BBH (Baltic Beverages Holding) and Carlsberg Asia joint ventures, respectively. In contrast, the company has yet to make a strong impression on North America and Australasia, with negligible volume shares in each of these regions in terms of its beer activities. In terms of sector representation, Carlsberg is mainly interested in lager on an international level, but also has some important local dark-beer brands, such as Tetley's in the UK.

Grupo Modelo

Mexican beer giant Grupo Modelo has a presence across six world regions, but is very much a minor player in most of these markets. The company's international presence is due to the wide distribution of its Corona Extra brand, which enjoys a particularly high profile in North America as the leading imported premium lager in the USA. The company is entirely focused on lager.

Regional specialists

There are a number of brewers that specialize in one or two regions. This group includes Coors, Asahi, Stingray and Amber. With the exception of Coors, all these companies are entirely, or almost entirely, focused on lager, due to a lack of demand for other beer types in their domestic markets.

Amber is positioned as a Latin American specialist, although the company plans to expand outside the region in the medium term. At present, the company is largely confined to Brazil, Venezuela, Uruguay and, more recently, Argentina and Chile, following its purchase of a 37.5 per cent stake in Quilmes in January 2003.

Because of its relatively marginal volume share outside its domestic US market, Coors is not in the major league of the world's overall beer market. In recent years, however, the company has made attempts to globalize its interests, most notably through its acquisition, in February 2002, of UK brewer Carling from Bass Brewers (Interbrew).

Tsingtao's strength lies in China, which has been the world's largest beer market in volume terms since 2002. However, the company is looking to expand its international presence, which remains negligible despite the fact that the company has extended its export market to around 40 countries.

Despite numerous alliances and agreements with foreign brewers, Asahi's core market remains the Asia-Pacific region, and in particular its domestic Japanese market. The company's strongest international market outside Asia-Pacific in 2002 was Greece, where it accounted for 0.1 per cent of beer volume sales.

Table 6.3 **Major beer manufacturers 2002 and their target markets**			
Manufacturer	**Country of origin**	**Regional presence**	**Main area of activity**
Anheuser-Busch Co., Inc.	USA	All except EE and AU	L
SABMiller plc	South Africa	Global	L, S
Heineken NV	Netherlands	Global	L
Interbrew NV SA	Belgium	Global	L, DB
AmBev	Brazil	LA	L
Modelo SA de CV, Grupo	Mexico	All except AME	L
Coors Co., Adolph	USA	WE and NA	L, DB
Carlsberg A/S	Denmark	All except NA and AU	L, DB
Tsingtao Brewery Co. Ltd	China	AP	L
Asahi Breweries Ltd	Japan	AP	L

Source: adapted from company reports and Euromonitor; EE = eastern Europe, LA = Latin America, WE = western Europe, NA = North America; AU = Australasia; AP = Asia-Pacific; AME = Africa and the Middle East; L = lager; S = stout; DB = dark beer

Eastern Europe

Figures suggest that in eastern Europe, Russia dominates with over 100 breweries, although this number continues to decline as larger brewers acquire smaller operations and then consolidate. A similar process is occurring throughout eastern Europe, with an estimated 80 breweries in Poland representing a dramatic reduction in the number active prior to the Second World War.

Following a period of restructuring that lasted throughout the 1990s, the Czech brewing industry has emerged as modernized and consolidated. Of about 70 breweries existing at the start of the decade, just over 50 have survived. Many regional breweries have gone bankrupt or been bought up by larger companies and merged.

The eastern European beer market exhibited dynamic volume growth during the review period, with overall sales increasing by 59.5 per cent to reach 18.8 billion litres. Growth was largely stimulated by increased external investment, as the market became increasingly attractive to foreign breweries. As competition from overseas companies intensified, local breweries also worked to upgrade their production facilities. However, volume growth slowed to 6 per cent in 2003, owing to increasing saturation, particularly within standard lager.

Table 6.4 **Eastern Europe: sales of beer by country** (*growth rates in constant local currency*)				
	2003 US$ million	**1998–2003 compound average growth rate**	**1998–2003 Total % growth**	**2003 litres per capita (retail volume)**
Bulgaria	262	−3.5	−16.1	42
Czech Republic	2048	4.1	22.3	82
Hungary	1088	2.0	10.7	52
Poland	4146	4.4	23.8	49
Romania	1128	−1.4	−6.6	41
Russia	10011	20.5	154.2	52
Slovakia	405	−4.5	−20.7	57
Ukraine	1235	4.4	24.2	31
Other eastern Europe	2098	–	–	44
Total eastern Europe	**22421**	**4.6**	**25.5**	**450**

Source: adapted from country reports, Euromonitor and other sources

Leading manufacturers in eastern Europe

Consolidation: the lager sector in eastern Europe is increasingly consolidated, with the top four players – BBH, SABMiller, Interbrew and Heineken – accounting for over 53 per cent of total volume sales in 2002. Smaller players are increasingly being squeezed out, and large and medium-sized businesses are also likely candidates for takeover bids from international conglomerates.

BBH – the market leader: BBH was the leading player in lager in 2002, with a volume share of 15.5 per cent, one percentage point ahead of SABMiller, its closest rival. The company is owned jointly by Carlsberg and Scottish & Newcastle, which purchased the 50 per cent shareholder Hartwall in 2002. BBH is primarily active via its Baltika range of lager in Russia and the Ukraine, with additional brewing interests in Latvia, Lithuania and Estonia. Baltic Beverages Holding AB (BBH) is a 50:50-owned joint venture between Danish Carlsberg Breweries A/S and UK-based Scottish & Newcastle plc (Hartwall plc) (see the accompanying figure). BBH operates 18 breweries in six countries in eastern Europe, including Russia where it is the market leader. BBH increased its regional volume share by 1.5 percentage points in 2002, consistent with the dynamic performance of the Russian market as a whole. During the review period, the company expanded its presence into various regions in Russia and updated all its local plants with more advanced brewing equipment. In 2003, the company opened two new breweries: one in Samara (the European part of the country), the other in Khabarovsk (Siberia). The Samara brewery cost US$50 mn and has a one billion-litre brewing capacity.

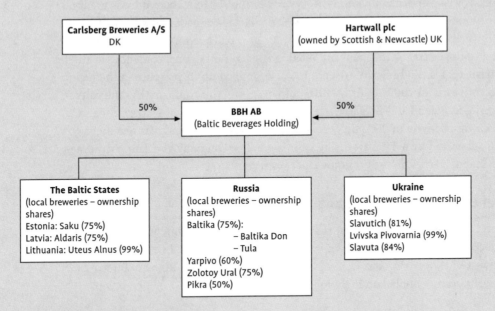

Figure 6.5 BBH ownership structure

SABMiller: SABMiller entered eastern Europe in 1993, following its purchase of Dreher, one of Hungary's largest breweries. Since then, the company has developed its regional presence through a series of acquisitions, most notably that of controlling interests in Plzensky Prazdroj and Pivovar Radegast, the leading brewers in the Czech Republic, in 1999. In 2002, SABMiller was the second largest player in lager with a volume share of 14.5 per cent, one percentage point behind sector leader BBH. The company owes much of its strength to the Czech Republic where it dominates sales with a 42 per cent volume share, 27 percentage points ahead of Budejovicky Budvar, its closest competitor. The company also owns Tyskie Gronie, the most popular brand of lager in Poland. In contrast, the company has yet to make much of an impact on the large Russian market.

Interbrew: third-placed Interbrew entered eastern Europe in 1991, following its purchase of Hungarian brewer Borsodi Sorgyar. Since then, the company has developed its regional presence through a series of acquisitions, most recently by taking a controlling stake in the Serbian brewer Apatin in September 2003. Interbrew saw its volume share contract by 0.78 percentage points in 2002, however, owing to a weak performance in Russia. This was reportedly due to a lack of PET and can capacity, which are the fastest-growing categories in terms of packaging.

Heineken: international brewer Heineken is also of note, taking a volume share of 10.4 per cent in 2002, an increase of 1.5 percentage points on the previous year. Growth was due primarily to the consolidation of Bravo International, the major Russian brewer, in early 2002. Heineken owns Zywiec, the third-ranking brand in the region, as well as Bochkarev, and is at its strongest in Poland where it leads the lager sector through Grupa Zywiec. In October 2003, Heineken acquired a majority stake in BBAG, the leading Austrian-based brewery group. The combined company will have a volume share of 15.2 per cent, making it a serious regional contender to BBH.

Carlsberg: Danish brewer Carlsberg has also stepped up its presence in the region in recent years. In addition to its BBH joint venture, the company has interests in breweries in Poland and Bulgaria, where it held volume shares of 14 per cent and 18 per cent respectively in 2002. In the former, the Carlsberg brand was relaunched in 2002, supported by a TV advertising campaign. The company also launched a new lager brand, Harnas, in the economy lager subsector.

Local companies retain strong presence

Beyond the four leading players, the sector is extremely fragmented, with a large number of mainly local breweries competing for volume share. Local players of note include Ochakovo Moscow Beer & Soft Drinks Enterprise (Russia), Budejovicky Budvar (Czech Republic) and Obolon ZAO (Ukraine).

Table 6.5 **Eastern Europe: company shares, beer 2000–2002 (% total volume/million litres)**

	2000 market share %	2000 million litres	2002 market share %	2002 million litres
BBH	12.4	1730	15.5	2580
SABMiller plc	–	–	14.5	2415
Interbrew NV SA	13.5	1891	12.9	2156
Heineken NV	9.7	1354	10.4	1728
Österreichische Brau-Beteiligungs AG Group (BBAG)	5.2	725	4.8	807
Carlsberg A/S	2.5	345	3.6	600
Ochakovo Moscow Beer & Soft Drinks Enterprise	2.7	382	3.4	573
Krasny Vostok OAO	1.7	240	2.5	425
Obolon ZAO	1.3	181	1.7	279
Budejovicky Budvar as	1.9	264	1.6	265
Rest (local breweries)	49.1	6860	29.1	4855
Total	**100.0**	**13972**	**100.0**	**16683**

Source: adapted from company reports and Euromonitor

The Russian beer market

The Russian beer market is considered to be one of the fastest growing in the world, with a 6.5 per cent increase in total market in 2003, bringing the total volume of domestic sales to 7400 million litres. Local per capita consumption of beer was 51 litres in 2003.

In general, the Russian beer market can be segmented as shown in the accompanying figure. BBH tries to be represented in all the large Russian population centres with its local beer production.

Questions

1 Which markets in eastern Europe should Carlsberg/BBH concentrate on?

2 Should Carlsberg use its own brand or use BBH's brands to penetrate the eastern European markets?

3 Should a marketing plan be drawn up for a single country or for the region as a whole?

Source: Carlsberg website and various public sources

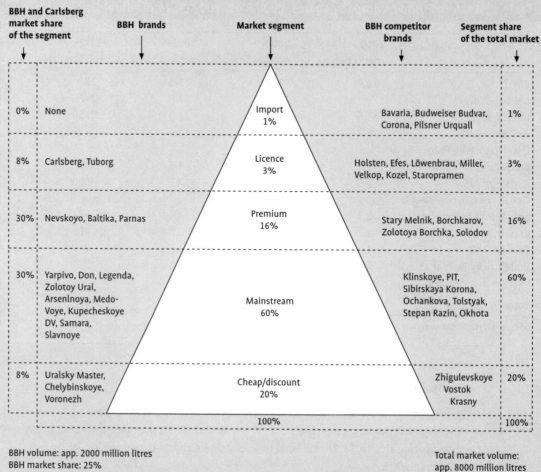

Figure 6.6 Segmentation of the Russian beer market

Marketing mix decisions I: product

Chapter contents

Learning Objectives

After studying this chapter you should be able to:

- define the terms product and product levels
- discuss the differences between services and goods
- explain the different product differentiation strategies
- discuss the steps in new product development processes
- explain the different product stretching strategies.

7.1 **Introduction**

So far, we have discussed the analysis that precedes, and is essential to, the development of detailed marketing programmes designed to meet corporate and strategic marketing objectives. In this and the following chapters, we will consider strategic decisions concerned with planning and implementing elements of the marketing mix (i.e. product, price, promotion and place decisions). In this chapter, we will start with the *product* element of the marketing mix.

Exhibit 7.1 **Harley-Davidson's 'total experience' product (HOG)**

Typically, there is more to an experience than merely the product itself. Outstanding service firms pay attention to the complete experience that customers have, from the first contact with the organization onwards. The more customer-focused manufacturing organizations have also learned this lesson. When people become Harley-Davidson customers, they buy into a brand experience and a way of life. Harley managers and dealers often refer to their business as 'fulfilling dreams through the experience of motorcycling'. An illustration of the company's appreciation of the total customer experience is its successful sponsorship of the Harley Owners Group (HOG).

Harley-Davidson established the Harley Owners Group in 1983 in response to a growing desire by Harley riders for an organized way to share their passion and show their pride. By 1985, 49 local chapters had sprouted around the United States, with a total membership of 60,000.

Rapid growth continued into the 1990s, and in 1991 HOG officially went international, with the first official European HOG rally in Cheltenham, England. Worldwide membership numbered 151,600, with 685 local chapters.

As the 1990s continued, HOG expansion spread into Asia, including new chapters in Singapore and Kuala Lumpur, Malaysia. By 1999, worldwide membership had hit the half-million mark, and the number of local chapters totalled 1157. Today, more than 900,000 members make HOG the largest factory-sponsored motorcycle organization in the world, and it shows absolutely no signs of slowing down.

Source: adapted from www.harley-davidson.com

7.2 **Product mix decisions**

In order to illustrate the range of decisions that the product strategy encompasses, it is useful to consider the hierarchy of related decisions from product item to product mix elements.

The first level of product decisions concerns individual products or services that a firm manufactures and markets. A *product item* is, then, by definition a separate product entity, identified by a certain design quality, features, packaging and branding. Individual product items that are closely related in some way to another are classed as *product lines*. The *product mix* (see Fig. 7.1) then constitutes the sum of individual product items and product lines.

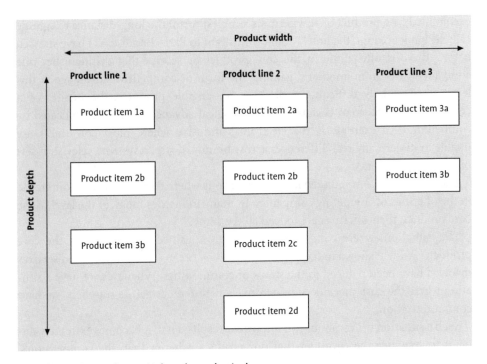

Figure 7.1 The product mix for a hypothetical company

The hypothetical company in Fig. 7.1 manufactures and markets three product lines (= product width). Product depth refers to the number of product items in each line – 3, 4 and 2 respectively – with the average being 3. By looking at Fig. 7.1 a strategic assessment of a company's product offering can be made. For example, the product width could be extended by adding more product lines. The same could be applied to the product depth.

Decisions about new products should reflect consistency with existing product lines in relation to previously determined marketing objectives set for product provision in specified markets. Hence the addition to the width of the mix and the depth within each product line should be compatible with the planned long-term marketing strategy, based on a set of evaluation criteria so that the decisions taken are rational and not purely emotional or opportunistic. Product mix strategy involves the management of existing successful products, the elimination of obsolete or non-profit-making ones, and the development and introduction of new products. Each of these elements of product strategy and management is important to the achievement of company objectives.

7.3 Different product levels

The core product is the basic element of the firm's offer to its customers. It has to be right in order for customers to consider the other elements. The core of the offer is exemplified by a product or service in its simplest form: the long-distance telephone call, the bank account, the hotel room or the flight to Paris. Because, as I have stressed before, there is often little in the core product or service that distinguishes one company's offer from another's, gaining any form of competitive advantage at this level is particularly difficult. In the case of tangible products, the quality of a company's product may, because of technological advances, easily be replicated by competitors. An example is the electronics industry where most consumers are unable to discern any real differences across brands of stereo systems, television sets or laptop computers.

The situation is compounded in those situations where there is in fact no difference in the offerings of competing companies. In many industries today, at the level of the core product, their offerings are indeed all the same.

This situation, where competitive advantage is gained at the level of the core product, is widely known today as *commoditization* because the products and services involved have been reduced to the status of commodities. Whenever we have a situation where the customer does not perceive any difference across suppliers, we have commoditization.

Such a situation brings about two important results. First, it becomes extremely difficult to convince the customer that our product is better than the competition's. Second, when nothing is done to differentiate the core product or service, customers will default to using price as the differentiating factor. This situation is obvious in many industries where the customer simply does not see any value in the core product because it is indistinguishable from those offered by others. In the classic definition of commodities, that is why consumers will often buy household products like flour and sugar based on the lowest price, and why we have petrol price wars and a very large percentage of customers will shop around for the lowest rates for car insurance and home mortgages.

Support services

This is the level where firms add services that are intended to create value for the customer by reducing non-monetary costs. Services such as deliveries, repairs, installation, warranties and payment plans help to differentiate a company and provide added value for customers by reducing psychological sources of irritation, time and energy costs. A customer who buys a home theatre system will appreciate the delivery of the components, the warranty, repair service and other support services. Because the technology and features are quite similar in a given price range, the manufacturer will differentiate its product by these added service features. The customer will then choose a specific brand or vendor based on the support services provided and how important these are to him or her. These services are easily replicated by the competition, however, and what was a differentiating factor can become a commodity in the marketplace.

Enhancing the core product through the addition of services is a very sound strategy, but many of the services and enhancements that we may consider adding are, as mentioned above, easily copied by the competition and have in fact become standard equipment in the value proposition of many companies: we all expect furniture retailers to deliver, and auto and appliance manufacturers to offer warranties.

At the technical performance level, companies strive to deliver on their promises and establish themselves as leaders in 'service excellence'. They are becoming more aware of this level as a driver of customer satisfaction because it is more difficult to achieve and for the competition to replicate. There is a positive relationship between customers' evaluations of service quality and assessments of service value. Customers evaluate service quality in five underlying dimensions: tangibles, reliability, responsiveness, assurance and empathy. Four of these five are dimensions of relationship growth and are directly related to the customer's overall perception of value.

Achieving excellence at this level depends on many factors. Top management commitment is essential since time and money must be spent in order to develop processes and technologies, as well as to attract, retain and train staff to perform at the highest level. The payback from this investment comes from the customer's perception of increased value. Customers who value excellence in service will be more satisfied and will tend to remain loyal.

To create value at this level, a firm can improve its performance and provide superior service. This increases what the customer gets because he or she can rely on the company to deliver on time and produce exactly what was promised. Thus, value is added through the addition of controls and systems to ensure that service is completed as and when it was said it would be. The company does whatever it takes to get it right. Some companies are now so confident of their ability to deliver for their customers that they are offering service guarantees.

In addition, companies can reduce the psychological cost to customers by making it easier for them to obtain information and advice. Many businesses now offer e-mailing or toll-free customer telephone lines, which allow customers to request service, seek advice on the use of a product or obtain information about where to take it for servicing.

Customers will decide whether to continue their patronage of some firms based largely on how they are handled by members of staff. Even when all aspects of the core product and its delivery are quite acceptable or even superb, poor treatment by staff can cause a customer to go elsewhere. For obvious reasons, customers prefer employees who are friendly, helpful, understanding, personable, courteous and empathetic. The interaction with staff influences the customer's assessment of the psychological costs associated with the interaction. Customers who are treated with respect, empathy and genuine concern will perceive psychological costs as low and benefits high, and will have a better view of the overall value of the interaction.

Exhibit 7.2 **Dell's online service programme**

Dell was one of the first companies to put its products on the Internet, launching www.dell.com in 1994. Today it is one of the highest volume Internet commercial sites in the world. The company receives 40 million visits per quarter to its websites in different countries. About 50 per cent of Dell's sales are currently web-enabled, with another 50 per cent of Dell's technical support activities occuring online.

When ordering online, customers are able to design a computer to meet their own needs. The web page immediately displays the price of the chosen system. As well as being able to customize the product, customers can track the progress of the order as it is produced and delivered. This can help them see the stages of the process and the likely delivery times. If changes are made in the specification, customers can see the price change immediately. A range of payment options is offered and, if customers wish, they can pay online. They can also check online the status of their computer as it moves through various production and test stages in the factory. A full after-sales support service is also offered over the Internet. Customers can access pages that give detailed instructions on how to resolve questions and issues. Information on new upgrades is also sent via e-mail to customers.

Dell has created many features and services online to help the customer see the whole purchasing process clearly. Customers can create and view their service records online. This includes product support, shipment and delivery dates. Each purchase comes with a service tag code, which can track the model bought and its service requirements. This allows Dell customer service representatives to handle requests quickly and efficiently.

This level of 24-hour customer service and fast response time helps Dell build strong customer relations, which of course is crucial for the company in its understanding of consumer needs. It is also a very cost-effective way of providing sales and support – cost savings that can be passed on in the form of better prices to customers.

Source: adapted from www.dell.com, www.business2000.ie

7.4 **Product differentiation**

Product differentiation seeks to increase the value of the product or service on offer to the customer. Levitt (1986) has suggested that products and services can be seen on at least four main levels. These are the core product, the expected product, the augmented product and the potential product. Figure 7.2 shows these levels in diagrammatic form. Differentiation is possible in all these respects.

At the centre of the model is the *core, or generic, product*. This is the central product or service offered. Beyond the generic product, however, is what customers expect in addition: the *expected product*. When buying petrol, for example, customers expect the possibility of paying by credit card, the availability of screenwash facilities, and so on. Since most petrol forecourts meet these expectations they do not serve to differentiate one supplier from another.

At the next level Levitt identifies the *augmented product*. This constitutes all the extra features and services that go above and beyond what the customer expects, to convey added value and hence serve to differentiate the offer from that of competitors. The petrol station where, in the self-serve 2000s, one attendant fills the car with petrol while another cleans the windscreen, headlamps and mirrors, is going beyond what is expected. Over time, however, these means of distinguishing can become copied, routine and ultimately merely part of what is expected.

Finally, Levitt describes the *potential product* as all those further additional features and benefits that could be offered. At the petrol station these may include a free car wash with every fifth fill up. While the model shows the potential product bounded, in reality it is bounded only by the imagination and ingenuity of the supplier.

In the past suppliers have concentrated on attempts to differentiate their offerings on the basis of the core and expected product, such that convergence is occurring at this level in many markets. As quality control, assurance and management methods become more widely understood and practised, delivering a performing, reliable, durable, conforming offer (a 'quality' product in the classic sense of the word) will no longer be adequate. In the future there will be greater emphasis on the augmented and potential product as ways of adding value, creating customer delight and hence creating competitive advantage.

Differentiating the core and expected product

Differentiation of the core product or benefit offers a different way of satisfying the same basic want or need. It is typically created by a step-change in technology, the application of innovation. For example, in mobile telephone technology, SMS messages represent a 'new' way of communicating.

7.5 Differentiating the augmented product

Differentiation of the augmented product can be achieved by offering more to customers on top of existing features (e.g. offering a lifetime guarantee on videotape rather than a one- or two-year guarantee) or by offering new features that are of value to customers. There are two main types of product feature that can create customer benefit; these are performance features and appearance features. Analysis of product features must relate these features to the benefits they offer to customers.

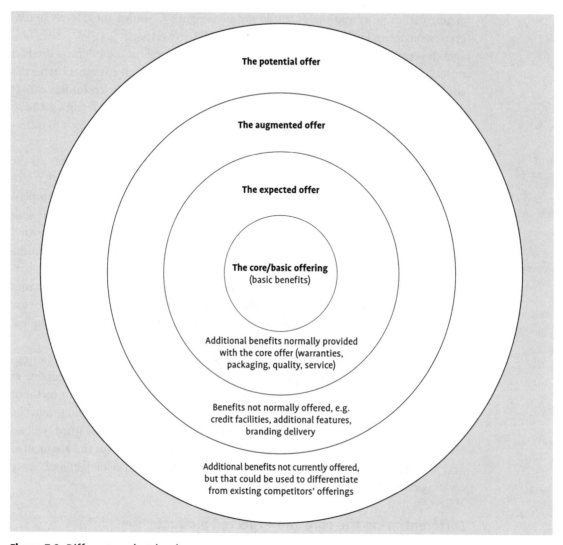

Figure 7.2 Different product levels

Quality

A prime factor in differentiating the product or service from that of competitors is quality. Quality concerns the fitness for purpose of a product or service. For manufactured products this can include the durability, appearance or grade of the product, while in services it often comes down to the tangible elements of the service, the reliability and responsiveness of the service provider, the assurance provided of the value of the service, and the empathy or caring attention received (see Parasuraman *et al.*, 1988). Quality can reflect heavily both on raw materials used and the degree of quality control exercised during manufacture and delivery. Of central importance is consumer perception of quality, which may not be the same as the manufacturer's perception.

Quality has been demonstrated by the PIMS project to be a major determinant of commercial success. Quality was shown to have a greater impact on ROI level and to be more effective at gaining market share than lower pricing.

Closely related to perceptions of quality are perceptions of style, particularly for products with a high emotional appeal (such as cosmetics). In fashion-conscious markets, such as clothes, design can be a very powerful way of differentiating.

Packaging

Packaging, too, can be used to differentiate the product. Packaging has five main functions, each of which can be used as a basis for differentiation.

1 Packaging *stores* the product, and hence can be used to extend shelf life or facilitate physical storage (e.g. tetra packs for fruit juice and other beverages).

2 Packaging *protects* the product during transit and prior to consumption, to ensure consistent quality (e.g. the use of foil packs for potato crisps to ensure freshness).

3 Packaging *facilitates* use of the product (e.g. applicator packs for floor cleaners, wine boxes, domestic liquid soap dispensers).

4 Packaging helps *create an image* for the product through its visual impact, quality of design, illustration of uses, etc.

5 Packaging helps *promote* the product through eye-catching, unusual colours and shapes, etc. Examples of the latter are the sales of the Absolut Vodka brand.

Branding

A particularly effective way of differentiating at the tangible product level is to create a unique brand with a favourable image and reputation. Brand and company reputation can be powerful marketing assets for a company.

The brand name or symbol is an indication of pedigree and a guarantee of what to expect from the product – a quality statement of a value-for-money signal. Heinz Baked Beans, for example, can command a premium price because of the assurance of quality the consumer gets in choosing the brand.

A great example of a brand that has a strong product/service competitive advantage is Dell. Dell takes orders straight from customers and builds each customer's personal computer according to demand. This means that customers get exactly what they want. Dell also gives its customers fast, convenient service that other companies can't match, including three-day delivery of PCs with all custom software preloaded. No other computer company can do what Dell does.

Branding is also a highly defensible competitive advantage. Once registered, competitors cannot use the same branding (name or symbol).

To a software-product vendor deciding the technology strategy and focus, legal protection of the product's special features is critical. If strong protection is difficult to obtain, the only way to maintain competitiveness is to pursue rapid innovation and bring out a continuous stream of upgrades that maintain the product's uniqueness. For software-service companies, intellectual property rights are less important. Companies rarely own the rights to the services they develop or to the knowledge generated during development. Thus they lack the experience and processes to handle intellectual property rights appropriately for a product-development plan.

Product complementarity

Software-product companies expend a lot of effort developing products that complement, support or enhance the functionality of existing and established products. By leveraging the potential for products to complement one another, vendors can gain larger marker size and make it more costly for customers to switch. For example, the initial success of i2 Technologies (a supply-chain solution provider) was due not only to its product's unique functionality, but also to how well the product complemented the leading enterprise resource planning (ERP) products. (ERP products provide companies with one comprehensive computer system that will integrate all the functions or tasks of the computer systems used by different departments or business units.)

According to Fig. 7.1, the last level of the product is the 'potential offer', but it is more or less impossible to differentiate benefits not currently offered.

7.6 **Brand equity**

It is recognized that marketing, as a discipline, sometimes uses and adapts concepts derived from other disciplines. The concept of added value can most notably be found in economics, accounting and marketing literature, and there is a distinct integration of ideas among these three disciplines. As far as marketing is concerned, the greatest degree of alignment is with the accounting literature. The concept of added value has evolved over time in the marketing literature such that there is much variation in the interpretation of the term. This variation in usage within marketing can be confusing, and the way that added value is used in marketing is incompatible with the accounting vocabulary.

What marketers call added value would better be termed 'added value agents'. Added value agents are the factors that create and help realize added value. Much marketing activity is based around managing added value agents, the outcomes of which are represented by added value itself. Added value agents are many and various, but branding is of major importance and gets significant coverage in the marketing literature. Clearly there is a relationship between what marketers and accountants call added value. By managing added value agents, marketers can significantly increase the added value that accrues to the organization.

An attempt to define the relationship between customers and brands produced the term 'brand equity' in the marketing literature. The term began to be used by US advertising practitioners in the early 1980s and led to academic interest. The concept of brand equity has been debated in both the accounting and marketing literature, and has highlighted the importance of having a long-term focus within brand management. Although there have been significant moves by companies to be strategic in the way that brands are managed, a lack of common terminology and philosophy within and between disciplines persists and may hinder communication.

Basically, brand equity refers to the value of a company's brand names. A brand that has high awareness, and perceives quality and brand loyalty among customers has high brand equity. A brand with strong brand equity is a valuable asset.

Brand equity, like the concepts of brand and added value, has proliferated into multiple meanings. Again, accountants tend to define brand equity differently from marketers, with the concept being defined both in terms of the relationship between customer and brand (consumer-orientated definitions), or as something that accrues to the brand owner (company-orientated definitions). Brand equity can be defined as:

- the total value of a brand as a separable asset – when it is sold or included on a balance sheet

- a measure of the strength of consumers' attachment to a brand

- a description of the associations and beliefs the consumer has about the brand.

The first of these is often called brand valuation or brand value, and is the meaning generally adopted by financial accountants.

Table 7.1 illustrates the process of valuing a brand. The first step is to forecast brand sales, operating margins and cash flow over a reasonable period, such as five years. It is important that the forecasts are based solely on brand sales and not any unbranded products that may be produced in parallel. Here brand sales are predicted to grow at 5 per cent a year, the operating margin is 15 per cent, the tax rate 30 per cent and net investment is estimated at 50 per cent of incremental revenue. The second step is to calculate the percentage of the earnings that accrue from the use of the brand name. A brand name creates value by adding emotive associations, over and above the product, that lead to additional sales or higher prices. There are a variety of methods for estimating this increment, depending on the type of brand and its market. Where the brand operates by enhancing the margin, the most direct approach is to compare the operating margin on the brand with the estimated margin on similar unbranded products. This difference, i.e. $(OM_{branded} - OM_{unbranded})$, should be attributable to the company's unique assets: its brands, patents, channel partnerships, and so on. In heavily branded markets, any residual earnings will be predominantly due to brands; in high-tech markets other intangible assets may be more critical. In Table 7.1 the margin on unbranded products is estimated at 7 per cent, implying that earnings from intangibles account for 8 per cent of sales (i.e. $15 - 7\%$). In this market, since there are no quality differences, it is assumed that the brand premium accounts for this residual. The brand cash flow associated with this premium in any one year is then:

$$CF_{brand} = \text{Sales} \, (OM_{branded} - OM_{unbranded})(1 - \text{Tax rate})$$

Table 7.1 Valuing the brand (£m)

		Year				
	Base	1	2	3	4	5
Sales	250.0	262.5	275.6	289.4	303.9	319.1
Operating margin	37.5	39.4	41.3	43.4	45.6	47.9
NOPAT (net operating profit after taxes)	26.3	27.6	28.9	30.4	31.9	33.5
Net investment		6.3	6.6	6.9	7.2	7.6
Cash flow		21.3	22.4	23.5	24.7	25.9
Brand cash flow = CF$_{brand}$		**14.7**	**15.4**	**16.2**	**17.0**	**17.9**
Discount factor ($r = 12\%$)		0.893	0.797	0.712	0.636	0.567
Discounted cash flow		13.1	12.3	11.5	10.8	10.1
Cumulative present value						57.9
PV of continuing value						84.5
Total brand value (brand equity)						**142.4**

Source: adapted from Doyle (2000)

For example, the brand cash flow for year 1 would be calculated like this:

Year 1: $CF_{brand} = Sales\ (OM_{branded} - OM_{unbranded})(1 - Tax\ rate)$

$\Leftrightarrow CF_{brand} = 262.5\ (15\% - 7\%)\ (1 - 0.3) = 14.7$

The final step is to estimate the brand discount rate. This will not be identical to the company's overall *cost of capital* since the brand's earnings may be more or less volatile than the average of the portfolio. The Interbrand Group, a pioneer of brand valuation methods, calculates the discount rate on the basis of a 'brand strength score', which measures the security that the brand name adds to the earnings stream. This rates such factors as the stability of the market, the brand's market share, its geographic spread, legal protection, and so on. In the example, the discount rate ($= r$) is calculated at *12 per cent*. The total brand value (brand equity) is then calculated by adding the cumulative present value with the estimate of present value of the future brand value. In Table 7.1 the result is *£142.4 mn*. As with all shareholder analyses, sensitivity analysis is important to explore alternative scenarios using different price and growth assumptions and different brand investment policies. This allows an assessment of the robustness of the brand, and the problems and opportunities it may face in the future.

When marketers use the term 'brand equity', they tend to mean brand description or brand strength. Brand strength and brand description are sometimes referred to as 'consumer brand equity' to distinguish them from the asset valuation meaning. Brand description is distinct because it would not be expected to be quantified, whereas brand strength and brand value are considered quantified (though the methods of quantification are not covered by this chapter). Brand value may be thought to be distinct as it refers to an actual or notional business transaction, while the other two focus on the consumer.

Brand equity exists in the minds of various stakeholders, shareholders, employees, end users and distribution channels in particular. The customer/end user of that dominates most analysis and has been defined as the differential effect of brand knowledge on consumer response to the marketing of the brand.

Aaker (1991) describes five components of brand equity: brand loyalty, name awareness, perceived quality, brand associations, and a bundle of intellectual properties such as patents, trademarks and channel relationships.

7.7 The new product development (NPD) process

Product development is the heart of the global marketing process. New products should be developed, or old ones modified, in order to fit new or changing customer needs on a global or regional basis. With the competition increasingly able to react quickly to new product introductions, a firm that adopts a worldwide approach is better able to develop products quickly, with basic specifications compatible on a worldwide scale. However, worldwide products should be adaptable in order to adjust features to unique market requirements whenever technically feasible. Some firms design their products to meet major market needs and then make adjustments for smaller markets on a country-by-country basis. For example, Suzuki develops lead-country models for the Far East that can, with minor changes, be made suitable for local sales in the majority of markets. Using this approach, Suzuki has been able to reduce its number of basic models considerably.

Some markets may require unique approaches. Some manufacturers enter developing markets, such as China, with cheaper products before selling them in more up-to-date versions.

A number of NPD frameworks have been developed to satisfy the needs of different organizations operating in different markets. Their goal is to bring products to market on time, to optimize business results by reducing cycle times and costs, and to manage the programmes according to agreed business plans over the products' life cycle. The majority of these NPD frameworks possess a number of similar important characteristics, which when executed in a balanced and effective manner significantly improve NPD performance. These characteristics generally include:

- use of a *structured development process*, providing the 'rules of the game', and describing entry and exit criteria between key programme milestones, primary tasks, schedules and resource assignments

- a team of senior executives, called a *review board*, which provides oversight of the programmes by resolving cross-project issues, setting project priorities, resolving issues and making 'go/kill' decisions

- use of *realization teams* (cross-functional execution teams), operating under a product 'champion' and reporting to the assigned senior management oversight board

■ *'phase or stage/gate reviews'* at major development milestones, when funding, resources and project schedules are approved or rejected by the review board.

These activities are generally organized into distinct phases that are carried out sequentially by the realization teams and separated by 'stage/gate' reviews held by the review board (see Fig. 7.3).

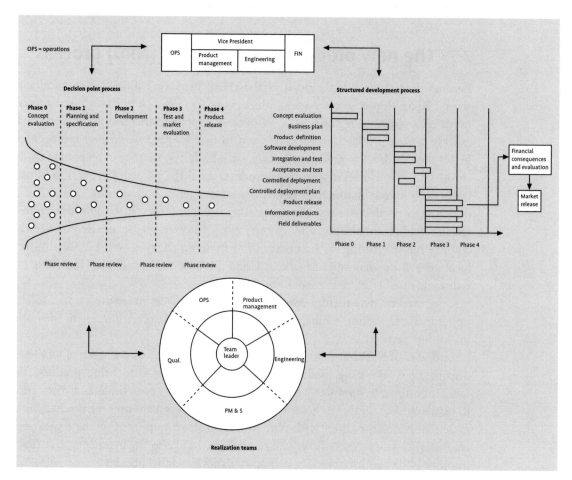

Figure 7.3 The NPD process model – as a phase review process

The phase review process can be viewed as a funnel, with many ideas entering at the concept phase and, through a series of screenings over the course of development, narrowed to a few appropriately resourced projects with high likelihood of market success. At the conclusion of each phase, a review is held to determine the direction of the project: proceed ('go'), cancel ('kill') or redirect.

Exhibit 7.3 **The NPD process for a medicine**

The life cycle for new pharmaceutical products is defined mainly by the different phases of clinical trials, as shown in the diagram.

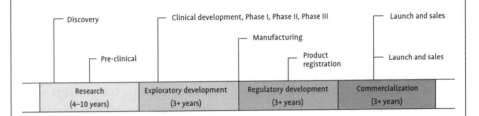

Phase I clinical trials (five to ten years pre-launch) are primarily designed to determine safe doses and administration methods (i.e. orally, intravenously, inhaled). These studies investigate how well the body metabolizes a drug and any side-effects that may result from increasing the dosage.

About two-thirds of drugs tested in Phase I continue to Phase II trials (three to five years pre-launch). At this stage the drug is tested for efficacy. In most Phase II trials, one group of volunteers may be given the experimental drug while another 'control' group will receive a placebo. Safety and effectiveness are examined in these trials. They do not give a final assessment of whether or not a particular drug will successfully treat an illness, although many patients may report experiencing same therapeutic benefits.

Phase III clinical trials (one to three years pre-launch) are then performed on the proportion of drugs that demonstrated favourable profiles in earlier trials. These studies measure how well a drug works in a large number of people. This helps fine-tune dosage amounts and procedures to ensure a drug's safety and effectiveness. Once these studies are all successfully completed, a dossier is submitted to the appropriate regulatory authorities (e.g. the Food and Drug Administration in the USA) for approval.

Clinical studies sometimes require Phase IV trials (post-launch) to examine the long-term safety and effectiveness of a drug, and these continue after the launch of a new product.

As a new drug progresses from one phase of clinical research to another, these represent key go/kill decision points in committing further financial investment to product development. Here pricing information forms an important input for the product forecast, in the decision to progress development and guide allocation of resources within the company product portfolio. With possible resource limitations, tough decisions have to be made as to whether to progress one product or another.

Source: adapted from Hanlon and Luery (2002)

Structured development processes (SDPs) offer a framework consisting of terms that describe what needs to be done in development, and which allow them to be applied consistently across all projects. For this, an SDP must be used uniformly across the company, and compliance must be mandatory. In this way, it forms part of the organizational culture. 'Best in class' companies create guidelines around the SDP to ensure that major tasks are performed across all projects and that mistakes, once identified, are not repeated. The clarity offered in these documents concerning key cross-functional linkages and responsibilities ensures an effective overlap of activities, improved hand-offs between functional groups, setting of realistic and more achievable schedules, and improved planning and control.

The major activities commonly seen to be executed within a typical NPD framework, after the original idea has been screened and accepted by management, are to:

■ develop and test the product concept

■ formulate a marketing strategy

■ analyse the impact on the business in terms of sales, cost and profit projections

■ develop the concept into a product

■ market test the product, and time its design and market strategy

■ build and launch the product.

The SDP offers the guidance to execute these activities in the company in an effective and co-ordinated fashion.

7.8 **Brand stretching**

Brand stretching – the use of an existing brand name for a new product in a different product class – has been used extensively by many consumer goods organizations. The use of existing brand names to access new markets is based on the premise that established brands have high name recognition and significant consumer loyalty, at least parts of which will get transferred to the new product. Brand stretching, on the other hand, involves the use of an existing brand name for introducing new products in the same product category. Whereas both strategies help reduce the risk of failure for the new product, neither is available as a strategic option to product managers of generic or own-label brands. This is a consequence of the common assumption that own-label has little brand equity that they could possibly leverage. One possible way to partially overcome this constraint is through ingredient branding, whereby own-label brands use national brand ingredients and also prominently display this association in their promotions as well as on product packaging. An example would be Safeway Select Chocolate Chip Cookies with Hershey Chocolate Chips. This way, even a relatively obscure own-label brand can get instant recognition and potentially a more favourable consumer evaluation.

A major distinction between ingredient branding and brand/line stretching is that ingredient branding does not involve introduction of a new product by the national brand-owning company. The national brand simply lends its branded product to be used as one of the ingredients for the own-label brand product. The end product still has to be sold under the own-brand label. This has two important implications. First, unlike in the case of brand or line stretching, a company other than the one that owns the established brand stands to benefit from it. Thus, unless or until there are gains associated with this alliance for both the partners, it is not likely to happen. Second, the alliance product has two brand names associated with it: the own-label for the product and the national brand for one of its ingredients. This is different from brand or line extensions where the national brand is typically the sole brand anchor for the new product.

An example of brand stretching in action is Kellogg's Special K Bar. Special K had built a reputation for tasty, nutritious breakfast cereals for people watching their figures. It was a relatively small functional stretch for the brand to offer a cereal bar. This met a real need by being tasty but having the same calories as just three potato crisps. The bar has added an incremental $20 million to the brand's sales in the UK.

With a purely functional stretch like this, there is no need for a change in brand personality and tone, leading to a branding solution as follows:

- the *purchase brand* that people bought and had a relationship with could stay the same
- a simple *descriptor* name was used to introduce the new product
- Kellogg's provided additional *endorsement* of quality and reliability.

Credibility depends on the stretch between current perceptions of the brand and the extension. The further the stretch, the more investment will be needed to overcome consumers' doubts and achieve trial. Big stretch *is* possible, but the level and duration of support needed may make a new brand a better alternative. Not one, but two dimensions need to be considered: functional and emotional. Taken together, these help highlight the boundaries of brand stretch and guide the optimum branding approach.

Exhibit 7.4 Athletics brand New Balance experiences brand hijacking

Brand hijacking takes place when a fashion brand is adopted by consumers that are not desirable in the eyes of the fashion house involved.

In 2002 the athletics shoe brand New Balance found itself being adopted by neo-Nazi groups in Germany, which drew parallels between the big 'N' on the side of the shoe and the SS 'lightning strike', a recognized Nazi symbol.

If a brand is hijacked like this the best course of action is to do nothing, but if the problem persists then drastic measures are required. The brand then has to go public in support of the other side, or put out a statement which points out that it in no way supports the cause by which it has been hijacked.

New Balance chose to take a course of action that undermined hijackers by sponsoring music events such as Rock Against Racism.

Source: adapted from Parry (2004)

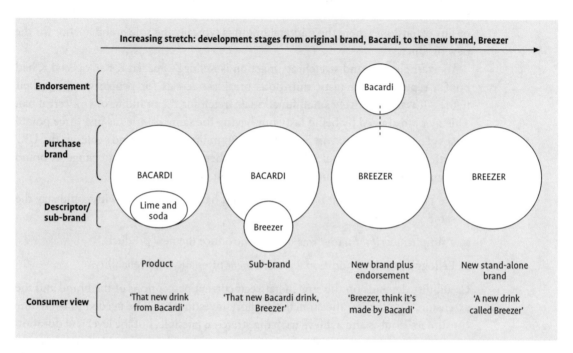

Figure 7.4 Branding options for different levels of stretch
Source: adapted from Taylor (2004)

Emotional stretch occurs when the personality, tone and style of the extension are different from those of the master brand. As with people, this is more difficult than changing jobs (i.e. functional stretch). A *sub-brand* allows more emotional stretch than a simple descriptor (e.g. Bacardi Breezer versus Bacardi Lime and Soda). Here, the extension starts to break out of the master brand's universe and take on more of its own personality. Like a son or daughter, the sub-brand shares the same family values and name, but has a life of its own. Launching a totally new brand, possibly with some low-key *endorsement,* gives even more stretch but less leverage of the master brand (Fig. 7.4).

Strong global brands are the key to winning international consumers, but creating effective campaigns across the complex barriers of nationality, geography, language and culture often proves a daunting task. Companies often flounder in their attempts to craft global branding because of the same fundamental flaw: they attempt to analyse their *brand* from a global perspective without first analysing their *consumers* from a global perspective. There is no real agreement on what makes a global brand; a typical definition would be 'a brand that is marketed under the same name in multiple countries with similar and centrally co-ordinated marketing strategies'. There are, however, some selected global brands that don't have the same name, but share some marketing programme elements (e.g. Mr Clean also sells under the Mr Proper and Maestro Limpio names, among others). A number of studies have attempted to quantify the definition of a global brand; typically, sales need to exceed $1 bn a year with a minimum amount generated outside of the marketer's home region or country (varying from 5 per cent to 20 per cent). Presence is also required in all of the mega-markets of the world. These definitions restrict the number of brands to be considered global to a few dozen. What is common in these definitions is the multi-market reach of products that are perceived as the same brand worldwide both by consumers and by internal constituents (Johansson and Ronkainen, 2004).

A global brand, in other words, is one that expresses the same values in all of its markets and owns a similar position *vis-à-vis* its competitors around the world. This creates several critical advantages, including:

- improved efficiency in costs for new product development and R&D because their outputs create revenues globally and not just locally or regionally

- increased leverage with channel partners, especially in the packaged goods sector, which faces the constant parallel challenge of a consolidating and globalizing retail industry

- economies of scale in marketing communication because copy can be produced along identical guidelines, and even shared, across markets, and

- improved alignment across the organization, boosting speed to market, workforce flexibility and the sharing of best practices.

That is the theory, anyway. The reality often proves quite different. Almost all companies that own 'global' brands are actually struggling to achieve those theoretical economies of scope and scale. That is because most of them are mired in the same basic melodrama: 'central marketing' (or whatever the function is called) tries to establish a set of guidelines for the brand. Sometimes the guidelines are more assertive, explaining the 'core consumer', describing the 'brand pyramid', and so on. This brand guidebook is then distributed to the 'country organizations' (they may be divided by country or region), which almost invariably choose what they want to use from the book and ignore the rest. When the central organization pushes for greater adherence, the country managers respond with classic refrain, 'But our market is different!'

What results is wasted energy. The central organization insists that global consistency in brand execution will help the company achieve greater consumer awareness and economies of scale, while the individual country organizations counter that their local markets are unique and require customized brand executions. While the debate careers back and forth, the brand itself is lost in the shuffle and its sought-after 'globalness' never materializes.

Of course, the debate over local versus global brand execution is part of a broader set of challenges faced by global companies as they seek to strike a balance between central and regional management – a set of challenges for which there is no 'one size fits all' answer. When it comes to the brand execution debate, it has been found that the main stumbling block centres on the issue of global consumers. A brand is designed to communicate a set of messages and values to consumers, so the assertion 'Our brand should be global' implies that there must be some set of consumers in every country or market that has a common set of beliefs and motivations that the brand will target.

Global branding must be driven by collaboration among local markets, both with each other and with central marketing. Because local markets do face unique competitive challenges, each country organization should bring to the table data on its own market. This process can be facilitated, but not forced, by the central marketing function.

It has been found that, with enough collaboration and creative thinking, common ground can often be discovered even where none appears to exist. For instance, when building a global segmentation for a washing powder manufacturer, we faced the seemingly intractable problem that frequency of clothes washing, obviously a key driver for the manufacturer, differs greatly across countries, often driven by water availability. However, further analysis revealed a specific group of appearance-conscious consumers in these less-developed countries who were finding ways to overcome their lack of water, acting in ways similar to consumers in the developed world. With this finding Procter & Gamble was able to create a segmentation that was 80 per cent global in its segment definitions, incorporating only a limited regional variation for less appearance-involved consumers. The result was a segmentation that was nearly 100 per cent global in its usefulness to all local countries.

To find such common ground, representatives of each country should sit down together, talk about their markets, and then jointly develop a set of hypotheses about what brands in the market, channels and consumers are shared across countries and regions. The group can then work through the available data and, if necessary, agree on what new data needs to be gathered in order to test those hypotheses and develop a common view. The goal is to replace the model in which each country organization relies on its own assumed knowledge of local consumers with one in which the entire organization uses the same view of the 'global' consumers. Data and consensus should overrule opinion and instinct.

Most companies that try to harmonize their brands across countries encounter a common problem: each country in question has done its own consumer research and none of the consumer segmentations is the same. This creates a genuine obstacle to brand alignment because it creates a roadblock in communication – you cannot align your brand around a common consumer target if everyone defines the target differently. Alignment requires a common view and a common language across the organization.

The need for a common view intuitively makes sense to most managers, but getting there can be hard. It is often the case that research methodology is one of the things that gets in the way. Most consumer segmentations conducted by market research agencies employ some sort of mathematical modelling of consumer segments. Probably the most frequently used method is simple factor-cluster analysis, in which drivers of consumer preference are grouped according to similarities in how they are answered by the entire sample (creating 'factors'), and then respondents are grouped according to similarities in how they responded to the factors (creating 'clusters'). These methodologies, and others like them, are sometimes called 'emergent methodologies' because the analytical solution 'emerges' from patterns inherent in the survey data. These emergent methods are tried and true, and have been used for decades. They tend to produce segments, or clusters, that are different in terms of preferences and attitudes, and have therefore historically been seen as useful for marketers, especially from the point of view of developing a distinctive brand position.

Summary

The first level of product decisions concerns the individual products or services that a firm manufactures and markets.

A *product item* is then by definition a separate product entity, identified by a certain design quality, features, packaging and branding. Individual product items that are closely related in some way to another are classed as *product lines* (product width). The *product mix* constitutes the sum of individual product items and product lines. Product width could be extended by adding more product lines. The same could be applied to product depth.

Decisions about new products should reflect consistency with existing product lines in relation to previously determined marketing objectives set for product provision in specified markets. Hence, the addition to the width of the mix and the depth within each product line should be compatible with the planned long-term marketing strategy.

Product mix strategy involves the management of existing successful products, the elimination of obsolete or non-profit-making ones and the development and introduction of new products. Each of these elements of product strategy and management is important to the achievement of company objectives.

The core product is the basic element of the firm's offer to its customers. It has to be right in order for customers to consider the other elements.

To create value, a company can improve its performance and provide superior service. This increases what the customer gets because he or she can rely on the company to deliver on time and produce exactly what was promised. Thus, value is added through the addition of controls and systems to ensure that service is completed as and when the company said it would be. The company does whatever it takes to get it right. Some companies are now so confident of their ability to deliver for their customers that they are offering service guarantees. In addition, companies can reduce psychological costs to customers by making it easier for them to obtain information and advice.

Product differentiation seeks to increase the value of the product or service on offer to the customer. Products and services can be seen on at least four main levels. These are the core product, the expected product, the augmented product and the potential product. Differentiation is possible in all these respects.

A prime factor in differentiating the product or service from that of competitors is quality. Quality concerns the fitness for purpose of a product or service. For manufactured products this could include the durability, appearance or grade of the product, while in services it often comes down to the tangible elements of the service, the reliability and responsiveness of the service provider, the assurance provided of the value of the service, and the empathy or caring attention received. Of central importance is consumer perception of quality, which may not be the same as the manufacturer's perception. Closely related to perceptions of quality are perceptions of style, particularly for products with a high emotional appeal.

A particularly effective way of differentiating at the tangible product level is to create a unique brand with a favourable image and reputation. Brand and company reputation can be powerful marketing assets for a company.

An attempt to define the relationship between customers and brands produced the term 'brand equity' in the marketing literature. Basically, brand equity refers to the value of a company's brand names. A brand that has high awareness, and perceives quality and brand loyalty among customers has high brand equity. A brand with strong brand equity is a valuable asset.

Product development is the heart of the global marketing process. New products should be developed, or old ones modified, in order to fit new or changing customer needs on a global or regional basis. With competition increasingly able to react quickly to new product introductions, a firm that adopts a worldwide approach is better able to develop products quickly with basic specifications compatible on a worldwide scale. However, worldwide products should be adaptable in order to adjust features to unique market requirements whenever technically feasible. Some firms design their products to meet major market needs and then make adjustments for smaller markets on a country-by-country basis.

Brand stretching – the use of an existing brand name for a new product in a different product class – has been used extensively by many consumer goods organizations. The use of existing brand names to access new markets is based on the premise that established brands have high name recognition and significant consumer loyalty, at least part of which will get transferred to the new product. Brand stretching, on the other hand, involves the use of an existing brand name when introducing new products in the same product category.

Questions for discussion

1 What do you think is the 'total product' offered by McDonald's? How does that company's understanding of a product give it a comparative advantage over its direct competitors?

2 Suggest ways in which a computer manufacturer could add to its product offering to provide a more acceptable 'total product'.

3 From the firm's perspective, what are the advantages and disadvantages of line and brand extensions?

4 What types of product might reach maturity more quickly than others? What are the implications for marketing planning?

5 How can you use research to support decisions about building brand equity?

6 For what kinds of product do you think customers need to be worldwide? Why?

7 In what ways does a product's packaging need changing when the product is being marketed in another country?

8 What factors decide whether a similar product can be marketed in different international markets and whether modifications are necessary?

References

Aaker, D. (1991) *Managing the Brand Equity: Capitalizing on the Value of the Brand Name*. New York: The Free Press.

Doyle, P. (2000) Valuing marketing's contribution. *European Management Journal* 18(3), pp. 233–45.

Hanlon, D. and Luery, D. (2002) The role of pricing research in assessing the commercial potential of new drugs development. *International Journal of Market Research*, Fourth Quarter, Vol. 44, pp. 423–47.

Johansson, J.K. and Ronkainen, I. (2004) The brand challenge – are global brands the right choice for your company. *Marketing Management*, March–April, pp. 54–5.

Levitt, T. (1986) *The Marketing Imagination*. New York, NY: The Free Press.

Parasuraman, A., Zeithaml, V.A. and Berry, L. (1988) SERVQUAL: a multiple-item scale for measuring customer perceptions of service quality. *Journal of Retailing*, Spring, pp. 12–40.

Parry. C. (2004) Fashion labels mixing with the wrong crowd. *Marketing Week*, 4 November, pp. 22–3.

Taylor, D. (2004) *Brand Stretch*. Chichester: John Wiley & Sons.

Case 7 *Vitakraft: transforming a 'small' German pet food brand into a global player

About Vitakraft

Vitakraft is a German family-owned business operating in the pet food industry. Its total net turnover in both 2003 and 2004 was about €250 mn. In 2004 the company made a net profit of about €15 mn. All in all, Vitakraft is quite well consolidated, with sufficient financial resources for global expansion. The parent company and head office are located together in Bremen.

Compared with other multinational pet food suppliers (like Mars and Nestlé) Vitakraft is a small company. Its strongest position is in its home market, Germany, where its market share is about 6 per cent in the dog food sector and 1 per cent in the cat food sector. Vitakraft also has good market positions in Austria and Switzerland. Worldwide in the pet food industry (dog and cat food), Vitakraft has a market share of about 0.3 per cent (see Table 7.2). In western Europe its market share is around 0.8 per cent. So although its total number of employees is around 2200, Vitakraft is still a very small player on the global pet food scene.

Vitakraft's products are sold in many different outlets: pet shops, supermarkets, drug stores, speciality stores for seeds and gardening appliances, DIY superstores and department stores.

Vitakraft has 11 foreign subsidiaries, mostly in European countries:

1 Vitakraft International AG, Buchs (Switzerland) (100 per cent)

2 Vitakraft-Simon Louis SA, Bruyeres-le-Chatel (France) (100 per cent)

3 Vitakraft Pet Products Company, Inc., Bound Brook, NJ (USA) (100 per cent)

4 Vitakraft H Wuehrmann KG, Vienna (Austria) (95 per cent)

5 Vitakraft AG, Buchs (Switzerland) (100 per cent)

6 Vitakraft Nederland BV, Eerbeek (Netherlands) (100 per cent)

7 Vitakraft Danmark A/S, Aarhus (Denmark) (100 per cent)

8 Vitakraft Burton Dene Ltd, Huddersfield (UK) (100 per cent)

9 Tier + Glueck Heimtiernahrung GmbH, Bremen (Germany) (100 per cent)

10 Vitakraft SA, Brussels (Belgium) (100 per cent)

11 Vitakraft Futtermittel GmbH, Vienna (Austria) (50 per cent).

The company's headquarters in Bremen, Germany, have decentralized a lot of the decision-making to these subsidiaries. The subsidiaries have fairly autonomous sales departments that deal with the pet and the grocery stores. In this way Vitakraft has close contact with its customers and can take their interests into consideration. At the same time changes and new trends are noticed and can be acted upon immediately.

* This case does not necessarily reflect the current strategy of Vitakraft

Table 7.2 **Dog and cat food, world (top 20 companies by market share, 2003 – % value)**

Rank	Company	Country of origin	2003 market share (%)	Leading brand (market share of this brand)
1	Nestlé SA (including Ralston Purina, USA)	Switzerland	25.7	Friskies (5.9%)
2	Mars, Inc.	USA	24.0	Pedigree (6.6%)
3	Procter & Gamble Co.	USA	6.9	Iams (4.9%)
4	Colgate-Palmolive Co.	USA	6.2	Hill's Science Diet (4.8%)
5	Heinz Co., HJ	USA	4.0	9 Lives (1.1%)
6	Royal Canin SA	France	1.8	Royal Canin (1.5%)
7	Nutro Products, Inc.	Canada	1.7	Nutro (1.0%)
8	Uni-Charm Corp	Japan	0.6	Gaines (0.2%)
9	Nisshin Flour Milling Co. Ltd	Japan	0.5	Nisshin (0.5%)
10	Philip Morris Co., Inc.	USA	0.5	Milk-Bone (0.5%)
11	Mogiana Alimentos SA	Brazil	0.5	Faro (0.2%)
12	Nippon Pet Food Ltd	Japan	0.4	Vita-One (0.4%)
13	Maruha Corp	Japan	0.4	Maruha (0.3%)
14	Pet Line Corp	–	0.3	Dog Bit (0.1%)
15	**Vitakraft-Werke Wührmann & Sohn**	**Germany**	**0.3**	**Vitakraft (0.2%)**
16	Tre Kök Doggy AB	Sweden	0.2	–
17	DoggyMan Hayashi KK	–	0.2	DoggyMan (0.2%)
18	Montedison SpA	Italy	0.2	–
19	Pets Ishibashi Co. Ltd	–	0.2	Pets Ishibashi (0.2%)
20	Süd-Chemie AG	Germany	0.2	Gimpet (0.2%)

Source: adapted from company reports and Euromonitor

In Germany, Austria and Switzerland, Vitakraft manufactures its products under the Vitakraft umbrella brand. The most important sub-brands include Cat-bonis, Flockis, Kanarien Perle, Pussy-Flakes, Sittich-Perle and Vitabon.

Important events in the history of Vitakraft

- **1837**: founding of the Wührmann company in Heiligenrode as a small rural business.

- **1930s**: Heino Wührmann takes over the family business in its fourth generation. The brand name Vitakraft is established. For the first time, different kinds of pet food are produced and packed industrially and sold as proprietary articles.

- **1950s**: in the 1950s the export side of the business is launched and the import side established. Today the different raw materials, seeds, and so on, are imported from over 50 different countries. The quality of all Vitakraft products is ensured through quality checks, and in labs and research centres.

- **1960s:** gradually some 24 delivery centres are established all over Germany. Deliveries not only go to pet stores, but also to specialized seed stores, drug stores, pharmacies, wholesalers and department stores. Large grocery store chains such as EDEKA, REWE, SPAR, and so on, carry an assortment of the basic Vitakraft products for budgies, canaries, exotic birds, parakeets and parrots. A special service for stock breeders is also established.

- **1962:** Vitakraft installs one of the most modern filling and packaging machines available in Europe at that time. The food is weighed out and then the packaging is filled up. Informative brochures are added later, then the packages are closed, packed in larger boxes and finally rolled to the dispatch department. In the early 1960s, this machine managed to weigh out and pack 160,000 packages of bird food per day. (Vitakraft is also one of Europe's biggest suppliers of flaked fish food and canned food for cats and dogs.)

- **1966:** more production centres, such as the fish food factory and laboratories, are built in Bremen-Arbergen, and later the large Vitakraft premises for production, storage and dispatch are added. A subsidiary company is founded in Switzerland.

- **1985:** a subsidiary company is founded in the USA – the first Vitakdraft subsidiary outside Europe.

- **2001:** the building of the new European headquarters in Bremen is completed.

Today, Vitakraft's product range includes more than 3500 different items for the proper feeding, care and keeping of animals (dogs, cats, birds, etc.) at home.

One of Vitakraft's strengths is of course the pet care sector, which ranges from dietary supplements to grooming products and pet clothing. This case will focus mainly on the cat- and dog-related aspects of the Vitakraft business.

Competition in the European and global pet food industry

Mars and Nestlé have both made major takeovers in the face of stagnating pet food sales in recent years, triggered by a shift in consumer demand towards premium and dry varieties, while these companies' offerings had been skewed towards wet and mid-priced products. Nestlé's purchase of US dry pet food specialist Ralston Purina in 2001 was followed a year later by Mars' takeover of French dry and super-premium pet food firm Royal Canin.

These takeovers have brought significant benefits to both companies, and the outlook for each has been considerably improved. But while both companies will remain very close in terms of pet food turnover for some time, it could be argued that Mars is set for stronger long-term growth. Nestlé leads in North America, while Mars is building on its dominant position in western Europe (see the accompanying table).

In terms of geographic penetration, Nestlé's takeover of Ralston Purina had the greater benefits. Nestlé became the dominant pet food company in North America, the world's largest pet food market, its share in the region leaping from 13 per cent in 2000 to over 30 per cent.

Being the dominant player in the USA also means that Nestlé has considerably improved its negotiating power with grocery retailers. Mars, whose position in North America is relatively weak – ranking third with a share of just over 10 per cent – now faces even tougher competition in US grocery stores.

In contrast, Mars' takeover of Royal Canin did not significantly change its pet food operations with regard to geographic reach. Royal Canin's main market is western Europe, a region in which Mars was already the dominant player. The takeover did, however, improve Mars' presence in the region within the specialist retail channel, Royal Canin's main point of distribution.

The main benefit of acquiring Royal Canin was the fact that this greatly enhanced Mars' dry and super-premium product portfolio. By moving into the fastest-growing sectors in dog and cat food, Mars may have gained an important edge over its rival.

While Nestlé also improved its dry portfolio, it failed to move into the super-premium end of the market, as Ralston Purina's products are positioned primarily within the economy and mid-priced platforms. Ralston's main brands, Dog and Cat Chow, lost share in their domestic US market in 2001 for this reason. Ralston Purina does have some premium brands, in particular Pro Plan and Purina ONE, but as both were launched relatively recently they are not yet competing fully against longer-established rival premium brands.

Globally, premium dry dog food is forecast to grow by 24 per cent between 2002 and 2007, while mid-priced dry dog food is expected to record only modest growth of just over 5 per cent. A similar trend can be identified for cat food. With an increasing number of premium and super-premium brands expected to appear in supermarkets, Nestlé is likely to face tougher competition in the long term.

Mars might consider introducing Royal Canin into supermarkets in Europe, and by doing so the company could capitalize on the growing popularity of super-premium products across distribution channels. Mars would furthermore be able to compete directly against Iams, whose distribution was expanded following its takeover by Procter & Gamble in 1999.

It is also likely to push sales for the brand in North America, as Royal Canin is well positioned to take on super-premium Hill's and Iams in the region. While Royal Canin had been present in North America for years, it was unable to establish itself successfully in this highly competitive market, mainly because it lacked the necessary financial resources and marketing support. This will undoubtedly change now that Royal Canin has the backing of a major firm with significant financial clout.

Mars: superior in innovation and long-term vision?

Long-term growth will be determined to some extent by innovation, something that Mars has already brought to pet food. Even prior to the takeover, the company proved to be able to turn around its pet food business through product reformulations and innovative packaging such as pouches for its ailing wet cat food business. Mars also supported its major brands through innovative advertising campaigns while, in comparison, Nestlé's advertising activity was less effective.

Moreover, Mars appears to have greater vision for its pet food business. Fully aware of the 'pet humanization phenomenon' (see below), Mars is keen to capitalize on the increasing trend for pet owners to spend money on ensuring their pets' well-being. As a result, it has ventured into added-value pet services, such as pet insurance, as well as animal hospitality through the takeover of UK pet hotel 'Triple A'.

Will Mars' and Nestlé's worldwide market leadership continue?

Currently Mars' and Nestlé's presence in the pet food market remains balanced, and as a result of their consolidation activity, the world pet food market is characterized by an even more pronounced duopoly. In terms of global pet food revenues, the two companies are now very close, and barring further acquisition activity this is likely to remain the case for the foreseeable future. However, unless Nestlé is able to improve its super-premium presence, the outlook appears more positive for Mars.

Pets as family members

The pet population in the USA is also growing at a strong rate, showing a 9 per cent increase between 1998 and 2002, which is in part linked to people's changing attitudes towards them. Increasingly pets occupy the place of valued family member and companion, deserving only the best in food and other pet products, and this improving status is proving as beneficial to superstore retailers as it is to pet product manufacturers.

The phenomenon of 'pet humanization' is gathering pace, and nowhere more so than in the USA. The status of the family pet has improved considerably there over the years, and according to leading global market analyst Euromonitor, expenditure per pet had reached an all-time high of nearly US$50 per year in 2002, an increase of 11 per cent since 1998.

Moreover, Americans seem to be spending as much on pampering their pets as they do on indulging themselves: per capita annual consumption in the USA of chocolate bars stood at US$19 in 2002, while overall expenditure per pet on dog and cat *treats* (e.g. dog snacks) was over US$25 in the same year. As US pet owners increasingly regard their pets as family members, they are opting for premium, functional products that not only sustain, but also contribute to improving their pets' quality of life.

Pet superstores take advantage

Taking advantage of this phenomenon, Petsmart and Petco, the USA's leading pet superstores, both recorded record results in 2001. The most significant distribution channels for pet products continue to be supermarkets and hypermarkets, accounting for nearly 40 per cent of total value sales. However, while this share declined slightly between 1998 and 2002, pet superstores are gaining in importance, increasing their share by three percentage points to over 22 per cent in the same period.

Pet superstores continue to benefit not only from increasing expenditure on pets, but also from a shift towards premium brands. Premium dog food, for instance, enjoyed year-on-year sales growth of 10 per cent in the USA during 2002, compared to 2.5 per cent for mid-priced dog food and a 0.1 per cent decline for economy dog food. A similar trend can be identified for cat food. Premium brands such as Hill's, Iams and Eukanuba are among the 10 top-selling dog and cat food brands in the USA. Iams was, in fact, the leading dog and cat food brand in the USA in 2001, followed closely by premium brand Hill's Science Diet.

Significantly, as pet superstores mainly stock premium pet products, they are the main beneficiaries of this ongoing trend towards high-end, functional food. Another reason for their resurgence is the shift of focus from pet food towards a wider range of pet-care products and pet services such as grooming and training. This enables the companies to differentiate themselves more distinctly from supermarkets, and to drive traffic to their stores in the long term. With a stronger focus on pet-care products, which range from dietary supplements to grooming products and pet clothing, pet superstores are satisfying increasing demand in the USA for such 'luxury' items. Between 1998 and 2002, pet-care products sales rose by over 20 per cent to more than US$5 bn.

Will this US retailing phenomenon also spread to Europe?

While this trend towards pet pampering is noticeable in all mature pet food markets, it is most pronounced in the USA, which boasts more pet superstores than anywhere else in the world. That this trend has not had an effect everywhere became evident in 2000 when Petsmart's expansion into the UK failed and the company decided, only a year after it had arrived, to exit the market at very high cost.

However, should people's attitudes towards pets evolve in other countries in a similar fashion, particularly in the mature western European markets, demographic trends would also support such a development in the region.

With falling birth rates and an ageing population in most western European countries, pets are increasingly likely to fill the void in childless families, and their already elevated status will only improve. Once pets have become more fully 'humanized', the time will perhaps be right for Petco and Petsmart to reconsider international expansion.

Global trends in dry/wet-type pet food products

Wet pet food – even premium alternatives – is in decline in virtually all the major world markets, due to the increasing popularity of premium dry food. Wet food is increasingly perceived as less healthy and insufficiently super-premium to dry alternatives, with the added inconvenience of requiring refrigeration and typically giving off an unpleasant odour (at least to the human nose!). In the dog food sector the wet type decreased from 29 per cent in 1996 to 23 per cent in 2000 and in the cat food sector the wet type fell from 63 to 58 per cent over the same period. So, in contrast to dog food, cat food is still led by wet varieties, even though sales have declined. This was partially due to the growing consumer preference for dry varieties across many national markets.

Sales of dog and cat food products by major geographical market

The world market for pet food and pet-care products totalled US$43.3 bn in 2000. The total market for pet food products was made up of the sectors shown in Table 7.3.

Table 7.3 The total market for pet food products

Pet food products	2000 (US$ bn)
Dog and cat food	30.5
Other pet food	2.0
Pet care products	10.8
Total	**43.3**

Source: adapted from company reports and Euromonitor figures

Dog and cat food sales are typically highest in the most developed national markets, notably the USA, Japan and the major markets of western Europe (see Table 7.4). Consumer affluence is highest in these countries, as reflected in the extravagant expenditure on prepared pet foods – increasingly higher-priced premium and super-premium varieties – as more consumers are inclined to indulge and pamper their cats and dogs.

Table 7.4 Top five world markets for dog and cat food

	2000 (US$ bn)
USA	11.6
Japan	3.1
UK	2.3
Brazil	2.1
Germany	1.7
Total	**20.8**

Source: adapted from company reports and Euromonitor figures

Global sales of dog and cat food are concentrated among the five major world markets, which accounted for a value share of 66 per cent (20.8 in a percentage of 30.5) of the world market in 2000.

The USA and Japan lead the world

The USA is by far the most valuable market, with sales of US$11.6 bn in 2000, equivalent to almost half of total global sales. This is directly attributable to the vast cat and dog population in the USA – the highest in the world – coupled with typically high levels of expenditure on prepared foods, including rising expenditure on dog and cat treats, and other luxury pet foods, among US pet owners.

Sales in the USA continued to rise in 2000, climbing nearly 1 per cent in real terms. In absolute terms, this represents an increase of US$434 mn, the highest increment of all national markets in that year. Growth in 2000 was very much attributable to sustained product development, stimulating consumer interest and fuelling the trend for premium products.

The growing mainstream acceptance of functional foods for cats and dogs – purporting to maintain urinary tract health, hair/coat condition, circulatory health and joint health, among other benefits – exemplifies the importance of product innovation in driving growth, serving to offset price competition, despite maturity of the US market.

Japan is the second most valuable market, with sales of dog and cat food exceeding US$3.1 bn in 2000. The country experienced particularly dynamic growth in 2000, rising by over 7 per cent in real terms – in absolute terms, the market expanded by some US$365 mn, the second largest value increment after the USA.

Reasons for growth are comparable to those in the USA – rising pet populations and pet ownership have been compounded by a strong consumer inclination to over-indulge pet cats and dogs, a trend fuelled by relentless product innovation and development. Total expenditure on dogs and cats in Japan is among the highest in the world – at US$176.4 per pet in 2000, compared to US$86 in the USA – and continues to escalate, with spending largely undeterred by lingering macro-economic difficulties.

Market slowdown in the UK and Germany

Expressed in US dollar terms, sales of cat and dog food among the major markets of western Europe all fell in 2000, due to adverse currency movements favouring the dollar over the euro. Growth in constant local currency terms varied, although maturity of demand saw sales stagnate in the three core markets of the UK, France and Germany.

The UK is the third most valuable national market, with sales of just under US$2.3 bn in 2000, although market stagnation was evident in a very marginal decline in real terms in 2000. Rising cat ownership in the UK was offset by a decline in the dog population, with overall sales undermined by maturity of demand for dog food.

Germany, the fifth most valuable market, saw more pronounced decline, dropping by over 1 per cent in real terms. This is mainly due to price competition and hard discounting through leading retailers, notably discounters such as Lidl and Aldi, exacerbated by competition from supermarkets such as Wal-Mart. As with other major markets, consumers in Germany are increasingly inclined to buy premium cat and dog food, although the availability of these products through discounters and supermarkets has undermined their higher price positioning. Declining dog ownership has also weakened volume sales.

Brazil

Other key growth markets such as Brazil enjoyed strong absolute growth over the review period, driven primarily by an increase in usage of prepared pet food. In Brazil, for example, penetration levels for pet food almost doubled over the survey period, and thus growth in market value escalated, although constant value growth was curtailed in 2000 due to currency devaluation.

Evolving attitudes towards pets in these countries, from being seen as working animals to members of the family, were instrumental in market expansion, with consumers wanting to supplement or replace scraps with perceived healthier foods. Manufacturers were vital to this shift, using advertising and promotional activities to educate consumers, and through the positioning of prepared products as the best method through which to provide a nutritionally balanced meal.

Demand for more exotic pets increases

While overall sales of most 'other' pet food tended to fall across the major markets, due to diminishing consumption in the core bird and fish niches, sales of other 'other' pet food tended to rise, leading growth in seven of the fifteen most valuable markets. This is indicative of a growing interest in small mammals and, increasingly, more exotic or distinctive animals, such as lizards and reptiles.

Rising sales of other 'other' pet food underpinned a near 4 per cent increase in France and around 8 per cent growth in Italy, two of the only major markets to record positive growth in 2000.

However, while consumer demand for more exotic pets rose in many countries, this partially undermined overall value growth through cannibalization of bird and fish sales. In Japan, for example, the fashion for more unusual pets, such as fruit bats and even jellyfish, was a significant factor in undermining sales of fish food – detrimental to overall value growth, due to the high average prices of fish food. In contrast, it is harder for manufacturers to develop products for more esoteric pets as diversity in pet ownership results in a fragmentation of the consumer base.

Many unusual pets, such as reptiles, eat insects, fruit or other animals rather than prepared foods, so a shift in ownership to such animals further undermined overall value sales of 'other' pet food. However, in 2000 the growth of pet food catering for the needs of more uncommon animals was evident in key markets such as the USA, with prepared foods for iguanas, turtles, chinchillas and ferrets emerging as nascent growth niches.

Questions

It is just before Christmas 2003 and Martin Schultz (Vitakraft's international marketing director) has to present a plan for the globalization of Vitakraft within the dog and cat food business. The plan has to be presented at the next board of directors meeting in Bremen (Germany). Martin is a little nervous and also sceptical about the international expansion plans into the global dog and cat food business, because until now Vitakraft has mainly been a market leader in Germany within the bird food sector. Historically, Vitakraft has specialized in the bird seed sector and in other kinds of food, mainly for smaller animals. However, the board of directors has given a signal that they regard this basis as too small for the globalization of the Vitakraft business. As a consequence the firm has launched several dog and cat food brands during the last two to three years, mainly for the domestic (German) market.

At the coming board meeting Martin is determined to give a comprehensive overview of the entire global pet food industry, and the opportunities and threats for Vitakraft within it.

You have just finished your degree in international marketing and Martin has asked you to give a preliminary evaluation of Vitakraft's opportunities in the global pet food industry. Specifically, he has requested you to answer the questions below. You are also welcome to seek further information about the products on the company website: www.vitakraft.de.

1 What are the criteria for success in the pet food industry and to what degree does Vitakraft meet them? Conclude your analysis by saying what you think are the chances of turning Vitakraft into an important global player in the pet food industry.

2 What product mix should be used by Vitakraft to 'attack' the world market for pet food?

Sources: www.vitakraft.de; McKinsey, P. (2003) Global trends. *Prepared Foods* 17(7), July, p. 9; Jones, J. (2003) Pet sauce. *Food Engineering & Ingredients* 28(3), June, p. 23; trade journals

Marketing mix decisions II: pricing

Chapter contents

Learning Objectives

After studying this chapter you should be able to:

- discuss the importance of pricing decisions to the individual firm
- explain the major steps in pricing decisions
- demonstrate how external factors influence pricing decisions
- explain how the product life cycle can affect the price decision
- understand the advantages of using a differentiated price strategy across segments
- discuss the special problems in international pricing.

8.1 **Introduction**

Pricing is one of the most important marketing mix decisions, price being the only marketing mix variable that generates revenues. Pricing is not a single concept, but a multidimensional one with different meanings and implications for the manufacturer, the middleman and the end customer. Pricing strategy is of great importance because it affects both revenue and buyer behaviour. The whole pricing environment is, therefore, considered in this chapter, first from the point of view of the company and its strategies and then from the perspective of the consumer. However, it must not be forgotten that there are other, external influences on pricing – not just from a firm's competitors but also from government and legislation. Once these factors have been taken into account in this chapter, various pricing strategies are reviewed and some attention is given to how best to implement those strategies, how pricing levels can be adjusted, and how such tactics affect buyer behaviour and company revenue.

The multidimensional character of price should be taken into account for the pricing of products and services. Pricing involves the determination (and adjustment) of a price structure and price levels, as well as decisions on short-term price changes. A more effective, goal-orientated approach to pricing is needed that explicitly takes into account the role of price as a marketing mix instrument and as a profit generator. This provides a framework for effective, goal-orientated pricing, and helps highlight the major aspects and factors of the pricing decision.

Figure 8.1 provides a schematic overview of the steps involved in effective price decisions. At the same time, it illustrates the sections covered in this chapter.

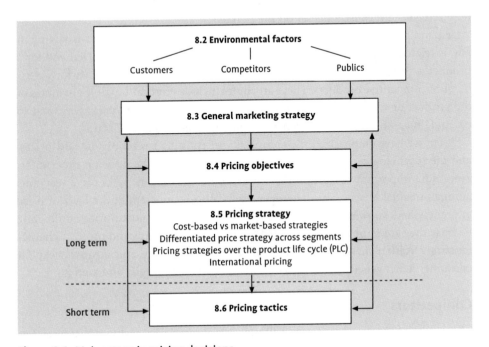

Figure 8.1 Major steps in pricing decisions

As the lines in Fig. 8.1 indicate, environmental characteristics influence each subsequent step, and feedback loops within one decision period and over time are bound to occur. In the following sections, the areas illustrated in Fig. 8.1 will be analysed in more detail.

8.2 Environmental factors

Customers

A key parameter affecting pricing decisions is essentially customer based. The upper limit to the price to be charged is set by the market – unless, of course, the customer *must* purchase the product and we are the sole supplier. Effectively, then, at least in competitive markets, demand (i.e. the price which customers are both willing and able to pay) is a major consideration in the selection of pricing strategies and levels.

Ideally, the marketing manager needs to know the demand schedule for the products and services to be priced. This means that we must take into consideration the time factor (i.e. demand must be specified for a given time period). For example, it is conventional to distinguish between short, medium and long-run time horizons when discussing demand. Certainly demand can, and does, vary over these different time periods. The time period must be explicit when evaluating demand concepts in the context of marketing.

The ability of the purchaser to buy products and services according to income levels and purchasing power converts the buyer's needs and wants into actual purchasing. The economist refers to this willingness and ability to purchase as 'effective demand'. For an organizational buyer, the ability to purchase is directly related to budget requirements and constraints set on the purchaser.

Demand for a product or service, and indeed the price the customer is willing to pay, is related to the attributes of competitive products being offered. Demand for a product is therefore closely related to how the customer perceives the various attributes of competitive products. These attributes include physical/tangible attributes of the product or service in question: for example, quality features, packaging, and so on, and 'intangible' attributes, such as brand/corporate image and status.

So far, we have emphasized the complexity of consumer reactions toward prices, and the psychological factors affecting the role of price in the decision process. An even more important observation is the enormous heterogeneity in price reactions among potential buyers. This heterogeneity is already apparent at the level of price awareness and knowledge. In addition, consumers may evaluate prices differently because they are more or less informed about prevailing prices and product characteristics. Decision-makers should recognize these differences, and positively exploit consumer heterogeneity in the development of pricing strategies and tactics.

Competitors

The results of the pricing strategy will not only depend on consumer response, but also on the reaction of competitors. Competitive behaviour varies considerably with market structure, intensity of competition, and the existence and nature of significant competitive advantages.

Competitors' prices are therefore more decisive for own pricing decisions in markets with many undifferentiated competitors. Market structure and intensity of competition change over the product life cycle (PLC) as new competitors enter the market and products become more homogeneous. Competition intensifies in most cases, and becomes especially severe in the maturity and decline stage, because sales growth can now only be accomplished at the expense of competitors' sales volumes.

Intense competition implies an increased likelihood of competitive reactions to pricing decisions (adjustments in price and/or other marketing mix variables). Besides market structure, the distribution of market shares, the sources and types of competitive advantage, and the marketing goals and strategies of competitors affect the likelihood and nature of competitive reactions. Competitive retaliation may attenuate pricing effects and sometimes provoke real price wars (prices are continually reduced, even to unprofitable levels). The analysis of competitive behaviour is therefore a prerequisite for effective pricing. Competitors respond to the actions of other market players by using those marketing variables that are their 'best weapons', such that price as well as non-price reactions should be monitored. Competitive response behaviour can be investigated in several ways – for example, by means of competitive response profiles.

Substantial deviations from competitors' price levels are feasible only through significant competitive advantages. The most important competitive advantages for pricing relate to costs and unique product values. Cost advantages exist when the product can be produced and/or distributed at a lower unit cost than competitors can achieve; they result from superior skills or resources.

Unique product value results from (tangible or intangible) product characteristics that are valued by consumers and differentiate the product from its substitutes. Unique product value reduces the price sensitivity of consumers, thereby enabling a firm to set prices above the competitors' level without experiencing a considerable decrease in demand.

The most important considerations with regard to competitor pricing include:

- competitors' prices, including discounts, credit terms and terms of trade
- competitors' resources, especially financial
- competitors' costs and profit margins
- likely competitor responses to a firm's pricing strategies and decisions
- likely potential competitors and barriers to market industry entry
- substitutes from other industries
- competitor marketing strategies, especially targeting, positioning and product differentiation.

Three of the most important competitor considerations that directly affect the extent to which an industry will be price competitive are:

189

1 the number of competitors

2 the degree of product differentiation between competitors

3 freedom of entry.

For example, where there is only one supplier (i.e. a monopoly), then the pricing decision-maker has substantial discretion over price. On the other hand, where products are undifferentiated, price competition is likely to be fierce. Finally, where competitors can enter an industry with relative ease, then the price setter will have less discretion over price and may be forced to set lower prices than might otherwise be the case, in order to deter new entrants.

Publics

In addition to customers and competitors, a number of other publics influence pricing decisions. The most important of these is government (legal constraints). Other individuals, groups or institutions may also have an impact on the pricing decision (e.g. financial institutions, workforce) but they are not discussed here.

A number of government laws set legal constraints on competitive pricing behaviour, consumer pricing, international pricing and (the control over) retailer pricing. Prohibited or restricted competitive pricing practices are price fixing, price discrimination and predatory pricing. Important legal constraints on consumer pricing are regulations against deceptive pricing and consumer price discrimination. Moreover, in specific product categories like pharmaceuticals or bread, governments exert direct price controls and establish ranges of legally acceptable consumer prices.

8.3 **General marketing strategy**

The pricing decision is only one part of the general marketing strategy. It must therefore be integrated with the other Ps of the global marketing mix. Price is the only area of the marketing mix where policy can be changed rapidly without large direct cost implications. However, this characteristic also results in the danger that pricing action may be resorted to as a quick fix instead of changes being made in accordance with the other elements of the overall international marketing strategy. It is important, then, that management realizes that constant fine-tuning of prices in international markets should be avoided, and that many problems are not best addressed with pricing action.

In addition to broader corporate objectives, pricing decisions must also reflect and support specific marketing strategies. In particular, pricing strategies need to be in line with market targeting and positioning strategies. Clearly, if a company produces a high-quality product or service aimed at the top end of the market and with a prestige image, it would not make much sense (indeed it would probably be a major mistake) to set a low price on the product even if cost efficiency allowed this. Pricing must therefore be consistent with the other elements of the marketing mix and the selected positioning strategy.

8.4 Pricing objectives

As mentioned earlier, pricing decisions are salient to the achievement of corporate and marketing objectives. Hence it is essential that pricing objectives and strategies are consistent with and supportive of these overall objectives. Environmental analysis provides crucial inputs for the specification of operational and attainable pricing objectives, which are in line with general company goals and strategies, and exploit the possibilities offered by the marketplace. Many pricing objectives can be pursued and these can be classified as follows:

- **profit-orientated objectives** (e.g. profit maximization, profit satisfaction, target return on investment)
- **cost-orientated objectives** (e.g. recover investment costs over a particular time period, generate volume so as to drive down costs)
- **demand/sales-orientated objectives** (e.g. sales growth or maintenance, market share growth or maintenance, use price of one product to sell other products in the line, build traffic), or
- **competition-orientated objectives** (e.g. be the price leader, discourage entry by new competitors, discourage others from lowering prices).

Companies may pursue more than one pricing objective; in such a case, pricing objectives should be mutually consistent, and priorities (or interrelationships) clearly defined. Managers often concentrate on cost-orientated pricing objectives because these can easily be translated into rules of thumb that simplify the pricing problem. In doing so, however, they disregard opportunities for profitable pricing based on factors other than cost.

8.5 Pricing strategy

Many different pricing strategies have been put forward by marketing academics and practitioners. Which of these are feasible in a given problem situation depends on three main factors (see also Fig. 8.1):

1 the characteristics of the environment

2 the general marketing strategy of the company

3 the pricing objectives of the company.

Some typical pricing strategies are highlighted below.

Cost-based versus market-based strategies

Cost-based pricing

The most widely used method for determining prices involves setting prices predominantly on the basis of the company's own costs. This method of pricing is often referred to as *cost-plus pricing*. In its simplest form, cost-plus pricing involves a company calculating average cost per unit and then allocating a specified mark-up, which may be related to rate of profit required by the company, to arrive at the selling price.

The major advantage of this method of pricing is its seeming simplicity. However, despite its widespread use by companies, it has long been severely criticized. The mechanics of cost-plus pricing involve calculating the variable costs per unit and adding to these an allocation of the total fixed costs. The first problem with cost-plus pricing is in both the calculation and allocation of these fixed costs. In many multi-product companies the allocation of fixed and semi-variable costs to individual products is often arbitrary. In practice, total fixed costs are allocated on the basis of either a standard volume or a forecast level of output.

A second problem with cost-plus pricing is the determination of the mark-up. As mentioned earlier, often the percentage mark-up is derived from a predetermined target rate of profit or return. The problem with such predetermined mark-up rates, however, is that they take no account of demand conditions.

With these disadvantages there must of course be good reason why cost-plus still remains widely used by companies. The advantages are as follows.

- If competitors are using cost-plus pricing, and provided they have similar costs and mark-ups, it can lead to price stability.

- The pricing decision-maker does not have to consider the difficult (if essential) area of demand and price sensitivity.

- It is often claimed that because prices are directly related to costs it is 'fair' to both competitors and customers.

None of these potential advantages compensates for the fact that cost-plus pricing, certainly in its most rigid form, is not at all market-orientated, and can lead to significant strategic disadvantages in the market.

Market-based pricing

Market-based pricing moves away from the focus on costs and instead concentrates on what the price should be, seen in a combination of two perspectives:

1 What are competitors' prices for similar products?

2 What is the perceived value of the product to customers?

The first perspective is based on several assumptions, including that of product image and the position of the company as being the same or very similar to that of the competition. Although it is vital to consider competitors' prices, costs, and so on (as we have seen) this information should be used to influence pricing rather than as a 'formula' for setting it.

The basic idea underpinning the perceived value-based approach to pricing is that when customers purchase a product they go through a complex process of balancing benefits against costs.

A customer will not purchase a product where the costs are seen as being greater than the benefits. It is important to stress that the costs may include more than just the purchase price, and again it is the customer's perception of these costs that is used in the evaluation process. For example, in assessing the costs of, say, a new car it is not just the initial purchase cost, but also maintenance, insurance, petrol and perhaps depreciation costs that the purchaser may consider. In addition, just as there are psychological benefits so too are there psychological costs. For example, a new car purchaser may well consider the costs of 'loss of status' if he buys a cheap eastern European car.

For the pricing decision-maker, of course, the difficulty in this method of pricing is in measuring how the customer perceives the company's offer against the competition. Moreover, value perceptions may vary considerably among consumers, and even over usage situations.

Different customers may use the 'same' product in different ways and hence make different cost/benefit evaluations. If the customer makes such a trade-off between costs and benefits it would seem sensible for the selling company to do the same. It is important to understand that the benefits involve a great deal more than the core attributes, and that in many choice situations it is the augmented product benefits that differentiate products.

Differentiated price strategy across segments

Any one price, even if it has been developed on the basis of market data in conjunction with overall marketing strategy, risks leaving a huge amount of money on the table. Because each customer – or, more realistically, each customer segment – makes a value/price judgement, developing an 'average' price at some midpoint along the spectrum of perceived value runs counter to the concept of aligning price and value. The result of this single 'average' price approach, represented in Fig. 8.2, is that the company ends up charging almost everyone the wrong price (Simon and Butscher, 2001).

For each of the customer segments that perceive more value than is represented by the single price, profit is being lost. On the other hand, the segments that perceive less value than is represented by the price simply will not buy the product. While effective marketing and sales communications may be able to move each segment's perception of value slightly, this will still capture only those segments whose perceived value is closest to the average price. At the high and low ends, substantial revenue and profit are being left on the table.

The ideal pricing strategy, then, should follow the natural segmentation of the market based on perceived value. By setting prices at or just below the value realized by each customer segment, a company will maximize revenue and profit. The role of marketing in this process is to identify the customer value segments and set prices accordingly. The role of sales is to maintain the differentiated pricing structure by selling on value, rather than just on price. To successfully implement differentiated pricing, marketing and sales must work together to understand customer needs and redefine the product/service offering in terms that intersect with these needs. This will maximize the perception of value. Often, definitions and perceptions of value differ within a single organization from one level of management to another. In such situations, success depends on identifying and targeting the level most likely to understand the full value of the complete product and service 'bundle' (Klompmaker *et al.*, 2003).

Price bundling is marketing two or more products in a single package for a special price. Examples include the sale of maintenance contracts with computer hardware and other office equipment.

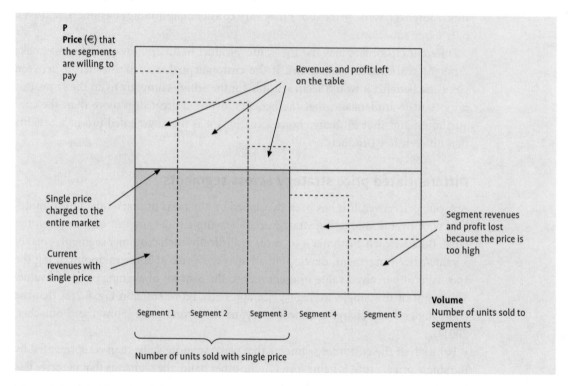

Figure 8.2 One-price approach vs price differentiation across segments

Auctions and Dutch auctions

The growth of the Internet has made customer-driven pricing models feasible on a large scale. In terms of price customization, auctions and Dutch auctions come close to the ideal situation in which every customer pays exactly the maximum of what he is willing to spend (Simon and Butscher, 2001). Auctions are an ancient form of pricing in which interested parties bid for a product that is for sale and have the chance to increase their original bid as other bidders top it. The product is typically sold to the party that in the end places the highest bid (there are alternatives where the second highest bid wins). Auctions require that all bidders are either physically present at the site of the auction or can participate via telephone or another technology. The Internet has made auctions a tool for the masses, as it enables everybody around the world with access to the Internet to participate in an auction on an auction website such as eBay or QXL. Auctions are becoming more and more popular in business-to-consumer, business-to-business and consumer-to-consumer scenarios.

Auctions are the best pricing strategy to extract the maximum 'willingness-to-pay' for a product that currently exists in the market, as determined by the highest bid. Of course, the highest bidder may have been willing to pay an even higher price.

In Dutch auctions, the starting price is an amount slightly above the highest price a seller thinks he can achieve. The price then begins to drop and the first customer to signal his willingness to buy at the current price gets the sale. Similar to regular auctions, this pricing system permits extraction of the maximum willingness-to-pay for a product that currently exists in the market, as it creates competition between customers. A customer could wait for the price to drop below his personal price limit, but then has to take the risk of another customer snatching the sale.

In order to make either auction form effective, however, it must be ensured that a large enough number of customers can and will participate in the auction. The participating audience should be an exact mirror of a firm's entire market or, ideally, all its potential customers should participate. The Internet is an excellent way to achieve this, but, depending on what market a firm is in, this might mean that it has to enable access to the auction through different technologies. For example, if its market has a low Internet penetration (i.e. small businesses, low-income consumer segments, etc.), it will have to allow access to the auction via mobile phone, conventional telephone, and the like.

Pricing strategies in the product life cycle (PLC)

As we have already seen, the competitive situation for a product changes throughout its life cycle. Each different phase in the cycle may require a different strategy. Pricing plays a particularly important role in this respect. Some of the ways in which price may be used at various stages of the product life cycle will now be examined. Once again, it should be noted that considerable care should be taken in interpreting the possible strategic implications of each of the life cycle stages.

Pricing in the introductory stage of the life cycle

With an innovatory product its developers can expect to have a competitive edge, at least for a period of time. With innovatory new products, a company can elect to choose between two extreme pricing strategies (Lancaster and Massingham, 2001):

1 **price skimming** – introducing new products at a high price level

2 **price penetration** – introducing new products at a low price level.

Price skimming

The setting of a high initial price can be interpreted as an assumption by management that, eventually, competition will enter the market and erode profit margins. The company therefore sets the price high so as to 'milk' the market and achieve the maximum profits available in the shortest period of time. This 'market skimming' strategy involves the company estimating the highest price the customer is willing or able to pay, which will involve assessing the benefits of the product to the potential customer. This strategy has in the past been used successfully by firms marketing innovative products with substantial consumer benefits.

After the initial introduction stage of the product the company will tend to lower the price of the product so as to draw in more price-conscious customers. When a company adopts this kind of strategy the following variables are usually present:

- demand for the product is high

- the high price will not attract early competition

- the high price gives the impression to the buyer of purchasing a high-quality product from a superior firm.

Price penetration

The setting of a low price strategy, or 'market penetration strategy', is carried out by companies whose prime objective is to capture a large market share in the quickest time period possible.

The conditions that usually prevail for penetrating pricing to be effective include:

- demand for the product is price sensitive

- a low price will tend to discourage competitors from entering the market

- potential economies of scale and/or significant experience curve effects.

Exhibit 8.1 **Pricing research in the early stage of pharmaceutical product development**

In early stages of drug development the product profile is highly uncertain. Only the mechanism of action, data on basic efficacy and safety at different doses will be in the process of being established. At this stage it may be difficult for physicians to comment on the value of product benefits, as these are not yet well defined. To a large extent, pricing research at this stage has to be qualitative in nature and tries to establish a sensible range of possible values (ceiling and floor prices), given possible best case and safety scenarios.

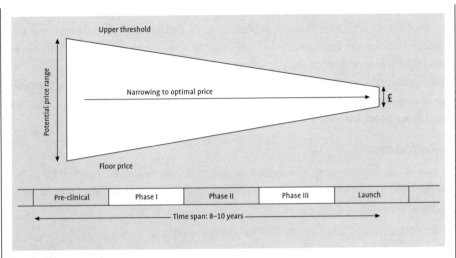

Narrowing the price range

Conducting pricing research with such a wide divergence from existing prices and price expectations requires approaching respondents with mind-sets that can think beyond the day-to-day drug budgeting and cost constraints. One should therefore try to establish an initial price range that, over time, research will narrow down to the optimal price.

In early-stage research a qualitative approach involving depth interviews with opinion leaders who may act, or have acted, as advisers to government authorities, and with a few clinicians is usually a good starting point from which to define the upper price limits and potential reference compounds. However, price acceptability will depend on product performance which at this stage of development will still be largely unknown.

One approach at this stage is to undertake some benchmarking or price referencing with respondents in relation to existing drugs on the market (not necessarily within the same therapy area) in order to be able to gauge the range of acceptable prices. This is particularly important for new chemical entities. The competitive environment must also be examined as the prices can vary widely.

Source: adapted from Hanlon and Luery (2002)

International pricing

Geographic pricing

Geographic pricing becomes an issue when a company serves geographically distant markets and transportation constitutes an important component of transaction costs. Depending on the competitive conditions in these markets and on the threat of entry, it may be more profitable to charge either uniform standardized prices in all markets or locally adapted prices.

Price setting within individual country markets is driven by typical corporate issues and objectives. Also, the major problem areas in international pricing have been meeting local competition, cost, lack of competitive information, distribution and channel factors, and government barriers.

Multinationals tend to make pricing decisions close to each market's prevailing conditions, but the relationship is symbiotic: co-ordination and strategic direction come from headquarters, yet short-term pricing decisions are made locally.

Price escalation

In preparing a quotation, the international marketer must be careful to include unique export-related costs as well as normal costs shared with the domestic side of the business, such as:

- the cost of modifying the product for foreign markets

- operational costs of the export operation (e.g. subsidiary costs) – personnel, market research, additional shipping and insurance costs, communications costs with foreign customers, and overseas promotional costs

- foreign market entry costs – tariffs and taxes, commercial credit and political risks associated with a buyer in a different market, and foreign exchange risks.

The combined effect of clear-cut and hidden costs causes export prices to accelerate. Price escalation can result in different-sized price increases across markets. Customers who shop around for lower prices, or distributors unhappy about their margins in certain markets, might force a marketer to abandon a market altogether. International marketers combat price escalation through accurate information and creative strategies such as the following methods, which emphasize cutting costs.

- Reorganize the channel of distribution: eliminate some distribution levels. However, shortening the value chain might incur other new costs such as new intermediaries' demands for better discounts.

- Adapt the product: use less expensive ingredients or unbundle costly features. Remaining features, such as packaging, can also be cheapened. If price escalation causes differentials between markets that customers might discover, alter the product by changing styling and packaging, for example.

- Emphasize non-price benefits: quality, after-sales service, warranties, etc. (not necessarily price concessions) can add to the value the customer receives, or at least perceives, from your offer.

- Assemble or produce the product overseas: through foreign sourcing, the exporter may receive an additional benefit to lower cost – duty drawbacks.

Transfer pricing

Transfer (intracorporate) pricing is the pricing of sales to members of the multinational corporate family. With rapid globalization and consolidation across borders, estimates have up to two-thirds of world trade taking place between related parties, including shipments and transfers from parent company to affiliates, as well as trade between alliance partners. Transfer pricing must be managed in a world of varying tax rates, foreign exchange rates, governmental regulations, and other economic and social challenges. Allocating resources among multinational units requires central management to achieve the following objectives:

- competitiveness in the international marketplace
- reduction of taxes and tariffs
- management of cash flows
- minimization of foreign exchange risks
- avoidance of conflicts with home and host governments, and
- allaying of internal concerns, such as goal congruence and motivation of subsidiary managers.

The euro and the 'price corridor'

The advent of the euro illustrates how all firms will need to re-examine the positioning of their businesses. The potential advantages of a single-currency Europe are considerable, but it also threatens businesses of all nationalities, sizes and types. More production and operating strategy decisions will be made on the basis of true cost differentials – proximity to specific inputs, materials, immobile skills or niche customers, for example. Consolidation will be the norm for many national business units whose existence was in some way perpetuated by using different currencies.

Intracompany transaction pricing – pricing among company business units and headquarters – becomes more troublesome with currency consolidation. Transparency allows tax authorities to easily enforce transfer price uniformity. If discrepancies among markets are not justified by market differences such as consumption preferences, competition or government interference, parallel importation may occur. Parallel imports into affluent markets will force prices to their lowest level as buyers simply go to the cheapest available source. For example, Portugal may influence prices in Germany through parallel imports and centralized buying power.

The price corridor solution

The recommended approach following the introduction of the euro is a 'price corridor' – a range within which national prices vary. A company sets the maximum and minimum prices that country organizations can charge – enough to allow flexibility as a result of differences in price elasticities, competition and positioning, but not enough to attract parallel imports that may start at price differences of 20 per cent and higher. The corridor would be much narrower for easily transportable items like photographic film than for immobile products such as industrial machinery. This approach moves pricing authority away from country managers and into the hands of regional management, and requires changes in management systems and incentive structures. In Europe, as in future regional currency consolidations, manufacturers will do well to compromise between individually market-optimized prices and a uniform regional price. Uniformity will occur over time as consumers and national economies slowly adjust.

Global pricing contracts

As globalization increases, customers will put pressure on suppliers to accept global pricing contracts (GPCs). Purchasers may promise international markets, guaranteed production volumes and improved economies of scale and scope, but what if they fail to deliver or if suppliers' global price transparency inspires them to make unrealistic demands? Suppliers must make three key decisions: whether to pursue a GPC, how to negotiate the best terms, and how to keep a global relationship on track. It has been found that the best tool for suppliers is solid information on customers. Good information can help a supplier make a sensible counter-proposal to demands for the highest levels of service at the lowest price.

Exhibit 8.2 **Barbie clothing: a case of brand stretching at high-end prices**

Mattel, the world's number one toy maker, has about 16 stand-alone stores in Japan selling Barbie clothes that are geared towards adults. It hoped to expand to 20 stores by the end of 2004. Barbie herself has always been a fashion icon and so creating her own label perhaps seemed only logical. Now Mattel also wants to penetrate the US home market. In June 2004, it showcased a new Barbie brand of vintage T-shirts, cocktail dresses, shoes and coats in New York at the International Licensing show.

The USA will see a limited debut of the line, with a few select pieces. The heritage of the Barbie brand in the United States is very sensitive and Mattel wants to reposition the Barbie brand as a fashion icon, not just a kitsch concept.

In July 2004 Mattel launched a Barbie vintage-style T-shirt inspired by the 1959 Barbie, priced between $40 and $60 at the high-end department store chain Nordstrom.

Source: adapted from Bhatnager (2004)

8.6 **Pricing tactics**

This section makes the following distinction between pricing strategies and pricing tactics: *pricing strategies* determine long-term price structure and price levels, and their evolution over time in response to long-term changes in the environment, while *pricing tactics* consist of short-term price decisions (mostly price reductions from the normal or long-term level) to induce immediate sales increases or to respond to short-term changes in the environment. Part of the confusion that may arise between the two stems from the fact that the same set of instruments and actions can serve both strategic and tactical purposes. This is, for instance, true for the use of price deals.

Price promotions

The measurement of sales promotion effects has generated a great deal of interest in recent years. While a variety of promotional activities is available, the bulk of sales promotion actions take the form of either a straight price cut or a more indirect price reduction. Typical of such price promotions is their temporary character; a large portion of the observed sales increase stems from brand switching.

All in all, temporary price reductions have about the weakest positive long-term effects of any below-the-line activity since they appeal to rational (financial) arguments rather than building brand image or franchise. While the evidence of positive long-run implications for brand sales is limited, there are indications that price deals lead to purchase acceleration and stockbuilding, followed by sales dips in the post-promotion period. In other words, sales promotions may partly 'borrow sales from the future'. More importantly, frequent price cuts may reduce the consumer's willingness to buy the product at the regular price and eventually damage product image.

So far, the discussion has implicitly concentrated on the impact of promotions directed at consumers. Manufacturers spend increasingly large budgets on trade promotions (i.e. temporary price cuts aimed at retailers). While the impact of trade promotions bears similarities to that of consumer promotions, their (long-run) implications are even more complex. Nevertheless, they may generate effects that extend over a longer period of time.

Summary

A whole set of complex factors affects pricing decisions, making this in fact one of the most complex and difficult areas of market planning. Pricing decisions are more than just a 'mechanical' exercise of adding margins for profit onto costs. Price setting must become an integral part of the marketing strategy of the company and must be consistent with corporate and marketing objectives and other elements of the mix. In addition to these inputs to pricing decisions, the marketer must consider demand, cost and competitors.

Based on environmental factors (customers, competitors and publics) and general marketing strategy, the major components of pricing decision-making are:

- pricing objectives (long term)
- pricing strategies (long term)
- pricing tactics (short term).

Companies use price skimming (high prices) as a pricing strategy for a new product when the product is perceived by the target market as having unique advantages. Penetration pricing means charging a relatively low price to capture a large market share.

The basic idea of price differentiation is simple: charge every market segment the price it is willing to pay. The Internet has made customer-driven pricing models feasible on a large scale.

As a product moves through its life cycle the management usually sets prices high during the introductory stage. Later on, as competition intensity increases, prices are likely to decrease.

In international pricing, companies have the possibility of using a 'price corridor'. A price corridor defines the range within which prices across borders may vary. This price corridor needs to be set as narrow as possible in order to avoid the threat of parallel imports.

Pricing tactics are short-term, fine-tuning pricing techniques. They include various sorts of discounts, promotional pricing and other special pricing tactics.

Questions for discussion

1 Why do customers sometimes believe high prices indicate high-quality products?

2 How does competition affect a company's prices? Briefly describe a major competitor-based pricing approach.

3 What could be the strategy behind having another pricing strategy outside the 'main season' (off-peak pricing)?

4 What are the drawbacks to using penetration pricing as the main strategy in entering a new market?

5 We know that several factors influence consumer responses to prices. What psychological factors should marketers keep in mind when using consumer-orientated pricing? Describe each factor.

6 Many firms enter a market as price leaders, but end up dominating the lower end of the market. What may be the reasons for this?

7 In what ways is the role of pricing in the international market (a) similar to and (b) different from the role of pricing in the domestic market?

8 What influence do distribution strategies have on international price setting?

9 Outline an international pricing strategy that offers a 'win-win' outcome for both manufacturer and importer.

10 Discuss the circumstances when one global price for all international markets is (a) the most appropriate course of action, and (b) an inappropriate course of action for a firm.

References

Bhatnager, P. (2004) Wanna dress like a Barbie? *CNN Money* (http://money.cnn.com), 14 June, New York.

Hanlon, D. and Luery, D (2002) The role of pricing research in assessing the commercial potential of new drugs development. *International Journal of Market Research* 44 fourth quarter, pp. 423–47.

Klompmaker, J.E., Rodgers, W.H. and Nygren, A.E. (2003) Value, not volume. *Marketing Management*, June, pp. 45–8.

Lancaster, G. and Massingham, L. (2001) *Marketing Management*, 3rd edn. UK: McGraw-Hill.

Simon, H. and Butscher, S.A. (2001) Individualized pricing: boosting profitability with a high art of power pricing. *European Management Journal* 19(2), pp. 109–14.

Case 8 Braun electric toothbrushes: is it wise to offer a low-priced battery version of Oral-B?

Braun as part of Gillette

Today the marketer of the Oral-B brand is Braun AG of Germany, which was acquired in 1967 by Gillette, thus entering the electric shaving and small electrical appliances sectors. In 1984, Gillette acquired Oral-B Laboratories, Inc., which added to its power toothbrushes business.

Gillette's core business is still its Blades and Razors division, which accounted for 40 per cent of its sales in 2002. Its Duracell division represented a further 22 per cent of sales in that year. Gillette's small electrical appliances, as defined in this case study, fall into two divisions: Oral Care and Braun, which together accounted for 27 per cent of revenue in 2002. The Oral Care business includes both manual and power toothbrushes sold under the Oral-B and Braun brands. The Braun division sells electric shavers under the Braun brand and hair depilators under the Silk-Epil brand, as well as a range of small household and personal diagnostic appliances under the Braun brand.

Gillette's smallest division, Personal Care, includes shaving preparations, after-shave products, and deodorants and antiperspirants.

Gillette's Braun subsidiary, which manufactures most of its small electrical appliances, is based in Germany but sells its products worldwide. This represented 12 per cent of Gillette's total sales in 2002.

Gillette operates a global production network, with 32 manufacturing facilities in 15 countries around the world. The Braun subsidiary has 10 plants in seven countries, namely Germany, Ireland, France, Spain, Mexico, the USA and China, and has a daily production output of around 250,000 units.

The new, low-priced Braun Power toothbrush product

Gillette's main threat in US power toothbrushes is Procter & Gamble, which acquired Dr John's Spinbrush in late 2000 and achieved phenomenal success when it was relaunched under the Crest brand name. In response to the erosion of its power toothbrush share by the low-priced Crest brand, Gillette launched the Oral-B CrossAction Power toothbrush in 2001, priced at less than US$10.

The Oral-B CrossAction Power toothbrush was designed to improve on the performance of the Oral-B CrossAction manual toothbrush. With its low price, CrossAction Power marks Gillette's entry in the budget battery toothbrush segment, the fastest-growing sector in the US oral care market, and is designed to encourage manual users to trade up to the battery segment and eventually to the premium rechargeable toothbrushes segment (e.g. the Oral-B Professional Care 7000 Series). The product uses Gillette's patented CrissCross bristle technology, which reaches deep between teeth and along the gum line to eliminate plaque, while the rotating PowerHead surrounds teeth to remove plaque from surfaces and hard-to-reach back teeth. The product also features an ultra-thin, manual-like handle with a soft, rubberized grip designed to provide greater comfort and control.

Gillette didn't stop there, however, but continued to innovate. In April 2003, the company introduced the Oral-B Professional Care 7000 Series in the premium power toothbrushes segment. The line features significantly faster brushing, at 40,000 pulsations and 8800 oscillations per minute. It also features a timer, which signals every 30 seconds to let users know when to brush a new quadrant of the mouth.

Power toothbrushes represent one of the smallest and most immature sectors of the small electrical appliances market, but this was the fastest growing sector over the review period. As a result, by 2002, it represented 5.2 per cent of small electrical appliances volume sales, compared with just 1.6 per cent in 1998.

The strong growth in this market was due to low household penetration and generally stemmed from low bases in most markets. The strongly declining prices of these products encouraged more consumers to purchase them, particularly in response to growing concerns over maintaining healthy teeth and gums. Recommendations by dentists to use electric toothbrushes in preference to manual brushing led to higher demand worldwide, although as these are still seen mainly as luxury purchases, sales are still very low in developing markets.

The main impetus to global growth was the phenomenal development of low-priced, mass-market battery-operated toothbrushes, particularly in the USA, but also worldwide. This was triggered in the United States by the acquisition of Dr John's Spinbrush by consumer products giant Procter & Gamble in late 2000. When the product was relaunched under the Crest name in 2001 it carried a retail price of just US$6. Hence, the market was opened up to a new segment of consumers than previously when prices were typically over US$60. Similar products soon followed from other dental care brands, including Colgate. The success of these small appliances also encouraged manufacturers with a longer heritage in the sector to offer products at lower price points, giving mass-market consumers a possible point of entry into their brands.

The global toothbrush market

The accompanying table shows the three general toothbrush market segments.

Table 8.1 Segmentation of the toothbrush market

Three toothbrush segments in the world market	Examples of brands	Typical retail consumer prices (€)
1. Manual toothbrushes	Jordan	3
2. Power toothbrush market, which can be divided into two sub-segments:		
(a) battery-powered toothbrushes	P&G Spinbrush	7–8
(b) electric toothbrushes (with rechargeable batteries)	Braun Oral-B	20

The main impetus to global growth was the phenomenal development of low-priced, mass-market battery-operated toothbrushes, particularly in the USA, but also worldwide.

Global sales

The global market for power toothbrushes amounted to just 47 million units in 2002, but this was a significant improvement on the level of 12.5 million units recorded in 1998. Exceptionally high growth levels of 46.2 per cent and 64.4 per cent were recorded in 2000 and 2001, with growth beginning to stabilize in 2002 at 29.2 per cent. Growth was underpinned by the development of cheap, battery-operated toothbrushes, which opened up a new market and allowed products to be sold through mass-market outlets at affordable prices.

Regional sales

North America far outweighed any other region in terms of power toothbrush sales by volume. The market developed very rapidly over the review period, overtaking western Europe by 2000, and accounting for 61.5 per cent of the global market by 2002. However, by value North America is much lower in importance. While still the largest regional market, sales in North America were only slightly ahead of those in western Europe by value, with the two markets combined representing almost 86 per cent of global value sales in 2002.

All regions recorded impressive growth over the review period – even Latin America, which suffered a decline in most markets. Nevertheless, growth rates were from relatively small bases. North America was the fastest growth region between 1998 and 2002, recording an increase of 804 per cent, while in Latin America sales progressed by 459.8 per cent, from just 32,000 to 180,000 units (see Table 8.2).

Table 8.2 **Power toothbrushes: sales by region (1998–2002)**				
000 units	**1998**	**2000**	**2002**	**% growth 1998–2002**
North America	3201	10282	28934	804.0
Western Europe	6457	8434	11965	85.3
Asia-Pacific	1765	2264	4519	156.1
Eastern Europe	343	306	542	57.9
Africa and the Middle East	339	385	443	30.6
Australasia	373	391	427	14.4
Latin America	32	75	180	459.8
WORLD	**12510**	**22137**	**47009**	**275.8**

US$ mn	1998	2000	2002	% growth 1998–2002
North America	167	264	511	205.4
Western Europe	377	415	468	24.2
Asia-Pacific	57	80	125	119.9
Australasia	11	12	13	11.6
Eastern Europe	11	8	10	−15.5
Africa and the Middle East	10	11	10	1.2
Latin America	3	3	4	45.0
WORLD	**636**	**792**	**1140**	**79.1**

Source: different company resources

Note: totals may not sum due to rounding

Leading national markets

The USA dominated the global market for power toothbrushes by volume in 2002 (see the accompanying table), accounting for more than half of total sales. Sales grew at a phenomenal rate of 1286 per cent over the review period, this being the fastest-growing and least mature sector of the small electrical appliances market in the USA. This is due to the introduction of new, low-priced battery-operated toothbrushes on the market, such as the Crest Spinbrush, which were accepted as mass-market items and sold through mass merchandisers.

The second largest market for power toothbrushes was Germany, although with sales of just 4.1 million units it lagged far behind the USA. Germany is the domestic market of the pioneer of electric toothbrushes, Gillette's subsidiary Braun, and therefore has a relatively long heritage in this type of appliance. Nevertheless, the German market continued to develop strongly over the 1998–2002 period, with volume sales up by 150 per cent during that time. This was again due to the fast rise of battery-powered brushes, whose low prices attracted many new users who were already aware of the positive publicity surrounding these products, but had hitherto been deterred by their high price.

The only other markets where sales of power toothbrushes reached more than three million units were the UK and Canada, closely followed by Japan. All three markets enjoyed strong growth, although the UK market is now showing signs of reaching maturity. In this market, ownership has clearly grown among key age groups, and the proliferation of cheaper battery alternatives widely available throughout the retail trade means that power toothbrushes are no longer the star performers they once were.

In Japan, sales of power toothbrushes exploded suddenly in 2002, due to the launch on to the Japanese market of low-priced products from Procter & Gamble and its competitors, which featured permanent brushes and dry-cell batteries. These became available through Japanese supermarkets and convenience stores, and opened up the market to manual users. Indeed, some low-end electric toothbrushes began to be retailed at less than ¥1,000 – down sharply from the ¥10,000 or more seen previously.

Sales of power toothbrushes are still negligible in many emerging markets, however, such as China and India.

Table 8.3 **Power toothbrushes: sales by leading countries (1998–2002)**			
000 units	**1998**	**2000**	**2002**
USA	1857	8629	25741
Germany	1643	2301	4116
UK	2250	3100	3400
Canada	1344	1653	3193
Japan	1090	1093	2727
France	560	660	1120
Spain	158	255	895
Australia	334	353	383
Sweden	400	415	380
Netherlands	205	261	281
Italy	132	185	252
Russia	200	150	250
Poland	70	90	200
South Africa	44	51	58
Portugal	18	20	22
Brazil	16	19	20
Hungary	5	5	6
Belgium	5	5	5
Greece	2	3	3

Source: adapted from company sources, databases and other trade sources

Product trends

The main development in the power toothbrushes sector, and that which caused the massive growth in the USA and hence global sales, was the introduction of low-priced, mass-market battery-operated toothbrushes. This was triggered by the aforementioned acquisition of Dr John's Spinbrush by consumer products giant Procter & Gamble in late 2000. The product was relaunched under the Crest name in 2001, as mentioned above, and carried a retail price of just US$6. Hence, the market was opened up to a new segment of consumers than previously when prices typically retailed at over US$60. Similar products soon followed from other dental care brands, including Colgate.

At the premium end of the market, Gillette introduced the Oral-B Professional Care 7000 Series in 2003, as we have seen, and in Japan, innovations in electric toothbrushes during the review period included an electric toothbrush launched by Japanese manufacturer Kagoshima Supersonic Technical Laboratory, which uses electricity and not toothpaste to clean. It claims to be able to clean teeth by creating an electrical current in the mouth via two strips of copper and magnesium that are embedded in the brush head. After initial rinsing with water, saliva in the mouth acts as a suitable conductor of electricity. The current of up to 1.8 volts apparently loosens plaque so that it can easily be brushed away, hence toothpaste is not required in the process. Matsushita launched another such innovative product under its Panasonic brand name, involving toothbrushes that have a camera stalk next to the vibrating bristles, thereby facilitating better visibility of the mouth cavity while teeth are being brushed.

Children's toothbrushes were a particular growth segment in many markets. In Germany, these increased sales by more than 400 per cent, compared with growth of just 41 per cent for adult models. This was due to new children's brushes, such as that offered by Gillette (Braun), and supported by substantial poster, window display and print advertising campaigns.

Global manufacturer and brand shares

The global market for power toothbrushes is largely in the hands of two players: Procter & Gamble and Gillette (see Table 8.4). Procter & Gamble significantly increased its lead by volume in 2002 to reach 34.3 per cent, due to its rapid growth in the US market following the launch of Crest Spinbrush in 2001. This product revolutionized the US electric toothbrush market by representing the first budget battery-operated model to retail for only US$6. With the launch of similar products by competitors in 2002, Procter & Gamble is unlikely to maintain this strong share in the future.

Gillette was the pioneer in the power toothbrushes market through its Braun subsidiary, which was the world market leader before Procter & Gamble acquired Dr John's Spinbrush in late 2000. As Braun manufactures products at the premium end of the spectrum, it undoubtedly remains the global leader in value terms. However, by volume its share fell slightly to 27.1 per cent in 2002 due to competition from cheaper versions.

Another major player in the power toothbrushes market is Colgate-Palmolive, with its Colgate brand (see the accompanying table) achieving a global share of 12.8 per cent in 2002. This also represented a significant decline on 2001 levels, due to competition from Procter & Gamble's Crest brand.

The only other manufacturer to achieve a share of more than 2 per cent in the global power toothbrushes sector was Philips with its Sonicare sonic power toothbrush line. Its share remained broadly stable in 2002 at 6.3 per cent.

Table 8.4 Power toothbrushes: global manufacturer market share (2001/2002)

Manufacturer	% volume 2001	% volume 2002
The Procter & Gamble Co.	26.9	34.3
The Gillette Co.	28.3	27.1
Colgate-Palmolive Co.	16.9	12.8
Philips Electronics NV	6.4	6.3
Matsushita Electric Industrial Co. Ltd	1.1	1.6
GlaxoSmithKline plc	1.5	1.5
Salton, Inc.	1.3	1.0
Sunstar, Inc.	0.7	0.7
Minimum Corp.	0.5	0.7
Unilever Group	0.6	0.6
Toray Industries, Inc.	0.4	0.6
Conair Corp.	0.2	0.1
Homedics, Inc.	0.1	0.1
Private label	1.6	1.7
Others	13.5	10.9
TOTAL	**100.0**	**100.0**

Source: adapted from databases, company reports and different public trade sources

Table 8.5 Power toothbrushes: global brand market share (2001/2002)

Brand	Manufacturer	% volume 2001	% volume 2002
Crest	The Procter & Gamble Co.	25.6	32.9
Oral-B	The Gillette Co.	16.0	17.2
Colgate	Colgate-Palmolive Co.	16.9	12.8
Braun	The Gillette Co.	12.3	9.9
Sonicare	Philips Electronics NV	3.6	3.2
Philips	Philips Electronics NV	2.8	3.1
National	Matsushita Electric Industrial Co. Ltd	1.1	1.6
Blend-a-Dent	The Procter & Gamble Co.	1.1	1.1
Aquafresh	GlaxoSmithKline plc	0.9	0.8
Minimum	Minimum Corp.	0.5	0.7
Sunstar	Sunstar, Inc.	0.7	0.7
Salton	Salton, Inc.	0.8	0.6
Toray Ireeve	Toray Industries, Inc.	0.4	0.6
Dr Best	GlaxoSmithKline plc	0.6	0.6
Signal	Unilever Group	0.6	0.5
Ultrasonex	Salton, Inc.	0.5	0.4
Blend-a-Med	The Procter & Gamble Co.	0.2	0.2

Binaca	GlaxoSmithKline plc	–	0.2
Interplak	Conair Corp.	0.2	0.1
Homedics	Homedics, Inc.	0.1	0.1
Others		15.1	12.7
TOTAL		**100.0**	**100.0**

Source: adapted from Internet databases, company reports and different public trade sources

Spinbrush success prompts influx of competing products

While Crest Spinbrush was the primary driver behind increased sales of battery-powered toothbrushes specifically, and power toothbrushes in general, other rival manufacturers also launched similar products in the final years of the review period to counter Spinbrush's overwhelming sales success. Indeed, Colgate-Palmolive's Colgate Actibrush was launched prior to Procter & Gamble's acquisition of Dr John's Spinbrush. In February 2001, Colgate followed up with its child-specific Colgate Actibrush Bzzz. However, at US$20, both Actibrush and Actibrush Bzzz carried a much higher price than comparable Crest Spinbrush products. To its credit, Actibrush partially justified its higher price point by featuring replaceable heads upon its debut. This feature did not reach Crest Spinbrush until April 2002.

Despite its replaceable heads, Colgate Actibrush has failed to compete successfully against Crest Spinbrush. Part of this stems from a relative lack of marketing support. However, it mostly stems from the large price discrepancy between the two brands. Colgate Actibrush is simply too expensive relative to its Procter & Gamble rival, and consumers have responded by largely eschewing the brand in favour of the cheaper Crest Spinbrush. As mentioned above, many US consumers are typically very price-sensitive in terms of their power toothbrush purchases.

The Gillette Company also entered the US battery-operated toothbrushes market in early 2001 by expanding its Braun Oral-B electric rechargeable toothbrush line with the Oral-B CrossAction Power toothbrush. Available in both adult and child-specific varieties, the Braun Oral-B battery-powered toothbrush leveraged its strong reputation in the electric toothbrush segment. Gillette quickly convinced many consumers that it was the best battery-powered toothbrush on the market.

Questions

1 Was it a wise strategic move to launch the low-priced Oral-B CrossAction toothbrush in the United States in 2001? List the pros and cons and draw up a conclusion.

2 Which country should be the next in which the lower-priced Oral-B CrossAction toothbrush should be offered?

3 Draw up a proposal for the future price strategy of the Oral-B power toothbrush product line.

Marketing mix decisions III: distribution

Chapter contents

Learning Objectives

After studying this chapter you should be able to:

- explain how distribution patterns affect the various aspects of international marketing

- understand the variety of distribution channels and how they affect cost and efficiency in marketing

- list the functions, advantages and disadvantages of various kinds of middlemen

- explain the different stages in the design of channel structure

- understand how distribution channels can be managed internationally.

9.1 **Introduction**

A product must be made accessible to the target market at an affordable price. Distribution decisions deal with the problems of moving products from points of origin to points of consumption. Often referred to as the *place* variable, distribution decisions are directed at ensuring that the right product is in the right place at the right time and in the right quantities. The creation of place, time and possession utility for a select group of customers located in a specific geographic location provides the focus of the logistics manager's efforts. The distribution network is referred to as a *marketing channel* – a team of marketing institutions that directs a flow of goods and services from the original producer to the final consumer.

Getting the product to the target market can be a costly process if inadequacies within the distribution structure cannot be overcome. Forging an aggressive and reliable channel of distribution may be the most critical and challenging task facing the international marketer.

9.2 **The role of the intermediary**

Channel intermediaries (e.g. wholesalers and agents) essentially solve the problem of the discrepancy between the various assortments of goods and services required by industrial and household consumers, and the assortments available directly from individual producers. In other words, manufacturers usually produce a large quantity of a limited number of products, whereas consumers purchase only a few items of a large number of diverse products. Middlemen reduce this discrepancy of assortments, thereby enabling consumers to avoid dealing directly with individual manufacturers in order to satisfy their needs. This is shown in Fig. 9.1.

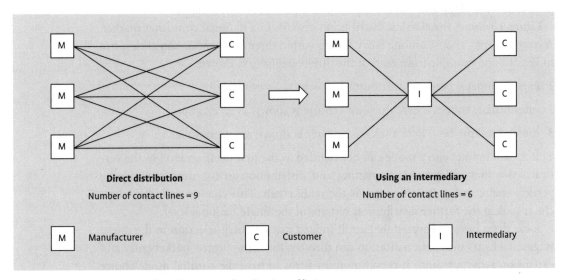

Figure 9.1 How an intermediary increases distribution efficiency
Source: *Marketing Management*, Hollensen, Pearson Education Limited (2003)

The middlemen may participate in the performance of any or all of the marketing flows (i.e. ownership, physical possession, information, financing, risk taking, negotiating, ordering and payment). However, the rationale for a wholesaler's existence boils down to the 'value adding' functions he performs for the suppliers and customers he serves, as illustrated in Fig. 9.2.

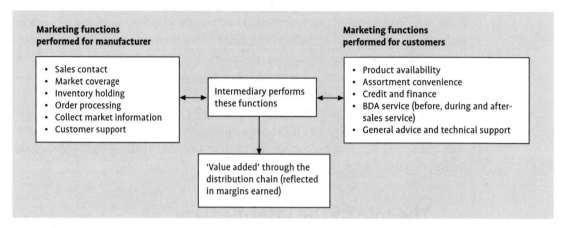

Figure 9.2 Value added by intermediary through performance of marketing functions for manufacturer and customers

9.3 **Entry mode strategy**

Once the firm has chosen its target markets abroad (as discussed in Chapter 6) the question arises as to the best way to enter those markets. An international market entry mode is an institutional arrangement necessary for the entry of a company's products, technology and human capital into a foreign country/market.

Figure 9.3 shows the classical distribution systems in a national consumer market. A company may choose among entry modes within three entry mode categories, and in Fig. 9.3 one example from each of the three categories is shown:

1 export modes – here the distributor is shown as an example

2 intermediate modes – here the joint venture is shown as an example

3 hierarchical modes – here a sales subsidiary is shown as an example.

The chosen market entry mode can be regarded as the first decision level in the vertical chain that will provide marketing and distribution to the next actor in the vertical chain; in Fig. 9.3 this actor is the retail chain. This chapter will also take a closer look at the further distribution systems at the single national level.

Some firms have discovered that an ill-judged market entry selection in the initial stages of a firm's internationalization can threaten the firm's future market entry and expansion activities. Since it is common for firms to have their initial mode choice institutionalized over time, as new products are sold through the same established

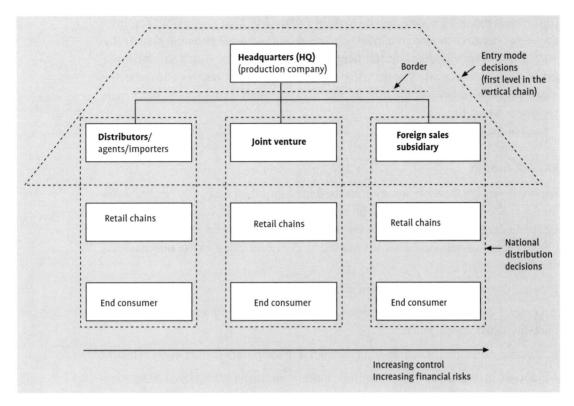

Figure 9.3 Examples of optional market entry modes in international consumer markets

channels and new markets are entered using the same entry method, a problematic initial entry mode choice can survive through the institutionalization of this mode. The inertia in the shift process of entry modes delays the transition to a new entry mode. The reluctance of firms to change entry modes once they are in place, and the difficulty involved in so doing, makes the mode of entry decision a key strategic issue for firms operating in today's rapidly internationalizing marketplace.

For most SMEs market entry represents a critical first step, but for established companies the problem is not how to enter new emerging markets, but how to exploit opportunities more effectively within the context of their existing network of international operations.

There is, however, no ideal market entry strategy, and different methods might be adopted by different firms entering the same market and/or by the same firm in different markets. The same firm may also use a combination of entry modes for a specific market (multiple-channel approach).

As shown in Fig. 9.3 three broad groupings emerge when one looks at the assortment of entry modes available to the firm when entering international markets. There are different degrees of control, risk and flexibility associated with each of these different market entry modes. For example, the use of hierarchical modes (investment modes) gives the firm ownership and thereby high control, but committing heavy resource to foreign markets also represents a higher potential risk. At the same time, heavy resource commitment creates exit barriers, which diminish the firm's ability to change the chosen entry mode in a quick and easy way. So the entry mode decision involves trade-offs, as the firm normally cannot have both high control and high flexibility.

Each of the three categories of entry mode is described in more detail below.

Export modes

Export modes are the most common method used for initial entry into international markets. The firm has to decide which functions will be the responsibility of the external international distributor and which will be handled by the firm itself. Arnold (2000) suggests seven guidelines for managing the relationship to the international distributor.

1 Select distributors – don't let them select you.

2 Look for distributors capable of developing markets, rather than those with a few obvious customer contacts.

3 Treat local distributors as long-term partners, not temporary market-entry vehicles.

4 Support market entry by committing money, managers and proven marketing ideas.

5 From the start, maintain control over marketing strategy.

6 Make sure distributors provide you with detailed market and financial performance data.

7 Build links among national concerns at the earliest opportunity.

Manufacturers get the most out of their international distributors if they let them do what they do best: implementing the local marketing strategy.

Intermediate modes

Intermediate entry modes are distinguished from export modes because they are primary vehicles for a closer transfer of knowledge and skills between the partners in a strategic alliance. They are distinct from the hierarchical entry modes in that there is no full ownership (by the parent firm) involved, but ownership and control can be shared between the parent firm and a local partner. This is the case with the (equity) joint venture.

Hierarchical modes

Here the firm owns and controls the foreign entry mode (e.g. the sales subsidiary, as illustrated in Fig. 9.3). The degree of control that the HQ would like to exert over the subsidiary will depend on how many and which value chain functions are transferred to the subsidiary. By using hierarchical modes, transactions between independent actors are substituted by intrafirm transactions, and market prices are substituted by internal transfer prices.

Many factors should be considered in deciding on the appropriate market entry mode. Hollensen (2004) discusses these different factors and how they influence the entry mode decision.

9.4 Designing and managing the channel structure

Once having considered and chosen the overall market entry strategy for a given foreign market, the management then needs to turn its attention to the task of designing the firm's channels of distribution within a given country. *Channel design* is the process of developing new channels where none had existed before, or making significant modifications to existing channels. The process of channel design and the management of it can be broken down into seven basic stages or phases:

1 setting distribution objectives

2 specifying the functions that need to be performed by the channel

3 considering alternative channel structures

4 choosing an 'optimal' channel structure

5 selecting the intermediaries

6 motivating the channel members

7 evaluating channel member performance.

We will now look at each of these in turn.

Setting distribution objectives

Distribution objectives refer to what the firm would like its channel strategy to accomplish in terms of how, when and where its products and services are provided to its target markets.

At the stage of channel design, distribution objectives need to be stated explicitly so that they can be made operational. Usually this means expressing the distribution objectives in quantifiable terms such as: within 12 months we would like to have XYZ cereal distributed in 80 per cent of the supermarkets in which consumers of this product are likely to shop.

Distribution objectives must also take into account the firm's broader marketing and corporate objectives so that there are no inconsistencies. A manufacturer of a luxury product, for example, would have to pay close attention to whether distribution objectives that seek to broaden the availability of its products would detract from the exclusive image of the goods.

Designing and managing distribution channels does not, of course, take place in a vacuum. All the other variables of the marketing mix are also in operation: hence channel strategy needs to be co-ordinated with the marketing mix. Such co-ordination should help reduce strategies and actions in the four areas of the marketing mix that work at cross-purposes. Ideally, good co-ordination should enhance the effectiveness of the firm's overall marketing mix strategy by creating synergies among the marketing mix variables rather than the debilitating incongruencies that can result from neglecting this important issue. To achieve such co-ordination, management needs to be aware of and sensitive to the many possible interfaces and relationships of channel strategy with product, price and promotional strategies.

Specifying the functions that need to be performed by the channel

The following factors should be considered as detailed distribution functions, which should be performed by the distribution channel.

- **Product and services flow (from manufacturer to final customer).** Inventory management, product transportation, product modification and after-sales service, customizing a product for the specific needs of clients/distributors, providing technical service, product maintenance and repair, procedure and handling of returned products, promoting product availability, packaging, specific packaging requirements, evaluating new products, and so on.

- **Communication flow (from manufacturer to final customers).** Sales promotion to final consumers, information about product features, advertising, providing sales force, packaging information, loyalty programmes, website participation, traceability information, and so on.

- **Information flow (from customers to manufacturer).** Sharing knowledge of local market, scanning data (access to computer data), complaints via website/service line, order frequency, order formats consideration, arrange information about consumption, and so on.

- **Payments and financial flows.** Conducting credit checks on final consumers, billing customers, caring for specific customer orders, arranging for credit provisions, price guarantees, financing, and so on.

This step provides a detailed overview of the chain and the distribution channels for a specific company. Management must therefore try to be as comprehensive and precise as possible in spelling out just what functions need to be performed to attain the distribution objectives.

Considering alternative channel structures

The form or shape that the channel of distribution takes to perform the distribution functions is the channel structure. Unless a direct channel structure from manufacturer to final customer is used, the structure will include some combination of independent intermediaries such as wholesalers, retailers, agents and brokers.

Management needs to be concerned with three dimensions of channel structure:

1 the length of the channels

2 the intensity at the various levels

3 the types of intermediary involved.

With regard to channel length, in developed countries management usually has only three or four options for the distribution of consumer goods ranging from direct up to possibly three levels of intermediaries. In channels for industrial products, the range of choice for levels in the channels is usually even more restricted.

The intensity dimension, which refers to the number of intermediaries to be used at each level of the channel, is usually characterized as:

- *intensive distribution* – where as many intermediaries as possible are used

- *selective distribution* – where the number of intermediaries to be used is limited through more careful selection

- *exclusive distribution* – where only one intermediary is used in a given geographical territory.

With regard to the types of intermediary to be used at each level in the channel structure, this can vary quite widely depending upon the industry in question.

Decisions involving any of the dimensions of channel structure, particularly those of intensity and type of intermediary, should be guided by channel strategy and the distribution objective being pursued, in order to avoid channel structures that are inappropriate to the strategy and objective. For instance, if a firm's objectives and strategy stress high levels of attention and service for final customers, this would generally be far more difficult to attain with an intensive distribution structure than with a more selective one because the very large numbers of channel members involved in intensive distribution would be harder to monitor and control than a small group of carefully chosen ones.

Choosing an 'optimal' channel structure

In practice it is not possible to choose an optimal channel structure in the strictest sense of that term. However, it is possible to choose an effective and efficient channel structure that can meet the firm's distribution objectives.

Many different approaches have been suggested over the years for choosing such a channel structure. The most popular are *judgemental* and *heuristic approaches* that rely on managerial judgement augmented by some data on distribution costs and profit potentials.

Of course, in the process of applying its best judgement, management also needs to take into consideration a number of key variables that are usually relevant when choosing channel structure. The most basic of these are:

- market variables
- product variables
- firm variables
- intermediary variables
- behavioural variables
- external environmental variables.

The location of final customers, the number of customers and their density, together with their patterns of buying behaviour, would all be key *market variables*.

Factors such as bulk and weight, unit value, newness, technical versus non-technical, and perishability are *product variables* that are frequently important.

The financial capacity of the firm, its size, expertise and desire for managerial control are some of the most important *firm variables*.

Cost, availability and services provided are indicative of significant *intermediary variables* that management needs to consider.

Factors such as the potential of particular channel structures to reduce conflict while maximizing power and communications effectiveness are critical *behavioural variables* for management to consider.

Finally, variables such as economic conditions, socio-cultural changes, competitive structure, technology and government regulations can all be important *environmental variables* to consider when choosing channel structure.

Selecting the intermediaries

The selection of intermediaries who will become channel members can be viewed as the last phase of channel design (choosing the channel structure), or as an independent channel management area if selection is not undertaken as part of an overall channel design decision. In any case, the selection of channel members essentially consists of four steps:

1 developing selection criteria

2 finding prospective channel members

3 assessment of the prospective channel members against the criteria

4 converting prospective channel members to become actual channel members.

Developing selection criteria

Each firm should develop a set of criteria for selecting channel members that is consistent with its own distribution objectives and strategies. Obviously, then, there is no universal list of selection criteria that would be applicable for all firms under all conditions. As a general rule, however, there is a basic guiding principle, or heuristic, that most firms can use, which can be stated as follows: the more selective the firm's distribution policy, the more numerous and stringent the criteria used for selection should be, and vice versa.

Thus the list of criteria for a firm practising highly selective distribution might include such factors as the prospective channel member's reputation, competing product lines carried and management succession. A firm using very intensive distribution might use little more than one criterion consisting of the ability of the prospective channel members to pay the manufacturer for the products it ships to them.

Finding prospective channel members

The search for prospective channel members can utilize a number of sources. If the manufacturer has its own outside field sales force, this is generally regarded as the best source because of the sales force's knowledge of prospective channel members in its territories.

Other useful sources include final customers, trade sources, advertising and trade shows. Usually, a combination of several of these sources is used to find prospective channel members whether these are at wholesale or retail levels.

Assessment of the prospective channel members against the criteria

Once the group of prospective channel members has been identified, they need to be assessed against the criteria to determine those who will actually be selected. This can be done by an individual manager (such as the sales manager) or by a committee. Depending upon the importance of the selection decision, such a decision might well include top management even up to and including the chairman of the board if the selection decision is of great strategic importance.

Converting prospective channel members to become actual channel members

The key issue of concern here is to recognize that the selection process is an interaction process. Not only do producers and manufacturers select intermediaries or various agents, but these intermediaries also select producers and manufacturers. Indeed, quite often it is the intermediaries, especially large and powerful distributors and wholesalers, who are in a powerful position when it comes to selection. Consequently, the manufacturer seeking to secure the services of quality channel members has to make a convincing case that carrying its products will be profitable for the channel members. Given the sophistication of today's retailers and wholesalers, owing to the excellent computerized information systems they use, manufacturers must make their cases very carefully and thoroughly to win the acceptance of such channel members.

Motivating the channel members

Motivation in the context of channel management refers to the actions taken by the manufacturer to secure channel member co-operation in implementing the manufacturer's channel strategies and achieving its distribution objectives. Because the manufacturer's efforts to motivate channel members take place in the inter-organizational setting of the marketing channel, the process is often more difficult and certainly less direct than would be the case for motivation in the intra-organizational setting of one firm.

Motivation management in the marketing channel can be viewed as a sequence of three steps:

1 learning about the needs and problems of channel members

2 offering support to channel members to help meet their needs and solve their problems

3 providing ongoing leadership.

Although the stages in the motivation process are sequential, the process is also iterative because of the continuous feedback from stages two and three.

Learning about the needs and problems of channel members

As mentioned earlier, channel members, as independent businesses, have their own objectives, strategies and operating procedures. But also as independent businesses they have their own needs and problems, which might be quite different from those of the manufacturer. Hence, if the manufacturer seeks strong co-operation from the channel members, it is incumbent on that manufacturer to discover the key needs and problems of channel members in order to be able to help meet those needs and solve those problems. This is not a simple or straightforward task for the manufacturer because the range of needs and problems of channel members can be legion. Small channel members may be overburdened with inventory, lack modern information systems, and need better managerial skills and newer ideas for competing against giant retailers. On the other hand, large retailers may face problems of how to reduce costs to operate profitably on small gross margins while being forced to carry larger and larger inventories as wholesalers disappear from the channel and new products proliferate. At the same time, wholesale channel members may be in desperate need of finding ways of competing successfully against power-buying retailers and customers who seek direct sales from the manufacturers. This list could go on and on for different channel members in particular industries, times and circumstances.

In order to foster better communication between manufacturer and channel member, an advisory committee consisting of representatives from wholesale- and/or retail-level channel members and key executives from the manufacturer meets on a regular basis (such as twice a year) in some neutral location. This type of close interaction between manufacturer and channel members can generate the kind of constructive dialogue needed to uncover channel member needs and problems, which may not emerge in the normal course of business.

Offering support to channel members

Offering support to channel members to help meet their needs and solve their problems can be done in a variety of ways, from an informal 'hit and miss', ad hoc, approach through to formal and carefully planned partnerships and strategic alliances.

The ad hoc approach, also called co-operative support, is the most common in loosely aligned traditional channels. Basically, advertising dollars, promotional support, incentives, contests and a host of other ad hoc activities are offered by the manufacturer to initiate channel members' efforts to push the manufacturer's products.

Partnerships and strategic alliances, in contrast, represent a more substantial and continuous commitment between the manufacturer and channel members. Support provided by the manufacturer is based on extensive knowledge of the needs and problems of the channel members, and tends to be carried out on a longer-term basis, with specific performance expectations that have been carefully worked out by the manufacturer in conjunction with channel members.

Providing ongoing leadership

Even a well-conceived motivation effort, based on a thorough attempt to understand channel member needs and problems, together with a carefully articulated support programme, still requires leadership on a continuing basis to achieve effective motivation of channel members. In other words, someone has to be in charge to deal with the inevitable changes and unforeseen problems that arise, such as new forms of competition, technological developments and government regulations. While the manufacturer cannot always assume the leadership role and immediately deal with any problems, it is important that support should be available to provide direction and input over the long term instead of only while a new motivation programme is being developed and then quickly left to channel members to deal with on a day-in-day-out basis.

Evaluating channel member performance

The evaluation of channel member performance is necessary to assess how successful the channel members have been in implementing the manufacturer's channel strategies and achieving distribution objectives. Evaluations require the manufacturer to gather information on the channel members. The manufacturer's ability to do this will be affected by:

- the degree of control of channel members

- the importance of the channel members

- the number of channel members.

Usually, the higher the degree of control, the more information the manufacturer can gather, and vice versa.

With regard to the importance of channel members, if the manufacturer relies heavily on them for the distribution of its products, it will tend to put more effort into evaluation than those who do not rely heavily on independent channel members.

Finally, when large numbers of channel members are used, such as in intensive distribution, evaluation tends to be much more cursory than when smaller, more carefully selected channel members are used. The actual performance evaluation essentially consists of three steps:

1 developing performance criteria

2 evaluating channel members against the performance criteria

3 taking corrective action if necessary.

Developing performance criteria

Although a wide variety of performance criteria can be used to evaluate channel members, by far the most commonly used are:

- sales performance

- inventory maintenance

- selling capabilities

- attitudes

- competitive products handled

- growth prospects.

Of course, this list can be supplemented to fit the particular circumstances of the manufacturer. The relative importance of each criterion may also vary considerably based on the policies of a particular manufacturer.

Evaluating channel members against criteria

The use of a list of criteria to evaluate channel members can be done in an informal, judgemental fashion or by using a more formal quantitative approach. In the former approach, criteria are used as a general benchmark of what the manufacturer is seeking. Channel members are then assessed against this list based on qualitative managerial judgements. In the latter approach, formal weighting schemes can be developed to specify precisely the importance of criteria relative to each other. Formal scoring systems such as a scale of 1 to 10 can then be used to rate each channel member against each criterion. It is then possible to arrive at an overall quantitative performance index for each channel member by multiplying the criteria weights by the scores and adding up the results.

Taking corrective action

The management purpose behind evaluation is not only to monitor performance but also to take the necessary action to improve the performance of those channel members that are below standard. Thus, an integral part of the evaluation process is to have a set of pre-planned steps to be taken to help channel members meet or exceed performance expectations. Termination of the relationship with the channel member should be the very last step in this pre-planned corrective process.

Exhibit 9.1 Dell's disintermediation in the distribution chain

Dell is the world's leading direct computer systems company, with 34,400 employees in 34 countries around the globe. At Dell, the traditional supply chain has two fundamental characteristics: *disintermediation* and *real-time production*. Dell sells directly to its customers, cutting out the middleman, the distributor and retailer. When a layer that exists between two other layers is removed like this, it is known as disintermediation. Dell manufactures the products and then sells them directly to the customer, thus it creates disintermediation – the outside retailer is cut out of the process. This reduces time and costs in the process and also ensures that Dell is better positioned to understand its customers' needs.

In this way, Dell's supply chain costs are reduced on the storage side, too, by the efficient relationship between orders and production. Each individual PC that is ordered is only manufactured *after* the order has been received and using only the freshest raw materials, which are delivered to the factory several times a day. This is known as just-in-time (JIT) production, or real-time production. There is no warehouse for either raw components or finished goods. Each computer has been paid for by, and built for, a specific customer before it is shipped.

Real-time production ensures that no costs are incurred from rising inventory stocks. Output is always driven by actual customer demand. Each individual product is created with the latest technology and each is custom-made to the customer's precise specifications.

Source: adapted from www.dell.com

9.5 Global distribution channel design

In every country and in every market, urban or rural, rich or poor, all consumer and industrial products eventually go through a distribution process. The *distribution process* includes the physical handling and distribution of goods, the passage of ownership (title) and – most important from the standpoint of marketing strategy – the buying and selling negotiations between producers and middlemen, and between middlemen and customers.

A host of policy and strategic channel-selection issues confronts the international marketing manager. These issues are not in themselves very different from those encountered in domestic distribution, but the resolution of the issues differs because of different channel alternatives and market patterns.

Each country market has a *distribution structure* through which goods pass from producer to user. Within this structure are a variety of middlemen whose customary functions, activities and services reflect existing competition, market characteristics, tradition and economic development.

In short, the behaviour of channel members is the result of the interactions between the cultural environment and the marketing process. Channel structures range from those with little developed marketing infrastructure, such as those found in many emerging markets, to the highly complex, multilayered system found in Japan.

Traditional channels in developing countries evolved from economies with a strong dependence on imported goods. In an *import-orientated*, or *traditional*, *distribution structure*, an importer controls a fixed supply of goods and the marketing system develops around the philosophy of selling a limited supply of goods at high prices to a small number of affluent customers. In the resulting seller's market, market penetration and mass distribution are not necessary because demand exceeds supply and, in most cases, the customer seeks the supply from a limited number of middlemen. Obviously, few countries fit the import-orientated model today.

Today, few countries are so sufficiently isolated that they are unaffected by global economic and political changes. These currents of change are altering all levels of the economic fabric, including the distribution structure. Traditional channel structures are giving way to new forms, new alliances and new processes – some more slowly than others, but all are changing. Pressures for change in a country come from within and without. Multinational marketers are seeking ways to profitably tap market segments that are served by costly, traditional distribution systems. Direct marketing, door-to-door selling, hypermarkets, discount houses, shopping malls, catalogue selling, the Internet and other distribution methods are being introduced in an attempt to provide efficient distribution channels.

Some important trends in distribution will eventually lead to greater commonality than disparity among middlemen in different countries. Wal-Mart, for example, is expanding all over the world – from Mexico to Brazil and from Europe to Asia. Avon is expanding into eastern Europe, Mary Kay Cosmetics and Amway into China, and Lands' End has made a successful entry into the Japanese market. The effect of all these intrusions into the traditional distribution systems is a change that will make discounting, self-service, supermarkets, mass merchandising and e-commerce concepts common all over the world, and that elevates the competitive climate to a level not known before.

The global channel design process

The actual process of building channels for international distribution is seldom easy, and many companies are halted in their efforts to develop international markets by their inability to construct a *satisfactory system* of channels.

Despite the special characteristics of each individual country's channel structure, it can still be possible to identify what middlemen should be used in a country to ensure that the strategic objectives of the marketing mix – the target segmentation and the desired product positioning – are reached. To do this requires an analysis of what the important functions in the channel network are (identification of what the key success factors are as they relate to channel choice) and then ensuring that the chosen intermediaries in each country measure up on those criteria.

To identify the channel requirements, the natural first step is to decide whether any of the firm-specific advantages (FSAs) and competencies are uniquely lodged in the distribution channels to be used.

Key success factors and FSAs may vary across countries. For example, many of the convenience products sold in western markets (packaged foods, cigarettes, soft drinks, and so on) require intensive distribution coverage, precisely because customers want them to be conveniently available.

If the firm cannot find relevant distribution partners it might invest in a dedicated network in order to supply the market. This is usually a big investment question and, as we have seen, there is no certainty of success. When the market is sufficiently large, as the US market almost always is, it might pay for the company to develop its own distribution network. But where the market is smaller and the gains consequently less, the investment might not be worth the risks involved.

The following sections go through the different stages in designing the global channel network (Baker, 2000):

- selection of the right international distributors
- contracting with the chosen distributor
- motivating middlemen (channel tie-up)
- co-ordination and control
- terminating contracts with distributors.

Selection of the right international distributors

Construction of the middleman network includes seeking out potential middlemen, selecting those who fit the company's requirements and establishing working relationships with them. In international marketing, the channel-building process is hardly routine. The closer the company wants to get to the consumer in its channel contact, the larger the sales force required.

The search for prospective middlemen should begin with a study of the market and determination of criteria for evaluating middlemen servicing that market. The checklist of criteria differs according to the type of middlemen being used and the nature of their relationship with the company. Basically, such lists are built around four subject areas: productivity or volume, financial strength, managerial stability and capability, and the nature and reputation of the business. Emphasis is usually placed on either the actual or potential productivity of the middleman.

Finding prospective middlemen is less a problem than determining which of them can perform satisfactorily. Low volume or low potential volume hampers most prospects, many are under-financed, and some simply cannot be trusted. In many cases, when a manufacturer is not well known abroad, the reputation of the middleman becomes the reputation of the manufacturer, so a poor choice at this point can be devastating.

The screening and selection process itself should include the following actions: an exploratory letter including product information and distributor requirements in the native language sent to each prospective middleman; a follow-up to the best respondents for more specific information concerning lines handled, territory covered, size of firm, number of sales people, and other background information; check of credit and references from other clients and customers of the prospective middleman; and, if possible, a personal check of the most promising firms.

Experienced international marketers suggest that the only way to select a middleman is to go the country in question in person and talk to ultimate users of the product to find who they consider to be the best distributors. Visit each possible middleman before selecting one to represent you; look for one with a key person who will take the new product to his or her heart and make it a personal objective to make the sale of that line a success. Further, international marketers stress that if you cannot sign up one of the two or three customer-recommended distributors, it might be better not to have a distributor in that country because having a worthless distributor will cost you time and money every year.

Contracting with the chosen distributor

Once a potential middleman is found and evaluated, there remains the task of detailing the arrangements with that middleman. So far the company is in a buying position; now it must shift into a selling and negotiating position to convince the middleman to handle the goods and accept a distribution agreement that is workable for the company. Agreements must spell out the specific responsibilities of the manufacturer and the middleman, including an annual sales minimum. The sales minimum serves as a basis for evaluation of the distributor; failure to meet sales minimums may give the exporter the right of termination.

Some international marketers recommend that initial contracts be signed for one year only. If the first year's performance is satisfactory, they should be reviewed for renewal for a longer period. This permits easier termination and, more important, after a year of working together in the market, a more workable arrangement can generally be reached.

Motivating middlemen (channel tie-up)

The level of distribution and the importance of the individual middleman to the company determine the activities undertaken to keep the middleman motivated. On all levels there is a clear correlation between the middleman's motivation and sales volume. Motivational techniques that can be employed to maintain middleman interest and support for the product may be grouped into five categories: financial rewards, psychological rewards, communication, company support and corporate rapport.

Where channel members are available to provide the functions necessary, they may still be unwilling to sign on with the new product unless special trade allowances bigger than those offered by the competition are made. There are reasons for making sure at this stage that the best units available are tied into, and it is customary for new entrants to pay a premium to established dealers to get them to accept the new product. For example, when Japanese car manufacturers entered the US auto market they offered higher dealer margins than had been customary for that size of auto.

The thrust behind signing up good distributors and dealers is not only that sales will be high, but also that they are the ones most likely to sustain the FSAs identified as necessary for the competitive success of the manufacturer.

Being human, middlemen and their sales people respond to psychological rewards and recognition of their efforts. A trip to the parent company's home or regional office is a great honour. Publicity in company media and local newspapers also builds esteem and involvement among foreign middlemen.

In all instances, the company should maintain a continuing flow of communication, in the form of letters, e-mails, newsletters and periodicals, to all its middlemen. The more personal these are, the better. One study of exporters indicated that the more intense the contact between the manufacturer and the distributor, the better the performance from the distributor. More and better contact naturally leads to less conflict and a smoother working relationship.

Finally, considerable attention must be paid to the establishment of close rapport between the company and its middlemen. In addition to the methods noted earlier, a company should be certain that the conflicts that arise are handled skilfully and diplomatically. Bear in mind that, all over the world, business is a personal and vital thing to the people involved.

Co-ordination and control

The extreme length of channels typically used in international distribution makes control of middlemen especially important. Marketing objectives must be spelled out both internally and to middlemen as explicitly as possible. Standards of performance should include sales volume objective, market share in each market, inventory turnover ratio, number of accounts per area, growth objective, price stability objective and quality of publicity. Cultural differences enter into all these areas of management.

The more involved a company is with the distribution, the more control it exerts. A company's own sales force affords the most control, but often at a cost that is not practical. Each type of channel arrangement provides a different level of control; as channels grow longer, the ability to control price, volume, promotion and types of outlet diminishes. If a company cannot sell directly to the end user or final retailer, an important selection criterion for middlemen should be the amount of control the marketer can maintain.

Terminating contracts with distributors

When middlemen do not perform up to standards or when market situations change, requiring a company to restructure its distribution, it may be necessary to terminate relationships. In some parts of the world (e.g. in the EU) the distributor often has legal protection that makes termination difficult. In other parts of the world (e.g. the USA) it is usually a simple action regardless of the type of middlemen: they are simply dismissed.

It is vital to secure competent legal advice when entering into distribution contracts with middlemen. But as many experienced international marketers know, the best rule is to avoid the need to terminate distributors by screening all prospective middlemen carefully in the first place. A poorly chosen distributor may not only fail to live up to expectations but may also adversely affect future business and prospects in the country.

Exhibit 9.2 De Beers is controlling distribution in China

A short history of diamonds in China and the rest of the world

Ancient Greeks and Romans believed diamonds were the tears of the gods and splinters from falling stars. In the East, some tradition is present with, for example in India, the first diamonds mined over 4000 years ago and largely used by Hindus as the eyes of some of their statues. They considered diamonds as symbols of power. However, in China, no such history is present and no positive preconceptions exist.

Diamonds have no roots in China, either in terms of culture or production. In Chinese culture, the colour white is considered unlucky and is linked with misfortune. Diamonds are viewed as white, therefore it is understandable that they have never been celebrated or even emphasized in Chinese history. Neither is China a diamond-producing country, so it would seem reasonable that the Chinese have little knowledge of diamonds.

Despite this background, however, diamonds occupy an important position in the minds of Chinese consumers today. In China, diamonds are now considered symbols of honour, luck, wealth, status and power (which is much like the current western perception of diamonds).

De Beers worldwide and in China

The De Beers Group was established in 1888 and since its initiation has been involved in all aspects of the diamond industry, including exploration, mining, recovery, sorting, valuation and marketing. The group comprises two main wings: De Beers Consolidated Mines Ltd and De Beers Centenary AG. The mining division focuses on the group's South Africa-based operations and activities, while De Beers Centenary AG administers those operations that are outside South Africa. An important arm of this operation is the Diamond Trading Company (DTC), based in the UK, which markets nearly two-thirds of the world supply. Since the late 1930s the DTC has developed and implemented some of the most effective promotional campaigns in the history of advertising (such as 'A Diamond is Forever' – recognized as the most effective slogan of the last millennium by *Advertising Age*).

For 100 years, throughout (largely) western economies, De Beers has driven the market to the extent that consumers currently equate diamonds with tradition, love and romance.

De Beers itself owns and operates mines that produce over 43 per cent of the total world value of rough-cut diamonds, and for over a century the De Beers Group has had de facto control over nearly 75 per cent of the rough-cut diamond market (through an international diamond cartel). Globally, De Beers spends about US$200 mn a year in the promotion of diamonds, based on the assumption that the company will be the primary beneficiary of such efforts. De Beers controls both sides of the consumption chain: supply and demand. Its mission in the Chinese market has been to cultivate and stimulate market demand, and serve the ultimate consumption market.

Indeed, De Beers' source of power in controlling diamond prices no longer comes from rough diamond production alone but from a complex network of marketing, sales and production arrangements that are all controlled and operated by the company. Such is the power and market coverage of De Beers that the firm is viewed as totally dominating the market, even more so in China than in other parts of the world.

The De Beers policy of controlling supply and demand for diamonds is also rehearsed fully elsewhere. Of more interest to strategic marketers, though, is the decision by De Beers to pursue a two-pronged strategy of (i) improved branding and market control, and (ii) market expansion into under-exploited markets.

In terms of branding and market control, in mid-2000 De Beers launched its 'Supplier of Choice' initiative, which aims to supply service to only those clients that are included in the DTC distribution channel, aided by a new identity known as the 'Forevermark'. In terms of market expansion, in 1999 the USA accounted for 48 per cent of retail diamond consumption, Japan 14 per cent, Europe 12 per cent, Asia-Pacific 10 per cent, Asia-Arabia 11 per cent and others 5 per cent. In this regard, China is clearly an underdeveloped market.

Before De Beers' entry in 1993 the Chinese market's underdevelopment was largely due to historical reasons and the fact that China does not produce and thus have experience of diamonds. There was little market demand and, in turn, jewellers had little motivation to push diamond sales. Consequently, as part of its market-driving approach, De Beers in China has proactively created purchase desire and developed specific market demand.

Creation of market demand for diamonds

By using an explicit market-driving strategy (see, e.g., Jaworski *et al.*, 2000; Harris and Cai, 2002) diamonds' retail value in the Chinese market had increased from US$169 mn in 1993 to US$800 mn in 2002.

Currently, De Beers divides the Chinese market into two main segments: female diamond jewellery and diamond wedding rings. Each of these segments has individually tailored promotional campaigns and in-store point-of-sale themes. Similar to the case in other countries, the wedding ring segment accounts for one-quarter of sales, while female diamond jewellery accounts for very nearly three-quarters of sales. Interestingly, De Beers estimates that significantly less than 5 per cent of the female population in China owns a piece of diamond jewellery.

How has De Beers created this development? It is changing customer preferences for diamonds

De Beers focused on modifying the existing preferences of customers. This manifestation of De Beers' tactic of changing customer perception of diamonds centres on a long-term education process, which De Beers' employees view as the 'education' of potential customers via 'rational information' to 'subjective association'. The supply of 'rational information' centres on educating the Chinese market in terms of what De Beers labels the '4Cs': cut, carat, colour and clarity. This process is viewed as fundamental to helping Chinese consumers choose suitable diamonds, while also achieving continuously increasing exposure of diamond images and the De Beers brand.

Changing 'subjective associations' pivoted on establishing in Chinese culture similar views regarding diamonds to those held in the West (and rather similar to those most Chinese consumers *currently* ascribe to diamonds).

Source: adapted from www.debeers.com; www.diamonds.net; www.forevermark.com; Jaworski, B., Kohli, A.K., and Sahay, A. (2000) Market-driven versus driving markets. *Journal of the Academy of Marketing Science* 28(1), pp. 45–54; Harris, L.C. and Cai, K.Y. (2002) Exploring market driving: a case study of De Beers in China. *Journal of Market-Focused Management* 5(3), pp. 171–96.

9.6 **Multiple channel strategy**

Distribution channels can be seen as sets of interdependent organizations involved in the process of making a product or service available for consumption or use. When making channel choices, firms can choose from a wide variety of alternatives. It should be noted, however, that companies are increasingly using a multiple channel strategy for most or all of their products.

A multiple channel strategy is employed when a firm makes a product available to the market through two or more channels of distribution. This strategy was expected to become the most popular channel design in the 1990s. The increasing popularity of this strategy results from the potential advantages provided: extended market coverage and increased sales volume; lower absolute or relative costs; better accommodation of customers' evolving needs; and more and better information. This strategy can also, however, produce potentially disruptive problems: consumer confusion; conflicts with intermediaries and/or internal distribution units; increased costs; loss of distinctiveness; and, eventually, increased organizational complexity.

A special case of multiple channel marketing is often referred to as *dual marketing*, where the same product is sold to both consumer and business customers at the same time (Biemans, 2001). For instance, in selling mobile phones, fax machines and audio equipment, Philips Electronics is confronted with a lot of similarities and overlap between both markets. For instance, small business owners also shop in consumer outlets and focus on price differences, while ignoring the differences in product functionality offered on both markets. Therefore, Philips uses different product versions, sales channels, prices and communication methods in an effort to tailor its offering to both groups of customers. In addition, it is faced with a continuous struggle to adapt the internal organization of the marketing function to the dynamics of the marketplace.

The use of dual marketing is also stimulated by a convergence of consumer marketing and business marketing. At the same time, consumers have become increasingly knowledgeable about products and product functions, such as personal computers and the health implications of food ingredients, making them more open to *rational* selling arguments. Finally, new interactive technologies allow firms to build one-to-one relationships with customers, whether these are large firms or individual consumers.

Although it is often impossible to completely separate the channels used for both markets, a supplier can enhance the differences between them by offering different versions of the same product and charging different prices. The success of this strategy depends on the extent to which the distribution channels can actually be separated.

Managing multiple channels

In managing multiple channels, companies demarcate products and models by channel, thus minimizing direct comparison. The demarcations, of course, work only when there are meaningful differences among products. Unfortunately, consumers do not come neatly segmented into such airtight compartments. There is considerable movement between segments and across purchases. Moreover, with accelerating product life cycles, proliferation of products and fragmentation of customer segments, multiple channel approaches are often the only way to provide market coverage. Different customers with different buying behaviours will seek the channels that best serve their needs.

Options are not, however, a perfect solution. Customers can infiltrate from other segments by patronizing both the full-service channel and the low-price channel (see Fig. 9.4). As long as higher price fairly reflects higher service, customers will be loyal to a particular channel, but if the service is unnecessary or can be obtained at a lower cost, customers will cross to the low-price channel. In some businesses, pre-sales service is a public good that customers can avail themselves of without making a purchase. For example, a customer can get a full-function demonstration at a high-street computer store and then buy the product from a low-cost mail-order retailer on the Internet. The customer thus gets a free ride on the full-service channel.

Multiple channels are most prevalent in fast-changing market environments. When the product market matures slowly, the channel has time to adapt to changes in customer buying patterns. Even if multiple channels are necessary to reflect market plurality, each channel is clearly specialized to serve a specific buying pattern. Crossovers are less common. Discount stores in the late 1970s and early 1980s were clearly targeted to the value-conscious shopper, and the service-conscious shopper continued to patronize the speciality stores. The two channels often stocked, displayed and sold different brands and attracted a very different clientele. This does not occur in more dynamic industries. Computer models that start out in speciality stores end up with the catalogue retailers in under six months. Early buyers may not face channel dissonance, but latecomers always do. While later buyers may seek the services of a speciality outlet, the price offered by a discount outlet is too tempting to pass up. Moreover, in dynamic environments, customers' shopping and buying behaviours, buying criteria and segments change frequently.

In coping with turbulence, channel diversity pays, but only if the arrangements are treated as options. Further, they must decide what to do with options as the market stabilizes.

The trend towards hybrid multiple channels

In a hybrid multiple distribution channel, the marketing functions are shared by the producer and the channel intermediary. The former usually handles promotion and customer-generation activities, whereas the intermediary is in charge of sales and distribution (Gabrielsson et al., 2002).

Another model is illustrated in Anderson et al. (1997). Both the supplier and its channel partners divide up the execution of the channel functions. The supplier performs some functions, such as sales negotiation and order generation, while its channel partners deliver physical distribution and order fulfilment. Other channel members might specialize in functions such as after-sales service. The members work together,

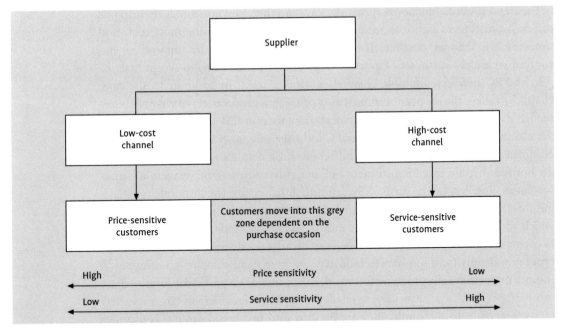

Figure 9.4 High- and low-cost channels

with certain members specializing in certain functions (see Fig. 9.5). The difference between the hybrid and conventional channels is the horizontal task allocation. A team of channel partners (including the supplier), each specializing in a few tasks, satisfies the customer's total needs. In the conventional channel, the hand-offs are vertical; each member performs the full channel functions that its immediate customers require.

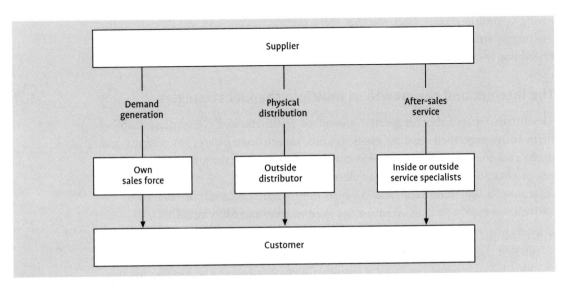

Figure 9.5 Hybrid multiple channels

The trend towards functional specialization (and therefore horizontal channels) is driven by customers' desire to receive products and services in the most cost- and time-efficient manner possible. If channel functions have to be unbundled and sourced separately, customers, especially large ones, will be willing to accept that.

In the PC industry, multiple channels are often used. In addition to the sales channel strategy, the PC producer must also consider a great variety of channel intermediaries at each channel level. (The vocabulary used in this instance, in respect to the channel members, is specific to the PC industry.) Channel intermediaries can be classified into distributors, resellers and retailers. By definition, distributors usually do not sell directly to end customers but use either resellers or retailers as intermediaries. Resellers can be further divided into dealer chains (or corporate resellers); local dealers; indirect fax, telephone or Internet resellers; and value-added resellers, which add software and services to the industrial organizations, whereas retailers sell to consumers through retail outlets. However, because the definitions of intermediary types vary greatly from industry to industry, and even from company to company, it is more important for a producer to consider the functions a particular intermediary can perform than to pay attention to labels per se. The sales channels target a variety of customers. In this example, they are divided into two broad groups: consumers (which includes people who buy the PCs from a personal budget); and business organizations from the different worlds of industry and services (Gabrielsson *et al.*, 2002).

Multiple channels, in the context of international business, have not previously been the object of an explicit study; the conventional view has been to consider channel decisions from a single channel viewpoint. Therefore, the multiple sales channel strategy alternatives, choice and development discussed here contribute by narrowing this research gap (see also Gabrielsson, 1999); for example, Figs 9.4 and 9.5 contribute by presenting the channel alternatives in relation to international marketing operation modes. Note too that this example has applied and developed the existing internationalization process and other theories, constructs and concepts in examining the multiple sales channels.

The Internet and the growth of multiple channel strategies

The Internet has turbocharged the growth of multi-channel companies, enabling them to leverage their existing assets, brands and customer bases for revenue and profit growth. Key to this leverage is correctly determining the strategic role of the online channel in combination with all other channels.

Here are a few important ideas on how multi-channels (and pure plays for that matter) can build competitive advantage (Vishwanath and Mulvin, 2001).

- **Define the Internet's role in your channel and operational portfolios.** The Internet means different things to different companies: a new channel, a place to unload slow-moving inventory, a customer service resource, a cost-reduction tool, a customer acquisition channel, or all of the above. Identifying where the Internet can help your business and where investment will pay off the most is the first step in extracting value from this flexible tool. Next you need to integrate the offline and online functions, both to cut costs and to raise service levels for customers. Only then can the natural advantages of multi-channels over both online pure plays and bricks-and-mortar companies be translated into profit.

■ **Identify and cater to your most profitable customer segments.** Whether you plan to make a large investment in the Internet or simply place 'a check in the box', you need to understand which groups of customers are providing the bulk of your profits, and how the Internet can best improve your offering for those customers. You can also learn to avoid unwanted customers: having the best website on the Internet won't do you any good if you are attracting unprofitable or fickle customers. Once you understand your best customers, you can execute a marketing plan to attract and retain new ones, and serve existing ones better. At heart, this is a decision about which customers you want to court in all media, and how. The Internet represents just one important facet of this plan.

■ **Invest in execution.** As we have seen, the companies that 'cash in' on their Internet sales sites best enjoy customer conversion rates up to eight times the industry average. Retention rates for online companies vary widely too. Differences in performance are achieved by being world-class in a small number of key areas: targeted, accurate and cost-efficient marketing; an intuitive, fast and easy-to-use site; sufficient product information available on the site, with non-Internet back-up options for customers; timely and accurate shipping; and a quick and simple transaction process. The companies that execute on these factors have seen significant improvements in their online performance; these improvements translate into profits that can be re-invested in their online presence.

■ **Take risks, but remain flexible.** The multi-channels have the pure-play dotcoms (and the venture capitalists who funded them) to thank for many early lessons and forward steps that we now take for granted: the dotcoms educated consumers, created awareness of the Internet, demanded and paid for infrastructure development, and dragged the bricks-and-mortar companies into the online arena far faster and further than they would otherwise have come. They also bore the brunt of some costly mistakes: it was dotcoms, for instance, that felt most acutely the disappointments of online advertising. Partly as a result, the pure plays are now on the wane, and the mantle of online leadership has passed to the multi-channels. It won't be easy for multi-channels to sit back and watch any more, and then just invest in the safer bets, so managers of multi-channel retailers will have to adjust their approach to investing in the Internet: they will have to become the risk takers and, like the pure plays before them, will have to place a number of bets, carefully monitor them to see which are panning out and redirect spending as their learning progresses.

9.7 **Grey (parallel) distribution**

Development in logistics coupled with floating exchange rates and widely different prices in different countries have led to the emergence of 'grey' trade through (parallel) distribution channels.

Grey distribution

Grey trade is the parallel distribution of genuine goods by intermediaries other than authorized channel members. Grey marketers are typically brokers who buy goods overseas either from the manufacturer or from authorized dealers at relatively low prices and then import them into a country where prevailing prices are higher. The grey marketers sell the merchandise at discounted prices in direct competition with authorized local distributors, often advertising the lower prices openly in print media and direct mail. The practice is not illegal per se, except under certain circumstances, but the activities tend to disturb existing trading relationships and are usually fought against by manufacturers as well as authorized distributors.

The World Wide Web has drastically increased grey market potential for both domestic and foreign goods. As an information medium, it raises a customer's awareness of special offers that were initially designed to be limited to specific regions, countries or classes of customers such as OEMs. Web-based grey marketers can also advertise merely by using a product's brand name or model number on their websites and waiting for search engines to direct consumers there. (Grey trade tends to serve as an arbitrage mechanism, equalizing prices between markets in different countries.)

The conditions necessary for grey market activity are similar to those in arbitrage, in which the same financial security is sold at the same time at different price levels in different financial markets. In either foreign or domestic grey marketing, the price differentials across markets must be great enough to justify the costs associated with buying a good in one market and selling it in another. However, unlike financial securities, a grey marketer may have significant transportation and holding costs, and deal with goods that have different brand names, are labelled in different languages and need to be modified to meet a particular country's safety standards. The basic principle is that significant price differences between markets are the stimuli for grey marketing.

The sources of foreign grey marketing are based largely on the need to charge different prices to different countries or regions based on wealth, excise taxes, competitive environments or government price caps in certain markets (such as on pharmaceutical products in the EU). Unfortunately, some of the goods exported to foreign countries are trans-shipped back to the original country. Unauthorized resellers can purchase goods from authorized resellers or manufacturers in a foreign country. Foreign wholesalers or manufacturers are aware that goods will be shipped to the original country.

Three main factors motivate entrepreneurs to engage in grey marketing:

1 **Wide price discrepancies**. There are substantial price differences between national markets, because of currency fluctuations for example.

2 **Limited availability**. There is limited availability of certain models or versions in one market. Demand outstrips supply and is likely to push local prices even higher relative to other markets. Certain Mercedes-Benz and Porsche models, for example, are unavailable in the United States, as was originally the case with some Lexus models in Japan, and this stimulated grey trade. Localization requirements, such as local certification of emissions controls on cars, have a dampening effect, but with sufficient margins grey traders will invest in conversion equipment (although sometimes the buyer gets stuck with that job).

3 **Inexpensive logistics**. Transportation and importation can be accomplished with relative ease. The increased availability of global modes of transportation and the added services offered by carriers and freight forwarders have meant that logistics problems are usually few. Grey traders can use independent middlemen.

Figure 9.6 shows some of the ways in which grey traders infiltrate the global distribution of Japanese watches. The Japanese companies (here Seiko is used as an illustration) export watches to the importer, often a sales subsidiary, in the various countries. From there the watches are shipped to the distributors and then on to retailers. These are the authorized channels where the company offers merchandising support and sales training, and in turn demands service support.

As can be seen in Fig. 9.6, the grey trade arises from several sources. Some of the distributors in price-competitive markets, such as China, will divert part of their shipment to more lucrative markets. They may sell directly to unauthorized (or even authorized) European or American distributors or retailers, getting higher prices that more than offset any transportation charges. Alternatively, Japanese distributors and retailers backed by a strong yen can go abroad to get watches from overseas distributors or retailers for sale at home.

Difficulties associated with grey market sales

While the grey market can lead to additional short-run sales revenues for manufacturers, the potential disruption is generally long-term in nature, as described below.

Difficulty in developing and maintaining a global image

Grey marketing can generate problems for firms seeking to build a global brand. With traditional channels, a marketer controls which product version is sold in a given country. In contrast, with grey market goods, products with different tastes, consistencies and sizes may be sold in a country where the product was never intended to be resold. For example, chocolate made for the UK market tends to be sweeter than chocolate sold in the rest of Europe. In other European markets with very warm climates, chocolate contains chemicals to retard melting, and this affects taste. Thus,

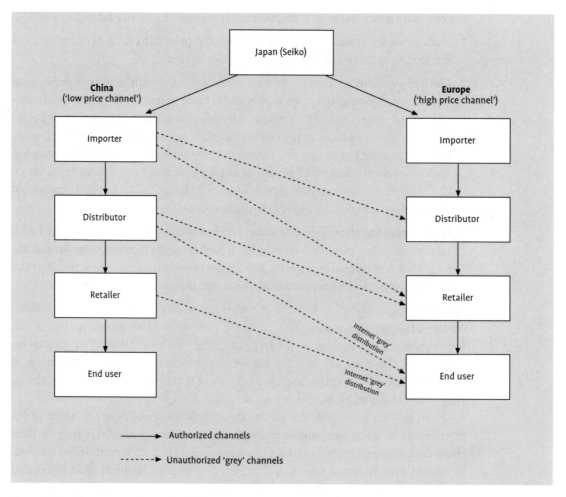

Figure 9.6 Seiko's 'grey' channels of distribution. Here two export markets – China and Europe – are used as illustration

says Benady (2003), two chocolate bars sold in the same country – one on the grey market, the other through traditional channels – may have different tastes.

Less control over a firm's overall marketing strategy

The grey market can result in a firm having less control over its marketing strategies. As stated earlier, because grey marketers are unauthorized dealers, manufacturers have no control over their selection or continuance. The traditional rewards and sanctions used by a firm to control its distributors are not present. Ironically, a firm's internal sales force is typically rewarded for the increased sales that lead to grey marketing.

Grey market activity can also affect other areas of market planning, such as a firm's new product introduction plans. Forecasted sales in a market may not be realized when there is a sudden influx of grey goods. Rollout campaign plans for new product introductions might have to be changed if grey traders introduce a product prematurely, as happens frequently with movie videos and popular music.

Coca-Cola, for example, was recently forced to bring forward the product launch date for its Vanilla Coke in the UK after discovering that the product had been sold in London and the south-east six months prior to its official launch date. The goods had been imported from Canada via the grey market.

Not all effects are negative, however. It is also possible to gain some advantages because grey trade tends to enlarge the market for a product through lower prices.

Erosion of a firm's traditional pricing strategy

The low prices offered by grey marketers may cause consumers to view the authorized reseller's price as being too high. And while an authorized dealer may be contractually obliged to run a complete service facility, purchase a manufacturer's full product line, participate in co-operative advertising and handle product recall responsibilities, grey marketers typically do not have to meet any of these obligations. Unfortunately, such augmented services may mean little to a price-conscious consumer. Continued low prices on grey market goods can also devalue a brand name whose image is associated with premium prices, as well as undermine a manufacturer's established list price and discount structure.

Problems in obtaining support from authorized resellers who 'play by the rules'

The grey market can generate difficulty in obtaining support from authorized dealers, who are particularly resentful of the pricing structure differences if a significant degree of free-riding occurs. With free-riding, customers visit authorized dealers for product information and then buy cheaper goods from grey market dealers. As a result, the latter benefit from the advertising, display and sales support of the authorized dealers. According to a recent KPMG study, 81 per cent of the IT distributors surveyed said that their competitive position would improve if all grey market activities were eliminated (KPMG, 2003).

The legal liabilities problem usually involves warranties that can't be honoured and performance criteria that can't be fulfilled. These problems are especially acute for pharmaceutical products because of the potential harm involved: taking medication that has expired or whose dosages are meant for adults can severely harm children, for instance.

Erosion of a brand's image

The erosion of a brand's image due to grey market activity may be the result of frequent sales at a low price, the existence of instructions in a foreign language, the absence of replacement parts for foreign goods, poor product quality (due to problems in the way foreign goods are stored and handled), and lack of manufacturer control over reseller selection. Because grey market sales are made through unauthorized channel members that have never been evaluated by their suppliers, some grey marketers can engage in unscrupulous behaviour, such as selling factory-remanufactured goods as new, reparing goods with parts manufactured by independent firms, selling supplies not made by the manufacturer and improperly adapting products to meet national safety standards.

Channel strategies for limiting grey market activity

Proactive strategies

These are designed to limit grey distribution even before the activity starts. The two most important proactive strategies are as follows.

1. *Reduce price differences across markets*

Because both domestic and foreign grey market activity are forms of market arbitrage, one obvious deterrent is to reduce the price differentials between market areas and adjust a firm's quantity discount schedule to prevent trans-shipping. For example, there is no economic reward for grey marketing when the price difference between two market areas is so small that it is less than shipping and inventory holding costs. An extreme example of a strategy to eliminate grey market activity is the Moët Hennessy – Louis Vuitton (LVMH) decision to price its TAG Heuer and Christian Dior watches the same worldwide. According to the firm's chairman, this strategy 'will dry out temptations for the grey market' (Shashidhar, 2002).

2. *Differentiate products sold to different markets*

A second strategy is to differentiate products sold to different markets: have products tailored to meet a region's unique regulatory requirements; use foreign labels; assign unique product numbers and names to foreign products. This provides legal rights in foreign grey market cases and reduces the consumer attraction of grey market goods. Set up a cross-border programme. For example, Canon uses different names and model numbers for cameras sold in lower-priced European and Asian markets.

Other proactive strategies

- Manufacturers can deter grey market goods by carefully checking their new and existing distributors. For example, they can employ cargo inspection firms to verify that foreign shipments are actually delivered to their specified location. They can also conduct compliance audits on an unscheduled basis to verify that goods have actually been sold to local final consumers.

- Manufacturers can also track down trans-shippers through a product's serial numbers, warranty card information and factory rebate data. Some manufacturers and wholesalers take a more aggressive position and employ 'shoppers' to purchase products from unauthorized resellers. Manufacturers and wholesalers should make resellers aware that they carefully monitor all reselling activity and will take away distributor or dealer status from authorized representatives that trans-ship goods. Most Japanese camera makers, for instance, use different model numbers and introduce slight differences in features between their Asian, North American and European markets. By stressing features and model numbers in the advertising, their global advertising copy can remain uniform with the same brand name (Minolta, Canon, Nikon) while at the same time alerting buyers when a grey import does not correspond to an 'authentic' model.

- Ironically, even as the web stimulates grey market activity, it also makes surveillance relatively easy. For example, manufacturers can easily search the web to determine the extent of sales by unauthorized resellers and the nature of price discounts, as well as the names and locations of grey marketers. They can also purchase grey market goods on the web to determine their condition and possibly trace their origin.

- Manufacturers can use their marketing information systems to monitor above-average purchases by specific wholesalers and retailers. Some manufacturers even hire investigators to approach wholesalers and retailers with offers to buy merchandise for diversion. Despite the importance of these deterrents, audits of channel partners are apparently rarely carried out.

- Consumer education and the use of rebates are two demand-side means of reducing grey market activity. Wella warns consumers not to buy its products outside of professional beauty supply stores and licensed beauty salons. According to its website (www.wellausa.com), 'diverted products usually pass through … many hands, travel great distances, [and] have been marked up 5 to 6 times before they finally make their way onto the retailer's shelves'. As a result, products are often old or damaged. Likewise, Kodak uses its website (www.kodak.com) to report that it is 'unable to govern the conditions under which these products are shipped. Film is very sensitive to heat and humidity, which means by the time a gray market film reaches you, it may be an inferior product.' A more constructive solution is to go on the attack and create stronger reasons for customers to patronize authorized dealers. This might involve aggressive price cutting, but other measures should be considered as well. Supporting authorized dealers in offering innovative credit plans, improved service and other customer-orientated initiatives is a possible tactic. Caterpillar, the heavy machinery company, helped authorized dealers develop customized warranties that the individual buyer could tailor to his or her own special needs. Manufacturers also support their dealers by regionalizing their offerings, and, as mentioned above, by differentiating model features and numbers between trade areas to make it possible to spot grey imports and restrict servicing liability.

Reactive strategies

The reactive strategies for fighting grey marketing once it has occurred are largely legal in nature. Many defences are most applicable when grey marketers sell goods that differ materially from the manufacturer's domestic goods, or when they seek to confuse customers. Trademark and state consumer protection laws can provide a basis for protecting manufacturers in such cases.

Legal actions, of course, may be quite costly and are not always successful. Suing grey marketers for breach of contract is difficult to enforce for two reasons: first, some grey market distributors may also be good customers for authorized products; second, in breach-of-contract cases, lost income due to diminished sales of lower prices must be proved.

A more drastic measure is to search for grey imports at the grey traders' outlets in the importing country and then ask the dealers – or help them – get rid of their inventory. Companies sometimes attempt simply to destroy grey merchandise in the stores. This kind of 'search and destroy' action requires a substantiated legal justification, such as an illegal change in the valid dates, or improper packaging, and is more common for counterfeit goods.

9.8 **Logistics**

Logistics involves all activities required to plan and move items from a material or manufacturing source to the point of consumption. While logistics has been defined as a discipline of its own, it is important to note that it is also a critical component of a firm's marketing capability. The right product, price and promotional mix are useless without dependable and timely product availability (place, or distribution). Timely availability creates value by allowing customers to purchase products or services where desired and if appropriate arrange delivery when and where desired. For a customer, availability or timely availability is as important as price and assortment.

While the role of logistics has not always been visible and well defined in commercial enterprises, transportation, inventory storage and customer service have always been performed. However, top management did not always fully understand the strategic importance and competitive impact of integrated logistics. Wide acceptance of enterprise operating philosophies such as just-in-time, total quality management, customer satisfaction and customer responsiveness served to enhance the role of logistics in achieving competitive advantage. A well-planned and well-executed logistics effort can achieve timely shipment arrival, undamaged product and satisfied customers at the lowest attainable total cost. Both the professional and popular press recognize the role of logistics in serving customers effectively.

Simply stated, customers expect nine 'rights' in any transaction:

1 the right product

2 the right quantity

3 the right quality

4 the right location

5 the right time

6 the right form

7 the right price

8 the right packaging

9 the right information.

Logistics plays a major role in achieving each of these customer expectations. The participants involved in logistical process management include wholesalers, distributors, retailers and third-party service providers necessary to provide warehousing, transportation and a wide range of other value-added services. The transportation service decision includes selection of transport modes and providers. The managerial aspect of logistics includes scheduling and execution of activities to respond to customers and facilitate shipments. Management or execution activities include order processing, selection and shipment. Measurement includes monitoring activities to ensure performance both satisfies customers and deploys the firm's resources effectively. Typical measures include customer service level, cost, productivity, asset utilization and quality.

Although not specifically stated, the discipline also includes activities related to recycling, returns handling and product recall.

The logistics value chain

The logistics value chain links all activities required to support profitable transactions as a single process linking a business with its customers. In some situations the value chain is owned by a vertically integrated firm, which controls all activities from raw material procurement to retail sales. Such vertical integration is found in the petroleum industry where firms control product value added from the drill to retail sales.

The more common value chain involves a number of independent firms such as material suppliers, manufacturers, wholesalers, retailers and logistics service firms. Due to the potential efficiency and effectiveness benefits, most firms linked together in a value chain seek to integrate some behaviours. Such collaboration is what distinguishes a traditional channel of distribution from a value chain.

A traditional channel of distribution comprises multiple chain members each attempting to optimize their individual performance. For example, each channel member may seek to minimize inventory investment rather than co-ordinate activities to reduce overall value chain inventory. The integrated value chain perspective attempts to co-ordinate value chain activities in an effort to reduce redundancy and duplication. It is the degree of collaboration in joint planning and co-ordinated operations that differentiates a traditional channel of distribution and an integrated value chain.

Value chains facilitate a combination of value-added flows. The primary three are inventory, information and financial flows. Information flow consists of sales activity, forecasts, plans and orders, which must be refined into deployment, manufacturing and procurement plans.

Another observation is that normal inventory flow towards end customers must at times be reversed. Product recall capability is a critical competency to accommodate increasingly rigid safety standards, product expiration and responsibility for hazardous material. Reverse logistics is also necessary due to the increasing number of laws prohibiting disposal and encouraging recycling of containers and packaging materials. Reverse logistics does not usually enjoy the scale economies characteristic of outbound movement. However, reverse movement capability is a social responsibility that must be accommodated in logistical system design.

Retailers and wholesalers typically link physical distribution and procurement activities even though no change in product form typically occurs. Nevertheless, wholesalers and retailers are key contributors to the value added process. Wholesalers develop assortments of products from multiple manufacturers, allowing retailers to purchase desired end combinations in smaller quantities. Retailers make a broad range of products conveniently available to customers. Such sorting and positioning is an essential element of the value added process.

Logistics activities

While it is appropriate to consider the logistics process across an integrated value chain, it is also useful to identify the major work required to accomplish the logistics mission. Traditional organizations incorporate four areas of logistics functionality:

1 customer service

2 transportation

3 inventory management, and

4 distribution operations.

Even though many firms have integrated the logistics process with other internal units, and externally with suppliers and customers, these work areas remain the heart of the logistics value chain. Each of these work areas is described below.

Customer service

Customer service manages the primary interface between a firm and its customers from an order fulfilment perspective. Customer service includes order taking and modification, order status inquiry and customer problem resolution. Customers expect the firm's customer service activity to be capable of providing accurate information regarding product availability, delivery time, product substitution, pricing and product customization options.

Transportation

Transportation controls product movement from manufacturing sites to distribution facilities to customers. The responsibilities include selecting the type of carrier, scheduling, routing and freight payment. In addition to managing the firm's shipping activities, transportation is responsible for monitoring carrier performance. Logistics is responsible for improving transportation service levels while simultaneously decreasing overall cost. The transportation management objective is to minimize total costs associated with all movements from suppliers to the final customer.

Inventory management

Inventory management consists of monitoring inventory levels and requirements at manufacturing plants and distribution facilities. The objective is to maintain enough inventory to satisfy customer demand while minimizing total asset deployment. Leading-edge firms gather knowledge regarding sales, customer demand, customer promotion plans, delivery times and replenishment cycles so that inventory can be synchronized with demand.

Distribution operations

Distribution operations have responsibility for the physical facilities and activities that take place at the distribution facilities used by a firm. The facilities include the buildings, offices, communications equipment, storage racks and material handling equipment. The activities include product receipt, storage, order selection and shipment. The distribution operations objective is to minimize expenses for receiving, storing and shipping product from a distribution facility. The historical operations focus has been to minimize the variable cost associated with handling or moving a product. A more comprehensive focus is to reduce assets required to support logistics while simultaneously increasing operating flexibility. Reduced assets remove distribution facilities and handling equipment from a company's books.

9.9 The internationalization of retailing

In spite of the power and sophistication of large-scale retailers, the process of internationalization has been slow and painful. In addition to legal, linguistic and logistical problems, it is difficult to export even the most successful of retail concepts into other markets. As noted earlier, competitive structures differ greatly and there are still major differences in consumer tastes and preferences. Difficult or not, the internationalization of retailing is, however, gaining in importance.

Motives for internationalization

The pressures towards/reasons for internationalization are diverse, but may be summarized as 'push', 'pull' or 'facilitating' factors.

- **Push factors** include the maturity or saturation of home markets, domestic trading restrictions, unfavourable economic conditions, rising costs, adverse demographic changes and imitation of trading styles.
- **Pull factors** include more enlightened corporate philosophies, perceptions of growth opportunities abroad (niche or underdeveloped markets), established bridgeheads in other countries and imitative 'bandwagon effects'.
- **Facilitating factors** include the lowering of political, economic and perceived barriers between countries, the broader vision of senior management, an

accumulation of expertise, the ability to assess other retailers' international moves and the improvement of communication technologies.

The particular mix of these factors often determines the most appropriate route to internationalization. Also relevant is the availability of capital, the level of understanding of market needs within other countries, and the compatibility of the domestic trading format(s) with those needs.

Prior to the 1980s, retailing was essentially a localized, domestic industry and thus retail operations were long considered poor candidates for international expansion. However, for the past two decades or so, retailers in mature markets have expanded their operations into overseas markets as a means for strategic growth. Retailers from Europe, the United States and Japan are now breaking into the developing markets of Asia, eastern Europe, and South America as the next step of their retail format expansion. A number of US-based retail giants, including Wal-Mart, Sears, Gap and Home Depot, have entered international markets in recent years. A similar trend is also evident in Europe, with the development of the European Union. European retailers derive a relatively large proportion of their turnover from operations outside their home market.

The internationalization of retailing has produced very diverse styles of operation, ranging from global to multinational. Global retailers such as Benetton vary their format very little across national boundaries, achieving the greatest economies of scale but showing the least local responsiveness. Multinationals, on the other hand, tend to develop or acquire a diversity of formats internationally, usually achieving rather lower benefits from integration. A middle course may be termed 'transnational' retailing, whereby a company seeks to achieve global efficiency while responding to national needs, opportunities and constraints. Some of the more recent developments by Marks & Spencer could best be described as transnational, recognizing that even the most successful retail formats within the domestic market may require adaptation to suit markets aboard.

Cross-border alliances have become a major element of international retail co-operation and expansion in recent years. The European Retail Alliance (ERA) and Associated Marketing Services (AMS), for instance, link retailers across Europe and open opportunities for many forms of co-operation, including purchasing, sourcing, logistics, product development, promotion and political lobbying.

Summary

Marketers must get their goods into the hands of consumers and must choose between handling all distribution or turning part or all of it over to various middlemen. Distribution channels vary depending on target market size, competition and available distribution intermediaries. It is evident that the international marketer has a broad range of alternatives for developing an economical, efficient, high-volume international distribution system.

The creation of globally co-ordinated channels has to start with a clear understanding of how the firm-specific advantages (FSAs) depend on distribution channel design. Key elements in distribution decisions include the functions performed by middlemen. The process of channel design and management of it can be broken into seven basic stages:

1 setting distribution objectives

2 specifying the functions that need to be performed by the channel

3 considering alternative channel structures

4 choosing an 'optimal' channel structure

5 selecting the intermediaries

6 motivating the channel members

7 evaluating channel member performance.

Parallel distribution and grey trade create control problems for the global firm and resellers, but can have some positive aspects too.

Global logistics are important determinants of financial performance, and their efficiency has been improving dramatically.

The wholesale and retail structure of a local market reflects the country's culture and economic progress, and the way business is done in that country; but new channel modes may be successful if timing and conditions are right.

Although international middlemen have become more numerous, more reliable and more sophisticated over the past decade, traditional channels are being challenged by the Internet, which is rapidly becoming an important alternative to many market segments. Such growth and development offer an ever wider range of possibilities for entering foreign markets.

Questions for discussion

1 Why is global distribution more difficult than domestic distribution?

2 What are the factors that affect the length, width and number of marketing channels?

3 Why might a firm choose not to use an intermediary in its efforts to reach its customers?

4 From the manufacturer's and the customer's perspective, how might a long channel be beneficial?

5 Suggest three products that might benefit from intensive distribution, and explain how this might be achieved.

6 What are the advantages and disadvantages for a clothing manufacturer of making products available via their own website or, alternatively, via a mail-order catalogue sent out to known customers?

7 Why is a good logistics strategy especially vital for foods and high-tech products?

8 What are the advantages and disadvantages of a firm establishing its own distribution in the international market, and what forms might this take?

9 How do the characteristics of the final consumers influence the structure of international distribution channels?

10 How does international physical distribution differ from international channel distribution?

References

Anderson, E., Day, G. and Rangan, V.K. (1997) Strategic channel design. *Sloan Management Review*, Summer, pp. 59–69.

Arnold, D. (2000) Seven rules of international distribution. *Harvard Business Review*, November–December, pp. 131–7.

Baker, M. (2000) *IEBM Encyclopedia of Marketing*, London: Thomson Learning.

Benady, D. (2003) Selling you a new past. *Independent*, 21 October, London, p. 18.

Biemans, W. (2001) Designing a dual marketing program. *European Management Journal* 19(6), pp. 670–7.

Gabrielsson, M. (1999) *Sales Channel Strategies for International Expansion – The Case of Large Companies in the European PC Industry*, doctoral dissertation. Helsinki: Helsinki School of Economics and Business Administration.

Gabrielsson, M., Kirpalani, V.H.M. and Luostarinen, R. (2002) Multiple channel strategies in the European personal computer industry. *Journal of International Marketing* 10(3), pp. 73–95.

Hollensen, S. (2003) *Marketing Management*. London: Financial Times/Prentice Hall, an imprint of Pearson Education.

Hollensen, S. (2004) *Global Marketing – A Decision-oriented Approach*, 3rd edn. London: Financial Times/Prentice Hall.

KPMG (2003) The grey market – a KPMG study in cooperation with the Anti-Gray Market Alliance, www.kpmg.co.uk/industries/t/pubs.cfm.

Shashidhar, A. (2002), 'Top Swiss watch brands cost the same worldwide – LVMH gears to check grey market', Business Line – Internet Edition, Oct. 5 (www.blonnet.com)

Vishwanath, V. and Mulvin, G. (2001) Multi-channels: the real winners in the B2C Internet wars. *Business Strategy Review* 12(1), pp. 25–33.

Case 9 Quiksilver

- Choosing distribution channels representing a causal lifestyle-driven and board-riding heritage

Based in Huntington Beach, California, Quiksilver is a designer and producer of apparel aimed at surfers, skateboarders and snowboarders. Quiksilver is a globally integrated company that designs, produces and distributes branded clothing, accessories and related products for young-minded people. Quiksilver brands represent a casual lifestyle—driven from the authentic board-riding heritage.

History of Quiksilver

In the late 1960's Australian surfers Alan Green and John Law chased a dream – to live in Torquay, make a living and go surfing. In 1969 Alan Green produced wetsuits (Rip Curl) on a $2500 loan from his father, the next product was sheepskin boots (UGG Boots), and in 1970 he and John Law formed the company named Quiksilver. The first product by the two Australian surfers was the famous Quiksilver boardshort. The Quiksilver boardshort, identified by its distinctive mountain and wave logo, became known in the core surfing world as a technically innovative and stylish product. By the mid-1970's, a small office/warehouse/distribution centre was opened in Newport Beach, California. The Quiksilver business was based on word of mouth, quality, service and their extensive personal contacts at surf shops on the coasts of the USA. The reputation and popularity of the Quiksilver boardshort grew, having been brought to the beaches of California and Southwest France in the 1970's by the founders of the company and Quiksilver Europe. Since the first boardshort, their product lines have been greatly expanded. In the 1990's they called on the Quiksilver heritage to reach out to the girls market by creating the Roxy brand for juniors, which has become their fastest growing brand. In 2004, they acquired the DC Shoes brand from its founders and expanded their presence in the action sports inspired footwear arena.

Quiksilver today

Over the last five years, Quiksilver revenues have grown from $519 million in fiscal 2000 to $1.3 billion in fiscal 2004. They design, produce and distribute clothing, accessories and related products exclusively in the consumer products industry. They operate in three geographic segments, the Americas, Europe and Asia/Pacific. By the end of 2004, Quiksilver had approximately 4,350 employees, consisting of approximately 2,450 in the United States, approximately 1,300 in Europe and approximately 600 in Asia/Pacific.

Quiksilver has three geographic segments, the Americas, Europe and Asia/Pacific. The Americas segment includes revenues primarily from the U.S. and Canada. The European segment includes revenues primarily from Western Europe. The Asia/Pacific segment includes revenues primarily from Australia, Japan, New Zealand and Indonesia.

Competition

The apparel and footwear industries are highly competitive. Quiksilver competes with numerous domestic and foreign designers, brands and manufacturers of apparel, footwear, accessories and other products, some of which are significantly larger and have greater resources than Quiksilver. The ability to compete effectively depends upon Quiksilver's continued ability to maintain the reputation for authenticity in the core boardriding market, the flexibility in responding to market demand and the ability to manage the branding process and offer fashion conscious consumers a wide variety of high quality apparel at competitive prices.

Competition is strong in each of the product markets in which Quiksilver operates. Each territory can have different competitors. The direct competitors in the United States differ depending on distribution channel. The principal competitors in the core channel of surf shops and Boardriders Clubs in the United States include Billabong, Volcom, O'Neill and Hurley. The competitors in the department store and specialty store channels in the United States include Tommy Hilfiger, Abercrombie and Fitch, Nautica and Calvin Klein. The principal competitors in the skateboard shoe market are Sole Technology, Inc. and DVS Shoe Company. In Europe, the principal competitors in the core channel include O'Neill, Billabong, Rip Curl, Oxbow and Chimsee. In Australia the primary competitors are Billabong and Rip Curl. In broader European distribution, and in Asia/Pacific, the competitors also include brands such as Nike, Adidas and Levis. The principal competitors both in the United States and Europe in the snowboardwear and snowboard markets, are Burton, K2 and a lot of smaller manufacturers.

The key success factors (KSFs) in the apparel industry depend in substantial part on the ability to anticipate, gauge and respond to changing consumer demand and fashion trends in a timely manner. Fashion trends may shift away from Quiksilver products, or if Quiksilver otherwise misjudge the market for their product lines, they may be faced with a significant amount of unsold finished goods inventory. The apparel and footwear industries historically have been subject to substantial cyclical variations, and a recession in the general economy or uncertainties regarding future economic prospects that affect consumer spending habits may have a serious effect on financial results.

Products and Brands

In addition to *Quiksilver*, *Roxy* and *DC Shoes*, Quiksilver has developed a stable of other brands to address a wide variety of consumers and markets. Quiksilver believes this multibrand strategy will allow them to continue to grow across a diverse range of products and distribution with broad appeal across gender, age groups and geographics.

Quiksilver's primary focus is apparel, footwear and related accessories for young men and young women under the Quiksilver, Roxy, DC Shoes, Raisins, Radio Fiji and Island Soul labels. Quiksilver also manufactures apparel, footwear and related accessories for boys (Quiksilver Boys and Hawk Clothing), girls (Roxy Girl, Teenie Wahine and Raisins Girls), men (Quiksilveredition and Fidra) and women (Leilani swimwear), as well as snowboards, snowboard boots and bindings under the Lib Technologies, Gnu, DC Shoes, Roxy and Bent Metal labels.

Quiksilver

The Quiksilver product line now includes shirts, walkshorts, t-shirts, fleece, trousers, jackets, snowboardwear, footwear, hats, backpacks, wetsuits, watches, eyewear and other accessories. Quiksilver has also expanded demographically and currently includes young men, boys and toddlers. Quiksilveredition is the brand targeted at men. In 2004, the Quiksilver line of products represented approximately app. 50% of the total revenues.

Roxy

The Roxy brand for young women is a surf-inspired collection that was introduced in fiscal 1991. The Roxy line is branded with a heart logo composed of back-to-back images of the Quiksilver mountain and wave logo and includes a full range of sportswear, swimwear, footwear, backpacks, snowboardwear, snowboards, snowboard boots, fragrance, beauty care, bedroom furnishings and other accessories for young women. Through fiscal 1997, Roxy included juniors' sizes only, but was then expanded as Teenie Wahine and Roxy Girl into the girls categories. In fiscal 2004, the Roxy product line accounted for approximately 33% of the total revenues.

DC Shoes

The recently acquired DC Shoes label specializes in performance skateboard shoes, snowboard boots, sandals and apparel for both young men and juniors. This brand enhances the footwear expertise and strengthens Quiksilver's presence in the core skateboard market. In 2004, the DC Shoes product line accounted for approximately 7% of the total revenues

The Quiksilver design and merchandising teams create seasonal product ranges for each of their brands. These design groups constantly monitor local and global fashion trends. They believe that their most valuable input comes from their own managers, employees, sponsored athletes and independent sales representatives who are actively involved in surfing, skateboarding, snowboarding and other sports in core markets.

The following table shows the approximate percentage of revenues attributable to each of the major product categories in 2004:

Products – 2004 Revenues

T-Shirts	19%
Accessories	14%
Jackets, sweaters and snowboardwear	12%
Trousers	10%
Shirts	9%
Footwear	9%
Swimwear, excluding boardshorts	7%
Fleece	5%
Shorts	5%
Boardshorts	4%
Tops and dresses	4%
Snowboards, snowboard boots, bindings and accessories	2%
	100%

Source: Adapted from www.quiksilver.com

Although the products are generally available throughout the year, demand for different categories of product changes in the different seasons of the year. Sales of shorts, short-sleeve shirts, t-shirts and swimwear are higher during the spring and summer seasons, and sales of trousers, long-sleeve shirts, fleece, jackets, sweaters, snowboardwear and snowboards are higher during the fall and holiday seasons.

Price

The U.S. retail prices for the apparel products range from approximately $18 for a t-shirt and $41 for a typical short to a range of $120 to $320 for a snowboard jacket. For European products, retail prices range from approximately $35 for a t-shirt and about $61 for a typical short to $220 for a basic snowboard jacket. Asia/Pacific t-shirts sell for approximately $32, while shorts sell for approximately $54, and a basic snowboard jacket sells for approximately $210. Retail prices for a typical skate shoe range from approximately $60 in the U.S. to approximately $117 in Europe.

Distribution

Quiksilver's products are sold throughout the world, primarily in surf shops, skate shops, snowboard shops and other specialty stores that provide an authentic retail experience for the customers.

Quiksilver's policy is to sell to retailers who provide an outstanding in-store experience for their customers and who merchandise the products in a manner consistent with the image of their brands and the quality of products. Quiksilver's customer base has for many years reflected the goal of diversification of distribution to include surf shops, skate shops, snowboard shops, other specialty stores, national specialty chains and select department stores.

The Quiksilver brand message is also carried over by specialty stores like Boardriders Clubs, with the use of point-of-sale materials. This core distribution channels serves as a base of legitimacy and long-term loyalty to the Quiksilver brand. Most of these stores stand alone or are part of small chains.

Quiksilver also sells to independent specialty or active lifestyle stores and specialty chains not specifically characterized as surf shops, skate shops or snowboard shops. This category includes chains such as Pacific Sunwear, Nordstrom, Zumiez, Chicks Sporting Goods and Journeys, as well as many independent active lifestyle stores and sports shops. They also sell to a limited number of department stores, including Macy's, Robinsons-May, Dillards, The Bon Marche and Burdines in the U.S.; Le Printemps and Galeries Lafayette in France; Corte Ingles in Spain; and Lillywhites in Great Britain.

Many of their brands are sold through the same retail accounts; however, distribution can be different depending on the brand and demographic group. The *Quiksilver* products are sold in the Americas to customers that have approximately 8,400 store locations combined. Likewise, *Roxy* products are sold in the Americas to customers with approximately 8,350 store locations. Most of these *Roxy* locations also carry *Quiksilver* product. In the Americas, *DC shoe* products are carried in approximately 5,000 stores, primarily in the U.S. and Canada.. Swimwear brands (*Raisins, Leilani* and *Radio Fiji*) are found in 10,400 stores, including many small. Quiksilver products are found in approximately 6,800 store locations in Europe, and in approximately 2,100 store locations in Asia/Pacific, in both cases primarily *Quiksilver* and *Roxy*. Distribution of *DC shoe* products in Europe and Asia/Pacific has been primarily through independent distributors.

The European segment accounted for approximately 39% of the total revenues during 2004. Asia/Pacific segment accounted for approximately 12% in 2004 (see following table).

The following table summarizes the approximate percentages of 2004 revenues by distribution channel and main geographic regions:

Distribution Channels – 2004 Revenues	Americas	Europe	Asia/Pacific	Consolidated
Boardriders Clubs, in-store specialty shops, surf, skate and snow shops	26%	37%	78%	36%
Specialty stores	52	46	6	45
Department stores	11	7	9	9
U.S. exports	11	—	—	5
Distributors	—	10	7	5
Total	100%	100%	100%	100%
Geographic segment (of total revenues)	49%	39%	12%	100%

Source: Adapted from www.quiksilver.com

The revenues are spread over a large customer base. During 2004, approximately 17% of the total revenues were from the ten largest customers and no single customer accounted for more than 4% of such revenues.

Quiksilver products are sold by approximately 310 independent sales representatives in the Americas, Europe and Asia/Pacific. In addition, Quiksilver use approximately 60 local distributors in Europe. The sales representatives are generally compensated on a commission basis. Quiksilver employs retail merchandise coordinators who travel between specified retail customers to further improve the presentation of the products and build the image at the retail level.

Retail Concepts

Quiksilver concept stores (*Boardriders Clubs*) are an important part of the global retail strategy. These stores are stocked primarily with *Quiksilver* and *Roxy* product, and their proprietary design demonstrates the Company's history, authenticity and commitment to surfing and other boardriding sports. They also have *Roxy* stores, which are dedicated to the juniors customer, *Quiksilver Youth* stores, *Hawk Clothing* stores, *Gotcha* stores in Europe, *Andaska* shops in Europe that carry multiple brands in the outdoor market, and other multibrand stores in Europe.

Quiksilver owns 170 stores in selected markets that provide enhanced brand-building opportunities. In territories where Quiksilver operates their own wholesale businesses, they had (in 2004) 64 stores with independent retailers under license. They do not receive royalty income from these stores. Rather, Quiksilver provide the independent retailer with their retail expertise and store design concepts in exchange for the independent retailer agreeing to maintain Quiksilver brands at a minimum of 80% of the store's inventory. Certain minimum purchase obligations are also required. Furthermore, in the Quiksilver licensed territories, such as Turkey and South Africa, their licensees operate 76 *Boardriders Clubs*. Quiksilver receives royalty income from sales in these stores based on wholesale volume.

Promotion and Advertising

Quiksilver's three-decade commitment to core marketing at the grass-roots level in the sport of surfing and other youth boardriding activities is the foundation of the promotion and advertising of their brands and products.

The sponsorship of high profile athletes in outdoor, individual sports, including surfing, skateboarding, snowboarding, windsurfing and golf is an important marketing vehicle for Quiksilver. Many of these athletes such as Kelly Slater, Lisa Anderson, Tom Carroll, Robbie Naish, Danny Kass and Ernie Els have achieved world champion status in their respective sports and are featured in Quiksilver's promotional content. They operate a promotional fund that is used to sponsor portions of the international team of leading athletes, produce promotional movies and videos featuring athletes wearing and/or using *Quiksilver* and *Roxy* products, and organize surf, skate and snow contests and other events that have international significance.

Quiksilver's core marketing is based on their sponsorship and support of surf, skateboard and snowboard contests in markets where they distribute product. These events reinforce the reputations of the brands as authentic among boardriders and non-boardriders alike. For example, the *Quiksilver in Memory of Eddie Aikau Big Wave Invitational* is held at Waimea Bay in Hawaii. *Quiksilver Pro* events are held on the Gold Coast of Australia, the beaches of Southwestern France and the beaches of Japan. The *Roxy Pro* is held in Hawaii and other international locations. Quiksilver also arrange many events in Europe, including the *Grommets Trophy* surfing event, the *Slopestyle Pro* snowboarding event and the *Bowlriders* skateboarding event. The *Quiksilver Airshows*, which feature aerial surf manoeuvres, are held in New Zealand, Japan, Indonesia and Australia.

Quiksilver sponsors also the *Quiksilver Crossing*, a continuing voyage of the Indies Trader, a surf exploration vessel whose mission is to explore new surfing regions around the world and document the state of the environment under a team of marine biologists. The *Quiksilver Crossing*, now in its sixth year, began its voyage in the South Pacific, continued on through the Suez Canal to Europe in 2002, visited the Caribbean in 2003, reached the east coast and Mississippi River of the U.S. in 2004 and is heading for the west coast of the U.S. in 2005.

Based on the international reputation for authenticity, compelling content and technical competence in the youth market, Quiksilver also enters into co-branding arrangements. For example, Peugeot has produced cars branded with *Quiksilver*, while Boost Mobile has produced and sold Roxy mobile phones in the U.S. and Quiksilver and Roxy mobile phones in

Australia, and Sony has produced a waterproof digital camera branded with *Quiksilver* and original Quiksilver artwork.

The Quiksilver **Entertainment division** is also producing television programming, documentaries and feature films, and publishing fiction and non-fiction books to transmit the boardriding lifestyle to the core and mainstream audiences. Quiksilver develops and produces (in USA) 54321, a weekly series on Fuel TV and Fox Sports Net, and they produced the Surf Girls reality series on MTV, which has aired in the U.S. and internationally. In 2004, they launched Union, a mainstream action sports film distribution company. Union distributes the highest quality action sports films from the leading producers in the action sports industry through a variety of mainstream channels, including over 1,000 retail locations in the U.S., Europe, Japan, China, and Australia.

The documentary film about big-wave surfing, "Riding Giants", opened the 2004 Sundance Film Festival. It was directed by Stacey Peralta, who shot to fame with 2001 Sundance winner "Dogtown," and "Z-Boys," a documentary about a gang of California kids in the '70s who transformed skateboarding-and youth culture. "Riding Giants" traces the evolution of big-wave surfing through the stories of three of the sport's they-must-be-insane pioneers, and in doing so explores the surfer ethos.

None of these film projects focus on Quiksilver brands or products. There are end credits and subtle logos, but this is not about product placement or even brand integration. Rather, it is about selling a special lifestyle with which Quiksilver is associated. The philosophy is: "If girls in Kansas, UK, Japan, Australia or Poland adopt the lifestyle of girls in California, Quiksilver is bound to benefit".

Latest development

In March 2005 Quiksilver announced an agreement in principle to acquire the Rossignol Group SA, one of the world leaders in winter sports. The Rossignol Group owns and operates a diversified portfolio of premier brands including Rossignol, Dynastar, Lange and Look in winter sports, as well as Cleveland Golf. The combination of Quiksilver and Rossignol will create a global leader in the outdoor sports lifestyle market.

Headquartered in Voiron, France, the Rossignol Group (www.rossignol.com) achieved total sales of approximately $625 million for financial year 2004 (Quiksilver achieved $1.3 Billion in the same period). The Rossignol Group is one the world's leading manufacturers of winter-sports equipment. It offers a full range of products for all disciplines (alpine, nordic, snowboard) and all product families (skis, bindings, boots, poles, and boards) under the brand names Rossignol, Dynastar, Lange, Look, Kerma, Hammer and Risport. Additionally, the Rossignol Group designs, manufactures, and markets golf products under the Cleveland Golf brand name. The Rossignol Group's product range also includes apparel and accessories.

Questions:

1 How will you characterize Quiksilver's current distribution strategy – intensive, selective or exclusive?

2 Please discuss to what degree Quiksilver should use a multiple channel strategy?

3 Should Quiksilver use the same distribution channels after the acquisition of the Rossignol Group?

4 Please propose a distribution strategy for the next five years?

Sources:
– www.quiksilver.com
– www.rossignol.com,
– BBC News, 22 March, 2005: Quiksilver buys French ski maker (http://news.bbc.co.uk/2/hi/business/4372679.stm)
– Bloom, J. (2004), Marketers should jump on Quiksilver's creative wave, Advertising Age, 19.07.2004, Vol. 75, Issue 29, pp.17–18

Marketing mix decisions IV: communication

Learning Objectives

After studying this chapter you should be able to:

- discuss the role of communication in the marketing mix

- describe the main elements of the promotional mix

- identify the local market characteristics that affect the advertising and promotion of products

- explain the five steps in developing an international advertising campaign

- discuss the role of personal selling in international marketing

- explain the considerations and steps in designing and managing an international sales force

- discuss how to design compensation systems for an international sales force

- explain the principles of multi-channel customer management.

10.1 Introduction

Without an effective marketing communications programme, a marketing strategy will fail. Target customers must be made aware of the product and its benefits, be continually reminded of these benefits, and stimulated to take action. Building awareness, message comprehension and interest are essential phases in building a high level of customer response.

Effective communication is the core aim of most promotion decisions. The marketing manager's job is to combine various forms of promotional activities to effectively communicate specific messages concerning the firm and its market offering to targeted consumers, channel partners, company shareholders and the general public. This promotion mix consists of such communications activities as advertising, sales promotion, personal selling, public relations and direct marketing.

A business's total marketing communications programme is called the 'promotional mix'. This consists of a blend of advertising, personal selling, sales promotion and public relations tools. The following sections describe the six key elements of the promotional mix (see Table 10.1) in more detail, and from an international marketing perspective in particular.

Table 10.1 Advantages and disadvantages of each element of the promotional mix

Mix element (section number)	Advantages	Disadvantages
Advertising (10.2) Any paid-for or non-personal communication of ideas or products in the prime media (i.e. television, newspapers, magazines, billboard posters, radio, cinema). Advertising is intended to persuade and to inform. The two basic aspects of advertising are the message (what you want your communication to say) and the medium (how to get your message across).	▪ Good for building awareness ▪ Effective at reaching a wide audience ▪ Repetition of main brand and product positioning helps build customer trust	▪ Impersonal – cannot answer all customer questions ▪ Not good at getting customers to make a final purchasing decision
Sales promotion (10.3) Providing incentives to customers or to the distribution channel to stimulate interest and demand for a product.	▪ Can stimulate quick increases in sales by targeting promotional incentives on particular products ▪ Good short-term tactical tool	▪ If used over the long term, customers may get used to the effect ▪ Too much promotion may damage the brand image

Public relations and sponsorship (10.4) The communication of a product, brand or business by placing information about it in the media without paying for the time or media space directly. PR communicates via a news release to definable news media in the hope of secondary exposure to a target audience through an editorial mention earned by the newsworthiness of the subject matter.	■ Often seen as more 'credible' – since the message seems to be coming from a third party (e.g. magazine, newspaper) ■ Cheap way of reaching many customers – if the publicity is achieved through the right media	■ Risk of losing control – cannot always control what other people write about your product
Internet promotion (10.5) The Internet represents a change away from a push strategy towards a pull strategy in which the manufacturer communicates directly with the customer. Examples of mix elements are banner ads, sponsorships, interstitials (TV-like commercials), mobile marketing (m-marketing) and viral marketing.	■ Interactive communication with customers ■ Reduced global advertising costs ■ Access to directories that guide people to visit the site	■ The promoted product cannot be touched (important for tangible products, not important for intangible products) ■ Online advertising messages are often perceived in a local context, and should be adapted to the local environment; this will increase total advertising costs
Direct marketing (10.6) Communicates person to person, but through an intervening channel, such as the post (direct mail), the telephone (telemarketing) or e-mail, guaranteeing exposure to a selected individual within a target market. For many years, the only form of direct marketing in use was direct mail.	■ Person-to-person interactive communication ■ Direct exposure to selected individuals within a target market ■ Messages can be targeted	■ Higher cost per recipient, but cheaper than 'personal selling'
Personal selling (10.7) Oral communication with potential buyers of a product with the intention of making a sale. Personal selling may focus initially on developing a relationship with the potential buyer, but will always ultimately end with an attempt to 'close the sale'.	■ Highly interactive – lots of communication between the buyer and seller ■ Excellent for communicating complex/detailed product information and features ■ Relationships can be built up – important if closing the sale may take a long time	■ Costly – employing a sales force has many hidden costs in addition to wages ■ Not suitable if there are thousands of important buyers

10.2 **Advertising**

Of all the elements of the marketing mix, decisions involving advertising are those most often affected by cultural differences among country markets. Consumers respond in terms of their culture, its style, feelings, value systems, attitudes, beliefs and perceptions. Because advertising's function is to interpret or translate the qualities of products and services in terms of consumer needs, wants, desires and aspirations, the emotional appeals, symbols, persuasive approaches and other characteristics of an advertisement must coincide with cultural norms if an ad is to be effective.

Global advertising can be defined as advertising that is more or less uniform across many countries, often, but not necessarily, in media vehicles with global reach. In many cases complete uniformity is unobtainable because of linguistic and regulatory differences between nations, or differences in media availability.

In contrast, *multidomestic advertising* is international advertising deliberately adapted to particular markets and audiences in terms of message and/or creative execution.

Several problems traditionally face the decision-maker in global advertising. One is how to allocate a given *advertising budget* among several market countries. Another is the *message* to use in these various markets. A third is what *media* to select. Even before tackling these management decisions, however, the advertiser needs to define the *objectives* of the advertising in the different countries.

Reconciling an international advertising campaign with the cultural uniqueness of markets is the challenge confronting the international or global marketer. The basic framework and concepts of international advertising are essentially the same wherever used. Five steps are involved (Baker, 2000):

1 strategic objectives

2 message creation

3 media selection

4 advertising budgeting

5 executing the campaign.

Of these five steps, developing messages almost always represents the most daunting task for international marketing managers, so that topic is emphasized here. The nuances of international media are then discussed. Advertising agencies are ordinarily involved in all five steps and are thus the subject of a separate section.

Strategic objectives

Most managers approach global advertising with the intention of using the global reach of media and the similarity of message to enhance the awareness and unique positioning of the brand or product. The boost to the *brand image* and global brand equity is usually the most immediate benefit. When the target market involves global consumers, the ability to reach these customers in many places throughout the world helps sustain a positive image of the brand. The traveller who recognizes a brand advertised in a foreign resort location may pay more attention to it there than he or she would at home. Global advertising helps create goodwill.

Unilever is introducing a new product-line extension, Dove Shampoo, in East Asian markets; and Russia's national airline Aeroflot is seeking to upgrade its quality image. Such marketing problems require careful marketing research, and thoughtful and creative advertising campaigns in country, regional and global markets, respectively.

Intense competition for world markets and the increasing sophistication of foreign consumers has led to a need for more sophisticated advertising strategies. Increased costs, problems of co-ordinating advertising programmes in multiple countries, and the desire for a broader company or product image caused multinational companies (MNCs) to seek greater control and efficiency without sacrificing local responsiveness.

Message creation

The effectiveness of promotional strategy can be jeopardized by so many factors that a marketer must be certain that no controllable influences are overlooked. Those international executives who understand the communications process are better equipped to manage the diversity they face in developing an international promotional programme.

In the international communications process, each of the seven identifiable stages listed below can ultimately affect the accuracy of that process. The process, then, consists of the following stages.

1 **An information source:** an international marketing executive with a product message to communicate.

2 **Encoding:** the message from the source converted into effective symbolism for transmission to a receiver.

3 **A message channel:** the sales force and/or advertising media that convey the encoded message to the intended receiver.

4 **Decoding:** the interpretation by the receiver of the symbolism transmitted from the information source.

5 **Receiver:** consumer action by those who receive the message and are the target for the thought transmitted.

6 **Feedback:** information about the effectiveness of the message that flows from the receiver (the intended target) back to the information source for evaluation of the effectiveness of the process.

7 **Noise:** uncontrollable and unpredictable influences, such as competitive activities and confusion, that detract from the process and affect any or all of the other six factors.

Noise comprises all other external influences, such as competitive advertising, other sales personnel, and confusion at the receiving end, that can detract from the ultimate effectiveness of the communication. Noise is a disruptive force that can interfere with the process at any stage and is frequently beyond the control of the sender or the receiver.

Unfortunately, the process is not as simple as just sending a message via a medium to a receiver and being certain that the intended message sent is the same one perceived by the receiver.

For good reasons, message creation and language translation are the aspects most consistently and thoroughly discussed in the literature on global advertising. Even experienced advertising people commit mistakes with ease.

Message translation is complicated because of the cultural diversity among the various countries of the world. Language difference is only the most obvious manifestation of this diversity.

Media selection

Although nearly every sizable nation essentially has the same kinds of media, there are a number of specific considerations, problems and differences that are likely to be encountered from one nation to another. In international advertising, an advertiser must consider the availability, cost, coverage and appropriateness of the media.

If message creation needs the collaboration of the agency and the advertiser (to ensure a unified positioning theme), media selection is one area where the agency and its local representative rule. The reason for this is primarily expertise. Local knowledge of the availability of media alternatives is absolutely necessary so that the optimal media, given the constraints, are chosen. It might be possible to direct an advertising campaign from overseas so far as budgeting, message creation and general direction go, but the media choices must be negotiated and made locally.

Rates of media usage are determined by a number of factors such as availability of commercial TV and radio, Internet, level of economic development, literacy rates, religion, and so forth, and reflect directly, of course, the actual media selection decisions made by the advertisers and agencies for the country in question.

What type of media to select hinges (within availability constraints) very much on the objectives and target segment(s) of the campaign.

For *awareness,* television serves well in many countries where it is generally available. In markets with lower rates of TV penetration, radio can often be used to supplement television advertising. Television in most cases has the advantage of a high attention value, especially in countries where it is relatively rare.

Once the media types have been decided upon, the particular vehicles to be used within each type are usually selected on the basis of some efficiency criterion such as cost per thousand (CPM). The use of an efficiency criterion requires information about how much advertising in a vehicle costs and how many people (in the target market) will be reached. Here a major problem is encountered in many markets. The available audience measurements are either incomplete (lacking audience demo-graphics, for example), unreliable or even non-existent at times. It can be very hard to find accurate figures.

Advertising budgeting

In domestic markets, a common method for advertising budgets is percentage-of-sales: setting a certain percentage of last year's sales as next year's budget. The figure arrived at can be adjusted by considering a changing competitive situation, increasing growth objectives or a squeeze on company profits; but percentage-of-sales has the advantage of establishing a stable and predictable expenditure level tied to revenues. The percentage chosen can be calibrated against the industry average ratio of adver-tising-to-sales, making for easy comparisons with competitors.

Although *percentage-of-sales* is popular among firms from most countries, it is not a very useful method for setting *global* advertising budgets. Even if total worldwide revenues can be used as a base, it is not clear what the appropriate percentage would be. Which country's industry average should be used as a starting point, for example? Different countries show widely different levels of advertising-to-sales ratios for the same industry, depending on media availability, competitive situation, and so on. Since the percentage-of-sales approach sets advertising on the basis of past sales, it is of little use when a shift from multidomestic to global advertising is contemplated. *Competitive parity* approaches, where advertising budgets are set on the basis of what competitors spend, are also of less relevance in global advertising. The main difficulty is in identifying the appropriate parity to actual and potential competitors from different countries, many of which have very different firm-specific advantages (FSAs) and market presence. Competitive parity is most appropriate when the major global competitors are from the same countries, as with Coca-Cola and Pepsi-Cola, or Sony, Matsushita, Sharp and other Japanese players in consumer electronics.

Budgeting for global advertising typically involves some version of the so-called *objective–task method* favoured domestically by more sophisticated marketers. In this method the objectives of the advertising are first made explicit and quantified, after which the requisite media spending to reach the required exposure levels is specified. Although precise calibration of spending is difficult because of the uncertainty in gauging worldwide audiences of media vehicles, the basic logic is sound. After the initial specification of the job to be done by advertising (target percentages for aware-ness, for example, or certain reach and frequency figures), the creative solutions and the media schedules likely to attain the desired levels are developed.

This is work requiring the expertise of an ad agency with a global network. The budgeting done for global advertising involves an unusually large amount of agency input, since assessing the feasibility and cost of global campaigns requires input from the local branches in the agencies' global network. Partly for this reason, the drive towards global advertising is often spearheaded by an agency with global reach.

Executing the campaign

The drive towards global advertising has to a large extent been initiated by global advertising agencies that have developed worldwide networks of subsidiaries or affiliates.

Advertising, being so close to the cultural traditions of a country, was long one of the more decentralized decisions in the multinational company. Headquarters would perhaps be setting the budget, but the basic positioning strategy would be determined by the local subsidiary and approved by headquarters. When it came to execution, including message creation and especially media selection, the advertising agency and its local branch were the prime movers.

The global advertiser, aiming to gain some benefits from a unified approach, has to take charge of this process more effectively. Positioning strategy has to be unified across countries and the unique selling propositions of the brand made clear – and the same – everywhere. That is the strategy part. As for execution, the global advertising manager needs to work closely with local personnel in the subsidiaries and in the agency network to get consensus on a message that transcends borders, reflects the brand accurately and has punch everywhere. As for media, although the agency must still be the main actor, the global advertiser will want to make sure that cost factors such as media discounts are properly taken into account. While doing all this, the global advertiser also needs to keep an open eye and open mind to suggestions from the local people, to quickly diffuse information through the various local affiliates, and to be flexible enough to change when new information and market research suggest this is necessary.

Standardization or adaptation of global advertising

The global advertiser faces a complex task. The communication has to be appropriate for each local market, while at the same time there is a need to co-ordinate campaigns and control expenditures across the globe. Because of the varying media availability in different countries, and the differing effectiveness of global media, the feasible channels for advertising will differ. But customizing the advertising to each individual country leads to increased costs and unwieldy control procedures.

The ads can be identical, usually with localization only in terms of language voiceover changes and simple copy translations. Pan-European advertising featuring Exxon gasoline's tiger in the tank and Marlboro cigarettes' cowboy are examples. In some cases the identical ads or commercials can be used without any translation at all. Levi's, the jeans manufacturer, uses cartoons with rock music and unintelligible, vaguely Esperanto-sounding vocals in one commercial where the Levi's-wearing hero rescues a beautiful woman from a burning building, an easily comprehended message. In other cases the commercials simply carry subtitles. IBM shows Italian-speaking nuns discussing the pros and cons of Internet surfing with subtitles translating the conversation: global ad with a local touch. It might be assumed that global products and brands need global advertising. This is often true. Campaigns for

Diesel, Club Med, Benetton and Reebok are very similar across continents. But there is often a need to do some local adaptation of global campaigns. For example, a global product and brand such as Levi's jeans targets specific segments with different appeals in each local market, since the positioning of the product and brand varies as the target markets differ.

Sometimes a brand's global campaign has misfired and the company has retreated to a more multidomestic adaptation. Parker Pen, a globally recognized American brand name, shifted to global advertising in the mid-1980s only to return to multidomestic advertising after sales slumped badly; the result was successful. The cause of the failure had been lack of co-operation on the part of the company's country subsidiaries, whose previously successful campaigns were discontinued.

In summary, global advertising is most powerful under the following conditions:

- the *image* communicated can be identical across countries
- the *symbols* used carry the same meaning across countries
- the product *features* desired are the same
- the *usage* conditions are similar across markets.

If all of these conditions hold, as they do in the case of the airlines, global advertising is a natural. When one or more are not fulfilled – as in the case of Levi's – even standardized products may need adapted multidomestic advertising. If the conditions are not right, global advertising will fail, which helps explain why there is still so much controversy about global versus multidomestic advertising.

Exhibit 10.1 Adaptation of Danone's international advertising

From small beginnings, Danone has grown to become a global business that makes yoghurts, yoghurt drinks and fromage frais, designed to make it easy for all the family to live a healthier life. Today Danone Group is the largest producer of fresh dairy products in the world. It produces 18 million tons of cheese, yoghurts and other dairy products per day.

Danone now employs in excess of 100,000 people worldwide and has a turnover of €15,000 mn (2004). It is the world market leader in the dairy products market, where it controls 15.5 per cent. It is also market leader in the bottled water market with its Volvic and Evian brands, and number two in sweet biscuits with Jacobs and Lu.

Danone has adapted its advertising messages to suit different European market expectations. In France, yoghurt is typically sold plain, a symbol of good health. Fruit and flavourings come later, as advertising emphasizes the health aspect. In the UK, the product is often associated with indulgence: fruit adds to the pleasure of eating yoghurt. In Spain or Portugal, where fruit is abundant, consumers prefer plain yogurt, eaten as much by children as by adults. In Italy, consumers prefer blended yoghurt, while flavoured varieties are positioned for very young children. Advertising messages are therefore adjusted accordingly to reflect these preferences.

Source: adapted from www.danone.com; www.business2000.ie

Consolidation of advertising agencies

As ad agencies expanded their global reach, many advertisers started to centralize their advertising spending and appointed a single firm as the global agency. This meant that many smaller agencies lost accounts as large firms consolidated their ad spending. As a result, smaller agencies merged and became part of larger global networks. According to researchers, the emphasis on pan-regional campaigns is mainly due to the emergence of regional groupings and trading blocs.

Local agencies are often preferable (and sometimes the only ones willing to accept the assignment) when the account is small. The reason is that global agencies, owing to their sheer size, tend to neglect smaller accounts.

A breed of generalist 'integrated marketing communications agencies' has recently developed, threatening to reduce the traditional full-service advertising agency's role to provider of one specialist service among many, and starting a reversal of the trend towards multiple delegation.

10.3 Sales promotion

Sales promotion communicates via a variety of promotions not encompassed by any of the definitions above, each aiming for exposure to a target audience and some furthermore offering an incentive to respond actively.

Sales promotions are marketing activities that stimulate consumer purchase and improve retailer or middleman effectiveness and co-operation. They are short-term efforts directed to the consumer or retailer to achieve such specific objectives as consumer product trial or immediate purchase, consumer introduction to the store, gaining retail point-of-purchase displays, encouraging stores to stock a product, and supporting and augmenting advertising and personal sales efforts.

As is the case with advertising, the success of a promotion may depend on local adaptation. Further, research shows that responses to promotions can vary across promotional types and cultures. Major constraints are imposed by local laws, which may not permit premiums or free gifts to be given. Some countries' laws control the amount of discount given at retail, others require permits for all sales promotions. In markets where the consumer is hard to reach because of media limitations, the percentage of the promotional budget allocated to sales promotions may need to be increased. In some less-developed countries, sales promotions constitute the major portion of the promotional effort in rural and less accessible parts of the market.

Different types of sales promotion

Price-based promotions

Discount pricing and sales

Discounting is a widely used form of promotion in a range of markets. It is only effective where the additional sales volume will compensate for the lost revenue, and in markets where a reduction in price will not be interpreted as a reduction in quality. Discounts are a relatively expensive form of promotion in that they provide a price reduction for all consumers, regardless of their price and promotion sensitivity. Discounting also carries with it the danger that it will undermine the consumer's expected reference price, so that they come to expect discounting and will resist a return to 'normal' prices.

Money-off coupons

Coupons are a very popular form of promotion, particularly in fmcg (fast moving consumer goods) markets. Coupons can be delivered by direct mail, in stores, as inserts in publications or on packages. The traditional disadvantages of couponing are in the logistical effort of the redemption-handling process, and consumer resistance to the need to physically clip and carry coupons. New technology may overcome all of these problems with innovations such as barcode scanning for coupons, and 'smart cards' for consumers that store information about coupon entitlements.

Improved payment terms

Interest-free credit and 'buy now, pay later' offers make purchase easier for consumers, and may reduce the real cost of purchase, while allowing the price to stay constant. Special payment terms are popular for relatively expensive consumer durables such as cars and domestic appliances.

Product-based promotions

Product samples

Samples are frequently used to encourage product trial for products such as foods, drinks and toiletries. There are a variety of methods of delivering samples, including direct mail, inserts within publications or packages, and sampling points inside stores. Sampling is a relatively expensive form of promotion, which often involves a high degree of wastage. It can also be difficult to assess its effectiveness, since there is no way to establish whether those who receive samples later go on to purchase (unless the sample is accompanied by a coupon).

Multipacks and multibuys

Offers of 'three for the price of two' are a useful means of getting consumers to stock up on a particular brand. Banding multiple product units or complementary

267

products together can now be accomplished electronically through the use of electronic point-of-sale (EPoS) systems, rather than banding them together physically.

Improved product quality or features

Major consumer durables such as cars or new homes are often marketed with additional free features such as a car stereo or a free fitted kitchen.

Opportunity-based promotions

Competitions

Competitions are a very versatile promotional tool that can be aimed at consumers, intermediaries or the sales force. Selecting the right prize can help to reinforce the brand's image. The limited number of winners and known cost of prizes generally make competitions a very cost-effective form of promotion, and one that can appeal to a wide range of consumers.

Promotional information

A great deal of promotional activity involves providing prospective customers with information that assists their purchasing process. The information provided can also be put into an entertaining and informative format that reinforces the image of the brand and its advertising. Some companies issue information with little in the way of a direct 'selling' message, which aims to educate consumers and hopefully make them likely to act in the company's favour. For example, Procter & Gamble's introduction of Ariel detergent in Egypt included the *Ariel Roadshow*, a puppet show that was taken to local markets in villages, where more than half of all Egyptians still live. The show drew huge crowds, entertained people, informed them about Ariel's better performance without the use of additives, and sold the brand through a distribution van at a nominal discount. Besides creating brand awareness for Ariel, the roadshow helped overcome the reluctance of rural retailers to handle the premium-priced Ariel.

There are many benefits of using sales promotions, but they have also limitations. They will neither compensate for fundamental weaknesses in the rest of the marketing mix, nor revive the fortunes of an outdated brand, and overuse can be counterproductive. Many companies fail to integrate sales promotions with the rest of the marketing strategy and mix.

10.4 **Public relations and sponsorship**

Public relations (PR)

Creating good relationships with the popular press and other media to help companies communicate messages to their publics – customers, the general public and government regulators – is the role of *public relations* (PR). The job consists not only of encouraging the press to cover positive stories about companies, but also of managing unfavourable rumours, stories and events. Effective damage control – actions taken to limit spillover into negative public opinion – requires both good PR and timing.

Corporate communications staff at headquarters and their counterparts in the various host countries serve as promoters of the corporation to various stakeholders interested in the company's foreign expansion. These stakeholders can include a wide variety of groups: stockholders, employees, customers, distributors, suppliers, the financial community, media, activist groups, the general public and government.

Public relations firms' billings in the international arena have been growing at double-digit rates for some years. Handling such international PR problems as global workplace standards is big business for companies serving corporate clients such as Mattel Toys, McDonald's and, of course, Nike. Fast growth is also being fuelled by the expanding international communications industry. New companies need public relations consultation in order to build an international profile.

Sponsorship

With the advent of global media the possibilities for global sponsorships are opening up. Sponsoring the soccer World Cup or the Olympic Games by plastering a brand name on bleachers and piggybacking on television broadcasts has helped companies establish a strong identity in the global marketplace. It is somewhat unsettling, however, to see newspaper pictures of the star-studded national soccer team of Brazil and find that it is sponsored by Nike. Global promotion knows no boundaries.

The global reach of sporting events, which has created opportunities for products to become associated with globally recognized sports stars, has made these stars rich as well as famous. Soccer player David Beckham, for instance, receives more money from endorsements than from playing soccer.

The use of well-known athletes has its downside, though. When the superhuman perfection of the stars is called into question – the cases of O.J. Simpson and Magic Johnson come to mind – sponsorship can be a liability rather than an asset. Athletes don't last for ever either: as part of its efforts to streamline marketing costs in order to compete more effectively in the athletic footwear industry Nike has ceased sponsoring a number of star athletes, including former world number one tennis player Pete Sampras.

Exhibit 10.2 Snickers sponsors key sporting events

Snickers and Mars are two of the largest confectionery 'single bar' brands in the world. At a local level, Snickers' manufacturer Masterfoods Ltd in Ireland invests heavily in maintaining and strengthening its brand image. In the case of Snickers, Masterfoods has found that one of the most effective and targeted marketing tools at its disposal is the sponsorship of key sporting events, the strategy being to position it squarely as an energy booster – it is 'the big eat when you are hungry'.

Source: adapted from: www.masterfooods.com; www.mars.com; www.business2000.ie

Celebrity endorsement

A recent estimate indicates that approximately 25 per cent of US commercials use celebrity endorsers (Silvera and Austad, 2004). In support of this practice, research indicates that celebrity endorsements can result in more favourable advertisement ratings and product evaluations, and can have a substantial positive impact on financial returns for the companies that use them. One possible explanation for the effectiveness of celebrity endorsers is that consumers tend to believe that major stars are motivated by genuine affection for the product rather than by endorsement fees. Celebrities are particularly effective endorsers because they are viewed as highly trustworthy, believable, persuasive and likeable. Although these results unequivocally support the use of celebrity endorsers, other research suggests that celebrity endorsements might vary in effectiveness depending on other factors like the 'fit' between the celebrity and the advertised product.

10.5 **Internet promotion**

The Internet is considered to be a global channel of communication, but advertising messages sent out via this medium are often perceived in the local context by the potential customer. Herein lies the dilemma that often causes the results of Internet promotion to be weaker than anticipated.

Traditional media have two capabilities: building brands and direct marketing. In general, most promotional forms are useful for one or the other. The Internet, however, has the characteristics of both broadcast mass media and direct response advertising.

In the traditional model of communications in the marketplace, there are clear distinctions between the sender, the message and the recipient, and control of the message is with the sender. In 'market space', control of the message is shared between sender and receiver because of the interactivity of the medium, the ability of the medium to carry a message back in reply to that sent, and the impact of the information technology on time, space and communication. The above impacts on the feedback loop are built into the Internet and hence give rise to interference. In general, however, this interference is more likely to be from Internet clutter than from external sources.

The web represents a change away from a push strategy in international promotion – where a producer focuses on convincing an intermediary to represent the products or services, or a distributor to stock its goods – and towards a pull strategy, in which the producer communicates directly with the customer. In this transition process promotional and other transaction costs are reduced. The feature that differentiates the Internet from other promotional vehicles is its interactivity. This results in the special feature that the Internet combines the attributes of both selling and advertising. Interactivity facilitates a completely new approach to reaching potential customers. Unlike television, for example, where the consumer passively observes, with the web there is an active intention to log on to the Internet, and a greater degree of attention to content as a result. With the Internet the potential customer has a high-involvement approach to advertising. A continual stream of decisions is demanded from the user:

each click represents a decision and therefore the web is a very high-involvement medium. In addition, unlike traditional media, the web is a medium by which the user can 'click through' and obtain more information or actually purchase a product. Web advertisements can be, and often are, targeted to a user profile that in turn affects the way the message will be received. Increasingly, ads displayed on the web are specific to user interests and appear as these interests are revealed while the user navigates the web.

In order to provide value to the potential international customer, and hold his or her interest, a website must be attractive and user-friendly. This involves an appealing design, being available in the buyer's language (or one with which the buyer is likely to be familiar) and being aesthetically aware in terms of colours and backgrounds used (taking into account buyers' cultural norms). A site should be easy to navigate, contain the information that the buyer is likely to want and be easy to access.

The most common form of advertising on the web (as opposed to advertising the existence of a website) is banners across the top of commercial sites, known as 'banner ads' (Fletcher *et al.*, 2004).

Effective online advertising strategies

An effective advertising strategy for online advertising aims to target the right advertisement message to the right person at the right time (Kumar and Shah, 2004).

Who to advertise to

Is online advertising for everyone? Experienced marketers will tell you that advertisement design depends on the type of product or service being sold and the desired target segment. Let us dig a layer deeper and divide the desired target segment into first-time visitors to the company's website, registered users and general information seekers. There is bound to be some overlap across these segments. However, this form of segmentation can provide useful insights when designing online advertising. Based on the user segment, a website can be programmed to respond appropriately. For example, every first-time visitor to a website can be made to see the same advertisement. Visitors identified as information seekers may be shown useful content instead of products and services, and registered users may see a customized advertisement message based on their profiles. Technologically, it is feasible to identify the type of user visiting a website by studying their browsing behaviour through clickstream data and by using files known as 'cookies' (a cookie is a piece of code that is retained on a computer user's hard disk, which enables a website to store information that can be retrieved later – the user's ID, preferences for that site, and so on).

How to advertise

After identifying the user or the website visitor, the next step is determining how to advertise or what format to use for advertising. There are several different formats currently being used for Internet advertisements. Interestingly, the form of advertising chosen by online marketers is undergoing a rapid transformation. What was previously dominant has now fallen out of favour, and what had been weak has now grown strong. The type of advertisement chosen should be directed towards not only 'pushing' the message across but also 'pulling' the customer to click deeper into the website by designing ads that contribute to the overall website experience. For example, a website with too many pop-up ads on its first page runs the risk of driving the user away.

What to advertise

People use the Internet to seek information as well as products and services. Marketers can be creative and design advertisements that simply offer helpful information to the user. For example, a user browsing for a digital camera may be offered useful tips and pointers on how to get the best results from digital photography. Non-commercial advertising like this may not have a short-term financial gain but may definitely contribute to a superior browsing experience leading to customer loyalty and repeat visits from the user.

If the customer's profile or past purchasing history is known, it is possible to predict future purchase behaviour. For example, let's assume that a user purchased a home appliance online. Given this information and the profile of the user (perhaps she is a woman, aged 30–40), it is possible to predict what she is most likely to buy next. The company can programme this information into its website code and the next time this user is detected returning to the website there will be an advertisement ready and waiting for her with the desired content. If deployed properly, this approach can help marketers to cross-sell products through combinations of online advertisement messaging.

When to advertise

The first three dimensions of the advertising strategy discussed so far will be rendered ineffective if the timing is not right. In the case of offline media, one can proactively call up the customer or send him/her a direct mailing at a specific time with a customized advertising message. However, these rules do not apply online; in the case of the Internet, users may decide to go online and visit the website during working hours, in the middle of the night or whenever they feel like it. Therefore, timing, in the Internet context, would refer to the time from the instant a user is detected online.

So when should the advertisement be triggered? As soon as the user comes online, after he/she has browsed for a while, or at the time of the first purchase? Studies conducted with Internet ad timings have indicated that generally response (clickthrough) to pop-ups is greater when the ad appears immediately after the user enters the site. However, the results could vary greatly depending on the user segment and the user's information-seeking purposes.

Amazon.com employs a subtle form of advertisement in real time. Basically, while performing a search for a particular book, the search also throws up a list on the side or bottom of the page of relevant books that may complement the book the user was originally considering for purchase. Also, when a user logs on to the site, Amazon pulls up their purchase history and profile to proactively suggest books or items that they may have a latent propensity to purchase next.

Where to advertise

It is crucial to make Internet ads visible at vantage points that maximize their hit rate with the intended target segment. Unlike other forms of media, where one can pick a well-defined spot within a finite set of possibilities, cyberspace offers an infinite number of possibilities across thousands of portals, search engines and online publishers, as well as multiple possibilities within the vendor's website. Identifying the perfect spot may seem like searching for a needle in a haystack.

There are two ways to tackle this. The first is to take the easy way out. Follow intuition and place advertisements at obvious locations, such as frequently visited portals and search engines. This is not, however, a cost-effective solution. A more sophisticated approach involves analysing the browsing pattern of an Internet user on a company's website using the website's log files. Analysis of these files can help model the browsing behaviour of a random visitor to the website. Based on this information, Internet ad displays may be placed at appropriate locations. Marketing managers can also leverage this model to sell complementary products to potential users. For example, a department store such as Marks & Spencer may advertise cosmetics on the page where a user is buying fragrances online. An electronics store like Best Buy may advertise the latest CD releases on the page listing different audio systems.

However, this form of analysis is limited to advertising within the company's website. A more advanced research approach involves modelling browsing behaviour at multiple websites using clickstream data. Information analysed in this manner renders a total view of a customer's online habits before purchase consideration. Such information is invaluable to marketers who are interested in knowing when and where they are most likely to find their potential customers and, based on that information, how they should place Internet advertisements in order to pull the relevant customers to their site.

Online performance tracking (metrics)

Having designed an online advertising strategy, the next critical step is to track its performance. Traditional offline media (radio, television and print advertisements) have well-defined and well-researched metrics in place that can accurately measure ad effectiveness. For example, there are many years of research testimony to show what a television commercial can do; Internet advertisements have a long way to go on this front.

Some of the most commonly used measures include:

- **clickthroughs** – the number of times that users click on an advertisement
- **cost per click** – the amount spent by the advertiser to generate one clickthrough
- **cost per action/lead (CPA/L)** – the amount spent by the advertiser to generate one lead, one desired action, or simply information on one likely user; the advertiser pays an amount based upon the number of users who fulfil the desired action
- **cost per sale (CPS)** – the amount spent by the advertiser to generate one sale; here, the advertiser pays an amount based upon how many users actually purchase something.

Increasingly, a large number of marketers claim to be optimizing their online campaigns using the 'cost per sale' metric, but it is clear that they are looking at sales (through online advertisements) as strictly margin transactions. The problem with this approach is that, while each individual transaction may look profitable to start with, this may not necessarily hold true over the lifetime duration of the customer. Similarly, initial returns that seem to be unprofitable may translate into very profitable transactions when measured over the lifetime value of the customer.

Therefore, customer lifetime value (CLV), which may be defined as the measure of expected value of profit to a business derived from customer relationships from the current time to some future point, is perhaps the most relevant of all metrics (see also Chapter 11). It provides a direct linkage on a customer-by-customer basis to what is most important for any company: profits. Marketing spend and outcome of advertisements guided by lifetime value measures would yield the most superior decision support system for a marketer. As companies become increasingly customer-centric, a switch to a customer lifetime value metric and building of buyer loyalty will become inevitable.

Building buyer loyalty

Using the web as a vehicle for building loyalty on the part of international buyers involves a number of different stages (Fletcher *et al.*, 2004), as described below.

Attract

Attract clients to visit the website. They do so on a voluntary basis and will not come simply because a site has been created. To create awareness of a site, it is necessary to use banner ads and links to other sites.

Engage

Engage visitors' attention. This is necessary in order to get the visitor to a site in order to participate and encourage interaction. Most sites fail as promotional mediums because they are boring and have poorly presented material. In this regard, the content of the site is most important.

Retain

Retain the visitor's interest in your site. This is important to ensure repeat visits to the site and the creation of a one-to-one relationship between the firm and its potential overseas customers. One way of achieving this is by persuading the customer to provide information on their requirements so that the firm can customize its offering and thereby increase switching costs.

Learn

Learn about the client and their preferences. This is enabled by providing on the site an easy-to-use facility for feedback and comment. The use of cookies can assist in this.

Relate

Adopt a deliberate policy of building relationships with site visitors. This is achieved by providing value-added content, by tailoring the product/service to the needs of each customer and promising customized delivery.

The web as a customer acquisition tool

Attracting visitors to a company's website is a big step, but it is only the first: turning them into buyers is a bigger challenge, and one at which many online sellers fail. The average sales conversion ratio across online B2C merchants is just 1.8 per cent (Vishwanath and Mulvin, 2001).

Companies lose potential customers at different stages in the purchasing process (see Fig. 10.1). The stages at which customers lose interest can be summarized under the following headings:

- homepage
- product search
- after product found
- shopping cart
- failure to repeat purchase.

One reason for defection that applies throughout each of these stages is unacceptable download times.

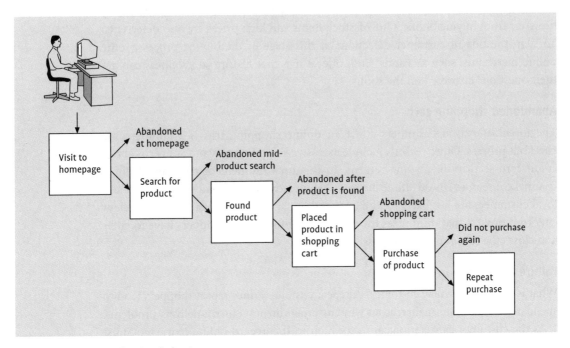

Figure 10.1 Internet buying behaviour

We will now look at each of these stages in turn.

Abandoned at homepage

There are many reasons why a visitor may take one look at your homepage and decide to leave. Errant advertising is a leading cause.

Established 'clicks-and-mortar' companies have an advantage over pure plays in attracting visitors. People know from experience what the company sells. But even well-established brands can lose a significant percentage of their homepage visitors. Often, it is poor design features such as slow download time or confusing navigation that drive them away.

Abandoned mid-product search

Customers who leave the website while they're still perusing merchandise typically do so when they can't find what they're looking for. Perhaps the selection is too limited or the shopper has run out of gift ideas. Best-practice merchants such as Victoria's Secret overcome such problems by feeding the visitor suggestions ('We think you'll also love …'), directing them to the recipient's wish list, or promoting online gift certificates.

Abandoned after product is found

Even after online customers find what they are looking for, many stop short of making a purchase. There are many reasons for this: for example, net shoppers who decide not to purchase gifts online may want to actually see the physical product before buying it. Tiny pictures and incomplete product information keep many browsers from buying online. Out-of-stock items and high prices are also deterrents. To stem the tide of customer defections at this stage of the buying process, some online merchants, such as Lands' End, offer a live chat feature so shoppers can get their questions answered on the spot.

Abandoned shopping cart

The foremost reason customers abort an online shopping trip is a cumbersome checkout process. Other reasons include excessive shipping costs and concerns about credit-card security or making returns. In this final moment of reckoning, multi-channel companies whose offline business has already established a strong brand and loyal customers are less likely to lose out on the sale. Retailers must have an efficient checkout process that minimizes the amount of information shoppers have to enter and closes the sale as quickly as possible.

Failure to repeat purchase

What is better than a new customer? A repeat customer, since repeat shoppers tend to spend more. One of the main reasons why customers do not return is delivery problems.

As the customer expectations are very high in this regard online marketers must make or buy a back-end system that will meet or exceed customer needs. Managing customer expectations is also important. In the case of stockouts or back orders, it is better to give shoppers the bad news *before* they submit an order rather than to send a follow-up e-mail, as some e-retailers do. While the result may be a lost sale, preserving the customer relationship is more profitable in the long run.

Unacceptable download times

Another factor in customer abandonment that is relevant at all points in the transaction chain is slow download and server response times. Five seconds is considered the current 'breaking point' for page downloads, above which customers will go elsewhere. Even this number would seem to be on the high side – the top 10 online retailers all have download times under two seconds. Meanwhile, consumer expectations are continually rising. Companies that decline to make the necessary investments to keep their websites fast may see declines in sales and retention; but they should be careful how they invest in their sites – fancy graphics and interactivity features designed to simplify the purchase process can actually slow down transaction times, especially since many potential customers do not have high bandwidth. Even if the servers are adequate, a data-rich website (such as one with lots of images, flash capabilities or sound) may render your site maddeningly slow and impractical for a large percentage of your potential customers. The key for retailers is to find the balance between the site's marketing impact, its functionality, and the ability of company and consumer infrastructure to handle the content.

Viral marketing

Another example of cost-effective internet promotion for online customer acquisition is *viral marketing*, the multiplier effect achieved when visitors to a website provide contact information not only for themselves but also for others who may be interested in a product or service, or when they pass on the site's information to others. Visitors to 1-800-flowers.com, for example, can choose from an assortment of flowers and vases to create and send a virtual bouquet – free of charge. In exchange, the company gets e-mail addresses for two potential customers – the flowers' sender and their recipient – to whom they can then market the real thing (Vishwanath and Mulvin, 2001).

M-marketing

Mobile marketing, or m-marketing, should be considered within the context of m-business and m-commerce. Emerging from recent developments in communications technology, m-business represents 'mobile' business and refers to the new communications and information delivery model created when telecommunications and the Internet converge. Thus m-marketing is defined as the application of marketing to the mobile environment of smart phones, mobile phones, personal digital assistants (PDAs) and telematics. M-marketing is characterized by both the interaction with the World Wide Web and the location-specific context, which enhances communication and delivery of information. Marketing communication and information can be delivered to mobile devices via voice-activated portals, or 'vortals', text applications such as SMS, using e-mail (the current I-mode application), and via web-mediated delivery using the 3G spectrum.

M-commerce combines the power and speed of the Internet with the geographic freedom of mobile telephony in terms of receiving and transmitting data and, importantly, the ability to conduct transactions. The emerging capacity to communicate with any individual, from any place, over any network and to any device, regardless of time or geographical location, provides enormous potential for marketers. For this reason, the impact on marketing strategies for direct marketers needs to be addressed.

The emphasis on real-world interactions is paramount and creates a compelling difference between m-applications and traditional web-based delivery. The mobile environment is not suitable for surfing the net, sorting through large and random accumulations of information requiring large amounts of time; therefore, information needs to be in small 'packets', and products and applications should be developed around business models that are likely to deliver real value using the unique features and immediacy of mobile interactivity to target customers. Volvo was the first company to use direct m-marketing in Australia, to launch the Volvo S60. This successful campaign using wireless hand-held palm pilots highlights the potential for targeting appropriate segments cost effectively by using opt-in e-mail (Mort and Drennan, 2002).

10.6 Direct marketing

Direct marketing is defined by the Direct Marketing Association (DMA) as 'an interactive marketing system that uses one or more advertising media to effect a measurable response and/or transaction at any location'. It is a more encompassing concept than direct sales, which simply refers to sales from the producer directly to the ultimate consumer, bypassing the channel middlemen. Direct marketing is not so much a promotional tool as a new distribution channel, but it grew out of direct mail, which is a traditional advertising medium. The traditional direct mail promotions of various products often offered 'direct response' options, including requests for more information, redeemable money-off coupons, and participation in contests and lottery draws. It was only a small step to a completed sale, and especially since credit cards have become common, direct mail has grown into an important promotion *and* sales channel.

The traditional direct marketing medium is *mail order*, with catalogues and sales offers sent directly to individual households, which then order via mail. The names and addresses are drawn from various lists – in the beginning often from subscription lists of newspapers and magazines but, today, more often from commercial data banks that can screen for key words and develop lists of qualified prospects. In recent years, *telemarketing*, selling via the telephone, has grown, and so has direct-response television (DRTV), where TV commercials will list telephone numbers that allow viewers to call and make purchases.

With the growing presence of the Internet, direct marketing has become a very important channel. There is no doubt that the Internet has changed the way people communicate. For many, email has virtually replaced traditional letters and even telephone calls as first choice for communication. Every day, billions of email messages are sent out. This has also influenced our way of doing business.

Email marketing

Done well, email marketing can be the most cost-effective communications tool you have. It is fast, inexpensive and effective, and its response rates are many times that of direct mail. Unfortunately, however, the email marketing landscape is littered with examples of marketers getting labelled as spammers, annoying customers, violators of privacy laws and worse.

A major strength of direct email is its ability to qualify leads. Appropriate software allows the firm to track who is reading and responding, along with the types of responses. This enables the firm to segment the audience accordingly, targeting future communications based on recipients' self-reported priorities.

The following is an example of a checklist for launching a successful email marketing campaign (Linkon, 2004).

- **Solid planning**. Have clear and measurable objectives, and plan your campaign as if it was a space shuttle launch.

- **Excellent content**. Standards are higher with email, so make sure you are offering genuine value to the subscriber.

- **Appropriate and real 'from' field**. This is the first thing recipients look at when they are deciding whether or not to open an email.

- **Strong 'subject' field**. The next place recipients look before deciding whether to open an email is the subject field. Make it compelling.

- **Right frequency and timing**. Do not overwhelm your audience. Do not send e-mails Friday to Monday or outside normal business hours.

- **Appropriate use of graphics**. Do not get carried away. If graphics add real value and aren't too big, use them. However, save most of them for your website.

- **Lead with your strength**. Do not bury your best content or offer. Make sure it is at the top or at the email equivalent of 'above the fold'.

- **Shorter is better**. Nobody reads a lot these days, and they read even less in email than elsewhere.

- **Personalize**. Use just three or four elements of personalization and your response rates can improve by 60 per cent. Try to go beyond just the first name. Learn about your subscribers.

- **Link to your website**. This is where richness of content and interactivity can really reside. Tease readers with the email so they will link to your website. Advertising can also be incorporated, serving the same role as the initial email: to create a desire in the audience for more information. The website catch page is crucial to this tactic and is often where many firms falter when integrating traditional advertising with online promotions. Let us say, for instance, that you are in the market for a small hand-held video camera and come across a magazine ad for exactly the product you need. The ad offers a web address, but when you go there you find the company's general website. It takes more than a dozen clicks before you find the product mentioned in the ad. You have gone from elation to frustration. A website catch page should fulfil your promise to the audience that when they go to the address, they will receive information on the offer that brought them there. From the catch page you can invite them to click to a more general website to make a donation, send a letter, sign a petition, learn who has endorsed your effort, or learn more about related causes, sales or promotions.

■ **Measure and improve**. The ability to measure basics such as open and click-through rates is one of the main advantages of email marketing, but do not stop there: also track sales or other conversions. Learn from what works and make the necessary adjustments.

Mobile telephone marketing (SMS ads)

A survey (Enpocket.com, 2003) showed that almost a quarter of people who receive SMS ad messages will show or pass them on to a friend. The findings conclude that 15 per cent of people will respond in some way to a mobile campaign. Responses to a mobile marketing campaign include replying to the message (8 per cent), visiting a website (6 per cent), watching TV (6 per cent), buying the advertised product (4 per cent), visiting a shop/retail outlet (4 per cent) and calling a phone number (2 per cent). This indicates that mobile telephone campaigns can outperform other response media channels, such as direct marketing and email.

10.7 **Personal selling**

Because of the importance of personal factors in selling, it is not surprising to find that good salesmanship varies across countries. Personal selling is usually the least global of all the marketing activities.

When a company wants to have more control than with independent distributors and takes over distribution in a country, it will usually end up establishing its own sales force. Doing this in a foreign country requires faith in the market and considerable resources. But some companies, especially those for which the selling function is a key success factor, have decided to take the plunge, and have done it successfully.

Structuring and managing a sales force (Cateora and Graham, 2004) involves:

■ designing the sales force

■ recruiting marketing and sales personnel

- selecting sales and marketing personnel
- training for international marketing
- motivating sales personnel
- designing compensation systems
- evaluating and controlling sales representatives.

We will now look at each of these in turn.

Designing the sales force

Based on analyses of current and potential customers, the selling environment, competition, and the firm's resources and capabilities, decisions must be made regarding the numbers, characteristics and assignments of sales personnel. All these design decisions are made more challenging by the wide variety of pertinent conditions and circumstances in international markets.

After decisions have been made about how many expatriates, local nationals or third-country nationals a particular market requires, then more intricate aspects of design can be dealt with, such as territory allocation and customer call plans.

Many things can differ across cultures: length of sales cycles, the kinds of customer relationships, and types of interaction with customers.

Recruiting marketing and sales personnel

The number of marketing management personnel from the home country assigned to foreign countries varies according to the size of the operation and the availability of qualified locals. The largest personnel requirement abroad for most companies is the sales force, recruited from three sources: expatriates, local nationals and third-country nationals. A company's staffing pattern may include all three types in any single foreign operation, depending on qualifications, availability and a company's needs.

The advantages and disadvantages of the three types of international sales force are summarized in Table 10.2.

Selecting sales and marketing personnel

To select personnel for international marketing positions effectively, management must define precisely what is expected of its people. A formal job description can aid management in expressing long-range needs as well as current needs. In addition to descriptions of each marketing position, the criteria should include special requirements indigenous to various countries.

International personnel require a kind of 'emotional stability' not demanded in domestic positions. Regardless of location, these people are living in cultures dissimilar to their own; to some extent they are always under scrutiny and always aware that they

Table 10.2 **Advantages and disadvantages of international sales force types**

Category	Advantages	Disadvantages
Expatriate (person sent out from home base – HQ)	■ Greater control is possible from home base (HQ) ■ Knowledge about product, technology, history and management policies ■ High service levels ■ Willing to learn as it is often training for later promotion	■ Highest costs ■ High training costs ■ Lack of local cultural understanding ■ High staff turnover
Host country (local person)	■ Economical, 'good' solution ■ Best cultural knowledge ■ High market knowledge ■ Local language skills ■ Access to local network of relevant decision-makers	■ Needs product training ■ May be held in low esteem ■ Importance of language skills declining ■ Difficult to ensure loyalty
Third country	■ Allows regional coverage ■ Cultural sensitivity ■ Language skills ■ Economical ■ May allow sales to country in conflict with the home country	■ May face identity problems ■ Income gaps ■ Needs product/company gaps ■ Blocked for promotion in the company ■ Resources needed for loyalty assurance

are official representatives of the company abroad. They need sensitivity to behavioural variations in different countries, but they cannot be so hypersensitive that their behaviour is adversely affected.

Managers or sales people operating in foreign countries need considerable breadth of knowledge of many subjects, both on and off the job. The ability to speak one or more additional languages is always preferable.

An international sales person must have a high level of flexibility, whether working in a foreign country or at home. Expatriates working in a foreign country must be particularly sensitive to the habits of the market; those working at home for a foreign company must adapt to the requirements and ways of the parent company.

Cultural empathy is also clearly part of the basic orientation because it is unlikely that anyone can be effective if they are confused about their environment. Finally, international sales and marketing personnel must be energetic and enjoy travel.

Selection mistakes are costly. When an expatriate assignment does not work out, a great deal of money has probably been wasted in expenses and lost time. Getting the right person to handle the job is also important in the selection of locals to work for foreign companies within their home country.

Training for international marketing

Many companies send their new sales reps into the field almost immediately upon hiring them, after only a cursory training programme. The rationale is that time is best spent prospecting and meeting with customers, rather than sitting in a training centre (Crittenden and Crittenden, 2004). It is true that detailed training can be costly and may result in lost opportunities when a seller is not in the field. Yet effective long-term sellers must not only have appropriate personal characteristics, but must also know and identify with the company and its products, understand customer buying motives, and be prepared to make an effective sales presentation, counter initial resistance, and close the sale. Moreover, to be successful, the seller has to know how to develop and maintain the records necessary to process orders, service customers and cultivate repeat sales.

The nature of a training programme depends largely on whether expatriate or local personnel are being trained for overseas positions. Training for expatriates focuses on customs and special foreign sales problems that will be encountered, whereas local personnel require greater emphasis on the company, its products, technical information and selling methods.

The Internet now makes some kinds of sales training much more efficient. Users can study text on-screen and participate in interactive assessment tests.

Firms may also need to devote resources towards training the trainers. Top sellers who move into positions where they also manage other reps do not necessarily have the appropriate skills, mind-set or disposition to train others.

Motivating sales personnel

Motivation is especially complicated because the firm is dealing with different cultures, different sources and different philosophies. Selling is hard, competitive work wherever it is undertaken, and a constant flow of inspiration is needed to keep personnel functioning at an optimal level. National differences must always be considered in motivating the marketing force.

Communications are also important in maintaining high levels of motivation; foreign managers need to know that the domestic office is interested in their operations, and, in turn, they want to know what is happening in the parent country. Everyone performs better when well informed. However, differences in language, culture and communication styles can make mutual understanding between managers and sales representatives difficult.

Designing compensation systems

Developing an equitable and functional compensation plan that combines balance, consistent motivation and flexibility is extremely challenging in international operations. Besides rewarding an individual's contribution to the firm, a compensation programme can be used effectively to recruit, develop, motivate or retain personnel.

International compensation programmes also provide additional payments for 'hardship' locations and special inducements to reluctant personnel to accept overseas employment and to remain in the position. The compensation plans of companies vary substantially around the world, reflecting the economic and cultural differences in the diverse markets served.

It is difficult to design compensation programmes that motivate sales forces without financially ruining a company. The sections below take a closer look at some of the payment plans available.

Straight salary

Perhaps the simplest reward system for sales people involves paying a fixed amount each pay period. The major benefits to a firm of paying by salary are greater control over wage levels and generally lower compensation for field sales people. With a salary plan, wages are a fixed cost to the firm, and the proportion of wage expense tends to decrease as sales increase.

Straight salary is common in industrial selling where service and engineering skills are important. It is also effective when sales people spend their time calling on retailers to set up displays, take inventory and arrange shelves. 'Pharmaceutical detail' people, for example, are not expected to make direct sales and are paid a salary to strengthen relations with doctors and pharmacists. Because pay is not tied directly to performance, salary systems are often criticized for failing to provide incentives for extra effort.

Straight commission

A straight commission plan rewards people for their accomplishments rather than for their time. Also, sales people who are paid commission typically make more money than they do with other wage programmes. Higher wages tend to attract better-qualified applicants and provide a strong incentive to work hard. Despite some obvious advantages, straight commission also has a number of drawbacks. The major problem is that sales managers have little control over sales people working on commission, and non-selling activities are likely to be neglected. Sales people working on commission are likely to be tempted to sell themselves rather than the company, as well as to service only the best accounts in their territories. Because sales people's wages are directly related to sales to particular accounts, sales people are often reluctant to have their territories changed in any way.

Combination plans

The most common compensation plan combines a base salary with a commission and/or bonus. The base salary provides sales people with income security and the commission and/or bonus offers an added incentive to meet the company's objectives. If an organization wants a modest incentive, a plan could be designed so that 70 per cent of the compensation is salary and 30 per cent is earned by commissions or bonuses. Firms that need more push to move their products could raise the incentive portion to 50 per cent or more.

Evaluating and controlling sales representatives

In evaluation and control of sales representatives in the United States, emphasis is often placed on individual performance, which can easily be measured by sales revenues generated (often compared with past performance, forecasts or quotas). However, in many countries the evaluation problem is more complex, particularly in relationship-orientated cultures (e.g. in some European and Asian countries) where teamwork is favoured over individual effort. Performance measures require closer observation and may include the opinions of customers, peers and supervisors. On the other hand, managers of sales forces operating in relationship-orientated cultures may see measures of individual performance as relatively unimportant.

10.8 **Push and pull strategies**

The distinguishing features of push and pull strategies are illustrated in Fig. 10.2 (note that both the wholesaler and the retailer are contained in the 'Distributor' box).

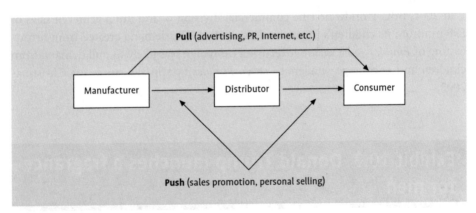

Figure 10.2 Push and pull strategies
Source: *Marketing Management*, Hollensen, Pearson Education Limited (2003)

Push strategy

A push promotional strategy makes use of a company's sales force, and trade promotion activities create distributor demand for a product. The producer promotes the product to wholesalers, the wholesalers promote it to retailers, and the retailers promote it to consumers. A good example of push selling is mobile phones, where the major handset manufacturers, such as Nokia, promote their products via retailers such as Carphone Warehouse. Personal selling and trade promotions are often the most effective promotional tools for companies such as Nokia – for example, offering subsidies on handsets to encourage retailers to sell higher volumes. With this type of strategy, personal selling, sales promotion and trade promotion are the most likely promotional tools.

Pull strategy

A pull selling strategy is one that requires high spending on advertising and consumer promotion to build up consumer demand for a product. If the strategy is successful, consumers will ask their retailers for the product, the retailers will ask the wholesalers, and the wholesalers will ask the producers.

A good example of a pull is the heavy advertising and promotion of children's toys, mainly on television. Consider the recent BBC promotional campaign for its new pre-school programme *Fimbles*. Aimed at two to four year olds, 130 episodes of *Fimbles* have been made so far, and they are featured every day on digital children's channel CBeebies as well as BBC2.

As part of its promotional campaign for *Fimbles*, the BBC has agreed a deal with toy maker Fisher-Price to market products based on the show, which it hopes will emulate the popularity of *Tweenies* (another successful TV series for young children). Under the terms of the deal, Fisher-Price develops, manufactures and distributes a range of *Fimbles* products, including soft, plastic and electronic learning toys, for the UK and Ireland.

In 2001, BBC Worldwide (the commercial division of the BBC) achieved sales of £90 mn from its children's brands and properties. The demand created from broadcasting of *Fimbles* and a major advertising campaign was likely to pull demand from children and encourage retailers to stock *Fimbles* toys in the stores for Christmas 2002.

Exhibit 10.3 **Donald Trump launches a fragrance for men**

In September 2004 Donald Trump announced a deal with Aramis and Designer Fragrances, a division of the Estée Lauder Company, to market his new business venture: Donald Trump, The Fragrance.

At the launch, Donald Trump said, 'My new partnership with Aramis and Designer Fragrances is huge. They are leaders in the industry. Donald Trump, The Fragrance, will be the best men's scent available and the must-have gift for the holidays.'

A spokeswoman for Estée Lauder said that the top note, or scent, of the cologne contains citrus notes with hints of mint, cucumber and black basil. The core note is made from an exotic plant – which the company keeps secret – that provides a green effect with woody undertones, rounded out with spicy, peppery accents. The finish comes from exotic woods and has earthy, herbaceous and spicy notes.

The geometric glass bottle in which the fragrance is sold is tall, slim and clear, and comes wrapped, of course, in gold packaging.

Aramis president Fabrice Weber said, 'We are confident that men of all ages want to experience some part of Mr Trump's passion and taste for luxury. People want to know him on every level.'

If you had responsibility for setting up an advertising plan for the Trump fragrance, what would your proposals be?

Source: adapted from Hargreaves (2004)

10.9 Combining communications and distribution: multi-channel customer management (MCCM)

Companies are moving towards the world of multichannel integration where we will see an increasing integration between *distribution channels* (through which products or services reach customers from suppliers, including transfer of title) and *communication channels* (through which customers and suppliers communicate with each other before, during and after distribution channels do their work).

A broad definition of the term 'multi-channel customer management' (MCCM) is as follows:

> Multi-channel customer management is the use of more than one channel or medium to manage customers in a way that is consistent and co-ordinated across all the channels or media used.

Note that this definition does not say that customers are managed in 'the same way', as different channels may be best used for different tasks. For example, in a complex, technical, business-to-business environment, a sales person may offer the best way to explain the product, meet objections, deal with queries and set up initial contacts, while the web or a call centre might be used for re-ordering or checking progress with delivery. Also, it may be that channels are used in a differentiated manner – for example, if a person wants to buy tickets for last-minute cancellations by other customers (anything from flights to equipment orders), they are referred to an auction website as other channels cannot support this kind of interaction cost effectively. Many companies are in a transition phase in terms of channel management:

- they are moving away from channels dedicated to restricted tasks and not communicating with each other, but are not certain how far to move towards channels that all work with the same data and to the same objectives

- they have seen some of the disadvantages of having different, and possibly incompatible, technology platforms for each channel, but are not certain of the benefits of moving to a single platform

- they have been through the process of setting up dotcoms as separate web channels

- separate web channels often had their own objectives, management, staff and systems, usually experienced escalating costs, provided a customer experience that was very different from that of other channels, and in some cases created brand damage and increased customer churn.

A multi-channel strategy is one that provides numerous customer touchpoints – the points at which products and services are purchased or serviced – across several distribution channels, such as:

- direct channels, e.g. telephone, Internet, mobile telephone (voice, SMS) and interactive television (iTV)

- counter and kiosk service in branch networks or retail outlets — partnerships and alliances – sales force

- service force.

In some cases, these may be supported by broadcast media, in which the customer is not necessarily identified (e.g. television, radio, press and some web applications).

Why is multi-channel customer management important now?

There are two main reasons for the current importance of multi-channel customer management.

1 **Developments in new channel technology:** increasing reliability and speed of storage and telecommunications technology, convergence of voice, video and data.

2 **Customer requirements and expectations:** some (not all) customers expect technology and processes to be used to manage them more consistently across channels.

Although it is now easier to ensure that every channel dealing directly with a given customer has the latest data on the state of interaction between supplier and customer, and follows related, connected processes, this is neither cost-free nor without technical problems. In particular, it should be noted that the companies for whom it is suggested that multi-channel customer management will yield the most benefits are those for whom achieving it is most problematic. They have the largest customer bases, the most complex lines and the longest history of systems development, with many business-critical systems that support the process of customer management being quite old. This applies, for example, to many companies in the financial services, logistics and manufacturing industries.

Drivers of multi-channel customer management

The seven factors discussed below are causing companies to focus on multi-channel management.

Customer demand

Customers' desire for convenience has partly fuelled the increasing requirement for multi-channel integration. Increased customer expectations translate to a demand for 24/7 high-speed access and choice in how they interact with a company. Customers often have strong preferences for using a specific channel for particular kinds of interaction – for example, they may use the in-store channel to commit to a buying decision, while using the more convenient online channel for exploring options.

Strategic competitive advantage and differentiation

Products can be copied within days (some fashion retailers can copy a design from the catwalk and get it on to the high street within a week). Pricing can be undercut within minutes. Apart from branding, multi-channel management is one of the few customer-facing differentiators that can deliver true sustainable competitive advantage.

Channel costs

Maintaining channels (including marketing, advertising and managing the channels themselves) can typically account for around 40 per cent of a company's costs. Channels tend to be managed and maintained in silos, with multiple infrastructures, management teams, technology and, possibly, different marketing strategies. The potential sharing and reuse of people, process and technology that can be achieved through an integrated channel strategy can, however, help improve an organization's channel cost structure. Furthermore, the mapping of high-value customer usage and preferences can help identify channel areas of over-investment and channels that are not providing their optimum ROI, consequently pinpointing those channels that require some form of disinvestment and asset reallocation.

Allowing customers to manage relationships

Badly executed customer relationship management (CRM) – as, sadly, many CRM implementations are – can result in the organization trying to control customers almost against their will through specific channels at specific times in the buying cycle. Customers can end up being made to feel like cattle being herded. Customer satisfaction and sales plummet. The term 'customer-managed relationship' (CMR) recognizes the possibility of the customer being in control and the idea that it is the supplier's job to nurture and service the relationship.

Convergence of channel roles

Traditionally, channels were usually silos with most, if not all, of the functions required in the customer-buying cycle being fulfilled through one channel. Now, at many companies, several channels are used during each customer-buying cycle and these need to be designed, maintained and measured appropriately.

Increased variety in customers' channel use patterns

Those who synchronize their distribution channels will preserve or gain market share. Research has shown that multi-channel shoppers in the financial services and retail sectors represent an increasingly large proportion of the attractive buying population. Furthermore, in the retail banking sector, multi-channel customers are 25 to 50 per cent more profitable than those using one channel, while retail shoppers who use multi-channel purchasing spend two to four times more than those who purchase through a single channel. These findings are reinforced by the Boston Consulting Group (BCG), whose research revealed that European retailers who have an offline presence and manage an integrated Internet channel enjoy a disproportionate market share, and that online satisfied customers spend 71 per cent more and transact 2.5 times more than dissatisfied ones (Stone, 2002).

Providing the target high-value multi-channel customer segment with increased convenience through integrated channel management thus not only encourages customer lock-on and brand loyalty, but results in improved customer lifetime value.

Regulatory pressure

In some sectors (e.g. financial services, the public sector) government has a strong interest in the cost effectiveness and quality of channel use, particularly where high channel costs lead to customers apparently getting poor value or even to customers being excluded or disenfranchised.

Benefits of and problems with multi-channel customer management (MCCM)

The benefits

The benefits of multi-channel customer management are numerous. These include benefits that work *through customers*, ones that work *for customers* and ones that work *through efficiency*, as described below.

The benefits for companies working with MCCM are:

- the identification and capture of opportunities for increasing value per customer

- increased convenience and an improved experience, reducing customer churn rates and increasing their motivation to buy more from the supplier

- the ability to leverage an established brand, creating positive impacts on brand perception and mitigating the risk of brand damage, increasing the incentive for customers to stay and buy more

- increased efficiency through the sharing of processes, technology and information

- increased organizational flexibility

- increased efficiency in dealing with business partners, so they can reduce their costs

- increased efficiency in exploiting customer data to identify customer needs, possibly indicating new paths for growth.

The benefits for customers are:

- increased choice in the way they can interact

- the ability to switch easily between the various channels, when it suits them and wherever they want to, depending on their preference and the type of interaction, whether it be the exploration or purchase of a product or service.

For the supplier, channel integration helps facilitate the sharing of customer data across channels to create a more complete customer profile, which will help maximize cross-selling opportunities.

Problems

Multi-channel integration does not come without its challenges, however. Problems experienced by companies include:

- heavy investment in unconvincing multi-channel strategies and technologies that result in a poor return on investment (ROI)

- problems in bringing together and standardizing data about customers or resulting from interactions with them

- problems unifying different systems that may have very different data models

- difficulties in reducing or abolishing organizational boundaries.

Managing multi-channel customer management

Determining channel functionality

Careful thought needs to be given to the use of each channel in multi-channel programmes – 'one channel fits all' is no longer the case. Car buyers don't just visit their local dealer any more, and television buyers no longer just go down to their local electrical store. Research shows that many customers use multiple channels throughout the buying cycle; some channels are used to research while others are used to purchase or service.

If a company decides to adopt a multi-channel strategy, it must consider whether all its channels should offer the same range of products and services, and whether all channels should support all functionality areas. If necessary, one channel can perform all three functions: online retailers or bricks-and-mortar retail outlets, for example.

It is essential to define the role of the various channels and how they interact. This helps identify and clarify target customer usage and preferences. Customer experience should be the starting point for defining required channel functionality.

Consistency

Suppliers should plan for consistency of their brand, customer information and the customer experience across different channels. Channel synchronization may be used to deliver a consistent customer experience. Consumers can become frustrated when suppliers' online channels sell only a selection of their offline products or services, or different products or services altogether. Many suppliers, however, offer either the same or fewer product categories online as in other channels. In order to improve consistency in the product/services offering, suppliers should stage online product rollouts, first focusing on depth in their core product/services categories, then adding breadth through new complementary products and, finally, once the depth and breadth of products online reach critical mass, suppliers should introduce less obvious categories and services, both on- and offline. Alternatively, the on- and offline channels should be clearly positioned as different.

Consistency in customer service and promotions

Services and promotions can be integrated across channels. Companies can use various strategies to achieve this: merging mailing lists to target e-mail and catalogue promotions better; launching cross-channel loyalty programmes to increase customer retention; rewarding customers for whichever channel they complete their transaction within; and using bricks-and-mortar stores to provide local services to improve customer convenience for online shoppers. Examples of the latter include accepting returns in-store from online shoppers and offering in-store pick-up to get online shoppers to favour them. Where companies fail to integrate services and promotions across channels this will shift the balance of business elsewhere as customers' expectations are not met.

Pricing

In making the transition from single-channel to multi-channel approach, companies face the challenge of pricing issues (i.e. can they charge different prices to their customers for the same product online and offline?). Many believe that charging different prices for the same product from the same company is not feasible; customers expect to be charged the same price whether purchasing online or offline, whether or not it is more cost effective for a supplier to sell online. The argument of suppliers is that a universal pricing strategy is not realistic, as offline customers must inevitably pay a premium for the added satisfaction of the in-store shopping experience. Therefore, in developing a channel strategy, companies must give consideration to the very real consumer pricing expectations: consumers expect prices to be competitive, whichever website they purchase from, and regardless of whether the site is a pure Internet operation or an online channel as part of a wider multi-channel operation.

Organizational issues

Multi-channel integration requires a new organizational model – one that adapts people, processes and technology to meet this co-ordinated approach to channel management. Redefining the organization, and the processes and technology that support it, to meet the multi-channel challenge, requires strong support from the chief executive and the senior management team. They need a clear vision of how channel integration will generate business value for the organization and where the main changes need to be in the organization. Decisions will need to be taken on the size of team and the skills needed to ensure the necessary resources and flexibility. Employees must have the right skills to understand increasingly sophisticated customers, analyse customer preferences and create value from these customer relationships.

An organization is unlikely to get it right first time, so it is vital to measure, monitor and review channel integration programmes. Financial measures are important, but they are a blunt instrument in a multi-channel world where not all channels are used to fulfil or close the deal. Instead a balanced scorecard approach is needed, in which a mixture of relevant strategic and operational measures are applied. This includes customer-focused measures, innovation and learning measures, and process measures, all of which drive the financial and value measures. Profit rather than sales targeting should be used (sales targeting focuses on promoting volume at the expense of profits and the quality of the customer base, while profit targeting focuses on contribution rather than volume and provides a basis for prioritizing multi-channel offers).

Consideration should be given to how to measure employees. They should be judged on customer profitability (present or ideally estimated future), as opposed to rewards being tied to a particular channel, as this can lead to focus on maximizing returns from that while organizations must train their employees to develop the right skills. Organizational processes must be redefined to overcome organizational barriers, reduce operational costs, increase efficiency and improve the cross-channel customer's experience. Organizational structures can be a barrier to multi-channel integration when a company is product- or function-focused rather than customer-focused.

While developing a new organizational model for multi-channel integration, organizations should consider cross-channel opportunities generated through channel co-operation. Online co-operation of retailers with their manufacturers can enhance sales through referrals.

The power of manufacturers online lies in their ability to affect retailers' sales, both online and offline. Consumers will take what they've learned while visiting manufacturer websites and spend their money in bricks-and-mortar stores and via catalogues. A bricks-and-mortar employee is unlikely to divert customers to a low-cost web channel if this reduces his or her bonus entitlement. Consequently, single-channel metrics should be replaced with cross-channel metrics. This may include crediting one channel for purchases through another channel, or rewarding different customer service representatives for their shared involvement in resolving a customer inquiry.

An example five-stage 'road map' for formulating a multi-channel strategy is as follows.

1 Analyse the industry structure; use market mapping and intermediation analysis.

2 Define channel chains to describe how channels combine to serve customers through their lifetime; consider both current and potential combinations and fit with customer life cycle.

3 Compare value proposition; use the channel curve to test whether a channel innovation will win market acceptance.

4 Set channel strategies; consider strategic options and the channel mix using the classic channel choice portfolio matrices for prioritizing.

5 Determine channel tactics; consider organizational structure, HR and reward systems, as well as project management and IT.

A starting point could be to transform yesterday's cost-intensive call centre into today's multi-channel customer interaction centre (CIC). The CIC is the first line of communication with customers and its 'hub-like' quality means that all customer touchpoints and departments connect to it. The solution can include call recording on a sampling basis, searchable tagging to route intelligence about customers to where it is needed most, and the ability to monitor any call at any time from any location. Another advantage is the ability to build and maintain a data-rich profile of each customer such that, even if a customer leaves and then returns, the company is able to view and maintain a complete record of the relationship.

Summary

Despite the pitfalls of standardized and translated messages, global ads have become an important alternative to adapted multidomestic advertising. For the global marketer, faced with increasing spending needs in all markets, a co-ordinated effort with synchronized campaigns, pattern standardization and unified image across trade regions is usually more effective and cost efficient than multidomestic campaigns. The major problem facing international advertisers is designing the best messages for each market served. The potential for cross-cultural misunderstandings is great in both public relations (PR) and in the various advertising media. The availability and quality of advertising media also vary substantially around the world.

Advances in communication technologies (particularly the Internet) are causing dramatic changes in the structure of the international advertising and communications industries.

Building an effective international sales force constitutes one of the international marketer's greatest concerns. The company's sales force represents the major alternative method of organizing a company for foreign distribution and, as such, is in the front line of a marketing organization.

The importance of personal selling to the achievement of company marketing objectives, and to the efficiency of the exchange process, must not be underestimated. Sales people provide information on their products and services, use persuasion and salesmanship to obtain and sustain a competitive advantage, and are responsible for building a relationship between a supplier and its customers. These activities are fundamental to both customer satisfaction and the competitiveness of the firm.

Consumers are becoming ever more multi-channel in behaviour – using specific channels at various stages of the interaction process. Consequently, companies must understand their customers' expectations, in particular their customers' interaction preferences and patterns of behaviour across different channels, particularly for those segments that are critical to the company's future. They must improve channel performance for these segments rather than trying to be all things to all customers.

Questions for discussion

1 How does the standardized-versus-localized debate apply to advertising?

2 Comment on the opinion that 'practically speaking, neither an entirely standardized nor an entirely localized advertising approach is necessarily best'.

3 How does each stage in the communications process require modification when communicating in international markets?

4 Why do more companies not standardize advertising messages worldwide? Identify the environmental constraints that act as barriers to the development and implementation of standardized global advertising campaigns.

5 Identify and discuss the problems associated with assessing advertising effectiveness in foreign markets.

6 Compare domestic communication with international communication. Explain why 'noise' is more likely to occur in the case of international communication processes.

7 Is international personal selling a reality? Or is all selling national, regardless of who performs it?

8 What is the role of public relations (PR) in global marketing?

9 Evaluate the 'percentage of sales' approach to setting advertising budgets in foreign markets.

10 Why are trade shows (exhibitions) an ideal medium for the exporter to introduce products in the international market?

11 How can trade shows (exhibitions) be used as a vehicle for researching opportunities in the international market?

12 When would you use a technical seminar in preference to a trade show (exhibition)?

13 Identify and discuss the problems associated with allocating the company's promotion budget across several foreign markets.

14 What effect will the Internet have on international marketing communications?

References

Baker, M. (2000) *IEBM Encyclopedia of Marketing.* London: Thomson Learning

Cateora, P.R. and Graham, J.L. (2004) *International Marketing,* 12th edn. McGraw-Hill.

Crittenden, V.L. and Crittenden, W.F. (2004) Developing the sales force, growing the business: the direct selling experience. *Business Horizons* 47(5), September–October, pp. 39–44.

Enpocket.com (2003) Enpocket declares mobile marketing highly effective after study of SMS ads. *New Media Age,* 13 February, p. 14.

Fletcher, R., Bell, J. and McNaughton, R. (2004) *International e-Business Marketing.* Thomson Learning.

Hargreaves, S. (2004) Trump: The Fragrance, *CNNMoney* (money.cnn.com), 23 September.

Hollensen, S. (2003) *Marketing Management.* London: Financial Times/Prentice Hall, an imprint of Pearson Education.

Kumar, V. and Shah, D. (2004) Pushing and pulling on the Internet. *Marketing Research* 16(1), Spring, pp. 28–33.

Linkon, N. (2004) Using e-mail marketing to build business. *TACTICS,* November, p. 16.

Mort, G.S. and Drennan, J. (2002) Mobile digital technology: emerging issues for marketing. *Journal of Database Marketing & Customer Strategy Management* 10(1), September, pp. 9–23.

Silvera, D.H. and Austad, B. (2004) Factors predicting the effectiveness of celebrity endorsement advertisements. *European Journal of Marketing* 38(11/12), pp. 1509–27.

Stone, M. (2002) Multichannel customer management: the benefits and challenges. *Journal of Database Marketing* 10, pp. 39–52.

Vishwanath, V. and Mulvin, G. (2001) Multi-channels: the real winners in the B2C Internet wars. *Business Strategy Review* 12(1).

Case 10 Playtex: the US conglomerate is seeking a foothold in the European lingerie market

On a sunny day in June, Mary Anderson, president of Playtex in the USA, packs her suitcase for her monthly trip to different European countries. In the US lingerie market, Playtex is a market leader in North America, but it has never made its way in Europe. While packing, she thinks about how the Playtex brand (on a European level) could break through the intensive European wall of international lingerie brands, like Triumph, Marie Joe and Chantelle.

Playtex's mother company: Sara Lee

Sara Lee Corporation has numerous leading brands and a wide global reach. It was founded in 1939 when Canadian entrepreneur Nathan Cummings purchased the C.D. Kenny Company, a small distributor of wholesale sugar, coffee and tea in Baltimore, Maryland. A remarkably innovative marketer, Cummings steadily expanded the corporation through the application of novel management techniques.

In 1942, Cummings acquired national packaged goods distributor Sprague, Warner & Company. He renamed the corporation Sprague Warner–Kenny Corporation, moved its headquarters to Chicago and began an aggressive expansion plan that set the tone for the next half-century. Cummings subsequently made many key acquisitions, including Reid, Murdoch & Company, and its nationally known Monarch brand. The second name change came in 1945, to Consolidated Grocers Corporation, to reflect the new growth initiative.

By 1953, sales had surpassed over $200 mn. The corporation was substantially diversified among food processing, packaging and distribution companies, and to emphasize this trend, a third name change took place. The company became Consolidated Foods Corporation, a name that would remain for the next 32 years.

In 1956, Consolidated Foods Corporation acquired Chicago-based Kitchens of Sara Lee to secure a strong position in frozen baked goods. This was followed by its first foreign investments: in Dutch canned goods producer Jonker Fris and a Venezuelan sauce and vinegar company. In 1966, its first acquisition of a non-foods company brought Oxford Chemical Corporation, a manufacturer of cleaning products, under the Consolidated Foods banner.

Through the early 1970s, the company continued to diversify. Additional food companies were acquired, including Bryan Foods, Hillshire Farm and Rudy's Farm. Consolidated Foods also entered the direct sales, apparel and personal care industries through acquisitions.

John H. Bryan was elected president and a director of Consolidated Foods in 1974. Chairman of the board since 1976 and chief executive officer since 1975, Mr Bryan has overseen both the globalization of the corporation and the development of early diversification initiatives into four distinct lines of business: Packaged Meats and Bakery; Coffee and Grocery; Household and Body Care; and Personal Products.

Mr Bryan also oversaw the fourth corporate name change in 1985 to Sara Lee Corporation. Over the past dozen years, Sara Lee Corporation has continued to aggressively develop each line of business, build brands and expand into new markets. Today, Sara Lee Corporation is a global food and consumer products company with more than $17.6 bn in sales and approximately 120,000 employees in more than 40 countries.

Although best known for its baked goods, Sara Lee is a diversified company also involved in the hot drinks, and cosmetics and toiletries markets, among others. The company's stated mission is to 'feed, clothe and care for consumers and their families the world over'. It produces the world's leading shoe polish (Kiwi) and some of Europe's leading brands of body-care products (Sanex, Radox), air fresheners (Ambi-Pur) and also insecticides (Ridsect in Malaysia and Vapona in the Netherlands).

Sara Lee's Direct Selling business, which is part of Household Products, distributes skin-care products, cosmetics, fragrances, toiletries and apparel directly to consumers in 17 countries through an independent sales force of more than 875,000. Its global operations are managed based on five business divisions, for which net sales are shown in the accompanying table.

Table 10.3 Sara Lee Corporation: sales by division (1998–2002)

US$ million	1998	2000	2002
Sara Lee Meats	4030	3662	3704
Sara Lee Bakery	1011	965	2976
Beverage	2720	2730	2539
Household Products	1843	1971	1962
Intimates & Underwear	**7066**	**7283**	**6455**
Inter-segment	−144	−157	−8
TOTAL	16526	16454	17628

Source: Sara Lee company reports

Sara Lee's Intimates & Underwear division accounted for the major share of net sales for the company in fiscal 2002, at approaching 37 per cent of the total, with sales worth US$6.5 bn. Sara Lee boasts a leading position in US sales of intimates and underwear, with leading global brand names such as Playtex, Hanes and Wonderbra.

Playtex

In 1991 Sara Lee acquired Playtex Apparel, Inc., an international manufacturer and marketer of intimate apparel products and lingerie. Today Sara Lee is one of America's leading suppliers of fashion lingerie, ladies' underwear, swimwear and nightwear, sold under the brand name Playtex (www.playtexnet.com). This case study will mainly concentrate on fashion lingerie and ladies' underwear, which together make up the majority of Sara Lee's turnover.

Over the years Playtex (Sara Lee) has developed from a production-orientated company with a main emphasis on women's underwear and knitwear, into a market-orientated company focusing on the design, sales and marketing of fashion lingerie in the medium-price segment.

All products are designed and developed by Playtex in the United States. Construction of lingerie is very complicated because its developers and manufacturers are dealing with a three-dimensional product. Bras are one of the most complex pieces of apparel to make. There are lots of different styles, and each style has at least a dozen different sizes and, within that, there are lots of colours. Furthermore, there is a great deal of product engineering involved. You've got hooks, you've got straps, there are usually two parts to every cup, and each requires a heavy amount of sewing. It is very component intensive. There is very little automation possible, compared to, say, a shirt where 40 per cent of the sewing process could be automated. The average bra has up to 20 differential materials, from lace, lining, foam, side panels and elastic, to hooks, eyes, wire and ribbon. For this reason, most of the production of Playtex's lingerie is outsourced – primarily to the Far East (China). However, the lace used in the lingerie is typically bought in France and then sent to China for the final production process.

Questions (part 1)

1 Evaluate the threats and opportunities for a brand like Playtex, if it decides to enter new markets in Europe.

2 Which marketing tools would be most effective in the attempt to capture market share for the Playtex brand in the European lingerie market?

Celebrity branding: a new idea for branding and communication to the European lingerie market

Launching lingerie with celebrity status is the latest weapon in the battle to gain market share in the lingerie industry. In 2003, Australian pop star Kylie Minogue came out with a line of lingerie called Love Kylie for European distribution, and supermodel Elle Macpherson expanded her Elle Macpherson Intimates (EMI) lingerie collection to the UK in 2002 from her native Australia. Since then, a number of Hollywood sex kittens and wannabe superstars from the worlds of TV, motion pictures and music videos, like Jessica Simpson, Anna Nicole Smith and Paris Hilton, have clinched lucrative lingerie deals in the volume arena. Even famed *Sports Illustrated* model Rachel Hunter is on the prowl for a licensing deal. Singer Christina Aguilera is the latest to jump on the celebrity fashion bandwagon – the petite pop star, who is as comfortable in a satin bustier as she is in leather chaps, wants to bring her idea of sexy to underwear. The Grammy award-winning singer is just the latest performer to express an interest in fashion, as stars and companies rush to capitalize on America's continuing fascination with celebrity. The list grows monthly, from Beyoncé Knowles to Pamela Anderson. Even the brand that has been pointed out as initiating lingerie's dynamism – Calvin Klein Underwear – turned to a celebrity in summer 2004: Academy Award-winning actress Hilary Swank, who starred in ads for its Calvin Klein Sensual Shapers line.

Let's get back to Mary Anderson (president of Playtex), who is in the middle of one of many meetings with her European marketing staff. At this meeting, one of her new marketing co-ordinators, Natalie Jones, suggests that Playtex should launch a sub-brand with a celebrity 'touch'.

Mary Anderson listens carefully to this suggestion, which is discussed intensively at the meeting but, finally, says:

> The Playtex brand is one that does not use a celebrity to promote its values. The strength and longevity of a brand is dependent upon its ability to successfully provide the correct product to its target market. A strong brand should be able to exist without celebrity backing. Celebrity backing could, of course, enhance the appeal of a strong brand, but may also work to its detriment if the celebrity chosen has waning appeal or is involved in scandalous behaviour. If the celebrity loses their lustre, their longevity becomes more like an entertainment or event licence – shorter and more volatile. The huge competition in the lingerie market can make it incredibly difficult to survive for long. It takes design skill, fashion forecasting ability, huge teamwork and a large media spend to make it work.

Mary concludes: 'If the product is right, the marketing is right and the brand is right, you don't need a celebrity.'

Natalie Jones does not give up that easily, however, and she argues:

> I know that the life cycle of a celebrity may be short. That is why we should always use Playtex as the master brand and only use the celebrity for the sub-branding. I think we can launch two to three celebrity brands each year in Europe under the Playtex master brand, each with a lifetime of around one to three years. Each of the celebrity brands will target different female target groups, but at the same time the celebrity brands should always reflect the core values of the Playtex brand. Celebrity brands are popular with celebrities too because it's great to be associated with something sexy, exciting, feminine and gorgeous, and it can increase their celebrity status. It also gives celebrities a chance to create their own business and many are now being lured by the success of brands such as Love Kylie. Therefore it would also be possible to make alliances with the companies behind the celebrity – for example, for a pop star, this would be the record company.

Questions (part 2)

3 What do you think of the idea of Playtex celebrity sub-brands? Evaluate the pros and cons of this idea and put forward your conclusion.

4 Draw up a proposal for a three-year European promotion plan that includes the idea of the Playtex celebrity sub-brands.

Source: Monget, K. (2004) Lingerie liaisons pick up steam. *Women's Wear Daily* 188(7), 12 July, pp. 18–19; Anderson, I. (2004) Lingerie brand to follow Kylie work with digital blitz. *Marketing* (UK), 22 February, pp. 4–5; www.playtex.com; other public sources

Implementing and managing the marketing plan

Developing and managing customer relationships

Chapter contents

Learning Objectives

After studying this chapter you should be able to:

- discuss loyalty, satisfaction and perception of value as determinants for development of the Customer Relationship Management (CRM) strategy

- understand how CRM, one-to-one marketing and GAM (Global Account Management) differ from each other

- explain how customer lifetime value can be measured.

11.1 **Introduction**

Simply put, marketing is all about *creating value* for customers. Many companies today profess to be dedicated to value creation or adding value for their customers. The sad fact, however, is that few really understand their customers well enough to know exactly how they should go about creating or adding value in ways that customers will recognize and appreciate. Many firms fall into the trap of attempting to create value for customers, using as a definition management's own view of what the customer wants.

Customer relationships may be viewed as long-term customer commitment or loyalty, which results from the fact that customers are satisfied not only by the company's products and services, but also by how they are treated by the company and its employees, and are made to feel as a result of their contact and association with the company.

Long-standing customer relationships represent a company's most valuable assets, assets that will pay dividends well into the future. By knowing how much equity really resides in its customer relationships, a company can have a very good understanding of how these relationships will pay returns to shareholders in the future through their contribution to a stream of revenue on which the company can rely.

The measurement of concepts such as service quality, customer satisfaction and customer relationship equity has to be tied directly to strategy. Many companies have established a corporate strategy of 'relationship marketing' on the premise that they will achieve success through the creation and enhancement of customer relationships.

About this chapter

This chapter is structured as illustrated in Fig. 11.1, which shows the forces (as discussed in Sections 11.2, 11.3 and 11.4) that determine the subsequent strategies:

- Customer Relationship Management (CRM) (Section 11.5)
- one-to-one marketing (Section 11.6) and
- Global Account Management (GAM) (Section 11.7).

It is important to understand that all three management concepts are part of the same relationship marketing paradigm.

In Section 11.8 we will examine how to create long-term customer value and how to measure customer lifetime value (CLV).

11.2 **Loyalty**

Loyalty, like so many other concepts that we encounter when discussing consumer psychology and marketing, is a state of mind. As is implied above, loyalty is a subjective concept, one that is best defined by customers themselves. There are, of course, *degrees* of loyalty: some customers are more loyal than others, and customers are very

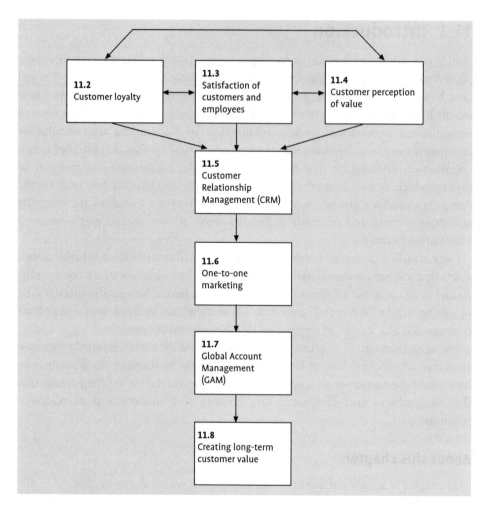

Figure 11.1 Structure of Chapter 11

loyal to some companies and less loyal to others. Some customers may be loyal to more than one company or brand within a product or service category. This is particularly so where to give one company all of one's business simply doesn't make sense, as in the case of restaurants. Very few people will be completely loyal to one restaurant to the point where it is the only restaurant they would ever patronize. But is possible to be loyal to a restaurant, or even to have a relationship with it, and yet visit it very infrequently.

Consumers and businesses will define loyalty in many different ways. Often longevity of customer patronage and repeat buying are used by businesses as proxies for loyalty. In other cases, loyalty is equated with or even defined as the percentage of total spending in the product or service category.

What are the main components of loyalty? Time, continuity and duration of the connection are indicators of loyalty, but these alone cannot lead us to conclude that a customer is loyal. A customer may patronize a business for many years without really being loyal to that business. Some bank customers, for instance, may deal with a bank for many years; however, if we look more closely at their financial services buying behaviour, we may find that they have recently purchased products from other financial institutions. Many may, in fact, be reluctant customers, feeling themselves locked into a relationship that they would really like to change.

Artificial or spurious loyalty illustrates a situation where customers appear to be loyal because they continue to do business with the firm, but these patterns of buying behaviour mask the reality. That reality is often defined by negative attitudes and feelings of frustration because customers, despite the fact that they continue to buy, wish they could move their business elsewhere. Such customers are not loyal, they are trapped.

This brings us to another aspect of loyalty that demands attention: *share of wallet.* When we assess a customer's loyalty, it is imperative that we consider the share of the customer's overall business we have secured for our products and services. If we think of our own dealings with, for example, hotels, airlines and retailers, it is obvious that we spread business around, often within a set of alternatives. This gives rise to situational loyalty, a sense of loyalty within bounds. We may be loyal to a certain restaurant in one market or for one occasion, and another restaurant at a different time or place.

The 'share of wallet' measure of customer loyalty is valid only in situations where spreading business around is feasible. Obviously, if one gives all one's electricity business to the local power company, it is not relevant to talk about spreading business.

Where a competitive marketplace operates, and products and services are bought regularly and frequently, the customer's share of wallet represents a reasonable indicator of loyalty. In other cases, where the range of products and services is much less homogeneous or comparable, the calculation of share of wallet as an indicator of loyalty is much less useful. This is the case in retail clothing and in situations where products and services are bought very infrequently. Many companies are not, however, in a position to make even a rough estimate of the share of a customer's wallet they enjoy. They don't know what total amount the customer spends with their firm and have no way of knowing what he or she is spending elsewhere.

Another measure of loyalty is the willingness of the customer to recommend a company to friends, family members and associates. Customers who are satisfied to the point of being prepared to refer others to a company are demonstrating their loyalty. Satisfied customers will be more likely to tell others about their experiences and to recommend the business. Loyal customers want to see the business thrive to the point where they feel a sense of ownership towards the company. They feel comfortable making a recommendation because they know that a friend or family member will not be disappointed.

Genuine customer loyalty cannot exist in the absence of an emotional connection. It is this evidence of emotion that transforms repeat buying behaviour into a relationship. Until the customer feels some sense of attachment or closeness to a service provider or other organization, then the connection between the customer and the company is not taking on the characteristics of a relationship. Customers themselves know, and are quite able to say, when there are stirrings of emotions between them and a company, or between them and an individual service provider. At what point would they describe this as a relationship, though? Possibly never. They may reserve that word for close family and other personal ties. However, they will admit to feeling a certain closeness or attachment to a company, and that they have a certain comfort level in dealing with it.

Customers demonstrate their loyalty to a firm or brand by making repeat purchases, buying additional products from the company and recommending the firm to others. Longevity should not be misconstrued as loyalty. There are many companies that customers have dealt with for many years, not because of an emotional connection or sense of loyalty, but because of convenience, price or inertia. By definition, these customers are not genuinely loyal. Their business is, in fact, vulnerable because their continued patronage is predicated not on any emotional connection that would bond the customer with the company in a meaningful sense, but on negative incentives or barriers to exiting, or on the absence of a viable or attractive alternative. It may simply be too much trouble to switch!

11.3 Satisfaction of customers and employees

The length of time a customer has been doing business with a firm is only one indicator of loyalty. Loyalty is, after all, very closely related to the concept of a relationship, as indicated above. Those individuals to whom we feel the closest are also those to whom we are the most loyal and who are probably most loyal to us. Genuine loyalty stems not from some artificial bond that makes it difficult for one of the parties to the relationship to leave. The foundation of loyalty is in sustained customer satisfaction; it is an emotional, attitudinal connection, not simply a behavioural one. To increase loyalty, we must increase each customer's level of satisfaction and sustain that level of satisfaction over time. To raise satisfaction, we need to add value to what we offer the customer. Adding value leaves customers feeling that they got more than they paid for or even expected. It does not necessarily mean lowering prices or providing more tangible product for their money.

Customers enter into purchase situations with certain expectations. Whether buying a car, a stereo or a vacation, attending a concert or donating to a charity, customers have ideas about how they want to feel when they complete the interaction and while they are using or experiencing the product or service. They have expectations for the purchase situation and for the performance and consumption of the product or service. To be satisfied, the customer must have both sets of expectations met.

Achieving the highest possible level of customer satisfaction is the ultimate goal of marketing. In fact, much attention has been paid recently to the concept of 'total' satisfaction, the implication being that achieving partial satisfaction is not sufficient to drive customer loyalty and retention. When customers are satisfied with how they have been handled during the purchase and how the product or service has performed, they are much more likely to come back to make additional purchases and to say good things to their friends and family members about the firm and its products; they are also less likely to defect to the competition. Sustained customer satisfaction over time leads to customer relationships that increase the long-term profitability of the firm. Marketing is not about single transactions and 'making the sale'; it is about satisfying the customer over and over again. When customers are satisfied, additional sales will follow.

The concept of service as a component of the offer to the customer may be viewed from a number of different perspectives. The essence of what is offered may itself be a service, in that it is an intangible. Air travel is a service, as are hotel accommodation and a haircut. Service may also be defined very formally as the elements of the 'package' of goods and services that a company includes with the purchase of a tangible product, or a core service that enhances the total offering. These elements of the offer include repairs, delivery, installation and warranty, and represent aspects of service that are quite inseparable from the core product or service itself.

These are not, however, the aspects of service a customer refers to when stating that he or she is no longer going to deal with a company because its 'service' is poor. The customer here is usually referring to the level of service that he or she experiences dealing with the company and its personnel, either face to face or on the telephone. This concerns how the customer is handled and treated, how he or she interacts with staff, and what his or her experience with service provision has been. The customer is talking about the speed of service, the responsiveness and attentiveness of employees, and the convenience experienced.

In this representation, customer satisfaction is seen to be a function of the value created for the customer through the quality of service provided by a firm and its employees. That satisfaction is seen as a major contributor to customer retention and, by extension, profitability.

Satisfied employees are more likely to provide superior levels of service; they stay longer with the firm and have a greater sense of commitment to the company and its customers. The concept of employee retention is as important, therefore, as customer retention, and is a major contributor to it. Employee churn is as much to be avoided as customer churn. Just as treating customers well leads to customer satisfaction, treating employees well leads to employee satisfaction. Thus, marketing and human resources meet.

When a firm provides value for its employees, it improves the value that will ultimately be delivered to its customers. Employees want many of the same things from their jobs that customers want from businesses: satisfaction, respect, quality and value are all important in the workplace. Employees who feel satisfied with their jobs and with their employer are more likely to want that employer to succeed and will work harder to ensure success. This often translates into better relationships among employees and between employees and management. It is no secret that satisfied employees are more likely to deliver higher-quality service, both within the company and to external customers, than those who are not satisfied in their jobs.

For this reason, companies who wish to deliver superior service and increased satisfaction among customers must first focus on the quality of service being delivered within the organization. This quality of service determines the satisfaction and loyalty of the employee. To improve satisfaction among employees, companies must improve the value the employee receives by working for the company.

In companies and organizations where service to the customer is important, the most important marketing decision made by management is who to hire: not only those who work with customers or develop marketing programmes and advertising campaigns, but all the employees in a company are responsible in some way for the marketing of that company. The way in which employees are treated and the level of employee satisfaction that results have an impact on customer satisfaction, retention, referral rates and overall profitability.

11.4 Value: customer perception of value

Many organizations attempt to add value, but if the customer does not feel that he or she is getting value, a company's efforts will not pay off in the shape of increased levels of customer satisfaction. In addition, as we have just observed, different things are valued by different customers and in different contexts. We cannot make blanket statements about value and expect them to apply to all customers; because each customer brings a unique background, value system and level of expectation to his or her interaction with a firm, each one's notion of value and what adds value is also unique.

Value is a predictor of customer choice and loyalty. Buyers who are considering a purchase in a particular product or service category will consider their options and develop a 'consideration set' that consists of all the brands or models they will consider purchasing. The customer will purchase the product or service that he or she perceives to deliver the most value. This assessment of value in the products or services being considered, and the post-purchase evaluation of value received, may take place at a very subjective, or even subconscious, level. The customer will probably not weigh each element of the product or service offer and mentally calculate which offers the best value or whether value has been received; he or she may not even use the term value, but may simply decide to buy one product or another. However, the customer is making an implicit determination of value whenever he or she faces the inevitable trade-off that characterizes a purchase situation or a decision whether to stay with a supplier. It will be a judgement call – very appropriate terminology for a situation that is highly judgemental. The customer will weigh anticipated benefits against current and anticipated costs.

The simple definition of value as what customers get for what they give is broad enough to allow for the incorporation of many different types of benefits and costs. The concept of give vs get goes far beyond the basics of money and core product or service, however. The costs that the customer might give in the exchange situation with a firm include money, time, energy or effort, and psychological costs.

The value proposition focuses the attention of the firm on what it can offer the customer that would be valued and would, as a result, contribute to increased customer satisfaction. Companies must have a holistic view of their value proposition: that it is literally everything that the company offers or is capable of doing for its customers. Conversely, the value proposition may be viewed as the collectivity of tools that the company can use to create or add value for existing or prospective customers.

Consider for a moment how online retailers create value for their customers. They do so not only by providing a variety of products for sale, but also by making it convenient for customers to buy from them. They also create value by offering various delivery and payment options, allowing customers to track the progress of their orders online, offering book reviews, virtual dressing rooms and joint shopping trips with a friend, and making suggestions on what would look good with that pair of jeans, or what book by that same author you might like to read.

When we examine the value proposition, we must look at the entire offering a firm provides or is capable of providing to its customers. This offering goes beyond the core product or service. It has the potential to meet the higher-order needs of customers and to create value at a level much higher than product features, price discounts and support services. However, many companies stop at this level, for various reasons. Some do not see any long-term benefit in trying to meet their customers' higher-order needs. Others see the benefit but are unwilling to spend the money in the short term. Some firms simply fail to recognize all of the needs that a customer brings to the purchase situation and the opportunities that are presented.

Different segments of customers perceive value in different ways. Customers combine various elements of the value proposition in order to define the value from their perspective. As a result, what is considered valuable or an important element of the value proposition by one customer is not considered valuable by another. Value may be created in different ways, and it is critical that marketers really understand what forms of value are considered most important by the segments of the market in which the firm is interested. In fact, an extremely lucrative way in which to segment markets is on the basis of the forms of value that contribute to satisfaction for the various segments. However, it is critical, first, that marketers and others understand how the customer defines value.

In an attempt to break away from the narrow interpretation of value as a function of what is received for the price paid, four sources of value can be identified.

1 **Process:** optimizing business processes and viewing time as a valuable customer resource.

2 **People:** employees are empowered and able to respond to the customer.

3 **Product/service/technology:** competitive features and benefits of products and services, lowering productivity interruptions.

4 **Support:** being there when the customer needs assistance.

Different customer segments value different combinations of things in assessing the attractiveness of a service offering. In addition, customers will place different weights on various components of value in certain circumstances, buying principally on low price in some situations and paying more in different circumstances to buy from a company that offers superior service or makes it easier for the customer to buy. Much of what may be considered impediments to value creation stems from the fact that customers view value in many different ways. They clearly know when value has not been added, or when some aspect of service that they valued has been removed.

Within customer value the goal should not be to increase customer loyalty across the board, but rather to acquire, retain and develop the most valuable customers. The first step is to understand the costs of acquiring and maintaining customers, and the value created by improvements in customer interactions. One can then create metrics such as customer lifetime value (CLV) and customer-level ROI, which will help to identify the most valuable customers. Rather than focusing solely on customer retention or market share, the more effective approach is to track the share of high-value customers and analyse trends such as movement between service tiers. By developing metrics aligned with their customer value growth objectives, companies can effectively analyse market trends and the effect of their initiatives on the bottom line (see Table 11.1).

Table 11.1 Customer-centric metrics for creating value

Not these	But these
Market share	<ul><li>Share of high-value customers</li><li>Tier movement among customers</li><li>Customer acquisition rate</li><li>Customer retention/turnover rate/tenure</li><li>Uptake of target programmes and promotions</li></ul>
Number of customers	<ul><li>Customer-level ROI</li><li>Customer Lifetime Value (CLV)</li><li>Relationship depth</li><li>Number of accounts per customer</li><li>Product mix</li><li>Share of wallet</li><li>Spending from repeat customers</li></ul>
Number of employees	<ul><li>Employee development (training) costs</li><li>Employee retention</li><li>Employee satisfaction</li><li>Staffing levels/mix for campaign and customer contact management</li></ul>
Direct costs	<ul><li>Cost per acquisition</li><li>Campaign efficiency</li><li>Channel usage and channel migration</li><li>Cost of campaign/customer service by channel</li></ul>

Using the right value metrics will help focus the organization on the activities and investments that are growing customer value. Such metrics can align the efforts of both customer-facing and internal departments.

11.5 Customer Relationship Management (CRM)

Customer Relationship Management (CRM) is a company-wide business strategy designed to optimize profitability, revenue and customer satisfaction by focusing on highly defined and precise customer groups. This is accomplished by organizing the company around customer segments, encouraging and tracking customer interaction with the company, fostering customer-satisfying behaviours, and linking all processes of the company from its customers through its suppliers.

A company using a CRM system must view its customers comprehensively, understanding that they interact, either directly or indirectly, with all components of the internal business system, from suppliers and manufacturers to wholesalers and retailers.

On the surface, CRM may appear to be a rather simplistic customer service strategy, but while customer service is part of the CRM process, it is only a small part of a totally integrated, holistic approach to building customer relationships. CRM is often described as a closed-loop system that builds relationships with customers.

To initiate the CRM cycle, a company must first establish customer relationships within the organization. This may simply entail learning who the customers are or where they are located, or it may require more complex information on the products and services they are using. For example, a bank may find it very beneficial to determine all the services a customer is using, such as loans, savings accounts, investment instruments, and so forth. Once the company identifies its customers and its popular products and services, it then determines the level of interaction each customer has with the company.

Based on its knowledge of the customer and his or her interaction with the company, the company can then acquire and capture all relevant information about the customer, including measures of satisfaction, response to targeted promotions, changes in account activity and even movement of assets.

Technology plays a major role in any CRM system. It is used not only to enhance the collection of customer data, as will be discussed later in this chapter, but also to store and integrate customer data throughout the company. Customer data are the actual first-hand responses that are obtained from customers through investigation or asking direct questions. These initial data, which might include individual responses to questionnaires, responses on warranty cards or lists of purchases recorded by electronic cash registers, have not yet been analysed or interpreted.

Data mining is an analytical process that compiles personal, pertinent, actionable data about the purchase habits of a firm's current and potential customers. (Data mining will be examined in greater detail later in the chapter.) Essentially, data mining transforms customer data into customer information, which consists of data that have been interpreted and to which narrative meaning has been attached. The data are subjected to a pattern-building procedure that profiles customers on variables such as profitability and risk. Customers may be categorized as highly profitable, unprofitable, high risk or low risk, and these categories may depend on the customer's affiliation with the business.

Implementing a CRM system

Companies that implement a CRM system adhere to a customer-centric focus or model. Customer-centric is an internal management philosophy similar to the marketing concept discussed in Chapter 1. Under this philosophy, the company customizes its product and service offering based on data generated through interactions between the customer and the company. This philosophy transcends all functional areas of the business (production, operations, accounting, etc.), producing an internal system where all decisions and actions of the company are a direct result of customer information. A customer-centric company builds its system on what satisfies and retains valuable customers, while learning those factors that build long-lasting relationships with those customers.

A customer-centric company and its representatives learn continually from customers about ways to enhance their product and service offerings. Learning in a CRM environment is normally an informal process of collecting customer information through customer comments and feedback on product or service performance. Dell Computer, for example, learned from its customers that they were experiencing difficulties unpacking its computers. The packaging was so strong that the customers were damaging the computers while trying to remove them from the box. Dell responded with a simpler, more efficient packaging design that allowed customers to disassemble the packaging material in one easy procedure.

The success of CRM – building lasting and profitable relationships – can be directly measured by the effectiveness of the interaction between the customer and the organization. In fact, what further differentiates CRM from other strategic initiatives, such as one-to-one marketing and market development, is the organization's ability to establish and manage interactions with its current customer base. The more latitude (empowerment) a company gives its representatives, the more likely it is that the interaction will conclude in a way that satisfies the customer.

CRM is a company-wide process that focuses on learning, managing customer knowledge and empowerment. It differs from one-to-one marketing in a very important way: one-to-one marketing is an individualized marketing method that utilizes customer information to build a long-term, personalized and profitable relationship with each customer; CRM is broad and systemic, whereas one-to-one marketing is focused and individualized. Some more aspects of one-to-one marketing will be dealt with in the next section.

Exhibit 11.1 Dell builds relationships with both customers and suppliers

Dell attributes its success to the direct relationship business model it has pioneered. This model works with both customers and suppliers.

Dell's customer relationship model

There are no retailers or other resellers between Dell and the customer. Dealing direct allows Dell to better understand its customers' expectations. The first contact is typically through the telephone or via the Internet; in the case of large corporate customers, it is more typically via a face-to-face meeting. In either case, an experienced sales representative advises the customer on the best possible computer for his/her needs and takes the customer's order. This is then entered on to the system and the order is downloaded to the factory.

At the manufacturing plant, a team of Dell employees assemble and test the entire computer system that has been ordered. Rapid delivery, award-winning technical support, customer service and ongoing feedback help ensure the highest-quality experience for Dell customers.

The direct relationship model with customers is based on the following core principles:

- **price for performance** – the company produces a range of high-performance products, which are competitively priced

- **customization** – every Dell system is built to order; customers get exactly, and only, what they want

- **service and support** – Dell uses knowledge gained from direct contact before and after sale to provide a good customer service

- **latest technology** – because a PC is assembled only when a customer orders it, the very latest technology can be used.

Dell's supplier relationship model

Dell has a strategic partnership with suppliers such as Intel and Microsoft. From the start the company decided it was better to buy in components rather than build them itself. By doing this, it can choose among the best providers in the world, often called best in class. This leaves Dell free to focus on what it does best: designing and building solutions for customers. It selects suppliers with the greatest level of expertise, experience and quality for any particular part.

Source: adapted from www.dell.com; www.business2000.ie

11.6 **One-to-one marketing**

One-to-one marketing is the ultimate goal of a new trend in marketing that focuses on understanding customers as individuals instead of as part of a group. To achieve this, contemporary marketers are making their communications more customer-specific.

Most businesses today use a mass-marketing approach designed to increase their market share by selling their products to the greatest number of people. For many businesses, however, it is more efficient and profitable to use one-to-one marketing to increase customer share – in other words, to sell more products to each customer. One-to-one marketing is an individualized marketing method that utilizes customer information to build long-term, personalized and profitable relationships with each customer. The goal is to reduce costs through customer retention and increase revenue through customer loyalty. Customer Relationship Management (CRM), which was discussed in the previous section, is a related marketing strategy that takes a broader approach.

The difference between one-to-one marketing and the traditional mass-marketing approach can be compared to shooting a rifle and a shotgun. If you have a good aim, a rifle is the most efficient weapon to use. A shotgun, on the other hand, increases your odds of hitting the target when it is more difficult to focus. Instead of scattering messages far and wide across the spectrum of mass media (the shotgun approach), one-to-one marketers are now homing in on ways to communicate with each individual customer (the rifle approach).

As one-to-one marketing takes hold, it is no longer enough to understand customers and prospects by aggregate profiles. The one-to-one future requires that marketers understand their customers and collaborate with them, rather than use them as targets. In fact, many early one-to-one marketing efforts failed because marketers bombarded customers with irrelevant, one-to-one communications before making an effort to understand the customers. The fundamental challenge of one-to-one marketing today is to combine the customer information gleaned from database technology with compelling marketing communications.

The one-to-one future is still a goal, not a reality, for most companies; but progress towards one-to-one marketing is evident in the increase in personalized communications and product customization. The battle for customers will be won by marketers who understand why and how their customers buy their products, and they will win them over one customer at a time.

Fundamentally, one-to-one marketing is no more than the relationship cultivated by a sales person with the customer. A successful sales person builds a relationship over time, constantly thinks about what the customer needs and wants, and is mindful of the trends and patterns in the customer's purchase history. A good sales person often knows what the customer needs even before the customer does! The sales person may also inform, educate and instruct the customer about new products, technology or applications in anticipation of the customer's future needs or requirements.

This kind of thoughtful attention is the basis of one-to-one marketing. Database technology provides the tools marketers need to 'get to know' their customers on a personal basis. Moreover, today's databases are capable of storing information about a company's customers, their purchasing history and their preferences, and then presenting it in a meaningful format that marketers can use to assess, analyse and anticipate customer needs.

Today's customers demand more choices; they seek to buy precisely what meets their needs and wants, and expect individualized attention. Technology now makes it possible for companies to interact with these customers in new ways, by allowing companies to create databases that pull data from, and feed information to, those interactions. Companies are using technology that makes it possible to tailor products, service and communications to meet those expectations.

Several forces have helped shape this new one-to-one focus on customers. They include the following.

- **A more diverse society:** a more diverse society has ruled that the one-size-fits-all marketing of yesteryear no longer fits. Consumers do not want to be treated like the masses. Instead, they want to be treated as the individuals they are, with their own unique sets of needs and wants. By its personalized nature, one-to-one marketing can fulfil this desire.

- **More demanding and time-poor consumers:** more direct and personal marketing efforts will continue to grow to meet the needs of consumers who no longer have the time to spend shopping and making purchase decisions. With the personal and targeted nature of one-to-one marketing, consumers can spend less time making purchase decisions and more time doing the things that are important to them.

- **Decline of brand loyalty:** consumers will be loyal only to those companies and brands that have earned their loyalty and reinforced it at every purchase occasion. One-to-one marketing techniques focus on finding a firm's best customers, rewarding them for their loyalty and thanking them for their business.

- **Explosion of new media alternatives:** mass-media approaches will decline in importance as advances in market research and database technology allow marketers to collect detailed information on their customers – not just the approximation offered by demographics, but specific names and addresses. One-to-one marketing will increase in importance and offer marketers a more cost-effective avenue to reach customers.

- **Marketing accountability:** the demand for accountability will drive the growth of one-to-one marketing (see Section 11.7 on Global Account Management) and justify its continued existence.

One-to-one marketing and the Internet

Undoubtedly, one of the most important trends in the field of one-to-one marketing is the emergence of one-to-one marketing over the Internet. While marketers have overwhelmingly adopted the Internet and World Wide Web as a new channel for promotions and commerce, many marketers are capitalizing on the web's full set of interactive marketing capabilities. Internet companies are learning more about their customers and using this information to fine-tune their marketing efforts and build relationships with each customer on a more individual level.

One advantage of online one-to-one marketing is the ability to deliver personalized promotional messages to each customer visiting a company's website. Past customer transaction history, clickstream data and survey responses are used to identify buying patterns and interests. Based on information known about the customer visiting its site, such as colour and brand preferences, geographic location and past customer transaction data, the marketer can develop a targeted and personalized online promotion or custom catalogue. For example, Amazon.com creates a personalized experience each time the same customer visits its website. Customers are greeted by name and instantly provided with a customized web page offering book, music and DVD suggestions based on their past purchasing and viewing behaviour.

To fund the new mobile marketing technology, mobile operators are looking for ways to increase mobile data service revenue. Many operators believe advertising revenue is the best option. Therefore, information technology research firms are working to improve mobile marketing technology. In the future, mobile marketing will be able to target messages based on both individual customer profiles and customer location. For instance, when a customer arrives at the grocery store, a message could be sent to remind him or her to purchase laundry detergent or to pick up a copy of a newly released DVD at the media store next door.

Of course, mobile marketing is not that sophisticated yet, but marketers do know that the advantages of mobile marketing will include interactivity, personalization, location awareness and always being with the user. In addition, mobile marketing will need to be personalized and permission based in order to be effective.

Increasingly, more and more companies are realizing that e-mail is the ideal one-to-one medium, capable of establishing and building enduring customer relationships with highly targeted lists of prospects. This technique works in much the same way as offline one-to-one marketing campaigns.

One-to-one e-mail marketing should be strictly permission based. That is, consumers should 'opt in' or give their permission to receive e-mail messages from a marketer. Amazon.com and other online booksellers ask customers to provide them with additional information about their likes and dislikes so that they can receive future book recommendations; but customers can indicate that they do not wish to receive these recommendations.

11.7 Global Account Management (GAM)

As a relatively new marketing phenomenon for supplier organizations, GAM is an organizational form employed by multinational/global supplier organizations and used to co-ordinate and manage worldwide activities of servicing a customer centrally by a managed team. GAM focuses on dealing with the needs of an important global customer (=Global Account GA) in the B2B market.

The development of a GAM relationship has a number of attributes that appeal to a global customer organization:

1 consistency in the application of policies throughout the world

2 co-ordination of marketing/selling activities to increase sales volume

3 effective utilization of marketing strategies and programmes in multiple locations

4 efficiency of management, in that there is a central contact for key accounts

5 establishment of a control mechanism relative to key accounts, to reduce the probability of account turnover

6 improvement in the two-way flow of communications with key accounts, thereby increasing the knowledge base in order to improve the quality of goods/services to these global clients, and

7 use as a means to pre-empt local/global competitors from securing business from these critical customers.

The co-ordination issues of short-run contracting also need to be assessed. In this situation, if a supplier is reactive in its relational behaviour, and forms a unilaterally dependent GAM relationship initiated and forced by the customer organizations, the supplier is motivated to adopt a defensive GAM strategy. The reactive short-run motivations to accept a GAM programme in spite of co-ordination issues are:

- **pressure from key accounts to improve global consistency** – global customers may force the supplier to institute GAM to maintain their global 'preferred' supplier status

- **pressure to 'standardize' pricing on a global basis** – global customers may attempt to use GAM as a means to lower prices globally in the guise of inferring that there should be equity/commonality of pricing throughout the global network of customer organizations

- **as a reaction to losing key customer sales in select foreign markets** – due to the 'unevenness' of selling and marketing activities globally (i.e. loss of sales in a foreign market to local suppliers), any departure from a high level of service or account attention to a global customer may stimulate the centralization of the management of key accounts

- **the loss of key accounts due to major competitors utilizing the GAM organizational strategy** – the focal organization may feel compelled to form a GAM team to match or counteract the strategy of key competitors.

A more proactive posture on the part of the supplier is demonstrated when a more proactive strategic reason for forming a GAM relationship can be employed in spite of high customer demands for supplier adaptation. The perceived long-run benefits of this are:

- **the development of relational contracting with large, global customers** – the co-operation between customer and supplier into long-term global relationships has a number of positive outcomes that provide the foundation for the formation of GAM teams (Wilson and Millman, 2003)

- **increasing the long-term dependency of the customer on the supplying organization** – if the supplier becomes the preferred source for products worldwide, it is more difficult for the customer to switch suppliers in one location; therefore, there is a tendency for the customer to become dependent on the supplier, shifting the balance of power in the relationship

- **development of synergistic strategies between the global customer and the supplier** – through the formation of the supplier–customer coalition, unique strategies can be implemented that are difficult for 'outside' competitors to duplicate due to the tacit knowledge developed in the relationship

- **development of a strategic 'fit' between the supplier and the customer** – to increase the effectiveness of the supplying organization, the supplier's strategies can be developed to be consistent with those of the key global account (e.g. providing the effectiveness/efficiency of co-ordinated and/or integrated strategies between the two organizations)

- **utilization of successful programmes throughout the world** – the GAM strategy allows the best strategies to be employed with key accounts throughout the world, thereby increasing their impact and reducing the cost of creating new programmes for each country/region

- **development of a network to increase global effectiveness and efficiency** – due to the relationship between supplier and customer, economies of scale, as well as of scope, can be utilized through the GAM strategy.

The power balance in GAM: the supplier–customer fit

The key strategic questions facing the supplier company are whether to create global accounts at all and, if the decision is made to do so, which customer relationships should be selected. In selecting the right customers to designate as global accounts, the two most important criteria are the balance of the power in the relationship and the potential for strategic synergy.

A professional buyer looking for standard worldwide pricing is, of course, looking for the lowest price to be applied everywhere. In most companies, the purchasing function is considerably more globally co-ordinated than the sales function, since it shows greater return to scale than the more execution-sensitive function of managing customer relationships. Therefore, it is surprising that so many global account relationships favour the customer at the expense of the supplier.

One key determinant of the balance of power in global account negotiations is the degree of internationalization of both the supplier and the buyer (see Fig. 11.2).

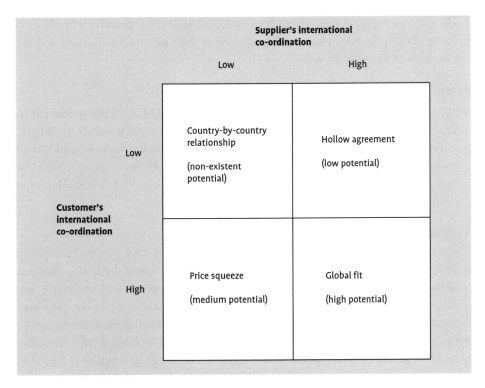

Figure 11.2 The supplier–customer balance

In the case of a customer's 'low' international co-ordination (as shown in Fig. 11.2) it may be difficult to talk about a global account (customer) at all. Consequently, the potential is also low or non-existent. In the 'Price squeeze' area, the supplier with low internationalization has access to a global player with a widespread network, which results in a 'medium potential'; but, as the supplier is 'under-globalized' in relation to the customer, the supplier will be in a rather vulnerable position. The supplier can end up servicing agreements in countries where it has no presence. For example, the supplier may receive a call demanding service from a customer at its plant in Thailand, though the supplier may not have any operation in that country; in such a case, rather than ignore the customer, this supplier may fly someone out from a neighbouring country, but this would be an expensive solution for the supplier.

In the 'Price squeeze' area, suppliers will not always face demand for low prices. Many far-sighted customers will choose to build a win–win relationship with their suppliers rather than squeeze them on price in the short term. Furthermore, some suppliers are skilful at increasing their power over their customers in other ways. They may try offsetting the central buying power of customers by negotiating contracts locally. Many local decision-makers of large GAMs prefer good local service from the supplier to very low prices.

As shown in Fig. 11.2, the 'Global fit' area is normally the alternative with the best potential. When the two sides are well matched in their internationalization, a GAM relationship can work very well.

Potential risks of entering GAM relationships

While the potential benefits associated with accepting a GAM relationship seem to be clear to the supplier, entering such a strategic arrangement is risky and should be prepared with the appropriate due diligence. The operational risks should be understood prior to adopting a GAM supply strategy. The issues/problems associated with the operational risks can be classified into the six categories described below (Harvey *et al.*, 2003).

Motivational issues/problems

The motivation for adopting the GAM supply strategy may have potentially negative implications for the supplier. The specific motivational issues refer to: customer information, customer panels, GAM revenue/profit measures, and incentives and compensation for the GAM team. In an effort to illustrate some of the problems associated with a reactive rationale, a number of potential consequences can be hypothesized. First, if the basic orientation to GAM is instituted as a defensive measure to keep an existing global customer, the management's support of the GAM relationship/strategy will be conditional. If the GAM strategy does not involve (i) an internal champion, (ii) extensive support by top management, or (iii) key functional heads, the probability of the GAM supply strategy being effective over time is minimal. Second, if the GAM strategy is implemented with a short-run, reactive perspective, the supplier may become strategically 'trapped' into an organizational solution that is not consistent with other strategies or structural considerations in the company. The dependency on the global customer may accentuate the path dependency of the supplier, given the 'derived' growth in sales volume/profit due to the GAM strategy.

Structural issues/problems

There are a number of potential structural issues inherent in a GAM relationship, such as customer demands for: resources co-ordination in being serviced; single point of contact; consistency in service quality and performance. The first and the most critical related problem is that the GAM solution can be perceived by the regional field operating managers as eviscerating their authority with the global customer, both at the national and the regional level. In particular, the supranational nature of the GAM team can blur the lines of authority as well as undermine the operating personnel's social capital with local representatives of the global account. This problem of overlapping authority is compounded by the fact that the local operating managers are frequently required to execute the policies/strategies formulated by the GAM team that may none the less conflict with established local practices. Therefore, to many experienced managers, the GAM structural design resembles a virtual matrix organization, with its attendant nightmares of parallel reporting, which are experienced by local and regional operating managers.

Relational richness

Another structural problem associated with GAM is that 'not all relationships with key customers are created equal' (i.e. there are different levels of relational richness in a GAM relationship). The concept of relational richness reflects the variation in the demands placed upon the supplier by the global customer, as well as the trust that it places in the supplier. The level of relational richness (i.e. how close the strategic intent/fit of two potential GAM members is) within a GAM relationship dictates, to a degree, the operating format of the policies/procedures for the supplier GAM team. Therefore, not all GAM relationships should be assumed to operate at the same level of supplier trust and commitment. As demand for the level of commitment and support to global customers can vary extensively, the interface at the boundary of the supplier organization needs to reflect the expected difference in 'service level'.

Personnel and team issues/problems

The personnel and issues influencing the supplier's GAM use include: the global account manager; the GAM support staff; the personnel evaluation policy; the reporting processes. The GAM team's composition entails a number of interrelated problems that could translate into operating impediments for the supplier. First, neglect of the team composition issue could present an initial barrier to the team's effectiveness, as far as who should be placed on the team. The appropriate functional representation of the team is essential to (i) gain acceptance in the organization, (ii) smooth reporting processes, and (iii) provide the GAM team with the expertise to be able to address cross-functional issues that will be salient when servicing a customer globally. Also, the team's leadership and the selection of the appropriate members from the various functional areas present another set of problems.

A specific related problem that needs to be addressed in a timely manner is the degree of heterogeneity of team membership. On one hand, the need for broad representation, both functionally and relative to global background/experience, could cause too much heterogeneity on the team, reducing the team's effectiveness. On the other hand, to assemble a team that possesses global expertise, it may be necessary to integrate a wide range of experiences and national orientations. The heterogeneity issue may necessitate the movement of international managers to organization headquarters so that they can be GAM team members.

Conflict issues/problems within/between organizations

There are a number of potential conflict issues within the supplier organization that is pursuing the GAM strategy. The issues are those that drive the demand for GAM, including: price uniformity; terms-of-trade uniformity; and service in markets in which the company has no customer operations. If the conflict issues are not addressed in a timely fashion, they may expand into conflict areas. Several of these conflict areas have already been mentioned, but there are others that could affect the functioning of the GAM relationship. The first conflict area originates from regional operating managers who see the GAM strategy as an intrusion into their sphere of authority. The conflict over who has the authority to make decisions concerning the global customer is heightened due to the need for the local operating manager to execute the GAM team's strategy. In this case, the operating manager in the foreign marketplace has the responsibility, but not the authority, to countermand or modify the strategy dictated by the GAM team. The second conflict area encompasses varying perceptions of 'fit' with the global customer organization; the perception gap can create a great deal of conflict and pressure in the GAM relationship.

Issues/problems of increased cost and potential for depressed profits

As with any addition to the organization/management of an organizational layer, there is potential for increased costs. This is particularly germane when considering the implementation of a GAM strategy, in that the GAM team in effect duplicates the costs of existing functional personnel, both at the supplier headquarters and at local market level. The overlay of another group or team of managers both improves the functioning of the GAM relationship and increases supplier costs, particularly in the initial stages of the GAM programme's implementation. Specifically, significant costs will also be incurred in the development of the infrastructure to support the GAM team. This operating platform must be endowed with adequate resources dedicated to ensuring quality service to global customers. In many cases, if not most, this infra-structure will not only separate, but also stand apart from, the existing support mechanisms in the local markets. In addition, providing the GAM team (i.e. the global account manager and support staff) with the ability to effectively communi-cate not only with the global customer organization but also with the operating units in its own organization, will increase costs at headquarters level.

There can also be implicit costs associated with the implementation of a GAM strategy; these include costs related to: (i) increased length of time to make decisions, (ii) resolving conflicts with the local operating units, (iii) co-ordination of commu-nications between operating units and the GAM team prior to communicating with the global customer, and (iv) resolving additional myriad time-consuming issues relative to embarking on a new organizational strategy.

Exhibit 11.2 International advertising agencies and their GAM strategies

Major advertising agencies and other business service providers must co-ordi-nate their services internationally. Service complexes need to provide every possible means to encourage communication between offices and specialists.

This will become critical as more firms form international account teams to serve multinational enterprises (MNEs).

Traditionally, advertising agencies go through a three-stage evolution internationally:

1 an imperial phase in which larger national agencies, mainly US, follow major GAs (Global Accounts) clients (GM, Ford, IBM, Kodak) overseas and establish offices staffed by expatriates in major metropolitan centres

2 a nationalization phase in which large agencies retrench from full to partial ownership of local affiliate agencies, and

3 a transnational phase in which a network of international agencies are co-ordinated by a central holding company under a mix of full and partial ownership arrangements.

Cordiant plc (formerly Saatchi & Saatchi) is an example of the transnational form of global ad agency under a central holding company.

Source: adapted from www.cordiant.com; Davis, T.R.V. (2004) Different service firms, different international strategies. *Business Horizons* 47(6), pp. 51–9

Step-by-step implementation plan for a GAM team

Once the GAM selection process has been established and the team members are assembled, the explicit mission and goals of the GAM team strategy concerning managing the GAM relationship can be established (see Fig. 11.3). There is an apparent paradox in selecting team members prior to the development of the team's mission and goals. But in reality, the team members must be a part of the initial charge of the team; therefore, it is recommended that the team be assembled first.

Each global customer will have specific requirements and expectations about the handling of their business on a global basis. A GAM team member's input on customizing the team effort is particularly critical when they have tacit knowledge of the account or have worked with the global customer prior to the formation of the GAM team. Also, the goals of the GAM team should be explicit, in order to permit the team's performance to be measured and to allow it to adapt to changes in the GAM relationship (i.e. relational richness) over the stages of the relationship. Specifically, the goals of the GAM team need to reflect the team's varying requirements – which vary due to differences in operating procedures relative to the functional units, since these units need to 'execute' the GAM strategy at the local level. This co-ordination of activities between the GAM and the functional unit levels is one of the primary concerns of the supplier. Without this collaboration, the effectiveness and, ultimately, the success of the GAM programme will be jeopardized.

Developing an operating strategy explicitly related to fostering co-ordination between the two organizations in the GAM programme is an essential step in implementation of the GAM strategy. However, managing between organizations is

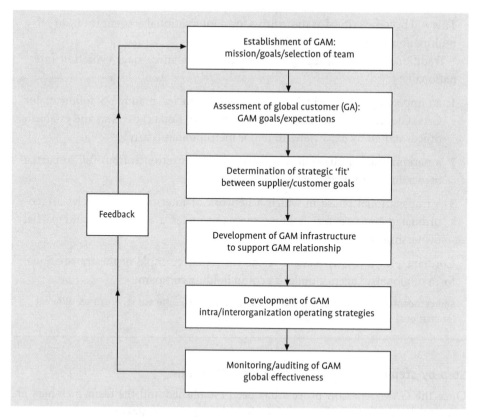

Figure 11.3 Step-by-step GAM operational plan
Source: adapted from Harvey *et al.* (2003)

one of the more difficult management tasks in the global marketplace. Most frequently, managers are trained to manage within their organizations, but with many GAM relationships, more and more of the key managers' time in the global network organization will be directed at obtaining co-operation/co-ordination with managers in organizations outside of their own.

Besides the interorganizational management format, the standard operating procedures for implementing the GAM strategy with key global customers must also be established in the supplier organization. Without the procedures clearly delineating the role of the GAM team and its mission, the support of operating managers for the GAM programme will be minimal. The likelihood of conflict over authority and responsibility is too great to be left to the chance that functional managers will bargain with the global customer in their markets.

The final stage of the GAM implementation/operating process is to institute an ongoing monitoring and auditing process to assess the direct and indirect impact of the GAM programme. This control process would have to elicit information from key managers in the global customer organization in order to validate the impact of the GAM supplier team. The central issue or problem related to the GAM control system is whether one system is effective when two organizations with different cultures are involved in a relationship spanning multiple national cultures.

As noted earlier, if the GAM relationship has no rationale other than sales, then the negotiations will focus on price, and the globalization of the relationship will result in pressure for volume discounts. The broadening of the relationship to include strategic development projects – such as new product development or customized service agreements – is the only way to make global accounts pay for suppliers. As with any sort of key account, the relationship shifts from price negotiations to strategic issues as you move through the customer's hierarchy. Today, most global account managers are recruited from the sales organization, from positions as regional sales manager or national sales manager in a small country. However, this approach is misguided because a global account is very different from a portfolio of regional or national accounts. True, many regional account managers do make good global account managers, but they have to learn some new skills to make the transition: internal co-ordination, taking a long-term perspective, nurturing the account not milking it, understanding SCM (supply chain management), and so on. Therefore some companies have had good experiences by appointing senior line management as global account managers (Arnold *et al.*, 2001).

11.8 **Creating long-term customer value**

Customer lifetime value (CLV) projects the future value of the customer over a period of years. One of the basic assumptions in any lifetime value calculation is that marketing to repeat customers is more profitable than marketing to first-time buyers. It is a well-known marketing fact that it costs more to find a new customer in terms of promotion and gaining trust than to sell more to a customer who is already loyal.

CLV has a number of uses: (i) it shows marketers how much they can spend to acquire a new customer; (ii) it provides a level of profitable spending to retain a customer; (iii) it provides a basis for targeting new customers who look like a company's most profitable customers. Lifetime value analysis allows a firm to identify its most valuable customers and profit from them over the long term by building relationships with them.

The increasing importance of the customer-centric approach to marketing is evident in the numerous CRM initiatives prevalent today, such as one-to-one marketing and database marketing. Most of these customer-centric marketing initiatives aim to increase the length of the customer life cycle as well as the value of the transaction between the firm and the customer during each stage of the life cycle. More and more firms are focusing on nurturing customer relationships for a long lifetime of customers with the firm and, subsequently, for higher profitability and growth. As a result of this approach, marketing activities and performance evaluations are increasingly being organized around relationships with customers rather than products. This has resulted in a totally different paradigm for making and evaluating marketing decisions. The focus on relationship management makes it extremely important to understand CLV because CLV models offer a systematic way of understanding and evaluating a firm's relationship with its customers.

CLV models have a variety of uses in all kinds of business organization. Particular use of such models, however, will depend on the type of products and customers a firm has. Firms having few and identifiable customers might benefit from models that measure the lifetime value of individual customers, whereas firms with large numbers of customers and with small sales to each customer might benefit from models that help segment the customer base on the basis of lifetime value.

CLV models can be very useful in helping firms make strategic as well as tactical decisions – that is, strategic decisions in terms of identifying who its customers are and their characteristics and which customers to go after in the long run, and tactical decisions in terms of short-term resource allocation among marketing variables and the focus of marketing activities.

CLV models help quantify the relationship of the firm with its customers and subsequently allow the firm to make more informed decisions in a structured framework. CLV models also help a firm to know who its profitable customers are, and customer profitability provides a metric for the allocation of marketing resources to consumers and market segments. Marketing efforts are best directed at the most profitable consumers.

The coming of the Internet has greatly increased the importance of CLV models. Many companies with a presence on the Internet do not have highly valued physical assets. Such companies can be valued correctly only when the value of their intangible assets is taken into account. Since the value of their customer base is the most important intangible asset that these companies have, understanding the lifetime value of the customers of these companies gives a more accurate picture of their potential.

The era of mass marketing is being replaced by an era of targeted marketing. Knowledge of CLV enables firms to develop customer-specific marketing programmes leading to an increase in the efficiency and effectiveness of such programmes. The Internet is undoubtedly a major instrument of such targeted marketing; the direct marketing concepts of CLV can be extended to be useful in interactive scenarios.

Problems in calculating customer lifetime value

The calculation of the CLV (see Fig. 11.4) is not problem free. Most of these problems, however, can be solved successfully if two main issues are taken into consideration.

1 The company applying this method has to define clearly from the beginning the purpose of using CLV analysis and the expected benefits.

2 The problems raised by the CLV analysis are often industry and company specific; as a result the company has to select the most appropriate way to apply this concept in its particular situation.

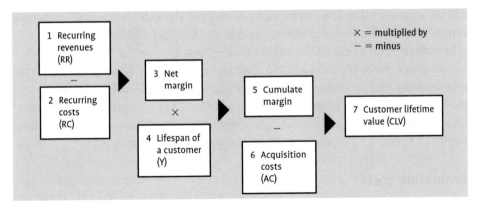

Figure 11.4 Seven-step process for measuring customer lifetime value

Figure 11.4 as a mathematical formula:

CLV = (RR − RC) × Y − AC   (1)
P = CLV × C   (2)
P = [(RR − RC) × Y − AC] × C   (3)

Where CLV = customer lifetime value (accumulated profitability of a customer during lifetime)

RR = recurring revenues   Y = lifespan of a customer or number of transactions
RC = recurring costs   AC = acquisition costs
P = total profits   C = number of customers

Defining a customer

The first challenge is to define the customer unit. Is it an individual, an account, a household or a business address? A second challenge is linking customer information to a single customer record when they leave and return multiple times during their lifetime. The answer to these questions is industry specific. The business organization has to identify the characteristics of its customer relationship and, on this basis, to define the customer unit and the customer lifetime cycle.

CLV for a firm is the net profit or loss to the firm from a customer over the entire life of transactions of that customer with the firm. Hence the lifetime value of a customer for a firm is the net of the revenues obtained from that customer over the lifetime of transactions with that customer minus the cost of attracting, selling and servicing that customer, taking into account the time value of money (see Fig. 11.4).

In the context of new customers, it is important to consider acquisition costs when thinking about the CLV. For example, consider a company that spends a million euros to attract customers. If only a few customers actually make a purchase worth a few euros each in the first period, then the costs incurred in the first period are acquisition costs, and ignoring this in the CLV models would give a positive lifetime value to each customer even though they may never make another purchase after their first purchase. Clearly the lifetime value of such customers cannot be positive. In short,

CLV is a concept that is forward looking, and the right definition and modelling should consider the *essence* of the concepts as against rigid definitions.

In mathematical terms, CLV consists of taking into account the total financial contribution (i.e. revenues minus costs) over the entire life of a customer's business relationship with a company. Despite its simplicity, the measurement of CLV requires great care. All cash flows involved in the process have to be identified and measured on a very detailed level, and allocated precisely to each customer or type of customer. Figure 11.4 represents a concise seven-step approach to measuring CLV.

Evaluating costs

The measurement of cost to the customer level poses the greatest challenge to customer lifetime value measurements. While revenue can usually be collected by customer from the appropriate billing system, cost information is aggregated into general ledger departments and accounts, and requires a good deal of analysis and disaggregation before it can meaningfully be attached to individual customers or customer segments. The indirect costs are especially difficult to divide and allocate. In solving these problems, three key costing principles should be applied.

1 Customer costs must be related to the revenues they generate.

2 Not all costs within the organization should be attributed down to a customer level.

3 It should be made absolutely clear who can influence different types of cost and revenues.

Evaluating the duration of customer loyalty

The duration of customer business relationships is difficult to measure in the present economic environment, characterized as it is by unpredictability and rapid change. Many companies are using as their main predictive tool the analysis of historical data about the past behaviour of their customers, identifying specific segments and extrapolating the behaviour of these segments into the future. This method can be used successfully only in relatively stable market environments because it assumes that:

■ customers will repeat their past behaviour in the future

■ market conditions will not change significantly.

The method is, however, completely useless in dynamic, fast-changing environments, such as the high-technology industries. In such sectors, customers' needs and perceptions change fast, competition is intense and market conditions fluctuate widely. It is important therefore to connect these predictions with the external market environment. Many CLV/profitability models neglect the external environment of the firm, and concentrate only on the relationship between the organization and its customers. It is, however, dangerous to forget that this relationship does not take place in a marketing void. Market conditions might, and indeed do, change over time, impacting on organizations' policies and on customer needs and perceptions.

The duration and intensity of customers' loyalty is determined and influenced by customer satisfaction. It can be assumed that as long as a company's offer satisfies a customer's need, that customer will be loyal to the firm. The measurement of customer satisfaction can therefore provide a platform for calculating, predicting and increasing customer profitability.

CLV is, therefore, much more than the simple forward projection of current spending levels. Ideally, we would like to be able to calculate the long-term profitability of a customer, but few firms capture the costs associated with serving a customer, and fewer still are able to associate specific costs with specific customers. In the absence of cost information, it makes sense to focus on the potential value of the customer in terms of the revenue that he or she can either generate directly or influence.

Summary

This chapter started by looking at the factors that determine the shape of the CRM strategy:

- customer loyalty

- customer satisfaction

- customer perception.

Customer loyalty is a subjective concept. Sometimes longevity of customer patronage and repeat buying are used as proxies for loyalty. Customer satisfaction is seen to be a function of the value created for the customer through the quality of service provided by the firm and its employees. Satisfied employees are more likely to provide superior levels of service. When a firm provides value for its employees it improves the value that will ultimately be delivered to its customers.

Different segments of customers perceive value in different ways. Customers combine various elements of the firm's value proposition in order to define the value from their own perspective.

CRM is a company-wide process that focuses on learning, managing customer knowledge, and empowerment. It differs from one-to-one marketing in a very important way: one-to-one marketing is an individualized marketing method that utilizes customer information to build a long-term, personalized and profitable relationship with each customer. CRM is broad and systemic, whereas one-to-one marketing is focused and individualized.

As a relatively new marketing phenomenon for supplier organizations, GAM is an organizational form employed by a multinational/global supplier organization in order to co-ordinate and manage worldwide activities of servicing a customer centrally by a managed team.

Customer lifetime value (CLV) projects the future value of the customer over a period of years. One of the basic assumptions in any lifetime value calculation is that marketing to repeat customers is more profitable than marketing to first-time buyers. It costs more to find a new customer, in terms of promotion and gaining trust, than it does to sell more to a customer who is already loyal.

Customer lifetime value has a number of uses: (i) it shows marketers how much they can spend to acquire a new customer; (ii) it provides a level of profitable spending to retain a customer; (iii) it provides a basis for targeting new customers who look like a company's most profitable customers. Lifetime value analysis allows a marketer to identify its most valuable customers and profit from them over the long term by building relationships with them.

In mathematical terms, CLV consists of taking into account the total financial contribution (i.e. revenues minus costs) over the entire life of a customer's business relationship with a company. Despite its simplicity, the measurement of CLV requires great care. All cash flows involved in the process have to be identified and measured on a very detailed level, and allocated precisely to each customer or type of customer. Figure 11.4 represented a concise seven-step approach to measuring CLV.

Questions for discussion

1 Which factors would encourage long-term relationships with customers?

2 Is it possible to identify market factors which would suggest that a relationship marketing (RM) approach is not appropriate?

3 If a relationship requires investment and customers require added value from relationships, how is it that relationships are worth building?

4 What are the arguments for spending money to keep existing customers loyal (customer retention)?

5 Why is it important to consider customer lifetime value (CLV)?

6 How can a firm increase its CLV?

7 Argue for and against the statement 'The customer is always right.'

8 What are the supplier's and buyer's motives for entering GAM?

9 Describe the different stages in GAM.

10 What are the most important factors for a supplier to consider in establishing and developing cross-cultural GAM relationships?

11 What do you consider the main requirements for ensuring longevity of alliances in international markets?

References

Arnold, D., Birkinshaw, J. and Toulan, O. (2001) Can selling be globalized? The pitfalls of Global Account Management. *California Management Review* 44(1).

Harvey, M., Myers, M.B. and Novicevic, M.M. (2003) The managerial issues associated with Global Account Management – a relational contract perspective. *Journal of Management Development* 22(2), pp. 103–29.

Wilson, K. and Millman, T. (2003) The global account manager as political entrepreneur. *Industrial Marketing Management* 32(2), pp. 151–8.

Case 11 Enercon: are buyer–seller relationships relevant in the wind turbine (WT) industry?

The historical development of wind turbines

In the 1980s, the USA had over half of the installed wind capacity worldwide. It gradually lost its leadership when the cuts Ronald Reagan made to Jimmy Carter's programmes to develop renewable energy began to undo this initial progress. Throughout the 1990s, continuing uncertainties in the US government's commitments to renewable energy have made investments in this budding industry a bit of a rollercoaster ride; one year, federal support is good, but the next year hardly anyone is willing to invest as governmental support is reconsidered. Wind turbines can run for decades, so a stable investment plan has to be based on price commitments that last longer than a few years.

Such price commitments are why Denmark and Germany have made up so much ground since the early 1990s. The political commitment to wind power in Germany and Denmark, for instance, crosses all parties: the current government is left-leaning (Social Democrats and Greens), but the government in Germany that first implemented price guarantees for wind-power producers in 1990 was the right-of-centre coalition under Helmut Kohl; 13 years later, these laws still applied. Today, three-quarters of the installed capacity worldwide is found in Europe.

Enercon

By founding Enercon in 1984, graduate engineer Aloys Wobben sparked an economic and ecological transformation of the German wind energy market. Wobben started construction of the first Enercon turbine in his own back garden in 1985, after realizing how much untapped wind potential lay hidden in the German region of East Frisia.

The extent of innovation at Enercon is determined by research and development. In 1985, Enercon started production with 55 kW turbines with a gearbox and variable speed, the first professional machine with variable speed ever installed. It was a very successful wind turbine and had a good market, but it was clear for Enercon that this was not the future of wind power. In 1992 the company switched to gearless turbines, which were more environmentally friendly as no oil was needed for the gearbox or hydraulics. In 1991 the company presaged this step by developing and manufacturing the E-40 as the world's first gearless wind energy converter.

The demand for the E-40 as the first gearless system, and the conceptional benefits of performance, reliability and service life, were followed in 1993 by a further logical step on the part of the company: the large-scale series production of Enercon wind energy converters with the development and in-house manufacture of the rotor and ring generator.

Since series production of the E-40 started the company has been able to maintain its position as German market leader in the wind energy sector. The technology has proved its worth over all continents and set standards in terms of technology, quality and reliability. In line with its corporate claim, Enercon is visibly stepping up its research and development activities as well as its production and international sales service.

As to markets for the company's products, in the near future Enercon will focus more on exports. Enercon policy is to collect data on potential markets – for instance, Estonia, Norway and Latvia – and determine which country is 'safe' to invest in, and which banks are willing to finance installations for customers.

Enercon's main production and R&D centre is in Germany, but it is also focusing on developing countries like India and Brazil. In these countries Enercon also has production lines for complete turbines and/or blades.

The total number of employees in the Enercon Group is around 1500. Total Enercon Group net sales have developed as follows.

- 2000: €570 mn

- 2001: €890 mn

- 2002: €1200 mn.

The world market for wind turbines

As shown in Table 11.2, the worldwide accumulated capacity of wind turbines by the end of 2003 was around 40,000 Mw, and the new installed capacity 8344 Mw. Of the 40,000 Mw, 73 per cent is installed in Europe (half of which is located in Germany alone), 17 per cent is installed in North America and 10 per cent in the rest of the world.

As the number of new wind turbines in 2003 was 6454, the average size of a new wind turbine in 2003 was 8344 divided by 6454 = 1.29 Mw. The yearly worldwide installed capacity has increased nearly 100 per cent from 2000 to 2003, from approximately 4000 Mw to 8000 Mw per year. Table 11.3 gives an overview of the market and competitive situation in 2003.

Table 11.2 **Wind turbines in main markets: market volume (2003)**

Market (Mw)	Germany	Spain	United States	India	Japan	Others	Total world
Total accumulated capacity – end of 2003	14612	6420	6361	2125	761	10022	40301
Total new installed capacity – 2003	2674	1377	1687	423	275	1908	8344

Table 11.3 Wind turbines in main markets: share market (2003)

Market share (%) Manufacturer, country	Germany	Spain	United States	India	Japan	Others	Total world
Vestas (merged with Micon in 2004), Denmark	23.5	– (represented by Gamesa)	20.9	8.3	42.0	n.a.	21.7
NEG Micon (merged with Vestas in 2004), Denmark	8.2	12.0	8.8	29.8	2.3	n.a.	10.2
Enercon, Germany	33.4	1.0	–	23.6	1.1	n.a.	14.6
GE Wind, USA	11.2	12.0	52.6	–	26.0	n.a.	18.0
Gamesa, Spain	–	50.7	3.3	–	–	n.a.	11.5
Bonus (Izar), Denmark	–	7.3	0.9	–	9.5	n.a.	6.6
RePower, Germany	10.7	–	–	–	–	n.a.	3.5
Nordex, Germany	4.8	–	–	–	–	n.a.	2.9
AN Windenergie, Germany	5.0	–	–	–	–	n.a.	2.0
Mitsubishi, Japan	–		12.1	–	7.8	n.a.	2.5
DeWind, Germany	–	–	–	–	7.7	n.a.	2.0
Made, Spain	–	14.0	–	–	–	n.a.	2.0
Ecotecnia, Spain	–	2.9	–	–	–	n.a.	1.5
Suzlon, India	–	–	–	34.6	–	n.a.	2.0
Others	3.2	0.1	1.4	3.7	3.6	n.a.	20.7
Total	100.0	100.0	100.0	100.0	100.0	100.0	100.0

n.a. = not available

Source: adapted from different sources (e.g. EWEA and BTM Consult)

Changes in the industry structure

Eight of the top 10 turbine manufacturing companies are European. Wind energy is an outstanding European success story, with European companies manufacturing more than 90 per cent of the turbines sold worldwide in 2002. In terms of electricity generation, in 2003 wind turbines generated 2.4 per cent of EU-15 electricity, in Denmark this figure is 15–20 per cent, while in Germany it is 6 per cent, and in Spain in 2002 the figure stood at 4 per cent.

Structural changes to the industry have taken place in recent years, and new companies have arrived. The increased size of wind farms, growth of business at approximately 30 per cent per annum, improved technology and, in particular, improved turbine availability have all allowed the wind energy business to be considered seriously by main players in the conventional power industry: Shell has formed a wind energy subsidiary, Shell Wind Energy; and the Enron subsidiary,

Enron Wind Corporation, was purchased by General Electric to form GE Wind Energy.

SIIF, a French company 35 per cent owned by Electricité de France, is emerging as a major player with global aspirations, recently purchasing the US operations and maintenance provider and developer enXco. The last year has also seen the separation of GamesaEolica, the leading supplier in the Spanish market, from its Danish partner, Vestas. This step has produced a major new competitor worldwide. The Indian company, Suzlon, has also emerged on the world market as a turbine supplier.

Over the past decade, the wind turbine manufacturing industry has become increasingly concentrated. This was emphasized by the announcement of a merger in December 2003 between the world's largest and third largest manufacturers, Vestas Wind Systems and NEG Micon. Together they will have a combined global market share of approximately 32 per cent (2003 figures).

Wind turbine customers

During the last two decades the majority of the WT market has switched from individual sales of WTs over to large wind farm developers with much larger buying power.

Smaller turbines may be installed in small wind farm configurations or as individual units. The vast majority of small WTs are less than 50 kW in capacity, with rotor diameters from 3 m up to around 15 m. Small turbines usually satisfy an individual power demand or property.

Included in this market sector are turbines that may be lowered in high winds, making them safe options for electricity generation in areas prone to storms. They may also be installed without the use of cranes – previously a limiting factor as many developing countries lack access to such hardware. The small WT sector can be divided into four segments:

1 individual use

2 isolated communities and industries

3 connected to electric distribution grids

4 power source for water pumps.

Wind farm developers

The principal European wind farm developers (both onshore and offshore) include:

- Airtricity – Ireland

- Elsam – Denmark

- Energia Hidroelectrica de Navarra (EHN) – Spain

- Italia Vento Power Corporation (IVPC) – Italy

- National Wind Power – UK

- Nuon Renewable Energy Projects – Netherlands

- P&T Technology – Germany
- Renewable Energy Systems (RES) – UK
- SIIF Energies – France
- Windkraft Nord (WKN) – Germany.

Airtricity is developing wind farms in the Republic of Ireland, Northern Ireland and Scotland. It is also developing the largest offshore wind farm in the world, off the Arklow coast in Ireland.

Elsam's offshore wind farm at Horns Rev comprises 80 wind turbines located 14–20 km off the coast of Denmark in the North Sea. It is the largest wind farm of its kind and produces enough electricity to supply 150,000 households year round.

At the end of 2002, Energia Hidroelectrica de Navarra (EHN) had installed a total of 1380 Mw. This represented approximately 30 per cent of Spain's installed capacity. The group, at the time of writing, has plans for a further 1000 Mw to be installed in the next few years. The wind energy production of the EHN group in 2003 was 1376 Gw hours, with a production share in Spain of 14 per cent.

Italia Vento Power Corporation (IVPC) has 10 wind farms in the regions of Foggia and Benevento in southern Italy, with an installed capacity of approximately 170 Mw.

P&T Technology has primarily concentrated on securing wind farm locations under leasehold agreements. In addition, a range of wind farms has been constructed: since 2000, this amounts to approximately 210 Mw.

Renewable Energy Systems (RES) has projects in the UK, Europe, North America, the Caribbean and Asia. At the end of 2003 RES had over 790 Mw of wind energy capacity built and more than 6000 Mw under development.

SIIF Energies operates the largest wind farm in Portugal (Pinheiro and Cabril), is selecting potential sites in Europe (France, Italy, Spain) and Latin America (Mexico and Brazil), and has interests in the USA and Scandinavia.

Questions

1 Evaluate Enercon's different strategic marketing alternatives.

2 Which international market should Enercon select as its next target?

3 Is it relevant for Enercon to consider the establishment and development of buyer–seller relationships? If so, in what segment of the WT market is it especially relevant?

Source: www.windenergy-hamburg.de and other public sources

Organizing and implementing the marketing plan

Chapter contents

Learning Objectives

After studying this chapter you should be able to:

- examine a typical conceptual framework for a marketing plan

- describe the structure of the marketing planning process

- explain the main contents of a marketing plan

- understand why the implementation part of the marketing plan is so important

- describe and evaluate the different ways of organizing the marketing department as part of the internationalization process of the company

- understand the important issues involved in implementing the marketing plan.

12.1 Introduction

We have now examined each of the components of a typical marketing mix. In developing a marketing plan an organization will need to give careful consideration to each of these, while at the same time being careful not to fall into the trap of viewing each one in isolation. The mix should be viewed as a collective whole, and opportunities for synergy will only be exploited if it is regarded as such. Each element of the mix should consistently reinforce the 'message' being conveyed by the other elements. To ensure that the plan does represent a coherent whole, its author should ensure that the organization's approach to each of the marketing elements is presented therein in a clear and easy-to-read format. It should then become obvious whether ambiguities are present, then corrective action can be taken.

12.2 The process of developing the international marketing plan

The purpose of this section is to summarize earlier chapters. It is well to remind ourselves at this point what the purpose of marketing planning is: to create sustainable competitive advantage. Basically, marketing planning is a logical sequence and a series of activities leading to the setting of marketing objectives and the formulation of plans for achieving them. Companies generally go through some kind of management process in developing marketing plans. In SMEs this process is usually informal. In larger, more diversified organizations, the process is often systematized. Figure 12.1 offers one example of how to systematize the process of developing an international marketing plan.

12.3 E-marketing and its effect on the international marketing mix

The Internet has changed the way we do business. No longer is there a need always to have face-to-face contact with a supplier, sales person or customer service representative to purchase goods when this can be done with the click of a mouse. Evans and Wurster (1997, 1999 and 2000) have argued that the Internet has given rise to a new economics of information, with the 'blowing up' of the trade-off between the richness of information involved in a transaction and the number of people that it can reach. The authors have argued that the Internet has made it possible for companies to reach a very wide audience, while at the same time doing so with richness of information through the enhanced volume, design and interactivity of content that is feasible on a website. Evans and Wurster identified three bases of competitive advantage: *reach* (referring to access and connection), *richness* (referring to detail and depth of information provided to customers), and *affiliation* (referring to whose interests the business represents).

The Internet has made inroads into both the business to consumer (B2C) and business to business (B2B) segments, and online business is predicted to be the biggest growth area in the next decade or so. Traditional companies, the so-called 'brick and mortars' (**B&Ms**), are being pressured to respond to this competitive threat from new e-business upstarts. The so-called Internet 'pure plays' have been able to create strong online brand recognition, provide good customer service, and are open 24 hours a day, seven days a week, 365 days a year. Some of them even give customers the option of customization and allow them to communicate with other customers through communities or discussion forums. The ability to customize service allows customers to build a relationship with the company while also being able to purchase products that they like. Physical stores can provide customers with good service but they cannot provide customers with the convenience and easy accessibility of purchasing online. In order for B&Ms to remain competitive and regain market share in their industries they have to make sense of how best to utilize the Internet.

Why should B&Ms go online?

The reason is quite simple: to remain competitive, to increase profits, to increase market share. However, the road to becoming a successful online company is not as easy as it sounds. Indeed the journey is fraught with traps and pitfalls, as many B&Ms have found.

There are important issues that B&Ms have to address in order to ensure a smooth and successful transition to an online business. First and foremost, B&Ms have to develop a strategic vision for their online business and how it integrates with their traditional business. Articulating a strategic vision in precise terms is probably futile since the dotcom business is changing so rapidly. As such, a more useful approach may be to view e-business as a continuous cycle involving building on current business models and creating future business models through selective experimentation.

One type of strategic vision is to focus on cost leadership. Web-based transactions usually save the company some money. For instance, the cost of Internet-based banking transactions is lower than the cost of a human teller transaction. Many companies that do not take advantage of this strategy may lose significant market share to those that compete on low cost. Another type of strategic vision is that of enhancing services. For example, car companies such as General Motors and Toyota have developed personalized interactions with potential customers through customized navigation paths on their websites.

B&Ms need to consider why a customer would buy from them online. A customer might buy online from a company because of:

- superior functionality of the website
- personalized interactions
- streamlined transactions
- security and privacy.

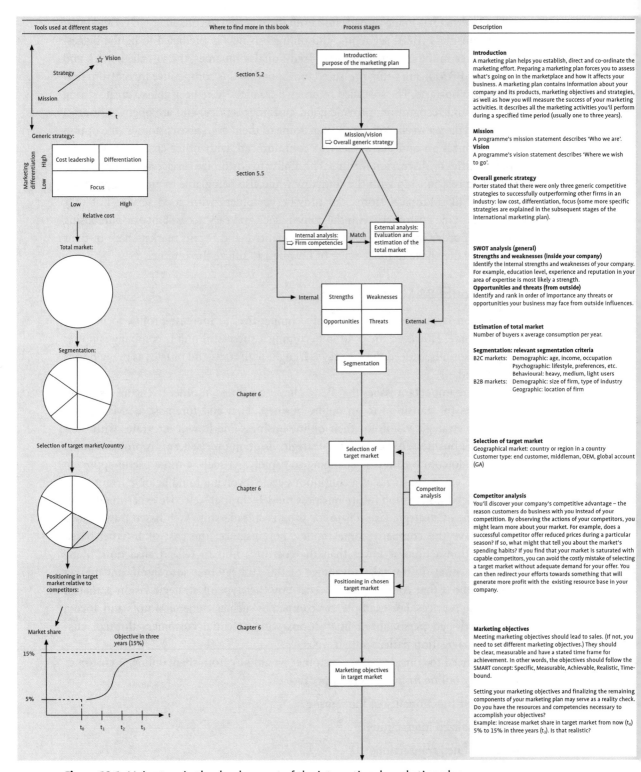

Figure 12.1 Main steps in the development of the international marketing plan

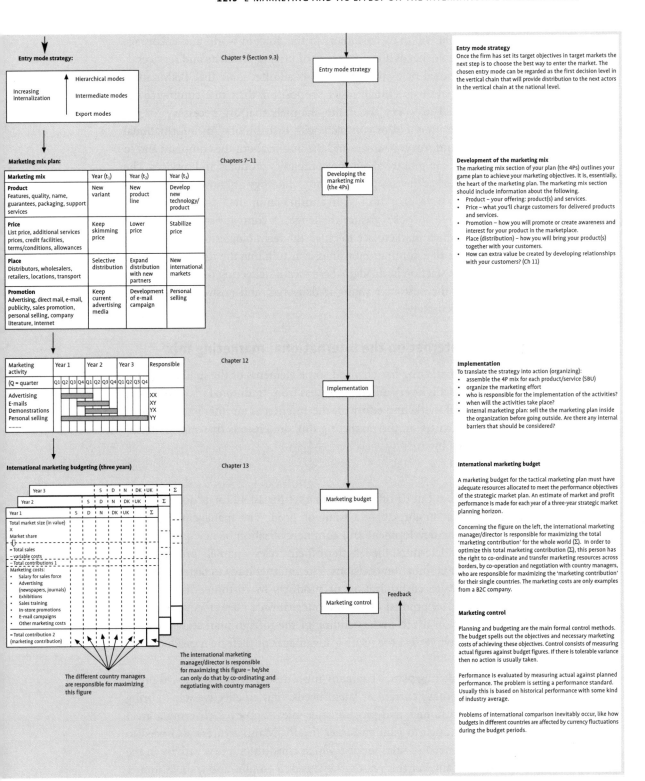

Figure 12.1 (continued)

These are all features that will draw customers to the dotcom world and encourage them to continue to use the net as a primary way of buying products and services.

Creating an informational or e-commerce site is another issue that B&Ms must address. An informational site is a much easier proposition than an e-commerce site because there is no need to worry about the channels that are necessary for the delivery of products, taxation and/or contracts with distributors. An informational site is used primarily to inform consumers and the public about the company, and to offer a place where they can inquire about the company's products and services. The main requirement is whether the company has the technology or know-how to maintain its website or has to outsource this task to another company.

Creating an e-commerce site poses greater challenges. A company must consider all the affected channels, which marketplace to enter, the technologies required, and so on. A major issue facing all e-commerce businesses is fulfilling the right order at the right time. Customer satisfaction in the digital era means delivering the right product when, where and how the customer wants it delivered, and answering customer inquiries quickly and accurately.

The effect of the Internet on the international marketing mix

International Internet marketing has changed some elements of the marketing mix. Marketing on the Internet is a very different process from traditional marketing. The key to a more successful marketing effort on the Internet is an interactive strategy. However, this section focuses on the marketing mix dimensions that may be facilitated through use of the Internet.

Product

A product is anything that can be offered to a market for attention, acquisition, use or consumption, or that might satisfy a want or need. The management of the product mix refers to the development and commercialization of new products, as well as to decisions that determine the length of their cycles – namely product rejuvenation and renewal or elimination decisions. The Internet leads to faster discovery of customer needs, greater customization of products to customer needs, faster product testing and shorter product life cycles. International marketers who use the Internet should have an in-depth understanding of the foreign marketing environment in order to be able to assess the relative advantages of their own products and services.

As part of a good marketing plan, a company must design new or improved products that meet the customer's current or latent needs, find an effective way to bring those products to the customer, and provide after-sales support. Delivering a great product is not, then, enough to gain customer loyalty. Manufacturers also need to provide online and offline after-sales service, which constitutes a new activity in the manufacturer's value chain. For this reason they need to employ and train customer service staff to service their customers on- and offline. Bulletin boards, user groups and virtual communities can also help customers to solve customer problems online, reducing the manufacturer's time and effort while strengthening its virtual community. In addition, remote service delivery plays a key role in shortening service delivery cycles.

The Internet can dramatically improve the entire product development process. This is especially true if the product being offered can be transformed into a digital product. For example, time zone differences provide a driver for software development. By using the Internet, development work on software or engineering prototypes can continue 24 hours a day through a relay of contractors working in different time zones. Microsoft, for instance, maintains a development centre in India for precisely this reason.

Price

The Internet has many influences on the price strategy; however, its use will lead to increasing standardization of prices across borders or to a narrowing of price differentials as customers become more aware of prices in different countries. For example, an international marketer's country-specific intermediates which advertise services locally (for the international marketer) have to recognize that there are international consequences to their promotions. For example, if an international publisher were to offer a 20 per cent discount on some products to its readers, readers all over the world can see this deal; but in some countries where the publisher already has distributors or does not need to discount in order to get business, the special offer is a problem. Furthermore, Smart agents (software programs that make meta-searches of the Internet for products meeting pre-specified criteria) may further combat attempts at price discrimination by uncovering different prices. Taken together, these factors suggest that use of the Internet will lead to increased standardization of prices across borders, or at least narrower price spreads across country markets.

In the B2B arena, it is expected that the bargaining power of customers is likely to be increased since they will become aware of alternative products and services. Besides, the ease of use of the Internet channel makes it easier for customers to swap between suppliers. It should be noted that there are still barriers to swapping: for instance, once a customer invests time in understanding how to use a website to select and purchase products, he or she may not want to learn how to use another service. It is for this reason that a company that offers a web-based service before its competitors has a competitive advantage.

The Internet has also made radically new pricing schemes possible, and these have encouraged start-ups to adopt pricing structures that depart a long way from traditional industry practice. The best-known example is the Priceline 'name-your-own-price' (C2B) model, which many people believed would become the dominant model for pricing, but is now seen as another variation on well-established pricing formulas. This approach works well with airline tickets because accurate, timely information about the best prices is hard to get and the seats must be sold before the flight. But customers must be willing to put up with the inconvenience of not being able to choose their airline or the time of day they will fly. Within this narrow niche, Priceline has a loyal and potentially profitable customer base. These conditions would not, however, apply to the long-distance telephone, automobile or mortgage markets, where prices are more transparent.

The final issue in the price dimension is currency rates. Shopping on the Internet needs to be convenient, which means trading in local currencies. Therefore, consumers are unlikely to search for information on currency conversion rates. Companies who wish to market their products internationally may consider adding a link from their web pages to a currency converter or providing an approximate conversion rate for each country to which they are prepared to make sales.

Distribution (place)

Physical distribution is the 'place' aspect of the marketing mix. The marketing channel can be defined as interdependent organizations involved in the process of making a product or service available for use or consumption. The Internet, by connecting end users and producers directly, will reduce the importance of traditional intermediaries (i.e. agents and distributors) in international marketing. To survive, such intermediaries may need to begin offering a different range of services. Their value-added will no longer be principally in the physical distribution of goods but rather in the collection, collation, interpretation and dissemination of a vast amount of information. For example, a hospital in Egypt can put out a request for proposal (RFP) for equipment over the Internet, secure bids and select a supplier without going through local brokers and distributors, and have the products delivered directly by DHL or Federal Express, say. Few buffer inventories will be needed in the worldwide distribution system and less working capital.

However, if intermediaries can perform a different mix of services, made necessary by the Internet, they will continue to play critical roles and extract value. The distribution system of the company must have some capabilities and competencies – for example, 24-hour order taking and customer service response capability, and regulatory and customer-handling expertise to ship internationally. Companies should consider providing information on how the products are shipped and the precautions taken to ensure their quality on arrival. Quality guarantees and/or special consideration for international returns or refunds may also be necessary.

Undoubtedly, the Internet has reduced many distribution issues. It is borderless and the opportunity to sell over the net in a standardized way eliminates many natural barriers to entry. In addition, any business connected to the Internet can source other businesses' products by ordering them from their websites. Companies no longer have to put together long and expensive distribution channels to bring their products to the customer.

The early Internet literature indicated that it would eliminate the need for intermediaries. Early predictions called for *disintermediation* – that is, the disappearance of physical distribution chains as people moved from buying through distributors and resellers to buying directly from manufacturers. The reality is that the Internet may eliminate the traditional 'physical' distributors, but in the transformation process of the value chain new types of intermediaries may appear. So the disintermediation process has come to be balanced by a 're-intermediation' force – the evolution of new intermediaries (e.g. infomediaries – aggregators of information on the Internet) tailor-made for the online world.

Promotion

Promotion refers to all the various ways an organization undertakes to communicate its products' merits and to persuade target customers to buy from it. The use of the Internet allows sales departments to have interactive communications with their customers. Hard-selling and advertiser-push promotion strategies do not work well on the Internet. Global advertising costs, as a barrier to entry, will be significantly reduced as the Internet makes it possible to reach a global audience more cheaply. However, there are many online promotion techniques. Paying to place links on pages with audiences that mirror or include a company's target customers is less expensive than traditional media. In addition, 'free' advertising on other sites can often be exchanged for mutual links. Postings on Internet discussion groups, on topics relevant to specific products or markets, are another way for marketers to attract visitors to their sites. There are many offline promotion techniques that work to attract potential customers to websites, such as traditional forms of advertising (e.g. magazine advertising or word of mouth).

However, there is one critical issue for international marketers who use the Internet in their marketing: the new challenge facing companies is the management of a global brand and corporate logo. Consumers may become confused if a company and its subsidiaries have different websites, each communicating a different format, image, message and content. Therefore, a company should clearly define its policies about branding on the Internet. Developing one site for each brand – while costly and limiting for cross-selling – is preferable when the brands have distinct markets and images. Finally, advertising on web pages other than the firm's own is possible (and increasingly common), but might not be well received. Customers merely wish to be presented with the hard facts about the subject matter on the pages they read. Note, moreover, that as more and more businesses establish an Internet presence, searching for potential suppliers will become impossible without the aid of high-quality directories to guide people towards relevant sites.

The 4Ps model does not explicitly include any interactive elements; furthermore, it does not indicate the nature and scope of such interactions. However, earlier changes in the 4Ps have been the result of the interactive nature of the Internet, which requires a shift in the marketing paradigm, towards a more relationship-orientated approach, as discussed in Chapter 11.

12.4 **Writing the international marketing plan document**

Marketing planning is widely adopted by firms from all sectors. The process of marketing planning integrates all elements of marketing management: marketing analysis, development of strategy and the implementation of the marketing mix. Marketing planning can, therefore, be regarded as a systematic process for assessing marketing opportunities and matching them with a firm's own resources and competencies. In this respect, the process helps businesses to effectively develop, co-ordinate and control marketing activities.

Basically, the major functions of the marketing plan are to determine where the firm is, where it wants to go and how it can get there. Marketing planning is able to fulfil these functions by driving the business through three kinds of activities: (i) analyses of the internal and external situations, (ii) development of marketing strategy, and (iii) design and implementation of marketing programmes.

The marketing planning process is linked to planning in other functional areas and to overall corporate strategy. It takes place within the larger strategic marketing management process of the corporation. To survive and prosper, the business marketer must properly balance the firm's resources with the objectives and opportunities of the environment. Marketing planning is a continuous process that involves the active participation of other functional areas.

The *marketing plan* itself is the written document that businesses develop to record the output of the marketing planning process. This document provides details of the analysis and strategic thinking that have been undertaken, and outlines the marketing objectives, marketing mix and the plan for implementation and control. As such, it plays a key role in informing organizational members about the plan, and any roles and responsibilities they may have within it. The plan also provides details of required resources and should highlight potential obstacles to the planning process, so that steps can be taken to overcome them. In some respects the marketing plan is a kind of road map, providing direction to help the business implement its strategies and achieve its objectives: the plan guides senior management and all functional areas within the organization.

Once the core marketing analyses are complete, the strategy development process follows. The key during this phase of marketing planning is to base any decisions on a detailed and objective view from the analyses. In this part of the plan, the most appropriate target markets will be identified, the basis for competing and positioning strategies determined, and detailed marketing objectives presented. As these choices will affect how the business proceeds in relation to its customers and competitors, there must be consistency with the company's overall corporate strategy. The marketing strategy must also be realistic and sufficiently detailed to form the basis for the marketing programmes that follow. Some of the most effective marketing strategies combine a realism that is grounded in a systematic review of the company's existing position with foresight about possible longer-term competitive advantages.

The final stage of the marketing planning process involves the determination of marketing mix programmes and their implementation. A detailed explanation is needed of exactly what marketing tasks must be undertaken, how, by whom and when. There needs to be a clear rationale connecting these marketing mix recommendations with the analyses and strategy preceding them. A common marketing planning weakness occurs when businesses press ahead with detailed marketing programmes that are not well connected with the earlier stages in the planning process, or that simply replicate existing marketing mix tactics without making adjustments to reflect the topical issues identified in the analyses. The result can be misdirected marketing activities that are not closely aimed at the key target segments or that fail to take into account the competitive or wider trading environment.

Assuming that appropriate attention has been devoted to the marketing analyses and marketing strategy that guide the marketing programmes, managers must next ensure that sufficient detail is provided to make the marketing mix genuinely implementable. This means that each component of the marketing programme – product, price, promotion, distribution (place) and people – must be discussed separately and the tasks required to action it explored fully.

Those involved in planning will usually prepare some form of written marketing plan document in which to explain the outputs of the process. Table 12.1 illustrates the typical section headers used in this kind of document. The marketing plan provides a useful reference point for the analytical and strategic thinking undertaken, the detailed marketing objectives and marketing programmes, and their implementation and control. Managers are able to refer back to the document for guidance and should update it regularly to ensure that a full record of marketing planning activities is available. This document helps focus the views of senior management, and explain the required marketing activities and target market strategy to other functional areas within the business, such as operations and finance (Dibb, 2002).

The key components of the final marketing plan are highlighted in Table 12.1 Note that the planning process format centres on clearly defined market segments, a thorough assessment of internal and external problems and opportunities, specific goals, and courses of action. Business marketing intelligence, market potential and sales forecasting are fundamental in the planning process.

Table 12.1 **Framework for a marketing plan**	
I	Title page
II	Table of contents
III	Executive summary
IV	Introduction and problem statement
V	Situational analysis
VI	Marketing objectives and goals
VII	Marketing strategies
VIII	Marketing programmes/action plans
IX	Budgets
X	Implementation and control
XI	Conclusion

Let us examine each section of the marketing plan structure in Table 12.1 in further detail.

I Title page

The title page is an identification document that provides the reader with the following essential information:

- legal name of business

- name of document ('Marketing Plan for …')

- date of preparation or modification of the document

- name, address, e-mail and phone number of the business or contact person

- name, address, e-mail and phone number of the individual or business who prepared the plan

- the planning period.

II Table of contents

This is the list of subjects covered in the marketing plan and where in the document to find them.

III Executive summary

This gives busy executives and managers a quick overview, in the form of a concise summary, of the key points in the marketing plan. This section encompasses a one-page (or thereabouts) summary of the basic factors involving the marketing of the product or service along with the results expected from implementing the plan.

IV Introduction and problem statement

The identification and clear presentation of the problem(s) or issue(s) facing the company is the most critical part of the introduction. Only a problem that has been properly defined can be addressed. You should move on to addressing the main problem fairly quickly. If there are sub-problems in the marketing plan that you feel you should identify, feel free to do so, but make sure you clearly identify the main problem. Be on the alert for symptoms posing as key issues and underlying problems – stick to the main issue as far as possible. Remember that strategic marketing problems are long term, involve large sums of money and affect multiple aspects of the firm.

V Situational analysis

Based on a comprehensive audit of the market environment, competitors, the market, products and the company itself, this section provides a condensed view of the market (size, structure and dynamics), prior to a detailed analysis of individual market segments, which form the heart of the marketing plan.

The process is based upon market segmentation – that is, homogeneous groups of customers with characteristics that can be exploited in marketing terms. This approach is taken because it is the one that is most useful for managers in developing their businesses. The alternative, product-orientated, approach is rarely appropriate, given the varying requirements of the different customer groups in the market in which most organizations compete.

It is necessary to summarize the unit's present position in its major markets, in the form of a SWOT analysis for each major market segment, product or business group. The word SWOT derives from the initial letters of the words strengths, weaknesses, opportunities and threats. The analysis includes the following issues.

The firm and its market

- Identification and evaluation of the competencies in the company (key personnel, experience, skills and capabilities, and resources), in comparison with those of your competitors.

- The structure of your marketing organization (lines of authority, functions and responsibilities).

- Description of your total potential market (i.e. your potential customers).

- How does your product/service satisfy the needs of this market?

- Describe the particular customers that you will target.

- Size of (i) total potential market (number of potential customers), and (ii) your target market. Support estimates with factual data.

- Growth potential of (i) total potential market, and (ii) your target market. Look at local, national and international markets. Support estimates with factual data.

- Your current market share (firm's sales divided by the total market sales in per cent).

Competitive environment

- Major competitors: name, location and market share.

- Compare your product/service with that of your major competitors (brand name, quality, image, price, etc.).

- Compare your firm with that of your major competitors (reputation, size, distribution channels, location, etc.).

- How easy is it for new competition to enter this market?

- What have you learned from watching your competition?

- Are competitors' sales increasing, decreasing, steady? Why?

Technological environment

- How is technology affecting this product/service?

- How soon can it be expected to become obsolete?

- Is your company equipped to adapt quickly to changes?

Socio-political environment

- Describe changing attitudes and trends. How flexible and responsive is your firm?

- New laws and regulations that may affect your business. What might be their financial impact?

Use SWOT analyses to assess the key issues that must be addressed. Summarize your internal and external assessment in form of a SWOT matrix using the key points from the situation analysis.

VI Marketing objectives and goals

This states precisely the marketing objectives and goals in terms of sales volume, market share, return on investment, or other objectives or goals for your marketing plan. State these objectives in precise, quantifiable terms and give the time needed to achieve each of them (e.g. 'To obtain a sales volume of 3000 units, equal to an increase in market share from 10 per cent to 12 per cent of total market, by the end of the next fiscal year').

What is the difference between a goal and an objective?

An objective is an overall goal. It is more general and may not be quantified. 'To establish our product as a market leader in the marketplace' is an objective. Goals are quantified: 'To sell 50,000 units next year' is a goal. Goals are also quantified in terms of sales, profits, market share, return on investment or other measurements. Make sure that your goals and objectives fit together. For example, your ability to capture a stated market share may require lower profits.

Objectives may also include societal objectives.

VII Marketing strategies

How will you reach your objectives and goals? That is what is covered in Chapter 5. Which strategic models from Chapter 5 should be used (new market penetration, penetration, market development, etc.)?

VIII Marketing programmes/action plans

Marketing programmes are the actionable means of achieving desired ends. They outline *what* needs to be done, *how* it will be done, *when* it will be done, and *who* will do it.

- How will you implement the above strategy?

- Product/service: quality, branding, packaging, modifications, location of service, etc.

- Pricing: how will you price your product/service so that it will be competitive, yet profitable?

- Promotion/advertising: how, where, when, etc.

- Selling methods: personal selling, mail order, etc. Include number of sales people, training required, etc.

- Distribution methods.

- Servicing of product.

- Necessary organizational development in the company.

- Other: add any other relevant information.

IX Budgets

Having detailed the steps that will be necessary to achieve the marketing objectives, the writer of the plan should then be in a position to cost the various proposals and to derive an overall marketing budget for the planning period. Of course, in reality, life is just not that easy. Cost will undoubtedly have been in the minds of marketing planners even before they commenced the marketing planning process. At the very least, the development of a suitable budget is likely in practice to have been an itera- tive process, with proposals being re-evaluated in the light of budgetary constraints.

There are a variety of ways of determining the marketing budget. The ideal would clearly be to specify the strategy and tactics that are felt necessary to achieve the marketing objectives, and then to cost these to arrive at an overall budget. This is usually referred to as the 'task method' of setting a marketing budget. Of course, in reality, this method is seldom employed since financial pressures from senior management, the budgeting/accounting practices of the organization, and uncertainty about resource attraction all hamper the derivation of an appropriate budget. In practice, therefore, budgets (concerning marketing costs) tend to be set using the following methods: percentage-of-sales, competitive parity or objective-task method (see Section 10.2).

- **Percentage of last year's sales:** there is a danger with this method in that if the organization has been suffering from poor performance of late, reducing the marketing budget in line with sales could actually serve to worsen the situation. Clearly, when sales fall there is a strong case for enhancing, not reducing, the marketing budget.

- **Competitor matching:** using the amounts spent on marketing by the competition and matching their resource allocation.

- **What can be afforded:** perhaps the least rational of all the methods of budget calculation, this one involves the senior management of the organization deciding what they believe they can afford to allocate to the marketing function in a particular year. Little or no reference is made to the marketing objectives, nor to the activities of competitors.

Irrespective of the method actually used, in practice it would be usual to specify how the eventual budget has been allocated and to include such a specification in the marketing plan itself. It would also be normal for an allowance to be made for contingencies in the event that monitoring by the organization suggests that the objectives will not be met. Sufficient resources should then exist for some form of corrective action to be taken.

A *budget of cash flows* should also drawn up. This identifies whether a company will have enough money to meet its cash requirements on a monthly basis. Some sales will be made in cash while others may be made on credit. Because sales made on credit will not result in the receipt of cash until a later date, they must not be recorded until the month in which the cash will actually be received. Therefore, the percentage of sales to be made in cash and the percentage to be made on credit must be estimated. The percentage of credit sales should be further broken down according to the business's different collection periods (30 days, 60 days, etc.).

X Implementation and control

As soon as the plan has been implemented, the marketing management will then have to take responsibility for monitoring the progress of the organization towards the goal specified. Managers will also need to concern themselves with the costs that have been incurred at each stage of implementation and monitor these against the budget. Thus, control mechanisms need to be put into place to monitor:

- the actual sales achieved, against the budget
- the actual costs incurred against those budgeted
- the performance of individual services against budget
- the overall strategic direction that the organization is taking – that is, will the overall corporate objectives be achieved in a manner commensurate with the organization's mission?

If variances are detected in any of these areas, corrective action can then be initiated, if necessary by utilizing resources allocated in the budget for contingency.

XI Conclusion

This section briefly concludes the problems stated at the beginning of the report, based on the analysis in the marketing plan. The conclusion is not a summary. The executive summary will normally also include the key results of the market analysis.

Exhibit 12.1 Seven steps to implementing personal selling and relationship building

Although personal selling as a profession and function has evolved and changed dramatically over recent decades, one of the oldest and most widely accepted paradigms in the sales discipline is commonly referred to as the 'seven steps of selling' (Dubinsky, 1980/81; Manning and Reece, 2001; Weitz *et al.*, 2001; Futrell, 2002). We will now look at each of these steps in turn.

1. Prospecting

Prospecting is the method by which sales people search for new customers and potential customers. One obvious reason for prospecting is to expand the customer base, which is important because most sales organizations lose customers every year. Many different methods of prospecting are available, such as referrals, networking, 'bird-dogging', cold canvassing and numerous others. Prospecting usually includes a discussion of qualifying the prospect and thus developing some type of screening procedure.

Traditionally, sales people were expected to find their own prospects. However, many sales organizations today are using telemarketers to perform the prospecting function. Once the prospect is found, the telemarketer may attempt a sale or may pass the lead to the appropriate sales person, depending on the structure of the organization. Use of the Internet now also allows potential prospects to approach the organization, and they are later contacted by a sales person. Technology has allowed the organization to become more cost efficient and effective in the prospecting step, freeing the sales person to focus on other sales functions. In particular, database marketing and CRM have enhanced marketing's ability to aid sales people in prospecting. As a result, the current evolution for prospecting means that sales people may no longer be performing the prospecting step as a systematic part of their job, but the step typically remains elsewhere within the organization.

2. Preapproach

The preapproach step includes all post-prospecting activities prior to the actual visit to a prospect or customer. The preapproach step occurs on virtually every sales call. Sellers are doing their research on the prospect or customer, familiarizing themselves with the customer's needs, reviewing previous correspondence, and pulling together any other new and relevant material that it might be appropriate to take along to the sales call itself. Preapproach activities also include talking with gatekeepers, doing homework on the customer (individual and organization), mentally preparing for the approach and presentation (rehearsal), and 'reading' the customer's office on entry. Today, a laptop computer loaded with customer data instantly makes a sales person highly customer knowledgeable. They have customer records at hand: their buying history and any personal information that might be useful. Well-executed CRM systems are excellent at providing the means to update any aspect of this customer information at any customer touchpoint (places where customers come in contact with the selling firm).

3. Approach

The approach usually takes the first minute or few minutes of a sale. It consists of the strategies and tactics employed by sales people when gaining an audience and establishing initial rapport with the customer. The approach includes opening 'small talk', the handshake, eye contact and generally making a good initial impression. A shift has occurred to a broader relationship approach where the sales person has probably already developed the foundation of an interpersonal network within the buying organization and the goal is to provide more information or solve some existing problem – that is, provide a solution. Because most sales do not occur on the first call but rather are a result of multiple calls and contacts with multiple people, establishing and building on this foundation is what eventually facilitates relationship selling.

4. Presentation

The presentation is the main body of the sales call and should occur after the sales person has predetermined the needs of the customer. This step can be one presentation or multiple presentations over a period of time. Goals for the sales presentation will vary. First-time buyers must get sufficient information to adequately understand the product's benefits, which may be facilitated by building the presentation around a product demonstration. Selling points and attributes are visualized and built around a call agenda or sales proposal. This step can be complex, and preparation is essential.

For many sales people, the presentation step has undergone a substantial transformation. Today's presentations are typically conducted over several meetings, with the sales person often doing more listening than talking.

The physical presentation has also undergone a transformation, spurred on by several factors. First, sales people can now use a PowerPoint-type presentation that can easily be adapted from call to call. Second, with the use of a laptop computer, a sales person can provide much greater depth of knowledge targeted to a specific customer. A third major transformative factor is the fact that today's presentations are often delivered by a team from the selling organization, rather than via the traditional approach of individual sales person presentations. Also more and more sales presentations are made to a buying centre, probably including a firm's executives, as opposed to a single purchaser. This change greatly affects the style and content of the presentation compared to the traditional way of presenting to a single purchaser.

5. Overcoming objections

Objections can broadly be defined as customer questions and hesitancies about the product or company. Sales people should expect that objections will be encountered in every sales presentation. A number of reasons exist for objections, and despite the fact that objections can delay the sales process, for the most part they should be perceived in a positive sense as useful. This is because, by revealing objections, true buyer needs can be uncovered. In the early days of selling, sales objections were viewed mostly as a hurdle that sales people had to overcome to get to the ultimate sale. More recently, a true objection might be viewed as a sign not to pursue the sale further because a need may not be met with a given product. Today's sales person, through either predetermined needs or multiple calls, is attempting to ascertain earlier and more precisely what the customer requires from the product. Listening and asking questions have become key elements of the transformation of the 'overcoming objections' step.

6. Close

The close is defined as the successful completion of the sales presentation, culminating in a commitment to buy the good or service. Once any objections have successfully been overcome, the sales person must actually ask for the order and thus begin the process of closing the sale. This step has traditionally been trumpeted as difficult for many sales people (especially new sales people) because many simply do not ask for the order. Many closing tactics are available.

The key goal of this step has moved beyond simply short-term physical closure to the successful realization of the mutual goals of both parties to the relationship, over the long run. Firms today focus on the lifetime value of a customer. The goals to be achieved between seller and buyer must be mutually beneficial. Developing a long-term relationship with customers whose ROI is negative is bad business.

7. Follow-up

The traditional follow-up was typically done with a phone call or letter thanking the customer for the sale and determining if the product is meeting expectations. Frequently, the sales person would 'drop by' to see if any problems were occurring. The key transformative factor here is increased effectiveness of communication through technology. Today, e-mail has become a dominant method of follow-up because of its ease of use and timeliness. In the era of relationship selling, the follow-up step has gained importance and is also now much quicker and more efficient to execute.

Customer relationship maintenance implies that the selling firm has assigned, on an ongoing basis, an individual or team to truly maintain all aspects of the business relationship. This may be the sales person him/herself or it may be turned over to others. Sales organizations are currently altering their control and reward systems to account for this shift towards more ongoing relationship maintenance, often to customers (MNEs) with a large global organization: the so-called global accounts. This is also the basic idea behind the concept of Global Account Management (GAM), which was discussed in Chapter 11.

Conclusion

The steps in the traditional seven-step selling process are sequential and cumulative in that a sales person starts with prospecting and works his/her way through to follow-up. The amount of time or effort in any one step may vary, but the traditional model requires that every step occur.

In contrast, the evolved selling process (Moncrief and Marshall, 2005) assumes that the sales person will typically perform the various steps of the process in some form, but that the steps do not necessarily occur for each sales call. Rather, they occur over time, accomplished by multiple people within the selling firm, and not necessarily in any given sequence. While the traditional seven steps reflect a selling orientation on the part of a firm, the evolved selling process reflects more of a customer orientation in that the focus is on *relationship selling* – that is, securing, building and maintaining long-term relationships with profitable customers.

Source: adapted from Dubinsky, A.J. (1980/81) A factor analytic study of the personal selling process. *Journal of Personal Selling & Sales Management* 1 (Fall/Winter), pp. 26–33; Futrell, C.M. (2002) *Fundamentals of Selling: Customers for Life* (7th edn). Boston, MA: McGraw-Hill/Irwin; Manning, G.L. and Reece, B.L. (2001) *Selling Today: Building Quality Partnerships* (8th edn). Upper Saddle River, NJ: Prentice Hall; Moncrief, W.C. and Marshall, G.W. (2005) The evolution of the seven steps of selling. *Industrial Marketing Management* 34(1), pp. 13–22; Weitz, B.A., Castleberry, S.B. and Tanner, J.F. (2001) *Selling: Building Partnerships* (4th edn). Boston, MA: McGraw-Hill/Irwin

12.5 Barriers impeding the implementation of marketing plans, and what to do about them

Even though the benefits of adopting marketing planning are well established, the effectiveness of the process is not guaranteed. A range of barriers to effective marketing planning have been highlighted in the literature. Careful attention is, therefore, needed to ensure that marketing planning is implemented effectively. The starting point should be an appreciation of the likely barriers, so that preventative and remedial action can be taken. The following list is an amalgamation of the key issues raised by researchers in the marketing planning literature (Dibb, 2002; Simkin 2002).

- **Lack of marketing competency in the organization:** insufficient marketing knowledge or skills, poor grasp of the marketing concept in general, poor understanding of the distinction between the marketing planning process and its outputs, management's failure to see across individual market sectors or brands to grasp the 'whole picture'.

- **Isolation of marketing planning from other areas of the business:** poor involvement of functions, lack of enthusiasm for planning among non-marketers, no power for marketers to talk to other functions and the need to understand them better; these are all facets of one underlying problem in much marketing planning – non-marketers have a wealth of knowledge and insights to bring to marketing planning; R&D personnel hear what is evolving elsewhere, technical managers understand what is feasible to produce/deliver, financial managers assist in bringing realism to the profitability debate.

- **Organizational barriers:** individual manager's 'empire-building' causes problems and detracts from the benefits to the company of structured planning. A lack of acknowledged corporate value given to planning, plus personal clashes, are facets of corporate life well known to most managers. The process of planning, however, requires sharing of information and ideas, effective communications, and a focus on the market rather than internal politics.

- **Too much short-term marketing planning:** too much emphasis on a one-year planning time frame, leading to plenty of short-term detail but little long-term vision.

- **Marketing plans developed in isolation rather than on marketing analyses:** inadequate marketing intelligence and/or lack of a marketing intelligence system (MIS), poor sharing of marketing intelligence, insufficient marketing analyses of customers, competitors and the wider trading environment, leading to a poor understanding of these areas.

- **Lack of managers' time resources for thorough marketing planning:** managers have difficulties balancing planning activities with the rest of their workload, so that the process is not fully implemented.

The need for a clearly defined process is fundamental to successful marketing planning. This process should incorporate the required analyses, strategic thinking and marketing programme development. However, if such a process is to be put into practice effectively and the barriers are to be avoided, businesses must also address certain infrastructure, processes and implementation requirements.

The recommendation is that marketers should use the following three solutions.

1 **Solution 1:** provide the necessary infrastructure and resources for marketing planning activities.

2 **Solution 2:** use a robust analytical process that is objective and complete in terms of the inclusion of the essential ingredients of marketing planning.

3 **Solution 3:** devote managerial time and attention to the ongoing management of the resulting plan's implementation.

We will now look at each of these solutions in greater detail.

Solution 1: infrastructure requirements

The infrastructure requirements for marketing planning can be conceptualized as a series of prerequisites that organizations should address at the outset of the process.

The need to manage internal communication extends far beyond the marketing function. A well-orchestrated programme to manage interfunctional co-ordination is paramount. It is vital to ensure that communication of the planning exercise and its outcomes extends throughout organizational hierarchies and right down the distribution channels.

In addition, any marketing initiative requires purpose, process and robust propositions, whether it is an externally deployed marketing mix programme or an infrastructure requisite for successful marketing planning. Busy personnel cannot be expected to take time out from routine operations to undertake strategic thinking and develop marketing plans without being provided with the resources for tackling such tasks. Too often, senior managers expect a few line managers to undertake additional weighty tasks without being provided with the necessary extra resources.

Solution 2: robust processes

There is no point determining tactical marketing mix programmes if no analysis of the marketplace has been undertaken or if the target market strategy has not been updated accordingly to reflect these findings. An effective marketing planning process should include a coherent and integrated process of analysis, strategizing and tactical programme recommendation.

The skills to undertake marketing analyses, facilitate a strategic review and to modify often entrenched marketing tactics accordingly must be inherent or bought in from external agencies.

Solution 3: facilitation of implementation

Strategy and planning activities will not occur by chance and must be managed: schedules, reviews, performance assessments and remedial actions, with praise and criticism from senior management in the ongoing evaluation process. Without attention to these requirements, much good marketing thinking fails to result in actionable recommendations being implemented.

The output from planning is normally summarized in the form of a detailed marketing plan document. The robustness of this document is a key factor in determining the success of the planning process. To be effective, the marketing plan document must explain the background analyses undertaken during the planning process before specifying all aspects of the proposed marketing strategy and of the marketing and sales programmes. The required marketing strategy elements should include details of target segments, an explanation of the basis for competing, and identification of product and brand positioning strategies. The marketing and sales programmes should encompass issues to do with product range, pricing terms, promotional tactics, methods and channels of distribution, and sales force planning. These recommendations must be seen to match the stated marketing objectives and arise out of the analyses of the market, customers, competitors and the wider trading environment that have been undertaken. That is, there must be a close connection between the desires, characteristics and buying behaviour of the company's target markets and the proposed marketing mix recommendations.

Three areas that are particularly vital to implementation, but that are sometimes overlooked in the marketing plan, warrant specific mention.

1 **Communicating planning outputs:** the importance of effective communication does not end once the marketing planning recommendations have been made. Instead, the emphasis shifts to ensuring clarity within and across functional areas, so that the newly designed marketing programmes can be consistently and thoroughly implemented. A detailed plan of communication activity is required that specifies how this can be achieved and who needs to be involved. This plan should extend beyond the organization itself to include all parts of the distribution structure.

2 **Specifying the required implementation resources:** an appropriate level of detail is needed to ensure sufficient finance, personnel and time are allocated to each of the marketing activities required. A weakness of many businesses' marketing plans is that they fail to provide these necessary implementation details, with the result that not all planned activities are put into practice. A key message is that marketing planning does not end when the marketing plan document has been prepared. At this stage, it is crucial that all aspects of the implementation details are attended to. Even once this part of the process is complete, the marketing plan document should continue to be updated on an ongoing basis.

3 **Handling changes in organizational structure, culture or distribution channels:** recognizing that planning may lead to organizational upheaval and change is an

important infrastructure prerequisite. However, in order to ensure that such change happens in practice, part of the marketing plan must specifically consider required changes in organizational or distribution channel structure. The level of detail provided is especially critical. For modifications in company structure this should include physical changes to the organizational chart, alterations in reporting structures, managerial responsibilities and communication channels. Alterations to the channel structure must be accompanied by a detailed explanation of the required system for physical distribution, together with any repercussions for the activities of the sales force or those involved in distributing the company's product base.

12.6 Organization structures for international marketing efforts

There are two main conditions to fulfil if a firm is to succeed: to pursue a suitable marketing strategy and to have adopted an appropriate organizational structure. The firm's organizational structure is a critical variable for the implementation of the firm's international marketing plans. The following list highlights the main reasons for this.

- There may be difficulties in co-ordinating and controlling operating units (subsidiaries) of different sizes and levels of complexity.

- Personnel in different markets may have different objectives, abilities and expectations, and organizing such a heterogeneous group can be problematic.

- There may be excessive head office control which can be a barrier for the local implementation of marketing plans.

Effective marketing planning only comes about when the marketing strategy and organizational structure match.

The question 'Do we have the right organization for our strategy?' is something that all chief executives should be asking, and a failure to do so may bring with it the risk of failure. This question can be broken down into four 'basic' parts, the first two of which concern themselves with the division of responsibility among the labour force, while the remaining questions focus on co-ordination and control.

- What tasks are required to put the strategies into operation?

- To whom should these tasks be assigned?

- How interdependent are these tasks?

- How can the organization be sure that the tasks assigned will be performed?

There are no right answers, and therefore right structures, for all organizations, but successful firms are those that tend to have organizational structures that fit their specific needs in terms of their corporate objectives, strategies, corporate culture, and so on.

There are many ways in which a multinational firm can be organized. These can be reduced to five organizational structure archetypes:

1 functional structure

2 international division structure

3 product-based structure

4 geographic structure

5 matrix structure.

We will now look at each of these in turn.

Functional structure

At this early stage of internationalization, the company has no international marketing specialist and the domestic marketing department may have responsibility for global marketing activities.

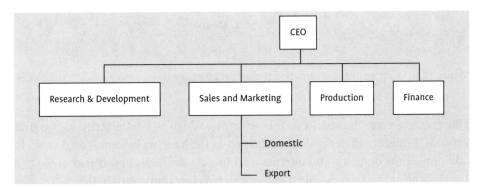

Figure 12.2 Example of the functional structure

The export department may be a sub-department of the sales and marketing department (see Fig. 12.2). The export department is the first real step in internationalizing the organizational structure. It is particularly suitable for SMEs, having low product and area diversities.

International division structure

As international sales grow, at some point an international division structure may emerge.

In Fig. 12.3, the firm's activities are separated into domestic and international divisions, with a major objective being to develop the firm's international business interests. This structure is most suited to firms that:

■ wish to develop international business and greater international expertise

■ do not have adequately trained executives to manage an international organization.

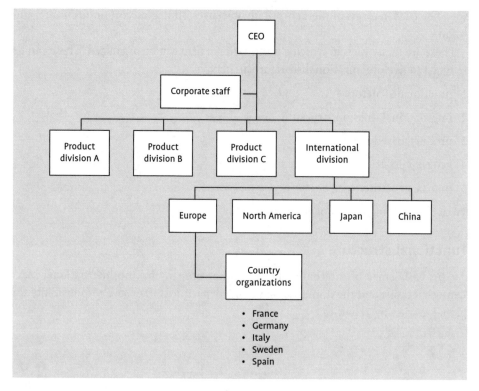

Figure 12.3 Example of the international division structure

However, there are drawbacks to this structure, which will be revealed as the firm expands, bringing problems of co-ordination as the business becomes too diverse. In addition, as the domestic and international spheres develop, conflict may emerge in the areas of product development and research & development (R&D).

Product-based structure

The product-based structure is suitable for companies with more international business experience and with diversified product lines.

Under the product-based structure the major focus is on product lines. The firm is divided along product lines and each division becomes a cost centre, with the divisional head responsible for profit margins. A key feature is the decentralization of the structure, which allows local managers greater freedom in their decision-making.

This structure suits firms that have:

- a diversified product line

- products that have potential for worldwide standardization

- a wide variety of final customers

- production sites in many locations.

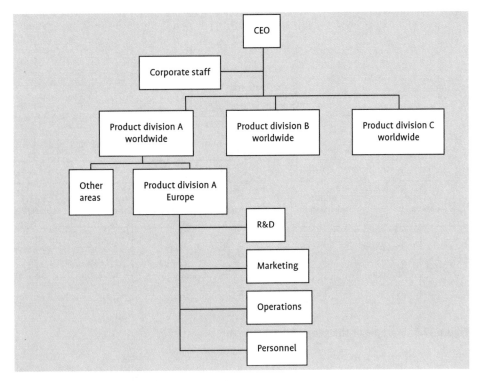

Figure 12.4 Example of the product-based structure

Major *advantages* of this structure are:

■ decentralization

■ a highly motivated group of divisional heads

■ product development and elimination can be achieved relatively easily, without affecting the rest of the firm's operations in any major way.

The *disadvantages* of this structure are:

■ co-ordination problems could arise

■ certain product areas may be overlooked, particular minor ones

■ when division heads move up the corporate ladder, there is a danger that they may bias policies in favour of their former product areas.

Geographic structure

If product acceptance and operating conditions vary considerably across world markets, then the geographical structure is the one to choose. This structure is especially useful for companies that have a homogeneous range of products, but at the same time need fast and efficient adaptation to local market conditions. Typically, the world is divided into regions, as illustrated in Fig. 12.5.

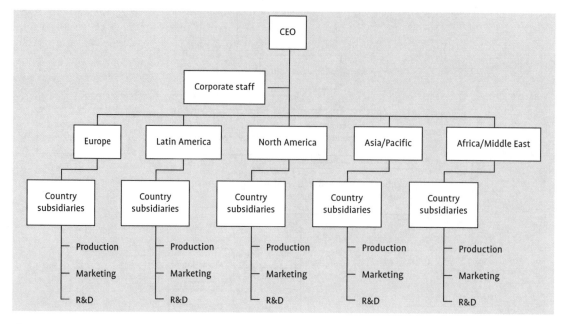

Figure 12.5 Example of the geographical structure

There are two main reasons for dividing into different regions:

1 When sales volume in a particular region becomes substantial there need to be some specialized staff to focus on that region, to realize more fully the potential of an already growing market.

2 Homogeneity within regions and heterogeneity between them necessitate treating each important region separately; therefore a regional management centre becomes an appropriate organizational feature.

Parallel to a regional centre, each country has its own organizational unit. Country-based subsidiaries are characterized by a high degree of adaptation to local conditions. Since each subsidiary develops its own unique activities and its own autonomy, it is sometimes relevant to combine local subsidiaries with a regional centre: for example, to utilize opportunities across European countries.

Firms may also organize their operations using a customer (key account or global account) structure, especially if the customer groups they serve are very different: for example, businesses and governments. Catering to these diverse groups may require the concentration of specialists in particular divisions. The product may be the same, but the buying processes of the various customer groups may differ.

The *advantages* of this type of structure are:

■ there is a clear demonstration of authority

■ the co-ordination of different functional areas of management is enhanced

■ resources could be pooled.

The *disadvantages* of this type of structure are:

- for it to work efficiently, the structure depends on a small group of highly effective managers
- there is the likelihood that certain product lines will be ignored as there is no overall responsibility for a specific product.

Matrix structure

The product-based structure tends to offer better opportunities to rationalize production across countries, thus gaining production cost efficiencies. On the other hand, the geographical structure is more responsive to local market trends and needs.

Some companies need both capabilities, so they have adopted a more complex structure: the matrix structure (see Fig. 12.6).

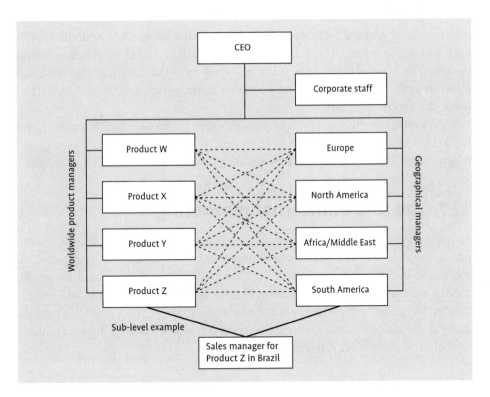

Figure 12.6 Example of the matrix structure

The strength of this structure is that it can respond to different political and economic environments because it incorporates the elements of product-based and geographic management. For example, the product manager would have worldwide responsibility for Product X, while geographic managers would be responsible for all product lines, including Product X, in the market. Thus both managers would

367

overlap and this is a good basis from which to make major decisions. Another feature of matrix structures is the duality that exists — in terms of dual budgeting, dual personnel evaluation systems, and so on. This could be seen as positive in that interdependence of opinion and contributions would be the outcome.

The major *disadvantages* of this structure are:

- the possibility of a power struggle as a result of the dual command structure – as illustrated in Fig. 12.6, the sales manager for Product Z in Brazil would have two superiors to refer to

- these structures tend to collapse in times of crisis

- communication becomes more complicated

- uncertainty exists in determining who decides what in certain circumstances.

Which organizational structure is best?

The structures adopted by firms tend to reflect their management outlook, experience and history; firms can even adapt the three basic types to produce hybrid models. The main point to bear in mind, however, is that the best organizational structure is the one that fits the organization's environment and internal characteristics (the SWOT approach).

If the strategy changes or the firm makes further internationalization moves, this has to have some effect on the organization structure. Also, the organization structure might change if the management experiences problems with its existing structure.

12.7 The role of internal marketing

As more companies come to appreciate the importance of people in the implementation process, they are becoming disenchanted with traditional approaches to marketing implementation. These forces for change have been caused by several factors: high rates of employee turnover and the associated costs of this, and continuing problems in the implementation of marketing strategy. These problems have led many organizations to adopt alternative approaches to marketing implementation. One of these alternatives is internal marketing.

The internal marketing approach

The concept of internal marketing comes primarily from service organizations, where it was first practised as a tactic for making all employees aware of the need for customer satisfaction. Generally speaking, internal marketing refers to the managerial actions necessary to make all members of the organization understand and accept their respective roles in implementing marketing strategy. This means that all employees, from the chief executive officer to frontline marketing personnel, must realize how each individual job assists in implementing the marketing strategy.

Under the internal marketing approach, every employee has two sets of customers: *external* and *internal*. In the end, successful marketing implementation comes from an accumulation of individual actions where all employees are responsible for implementing the marketing strategy.

The internal marketing process

In the case of service organizations, the 4Ps marketing mix is felt to be inadequate. Some authors have suggested extending this to include people, process and physical evidence (the so-called 7Ps). To an organization providing a service to clients, the people element of the marketing mix is arguably the most important. After all, it may reaonably be argued that the people *are* the organization, so the internal marketing process is important.

Ensuring that all staff, whatever their status, deliver a service of the highest quality is a key issue for all organizations. The inseparability of services makes it impossible to distinguish between service production and service delivery, and it is the people of the organization who are, therefore, responsible for both. In this section of the marketing plan the organization must, therefore, give consideration to the people skills it will need in order to provide its service and, indeed, deliver every component of the marketing plan. This can then be matched against the profile of the existing human resource and appropriate gaps identified. The organization can then ensure that those 'gaps' are represented in the staff recruitment programme and that the appropriate person specifications are in place.

The interaction between the internal and external marketing programmes is illustrated in Fig. 12.7.

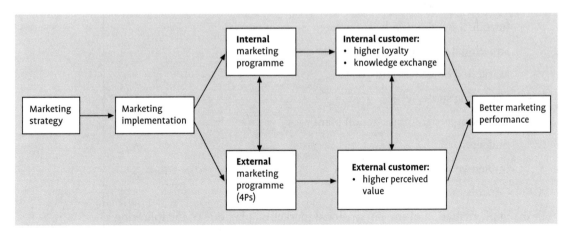

Figure 12.7 Internal marketing: a framework

It is, of course, usually much easier to develop and retain existing staff than it is to attain new ones. The second focus of this section of the plan is hence to identify what steps need to be taken in order to retain existing personnel. By far the easiest way of

369

achieving this is probably to survey those who decide to leave and, having discovered their reasons for dissatisfaction, implement any changes that may be necessary to ensure that these problems are corrected. One can also ensure that an ongoing dialogue is maintained with existing staff so that they do not feel compelled to leave in the first place.

Summary

The success of a company depends mainly upon its marketing activities and the effectiveness of these activities. In order to find out if the marketing function of the company is effective all aspects need to be analysed. With this information a strategic marketing plan can be created and applied in the years to come.

By analysing current marketing data, flaws in the planning and weaknesses in the company's (or the competitor's) products or strategies can be discovered. Appropriate action can then be taken to ensure a better functioning of the weak parts of the marketing engine or to make better use of the competition's weaknesses and flaws. This can best be done by performing a marketing analysis before writing a marketing plan. (If you have the marketing data readily available this is not necessary.)

The marketing plan has the following framework:

I   Title page

II   Table of contents

III   Executive summary

IV   Introduction and problem statement

V   Situational analysis

VI   Marketing objectives and goals

VII   Marketing strategies

VIII   Marketing programmes/action plans

IX   Budgets

X   Implementation and control

XI   Conclusion

In the implementation of the international marketing plan one of the following organizational structures may be used:

- functional structure

- international division structure

- product-based structure

- geographic structure

- matrix structure.

The success of a marketing plan depends on three areas:

1 the process that is followed

2 the infrastructure that is established prior to and throughout the process

3 the implementation controls that are put in place; it is self-evident that effective marketing planning must be based on a clearly structured and well-articulated process; those involved in planning must understand the expectations that are being placed upon them and be provided with clear guidance as to what they must do; however, putting this process in place is not enough on its own to ensure success.

No matter how sound the analysis undertaken during the process, or the strategy and marketing programmes determined, insufficient attention at this final stage can lead to implementation breakdown. Care must also be taken to ensure that adequate implementation resources are made available and also to fully communicate the outcomes of the plan to all interested parties. Finally, the planning process and the resulting implementation of the plan's recommendations must be monitored closely so that remedial action may quickly be carried out in order to rectify any problems and remove obstacles to the successful implementation of the plan.

Questions for discussion

1 What kind of market information would be necessary for international marketing planning, and how might it be obtained?

2 What are the major challenges faced by marketers in developing and implementing international marketing plans?

3 Compare and contrast the marketing plan for an established product with that for a new product.

4 What are the practical internal issues to be addressed by marketers when developing an international marketing plan?

5 Comment on the view that companies will derive as much benefit from the planning exercise as from the marketing plan itself.

6 What are the main problems associated with the links between international marketing strategy and organizational structure?

7 What are the principal issues to be considered in organizational design?

8 How does a firm's size at home and abroad influence the organizational structure?

9 Outline the main organizational structure types that are used by international organizations.

10 What are the advantages and disadvantages in adopting a matrix approach to organizational structure?

References

Dibb, S. (2002) Marketing planning best practices. *Marketing Review* 2, pp. 441–59.

Evans, P.B. and Wurster, T.S. (1997) Strategy and the new economics of information. *Harvard Business Review* 75(5), September–October, pp. 70–82.

Evans, P.B. and Wurster, T.S. (1999) Getting real about virtual commerce. *Harvard Business Review* 77(6), November–December, pp. 85–94.

Evans, P.B. and Wurster, T.S. (2000) *Blown to Bits: How the New Economics of Information Transforms Strategy*. Boston: Harvard Business School Press.

Simkin, L. (2002) Tackling implementation impediments to marketing planning. *Marketing Intelligence & Planning* 20(2), pp. 120–6.

Case 12 *Bob Martin Company: the UK's leading brand name for pet healthcare is seeking a foothold in Japan

Bob Martin Ltd (http://www.bobmartin.co.uk) was founded in 1892 and became famous for its conditioning powders for dogs. The company, based in Somerset, England, has since produced a range of over-the-counter medicines and petcare products to look after a wide range of pets, including dogs, cats, small animals and birds. The number of employees is approximately 140.

Bob Martin has been a family-owned company since it started, and today is financially very well consolidated. So the company has enough financial resources for an international expansion.

Until now, Bob Martin's products have been marketed actively only on the UK market. However, it has been a market leader in its niche there for several years.

At the last board of directors meeting in November 2003, the chairman, Sir Bruce Martin, said that he had seen in a journal that over 70 per cent of Japanese dogs and cats have serious dental health problems by the time they are three years old. Sir Bruce knows that the company is launching a brand new range of oral hygiene products for dogs and cats. The range contains large and small dental chews for dogs, uniquely designed toothbrushes for dogs and cats, as well as a toothpaste for dogs and cats. With this in mind, Sir Bruce Martin has asked you, as an international marketing specialist, to present an evaluation of Bob Martin's possible entry into the Japanese market at the next board of directors meeting. The following sections offer some background information that may help you.

Bob Martin's positioning in its home market: the UK

The company enhanced its position in 2002 with the redesign of its packaging and by adding new products to its range. Petcare products in the UK continued to perform strongly in 2002, growing by 5 per cent in current value terms to £394 mn. The principle reason behind this rise is the growing number of people who are prepared to spend increasing amounts pampering and looking after their pets. One industry expert has broken down pet owners into the following categories:

- owners who treat their pets like a member of the family
- owners who keep pets as a hobby
- owners who like having pets but do not take any extra care
- owners who should not have animals.

It is those in the first group that are increasing in number and who are also willing to spend more on their pets than before. This has been particularly beneficial to other petcare products, which saw stronger than average growth in 2002 of just over 4 per

* This case does not necessarily reflect the current strategy of Bob Martin Ltd

cent. It is in the more pampering-type products where there was significant growth, such as special cat and dog beds and animal toys. Growth in animal beds is particularly strong due to the popularity of special soft cloth beds, which have the added advantage that they can be washed.

The increasing number of people concerned with their pets' well-being has spread to healthcare and dietary supplements, which saw over 9 per cent and 8 per cent growth in current value terms, respectively, in 2002. Dietary supplements are perhaps the best example of this in practice. This niche is principally made up of worming products and vitamins/mineral supplements, with sales of each worth around £20 million in 2002. Both saw strong growth, as pet owners became more concerned about and aware of their animals' health – for example, owners are starting to use worming products more frequently.

This also explains the fast growth of pet vitamins and dietary supplements. Growth of these products, according to one industry source, is not being hindered by the increasing number of food products with added nutrients. Indeed, if anything, it seems to be helping to drive growth by increasing awareness among owners of the importance of vitamins and dietary supplements, although another factor could be that owners are not entirely confident that the food provides enough of these nutrients.

Others factors boosting sales

There are other factors driving growth in pet healthcare and dietary supplements. A major factor has been the increasing hard selling by vets of these products. A growing number of these practices have become more business focused, so rather than just treating the animal vets are also pushing more products. Thus as more owners are going to the vet, they are also being increasingly pressurized to buy products.

Within pet healthcare, growth has also been driven by the changing living conditions of pets and the emergence of more powerful and convenient anti-flea products. Anti-flea products, which make up around £35 mn of pet healthcare sales, saw strong growth in the latter part of the review period as the more powerful products became available. These products, launched in 2002 by Bob Martin, not only kill the fleas themselves but also destroy their larvae. In addition, they also have the benefit of being relatively easy to administer, as they are in liquid form and just need to be applied to the skin on the back of the pet's neck.

Sales have also been helped by the conditions in which animals are kept. Pets are increasingly being kept in warm centrally heated houses, which, combined with moisture, offer ideal conditions for fleas to breed. So whereas, before, the main flea season was the summer months, an increasing number of products are now being sold throughout the year.

Natural herbal and homeopathic products still remain a small niche within petcare; however, they are matching sales of the medical products. Herbal and homeopathic products are popular among a certain group of pet owners who dislike pharmaceutical-type treatments. The vast majority of pet owners still and will continue to prefer pharmaceutical treatments, however, as they want quick, easy and effective treatments for their loved ones.

Table 12.2 Retail sales of petcare products by sub-sector: value, 1998–2002

£ mn at current prices	1998	1999	2000	2001	2002
Cat litter	56.7	57.9	59.3	60.9	62.8
Healthcare	28.0	30.5	33.6	36.8	40.2
Dietary supplements	32.5	33.8	36.8	40.1	43.4
Other petcare products	219.0	224.3	229.6	237.8	247.5
Petcare products total	**336.2**	**346.5**	**359.3**	**375.6**	**393.9**

Source: trade press, store checks, trade interviews, Euromonitor estimates

---

Table 12.3 Retail sales of petcare products by sub-sector: % value growth, 1998–2002

% current growth	2001/02	1998–02 CAGR	1998/02 total
Cat litter	3.1	2.6	10.8
Healthcare	9.2	9.5	43.6
Dietary supplements	8.2	7.5	33.5
Other petcare products	4.1	3.1	13.0
Petcare products total	**4.9**	**4.0**	**17.2**

Source: trade press, store checks, trade interviews, Euromonitor estimates

---

A major factor that is likely to hold back growth in pet healthcare and dietary supplements will be the levelling off in the number of pets. Thus there will be only a limited degree of organic growth from increased usage, such as with worming and flea-control products. While growth of flea-control products during the review period came from the introduction of more powerful and costly vet-type products, there is, according to an industry expert, little sign (at least in the short to medium term) of new products becoming widely available. However, sales of anti-flea products could well be boosted if there are a number of hot summers during the forecast period. Meanwhile, the lack of product innovation in worming products will stifle growth in dietary supplements.

A bigger factor in the slowing-down of growth in dietary supplements will be specially prepared animal food with added vitamins and nutrients. At present, growth in the popularity of this food is boosting sales of pet vitamins and dietary supplements by helping to raise awareness. However, by the middle of the forecast period, sales of vitamins and dietary supplements will be hit as consumers go for the more convenient and cheaper all-in food.

Pet healthcare in the UK continues to be dominated by the two leading manufacturers, Bob Martin Company and Johnson's Veterinary Products, which took a combined value share of 72 per cent in 2001. Bob Martin has managed to extend its brand share with the launch of its vet-strength flea treatment in June 2001 and its strong presence in the multiple retailers. This was due to the detriment of Johnson's Veterinary Products, which saw sales grow but lost value share due to lack of brand presence.

Table 12.4 Uk healthcare brand share, 2000–01

% retail value

Brand	Company	2000	2001
Bob Martin	Bob Martin Company	40.8	42.0
Johnson's	Johnson's Veterinary Products Ltd	30.9	30.0
Hartz	Hartz Mountain Corp., The	8.2	7.5
Sinclair	William Sinclair Holdings plc	4.0	4.5
Hatchwell	Hatchwell Co. Ltd, The	3.6	3.5
Private label		3.1	3.0
Others		9.4	9.5
Total		**100.0**	**100.0**

Source: adapted from Euromonitor estimates

The Japanese pet healthcare market

In 1994, the Japan Pet Food Manufacturers' Association (JPFMA) began to compile data on the cat and dog population in the country. According to the JPFMA, since its peak in 2002 the dog and cat population has been in a steady decline, with the dog population falling by 4 per cent since 2000 to an expected total in 2002 of less than 9.7 million animals. The decline in the cat population has been even more marked, with a fall of more than 5 per cent since 2000, to an expected total of 7.3 million animals in 2002.

Pedigree breeds remain popular

Although the dog population is declining; the Japanese situation remains quite distinct, with the JPFMA believing that approximately 55 per cent of the dog population is comprised of pedigree animals, with the most popular breeds including the golden retriever and, more recently, miniature dogs such as poodles and shih-tzus. Small dogs are especially popular with the Japanese due to their manageability, and are particularly well suited to the often rather cramped apartments in which Japanese people live.

The decline in the cat population has, however, seen significant change over the review period, with the number classified as outdoor cats declining significantly, by 22 per cent to little over 900,000 animals, while the house cat population has continued to increase by 1 per cent, to 6.6 million animals. Cats have long been favoured for their independent nature, low maintenance costs and, like small dogs, their suitability to life in small Japanese homes. While cross-breeds are the most common cats in Japan, Persian and Siamese breeds are also very popular, with pure-bred cats accounting for 12 per cent of the total pet cat population in 2000.

Economic reality bites deep

Although keeping dogs and cats remains extremely popular in Japan, economic retrenchment of household budgets has limited the number of consumers willing to take on the responsibility and cost of keeping a pet. For the most part, the decline in pet population has occurred as a result of the ageing Japanese pet population. Many pets were first purchased in the early 1990s, during the first great wave of Japan's pet boom, and since the turn of the new millennium this pet population has begun to die off, while current economic instability has discouraged owners from replacing their departed pets. With a soaring number of strays and abandoned animals, enthusiasm for keeping pets in Japan's second pet boom of the late 1990s may well represent a short-term fad rather than a deep-seated change in national culture.

Birds continue to soar

Pet birds saw increasing popularity in Japan over the review period. Budgerigars, finches and canaries have long been favoured as feathered companions in the home. The bird population has increased by an estimated 10 per cent since 2000 to reach an expected total of 21.3 million in 2002. This is due to the continued popularity of traditional bird-keeping, and the more recent development of enthusiasm for exotic varieties such as cockatiels, parrots and macaws.

Table 12.5 **Pet populations, Japan 1998–2002**					
000s of animals	**1998**	**1999**	**2000**	**2001**	**2002**
Dogs	9,895.0	9,567.0	10,054.0	9,867.0	9,650.0
Cats	7,467.0	7,540.0	7,718.0	7,517.0	7,300.0
Birds	17,800.0	18,779.0	19,362.0	20,525.0	21,300.0
Fish	36,000.0	36,400.0	35,200.0	34,500.0	34,100.0
Small mammals	2,550.0	2,830.0	3,286.0	3,100.0	3,000.0
Reptiles	20.0	20.0	21.0	21.5	22.0

Source: official statistics (Japanese Ministry of Agriculture, Fisheries and Food), trade associations (Japan Pet Food Manufacturers Association), trade press (*Nikkei Marketing Journal, Nikkei Weekly*)

Dog- and cat-owning households

Until the 1960s, pets were not common in Japanese households. Over the past 30 years, however, the pet population has grown steadily until, by 2000, 18.1 per cent of Japanese households owned a dog, while 11.6 per cent of households owned cats. The year 2000 represented the peak of cat and dog ownership levels, with 2001 and 2002 experiencing declines in the pet population. Estimated dog ownership per Japanese household in 2002 stood at 17.3 per cent, while for cats the figure stood at 10.8 per cent (see the accompanying table).

Table 12.6 Dog- and cat-owning households: % analysis, Japan 1998–2002

% households	1998	2002
Dog	17.7	17.3
Cat	11.2	10.8

Source: adapted from official statistics (Japanese Ministry of Agriculture, Fisheries and Food), trade associations (Japan Pet Food Manufacturers Association), trade press (*Nikkei Marketing Journal, Nikkei Weekly*)

Petcare products' performance

Sales of petcare products were expected to decline slightly in 2002, falling by 1.3 per cent in current value terms. Dietary supplements and other petcare products were expected to decline just over 3 per cent and almost 5 per cent respectively, while cat litter was expected to fall by just under 1 per cent. The Japanese have a great passion for looking after their pets, as evidenced by the value of petcare product sales, which were expected to be worth some ¥264 million in 2002. Products available include items such as dog bowls, cat clothes and even Gucci-branded frisbees. However, wider demographic and economic factors have taken their toll on demand for such products.

With the expansion in the pet population reaching a plateau in 2001 and 2002, coupled with the deflationary nature of the Japanese economy, expenditure on petcare products has stalled. Evidence of this is clear in cat litter, where demand remains strong as an increasing number of cats are kept exclusively within the home, which has definitely increased reliance on such products; however, competition between manufacturers and retailers in the economic environment placed downward pressure on prices, thereby constraining value growth potential.

Healthcare products buck overall trend

The performance of pet healthcare products was expected to contrast with that of other petcare products in 2002, with an increase in current value terms of 6.8 per cent expected. Increasing health-consciousness among consumers has spread to the pet world, with owners spending increasing amounts on maintaining their pets' health.

Veterinary bills can often be extremely high in Japan, and this has increased demand for home care and preventative products that pet owners can use in the home. The ageing of the pet population in Japan has also stimulated demand for healthcare products, as owners seek to maintain the health of their pets as the animals grow older.

Developments in pet food reduce demand for dietary supplements

Dietary supplements were expected to see sales decline by 3.1 per cent in current value terms in 2002. This was largely due to increased sales of super-premium food products, which give owners a choice of pet products that are often fortified with vitamins and minerals that are designed to maintain animal health. Marketing initiatives by companies such as Iams and Hill's have made dietary supplements seem redundant in the eyes of many pet owners.

Table 12.7 Retail sales of petcare products by sub-sector, 1998–2002

¥ bn at current prices (¥ = £0.0055)	1998	1999	2000	2001	2002
Cat litter	103.0	105.0	107.0	106.0	105.0
Healthcare	36.5	39.9	41.3	44.0	47.0
Dietary supplements	10.8	11.2	12.1	12.7	12.3
Other petcare products	102.0	106.0	110.0	105.0	100.0
Petcare products total	**252.3**	**262.1**	**270.4**	**267.7**	**264.3**

Source: adapted from Euromonitor statistics and other public sources

Table 12.8 Retail sales of petcare products by sub-sector: % value growth, 1998–2002

% current value growth	2001–02	1998–02 CAGR	1998–02 total
Cat litter	−0.9	0.5	1.9
Healthcare	6.8	6.5	28.8
Dietary supplements	−3.1	3.3	13.9
Other petcare products	−4.8	−0.5	−2.0
Petcare products total	**−1.3**	**1.2**	**4.8**

Source: adapted from Euromonitor statistics and other public sources

Competitors in the Japanese pet healthcare market

Gendai Pharmaceutical Co. Ltd remained the leading player in healthcare products in 2001 with its eponymous range of products, which accounted for a value share of 40 per cent, up four percentage points on 2000. Gendai continued to benefit from its increasing penetration within larger-scale retailers, where much of the recent growth in retailer activity has been contained.

Yamahisa Pet Co. Ltd and DoggyMan Hayashi KK were the two only other major manufacturers of note, with value shares of 25 per cent and 16.8 per cent respectively in 2001. A wide range of smaller companies' products and imports is also available, as well as some private-label products.

Table 12.9 Pet healthcare brand shares 2000–01

% retail value – retail sales prices (RSP)

Brand	Company	2000	2001
Gendai	Gendai Pharmaceutical Co. Ltd	36.0	40.0
Dr Petio	Yamahisa Pet Co. Ltd	27.0	25.0
DoggyMan	DoggyMan Hayashi KK	16.4	16.8
Private label		1.0	0.8
Others		19.6	17.4
Total		**100.0**	**100.0**

Dietary supplements shares

Gendai Pharmaceutical led sales of pet dietary supplements in 2001 with a value share of 18 per cent, an increase of three percentage points on 2000, achieved through consumer familiarity with its eponymous brand at a time when other manufacturers were retreating from dietary supplements.

Smack Co. Ltd and Yamahisa Pet Co. Ltd were two other major manufacturers in pet dietary supplements, with value shares of 15.5 per cent and 13 per cent respectively in 2001.

Table 12.10 Market share of brands in dietary supplements, 2000–01

% retail value (RSP)

Brand	Company	2000	2001
Gendai	Gendai Pharmaceutical Co. Ltd	15.0	18.0
Smack	Smack Co. Ltd	14.0	15.5
Dr Petio	Yamahisa Pet Co. Ltd	14.0	13.0
Tokyo Pet	Tokyo Pet Co. Ltd	10.5	9.5
Pervinal	YK Enterprise Co. Ltd	5.1	4.0
Enervite	YK Enterprise Co. Ltd	3.4	2.0
Private label		8.0	9.0
Others		30.0	29.0
Total		**100.0**	**100.0**

Source: official statistics (Japanese Ministry of Agriculture, Fisheries and Food), trade associations (Japan Pet Food Manufacturers Association), trade press (*Nikkei Marketing Journal, Nikkei Weekly*)

Petcare product forecasts

Sales of petcare products are expected to be flat over the forecast period, with a 1.5 per cent decline in constant value terms to just over ¥260 mn in 2007. This decline is predicted as the factors that affected performance over the review period continue, and in some cases become increasingly significant.

A further decline in the number of cats and dogs kept as domestic pets is expected to undermine demand for other petcare products, which was largely built on the two pet booms Japan experienced during the 1990s. Fewer pets overall, as well as a weak economic performance, is likely to see other petcare products contract by as much as ¥15 mn over the forecast period – some 15 per cent – to stand at ¥85 bn in 2007.

Deflation to stump growth

Similar to events in 2002, the deflationary effect on sales of the wider economic situation is epitomized by the slight decline in value predicted for cat litter, which is expected to fall by 2.1 per cent in constant terms through to 2007. Although volume sales are predicted to rise as cat owners belatedly move over to cat-litter products, both retailer and manufacturer competition – encouraged by cheap imports – is expected to underpin a continued decline in average unit prices.

Dietary products are likely to suffer from the development of dry premium pet food products, which offer similar nutritional benefits to dietary supplements, thereby reducing the perceived need for the latter. The further development of life-stage and breed-specific products will further undermine demand for dietary supplements.

Generally, with an ageing pet population, and increasing awareness of health issues among consumers, sales of pet healthcare products are predicted to increase as owners are willing to pay handsomely for the maintenance of their pets' health. Overall, pet healthcare products are expected to see growth in the coming years.

Questions

1 How should Bob Martin Company penetrate the Japanese market with its products?

2 What are its chances of success in the Japanese market?

3 How could Bob Martin prepare its sales force for future cross-cultural negotiations in Japan?

4 How should Bob Martin apply the GAM concept for the Japanese market?

Source: adapted from Euromonitor database, official statistics (Japanese Ministry of Agriculture, Fisheries and Food), trade associations (Japan Pet Food Manufacturers Association), trade press (*Nikkei Marketing Journal, Nikkei Weekly*)

Budgeting and control

Learning Objectives

After studying this chapter you should be able to:

- understand why customer profitability is important

- define the concept of Customer Life Time Value (CLTV)

- understand why CLTV is important

- describe the key elements of the marketing control system

- list the most important measures for marketing performance

- understand the need for evaluation and control of marketing plans and their implementation

- explain how a marketing budget is established.

13.1 **Introduction**

An organization needs to budget in order to ensure that its expenditure does not exceed its planned revenue. This chapter discusses how to use a rational process for developing budgets and allocating resources. Furthermore, the chapter will outline the need for a control system to oversee the marketing operations of the company.

13.2 **Marketing productivity and economic results**

The productivity of an operation is related to how effectively the resources that are input in a process (manufacturing process, service process) are transformed into economic results for the service provider and value for its customers. The traditional productivity concept has been developed for manufacturers of physical goods as a production efficiency concept. Existing productivity models and productivity measurement instruments are also geared to the context of manufacturers. Moreover, they are based on assumptions that production and consumption are separate processes and that customers do not participate in the production process.

High productivity is generally assumed to be a 'good thing' in so far as a productive operation is more likely to have lower costs. It is this close connection with the cost performance of an operation or process that accounts for the interest in understanding and measuring productivity. Although the definition of productivity appears straightforward, productivity can be difficult to deal with for several different reasons; first of all, the outputs are usually expressed in different forms to the inputs. Outputs are often measured in physical terms such as units (e.g. cars produced), tonnes (of paper), kilowatts (of electricity) or value (euros), for example. However, inputs are usually physically different and include measures of people (numbers, skills, hours worked or costs), and cost of input resources or marketing actions (Johnston and Jones, 2004) (see Fig. 13.1).

This complexity of relationships between inputs and outputs is affected by both the number of inputs and outputs as well as their measurement units, because different combinations of number and type of units can result in a huge number of productivity metrics, each having its own information value and reflecting different things.

In particular, the intangible nature of many services means that it is difficult to objectively define and measure the service outputs being provided. The measurement and management of inputs and outputs is also complicated because of the simultaneous production and consumption of many services, as well as their perishability and heterogeneity, as service encounters are experienced differently by different people or even by the same people in different circumstances.

Because the service (production) process and service consumption to a large extent are simultaneous processes, where customers participate actively, the resources or inputs used to produce services cannot be standardized more than to a certain degree. It is difficult to relate a given number of inputs, in volume or value terms, to a given amount of outputs. Frequently, it is even difficult to define 'one unit of service'. According to the traditional manufacturing-related productivity concept, productivity is defined as the ratio between outputs produced and inputs used, given that the quality of the outputs is kept constant (the constant quality assumption), or (according to Grönroos and Ojasalo, 2004):

$$\text{Productivity} = \frac{\text{Outputs produced}}{\text{Inputs used}} \mid \text{Constant quality of outputs}$$

Only if the quality of the production output is constant, and there is no significant variation in the ratio between inputs used and outputs produced with these inputs, can productivity be measured with traditional methods. The constant quality assumption is normally taken for granted and not expressed explicitly. Therefore, the critical importance of this assumption is easily forgotten. However, in most service processes it does not apply. In services, it is not only the inputs that are difficult to calculate, it is also difficult to get a useful measurement of the outputs. Output measured as volume is useful only if customers are willing to buy this output. In manufacturing, where the constant quality assumption applies, customers can be expected to buy an output produced with an altered input or resource structure. However, in services we do not know whether customers will purchase the output produced with a different input structure. It depends on the effects of the new resources or inputs used on perceived process-related and outcome-related quality.

Hence, productivity cannot be understood without taking into account the interrelationship between the use of inputs or production resources and the perceived quality of the output produced with these resources. The interrelationship between internal efficiency and external efficiency is crucial for understanding and managing service productivity.

We first need to clarify the ways in which marketing activities build shareholder value. For example, when we talk of marketing 'investment', we must identify the marketing assets in which we invest and understand how the assets contribute to profits in the short run, and provide potential for growth and sustained profits in the long run. In this context, the spotlight is not on underlying products, pricing or customer relationships, but on marketing expenditures (e.g. marketing communications, promotions and other activities) and how these expenditures influence marketplace performance. The firm should have a business model that tracks how marketing expenditures influence what customers know, believe and feel, and, ultimately, how they behave. These intermediate outcomes are usually measured by non-financial means such as attitudes and behavioural intentions. The central problem we address here is how non-financial measures of marketing effectiveness drive financial performance measures such as sales, profits and shareholder value in both the short and the long run (Rust *et al.*, 2004).

It is important to understand that marketing actions, such as advertising, service improvements or new product launches, can help build long-term assets (e.g. brand equity, customer equity). These assets can be leveraged to deliver short-term profitability. Thus, marketing actions both create and leverage market-based assets. It is also important to distinguish between the 'effectiveness' and the 'efficiency' of marketing actions. For example, price promotions can be efficient in that they deliver short-term revenues and cash flows. However, to the extent that they invite competitive actions and destroy long-term profitability and brand equity, they may not be effective. Consequently, we will examine both tactical and strategic marketing actions, and their implications.

Factors influencing 'marketing productivity'

You may find it useful to read this section in conjunction with Fig. 13.1.

Input variables

Resource structure
Resources are the basic input into the business processes – that is technological, human, financial and organizational resources.

Marketing strategy
Marketing strategy and elements of it play a central role as input variables for winning and retaining customers, ensuring business growth and renewal, developing sustainable competitive advantages, and driving financial performance through business processes. A significant proportion of the market value of firms today lies in intangible off-balance-sheet assets, such as brands, market networks and intellectual property, rather than in tangible book assets. The leveraging of intangible assets to enhance corporate performance requires managers to move beyond the traditional inputs and outputs of marketing analysis and to incorporate an understanding of the financial consequences of marketing decisions, which include their impact on cash flows. On a more tactical level, managers implement marketing initiatives to increase short-term profitability. In most settings, this effort requires management of margins and turnover. Because better value to customers (or superior brands) can be tapped in terms of either price or volume, managers need to trade off prices (and therefore margins) against market share. Various programmes can be developed to enhance and sustain profitability (e.g. loyalty programmes, cross-selling, up-selling); how managers proceed is a matter of strategy. The question is, what type of expenditure has a greater influence on the value of a firm's customer base: a new campaign for advertisements or improvements in the quality of service? How do elements of a co-ordinated marketing strategy influence the purchase behaviour of different marketing segments over time, and how does this affect the firm's revenue streams? What are the disproportionate effects of changes in the structure of pricing on customer acquisition, retention and cross-buying? How do marketing and operations elements interact to grow or to diminish customer value?

Competitor basis

The competitive environment has a profound influence on the nature of marketing productivity. Marketing expenditure decisions, such as those about advertising, are often made with competitors in mind. Studies on advertising spending have identified two separate effects. On the one hand, competition can drive marketing spending higher, thus producing an escalation effect. Driven by a belief that gaining market share increases profit and enhances firm value, firms increase marketing expenditures to gain market share, even as rivals do the same. Little evidence suggests that the expenditures have the anticipated results.

Cost of input resources

These input variables will mainly have an impact on the financial metrics, like ROI.

Process variables

Value added is mainly created in the heads of the customers. It is only their evaluations that count in the end.

Customer process

To assess the impact of marketing expenditures on customers, it is important to understand the following five key dimensions, which can be considered particularly important measures of the customer mind-set.

1 **Customer awareness:** the extent to and ease with which customers recall and recognize the firm, and the extent to which they can identify the products and services associated with the firm.

2 **Customer associations:** the strength, favourability and uniqueness of perceived attributes and benefits for the firm and the brand.

3 **Customer attitudes:** the customer's overall evaluations of the firm and the brand in terms of its quality and the satisfaction it generates.

4 **Customer experience:** the extent to which customers use the brand overall, talk to others about the brand, and seek out brand and information, promotions, events, and so on.

5 **Customer loyalty:** how loyal the customer is towards the firm and the brand.

Because the strength and length of the customer or brand relationship matters, the firm must consider multiple aspects of each customer's purchase behaviour, not just retention probabilities. Consequently, researchers have begun to model other purchase behaviours, such as cross-selling, word-of-mouth behaviour and profitable lifetime duration of customers. These behaviours, at the individual customer level, influence the aggregate level of the marketing assets of the firm.

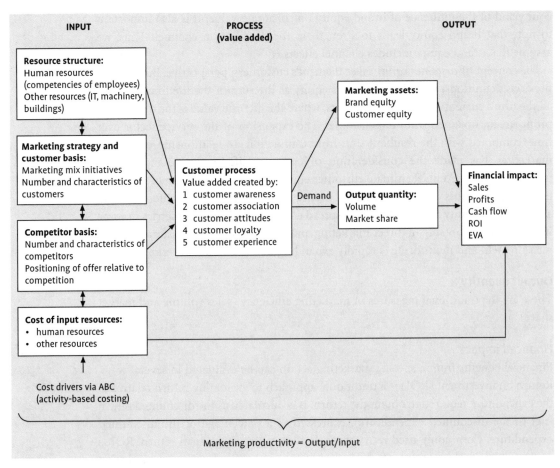

Figure 13.1 Model of marketing productivity

Output variables

Marketing assets

Marketing assets are customer-focused measures of the value of the firm (and its offerings) that may enhance the firm's long-term value. We focus on two approaches to assessing marketing assets that have received considerable attention in the marketing literature: brand equity and customer equity.

The concept of *brand equity* has emerged in the past 20 years as a core concept of marketing. One view of brand equity suggests that its value arises from the incremental discounted cash flow from the sale of a set of products or services, as a result of the brand being associated with those products or services. Research on brand equity has sought to understand the conceptual basis for this remarkable value and its implications. The fruits of this research are changing how people think about brands and manage them. Managers have a deeper understanding of the elements of brand equity, of how brand equity affects buyer behaviour, of how to measure brand equity and of the influence of brand equity on corporate value. It is also important to note that brand equity leads to strength in the distribution channel. Thus, we assume that brand equity includes channel effects.

The concept of *customer equity* takes the firm's customers' perspective. Building on previous definitions, we define customer equity as the sum of the lifetime values of all the firm's current and future customers, where the lifetime value is the discounted profit stream obtained from the customer. The expansion of the service sector over time, combined with the resultant shift from transaction- to relationship-orientated marketing, has made the consideration of customer lifetime value increasingly important. These events legitimate customer equity (i.e. the aggregation of customer lifetime value across customers) as a key metric of the firm. Customer lifetime value and customer equity are already in widespread use as marketing asset metrics in some industries, most notably in direct marketing and financial services. Customer equity measurement and monitoring is rapidly expanding in other industries too.

Output quantity
These are the traditional measures of marketing efficiency (sales volume and market share).

Financial impact
Financial benefits from a specific marketing action can be evaluated in several ways. Return on investment (ROI) is a traditional approach to evaluating return relative to the expenditure required to obtain the return. It is calculated as the discounted return (net of the discounted expenditure), expressed as a percentage of the discounted expenditure. Commonly used retrospectively to measure short-term return, ROI is controversial in the context of marketing effectiveness. Because many marketing expenditures play out over the long run, short-term ROI is often prejudicial against marketing expenditures. The correct usage of ROI measures in marketing requires an analysis of future cash flows. It is also worth noting that the maximization of ROI as a management principle is not recommended (unless management's goal is efficiency rather than effectiveness), because it is inconsistent with profit maximization – a point that has long been noted in the marketing literature.

Other financial impact measures include the internal rate of return, which is the discount rate that would make the discounted return exactly equal to the discounted expenditure; the net present value, which is the discounted return minus the net present value of the expenditure; and the economic value added (EVA), which is the net operating profit minus the cost of capital.

In each case, the measures of financial impact weigh the return generated by the marketing action against the expenditure required to produce that return. The financial impact affects the financial position of the firm, as measured by profits, cash flow and other measures of financial health.

If we take a look at the perceived service quality following from a given resource structure as inputs in a service process, it creates sales at a certain level. If the resource structure is changed, the cost level changes and so do perceived quality and the revenue-generating capability of the service provider. From this it follows that the productivity of service processes can be measured as the ratio between revenues and costs. This is a true measurement of service productivity. If revenues increase more than costs, productivity goes up. On the other hand, if a cost reduction leads to lost revenues, but the decline in revenues is less than the cost savings that have been achieved, productivity still improves. However, this may be a less recommendable strategy because in the long run it may lead to a negative image and unfavourable word of mouth, which can have a further negative effect on revenues.

Thus, cost reductions may lead to a bigger drop in revenues than the savings on the cost side. If this is the case, service productivity declines in the long run. Service-orientated productivity measures could be derived from the formulas above. However, one should keep in mind that there are problems with financial measures that have to be observed. Revenues are not always a good measure of output, since price does not always reflect perceived service quality. It may also be difficult to assign capital costs correctly to each type of revenue respectively. Further, if businesses are subsidized by government, if prices are regulated or if competition is monopolistic, revenues may be a poor measure of quality. In addition, in all industries and competitive situations price may not reflect perceived quality very well. This is the case for many professional services, for example.

13.3 **Marketing budgeting**

The purpose of a marketing budget is to pull all the revenues and costs involved in marketing together into one comprehensive document. This is a managerial tool that balances what needs to be spent against what can be afforded, and helps its users make choices about priorities. It is then used in monitoring the performance in practice.

Budgeting is also an organization process that involves making forecasts based on the proposed marketing strategy and programmes. The forecasts then are used to construct a budgeted profit-and-loss statement (i.e. profitability). An important aspect of budgeting is deciding how to allocate the last available money across all of the proposed programmes within the marketing plan.

The marketing plans and the annual budget are interlinked in many ways: the sales forecast, the pricing policy, the marketing expenditure budget and the allocation of resources. A budget is a detailed plan outlining the acquisition and use of financial and other resources over some given time period. The annual budget is commonly referred to as the 'master budget'. It has three principal parts: the operating budget, the cash budget and the capital expenditure budget. It is driven by the sales forecast. It has been noted that a sales budget for a company serves as a limit to be observed in establishing production budgets, selling and administrative budgets, cash budgets and budget plans. The budget plays a key role in an organization. It moves the organization from an informal reaction method of management to a formal controlled method of management. It can also act as a motivator and communicator, as well as assist in functional co-ordination and performance evaluation.

There are four uses of a budget: first, to fine-tune the strategic plan; second, to help co-ordinate the activities of the several parts of the organization; third, to assign responsibilities to managers; and, fourth, to obtain a commitment that is the basis for evaluating a manager's actual performance.

Four major advantages of budgeting appear: first, it gives planning top priority; second, it provides managers with a way to finalize their planning efforts; third, it overcomes potential bottlenecks before they occur; and, fourth, it co-ordinates the activities of the entire organization by integrating the plans and objectives of the various parts.

In summary, there are four main aspects to budgeting: the motivations aspect; the co-ordination of resources for their best use; setting benchmarks for performance; and as a cost control mechanism. The marketing plan is put together by members of the marketing team with input from the sales, finance and production departments. It is critical that senior executives accept the plan and lend their weight to it so that it is implemented. Both the annual budget as well as the marketing plan are used by firms as a short-term planning and control process. An integrated approach should enhance an organization's planning capabilities. The differences between the annual budget and the marketing plan are shown in Table 13.1.

Table 13.1 Comparison between the marketing plan and the annual budget

Marketing plan	Annual budget
Short term, most often annual	Annual, short term
Compiled by marketing department with input from other areas	Compiled by finance with input from other areas
Integrated into the strategic plan	Integrated into the strategic plan
Used to implement and control an organization's marketing activities	Used to co-ordinate functions and evaluate the performance of individuals
Concerns the use of company resources	Outlines the use of financial and other resources
Establishes benchmarks against which marketing accomplishments can be judged	Establishes benchmarks against which the company's performance can be measured
Has the sales budget as one of its outputs	Has the sales budget as its foundation

Source: adapted from Abratt et al. (1994)

It is clear that the annual budget and the marketing plan are interwoven and should be part of the same process in organizations. The management implications are important. An organization works effectively when there is clear communication and co-ordination across functional lines. For effective implementation of an organization's strategy, the firm must serve customers in the best manner possible. This will mean that all management policies and systems should be reviewed. An analysis of budgeting procedures, marketing planning processes and transaction flows will have to be undertaken. This analysis will have to be performed by both departments: whether it be a marketing audit, a budgeting process or a marketing planning exercise, personnel from both departments must be involved.

Profitability analysis

Regardless of the organizational level, control involves some form of profitability analysis. In brief, *profitability analysis* requires that analysts determine the costs associated with specific marketing activities to find out the profitability of such units as different market segments, products, customer accounts and distribution channels (intermediaries).

Profitability is probably the single most important measure of performance, but it has limitations. These are that (i) many objectives can best be measured in non-financial terms (maintaining market share); (ii) profit is a short-term measure and can be manipulated by taking actions that may prove dysfunctional in the longer term (reducing R&D expenses); and (iii) profits can be affected by factors over which management has no control (e.g. the weather).

Contribution analysis is helpful in determining the yield derived from the application of additional resources (for instance, to certain sales territories). Contribution analysis attempts to determine the amount of output (revenues) that can be expected from a given set of inputs (costs). (You are probably familiar with break-even analysis, a type of contribution analysis used to determine the amount of revenue necessary to cover both variable and fixed costs.)

There are three ways to build a marketing budget that is based on a specific strategic market plan and the tactical marketing strategy designed to achieve the target level of performance.

1 **Top-down budget**: a new marketing budget based on projected sales objectives is determined, using past marketing expenses as a percentage of sales.

2 **Customer mix budget**: the cost of customer acquisition and retention, and the combination of new and retained customers are used to derive a new marketing budget.

3 **Bottom-up budget**: each element of the marketing effort is budgeted for specific tasks identified in the marketing plan.

As this book has a customer-orientated approach the customer mix budget will be discussed in the following section.

Customer mix budgets

Recognizing the customer as the primary unit of focus, a market-based business will expand its focus to customers and markets, not just products or units sold. This is an important strategic distinction because there are a finite number of potential customers, but a larger range of products and services can be sold to each customer. As shown in Fig. 13.2, a business's volume is its customer share in a market with a finite number of customers at any point in time, not the number of units sold.

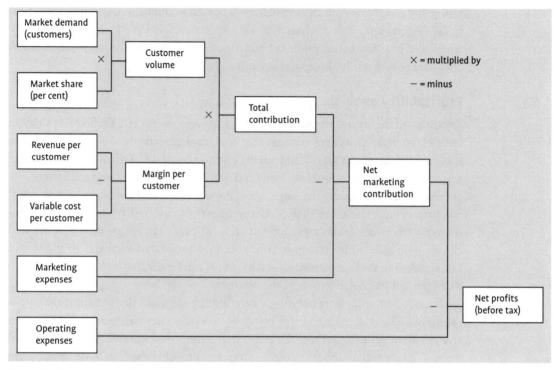

Figure 13.2 A customer-based model of marketing contribution and net profits
Source: *Marketing Management*, Hollensen, Pearson Education Limited (2003)

Customer volume = Market demand (customers) = Market share (percentage)

Figure 13.2 presents an overall flowchart of how market-based net profits are derived. Customer volume, at the top of this diagram, is derived from a certain level of customer market demand and a business's share of that customer demand. Without a sufficient volume of customers, net profit will be impossible to obtain. Marketing strategies that affect customer volume include marketing strategies that:

- attract new customers to grow market share
- grow the market demand by bringing more customers into a market
- enter new markets to create new sources of customer volume.

Each of these customer-focused marketing strategies affects net profits, invested assets, cash flow and, as we will see later, shareholder value. Thus, a key component of profitability and financial performance is customer purchases and the collective customer volume produced. Without customer purchases, there is no positive cash flow or potential for net profits or shareholder value.

Figure 13.2 is a 'DuPont'-like illustration of the different budget element. Figure 13.3 is an illustration of the traditional marketing budget (per customer group or country) and its underlying determinants.

Customer-based budgeting recognizes that companies are increasingly turning away from traditional accounting methods, which identify costs according to various

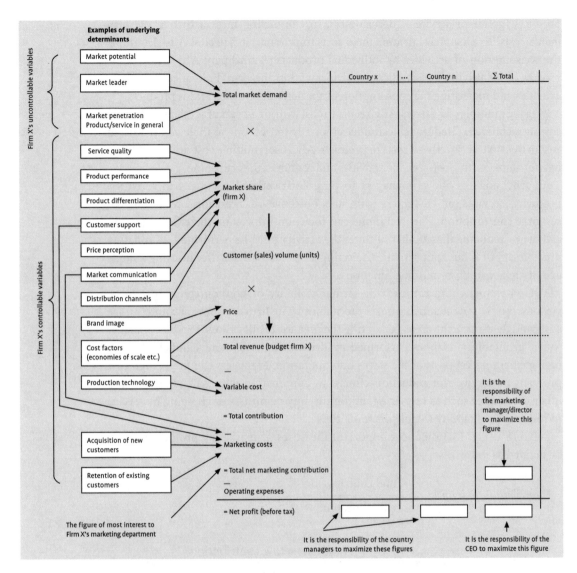

Figure 13.3 The international marketing budget and its underlying determinants
Source: *Marketing Management*, Hollensen, Pearson Education Limited (2003)

expense categories, and moving towards activity-based costing (ABC), which bases costs on the different tasks involved in performing a given activity.

The international marketing budget in Fig. 13.3 gives an indication of some of the underlying cost drivers in activity-based costing (ABC).

Activity-based costing (ABC)

To understand ABC systems, it is helpful to view the business as an entity that is engaged in performing a series of activities (e.g. research & development, product design, manu-facturing, marketing, distribution and customer service) for the purpose of providing products (goods or services) to customers. In conducting these activities, the firm incurs costs. To accurately attribute these costs to products it is necessary to determine the consumption of activities by individual products. Accordingly, ABC involves the process of identifying the significant activities within the firm, linking costs to these activities and measuring the consumption of the activities by the various products.

By using multiple cost drivers, ABC relates to cost with greater accuracy than traditional costing techniques. Traditional techniques typically rely on one to three volume-based cost drivers to trace overhead costs to products. ABC uses multiple cost drivers to reflect relationships existing between the activities and resources they consume.

An ABC analysis allows managers to pinpoint overhead resources to activities, products, services or customers with the objective of reducing or eliminating resource consumption. This technique can focus on improving the efficiency of an activity by reducing the number of times the activity must be performed, eliminating unnecessary or redundant activities, selecting a less costly alternative or using a single activity to accomplish multiple functions.

ABC implementation can provide greater visibility of how differently products, customers or supply channels impact profitability. The firm can more accurately trace costs and determine the areas generating the greatest profit or loss. Product and customer profitability analyses performed by firms using ABC may significantly alter management perceptions of the status quo operation. Managers can target high cost products or services for reduction efforts. In conjunction with ABC, they can use other techniques such as re-pricing, minimum buy quantities or charging by service to improve profitability (Stapleton *et al.*, 2004).

Looking at Fig. 13.3 the most important measures of marketing profitability may be defined as follows.

$$\textit{Contribution margin} \% = \frac{\text{Total contribution}}{\text{Total revenue}} \times 100$$

$$\textit{Marketing contribution margin} \% = \frac{\text{Total marketing contribution}}{\text{Total revenue}} \times 100$$

$$\textit{Profit margin} \% = \frac{\text{Net profit (before tax)}}{\text{Total revenue}} \times 100$$

If we had information about the size of assets (accounts receivable + inventory + cash + plant + equipment) we could also define:

$$\textit{Return on assets} \, (\text{ROA}) = \frac{\text{Net profit (before tax)}}{\text{Assets}}$$

(ROA is similar to the well-known measure ROI = return on investment.)

ROI and its applications

Customer profitability management requires a multi-level marketing ROI analysis covering a series of marketing activities that can be integrated and optimized for a customer or customer segment (Lenskold, 2004).

To apply marketing ROI at the customer level, it is necessary to have reasonable marketing ROI processes in place at the campaign level, including a corporate ROI threshold (or hurdle rate) at which the company will fund marketing programmes. There are three levels of marketing ROI analysis that should be applied where possible to guide marketing decisions: independent ROI, incremental ROI and aggregated ROI. Each of these can be effective at assessing and comparing marketing opportunities. When used together, the opportunity exists to truly optimize decisions that maximize customer profitability and total profits.

Independent ROI

The independent ROI analysis is completed for each decision that can stand alone. When managing marketing decisions at the customer level, this would involve assessing the independent campaigns directed at each customer. If the independent ROI exceeds the ROI threshold, that investment is generally justified unless the aggregated ROI analysis shows a higher-performing alternative. If the independent ROI does not meet the ROI threshold, this marketing activity may still be viable when assessed as part of a larger-scale customer-centric marketing programme.

Incremental ROI

When marketing activities are either dependent upon or can be influenced by other marketing activities, an incremental ROI analysis should be completed. This ROI analysis isolates the incremental impact where interdependencies between campaigns exist. For example, an 'investment' in a cross-sell campaign on its own may generate a significant ROI but decrease the impact of an existing retention marketing campaign that follows. In such a case, the incremental ROI analysis would take into consideration both the additional profits from the cross-sell campaign and the lost profits from its impact on the subsequent retention campaign to determine if the investment into the cross-sell campaign should be made. Incremental ROI assessments help to protect against decisions based on ROI figures that represent the average of high-performing marketing efforts blended with low-performing marketing efforts.

The incremental ROI may be defined as:

$$\text{ROI} = \frac{\text{Incremental total contribution} - \text{Marketing 'investment'}}{\text{Marketing 'investment'}}$$

(Marketing 'investment' is a part of marketing costs in Figure 13.3.)

Aggregated ROI

The aggregated ROI analysis is based on the total returns relative to the total investment for a series of marketing activities directed to a specific customer or customer segment. This analysis works best when it aggregates only those marketing activities that can be decided upon collectively.

This could be a series of campaigns from a specific business unit within the company, all activity directed to the customer for a period of time or the entire lifetime of marketing activity, depending upon the business model and management structure. Aggregated ROI analysis prioritizes total collective profitability ahead of independent campaign profitability, creating new opportunities to gain additional profits from existing marketing activities. This multi-level profitability analysis is beneficial to support customer-centric companies striving to integrate marketing activities across the customer relationship. For more product-orientated companies, it can also provide the financial insight necessary to motivate greater collaboration across the organization, eventually centring the planning and strategies on the customer.

Exhibit 13.1 External and internal marketing metrics

To ensure the marketing organization's continued existence and health, we must change senior executives' prevailing perception of marketing as an expense, to one of marketing as an investment that enhances a firm's overall profitability.

In today's competitive environment, many companies employ a balance-the-budget type of management. When revenue streams are good, these organizations allow the marketing expense to flow. When profits decline, they employ quick-fix measures to address financial problems. To reduce expenditures, some businesses cut marketing costs so that budgeted financial resources can flow directly to the bottom line. Others undertake strong marketing campaigns with the desired effect of immediately lifting revenue. Still others simply outsource their marketing functions to lower costs. The philosophy underlying these quick fixes is that marketing is an expense for which there is no appreciable or known return. At best, these approaches produce a short-term boost in profitability, but they produce little value in the longer term. Clearly, in these organizations the marketing investment is not appreciated. As marketers, we must turn around such myopic thinking. Our survival depends on it.

In order to change perceptions, we need to convince senior executives that a reduction in the amount of money budgeted to marketing activities prevents immediate and future returns on the corporate balance sheet. In this regard, perhaps the most significant activity marketers can engage in is to directly tie change (ROI) to specific marketing activities. The first step is to focus our marketing efforts and make causal connections between marketing activities and returns to the business. We can do this by establishing short-term and long-term metrics, getting senior management's agreement on these metrics, setting performance goals based on these metrics and measuring our success against them.

A 'metric' is a performance measure that top management should review. It is a measure that matters to the whole business. The term comes from music and implies regularity: the reviews should typically take place yearly or half-yearly. A metric is not just another word for measure – while all metrics are measures, not all measures are metrics. Metrics should be necessary, precise, consistent and sufficient (i.e. comprehensive) for review purposes. Metrics may be financial (usually from the profit and loss account), from the marketplace or from non-financial internal sources (innovation and employees).

Metrics help the firm achieve its specific goals. This puts pressure on the board to explain what 'success' will look like. Firms need multiple measures and these measures need to be relevant to the company's situation. It is important for each firm to determine the relevant-to-them indicators of internal and external marketing 'health'.

External marketing metrics

Performance can be expressed as short-term (profit and loss account) financial measures 'adjusted' by the change in brand equity. Unfortunately, brand equity needs many non-financial measures, so the adjustment is conceptual, not in cash. It is this non-financial adjustment that distinguishes best practice metrics companies from the rest.

Among the most important external marketing metrics are those shown in the table.

Customer metric	Measured by
Relative satisfaction	Consumer preference or satisfaction relative to average for market/competitor(s). The competitive benchmark should be stated.
Commitment	Index of switchability (or some similar measure of retention, loyalty, purchase intent or bonding).
Relative perceived quality	Perceived quality satisfaction relative to average for market/competitor(s). The competitive benchmark should be stated.
Relative price	Market share (value)/market share (volume).
Availability	Distribution, e.g. value-weighted per cent of retail outlets carrying the brand.

The above-mentioned external metrics are calculated differently in different sectors. For example, loyalty may be the share of category requirements in packaged goods markets (e.g. the amount of Persil a user buys as a percentage of total laundry detergent purchases over a year), or the churn rate (percentage of customers lost over a given time period) in communications businesses such as mobile telephony.

So far we have focused on customers at various levels through to the ultimate users. For many metrics the question is not how satisfied the customer is, but how this compares with how satisfied the competitors' customers are. They may even be the same people. An 80 per cent satisfaction level is great if the rate for the competition is 70 per cent, but not so good if theirs is 90 per cent.

Internal marketing metrics

Monitoring the firm's internal market takes two forms. We need to assess two things:

1 innovation health (i.e. how good your firm is at achieving the kind of innovation you want)

2 how well attuned the staff are to understanding what the firm is trying to achieve and how committed they are to doing it; in a sense, the firm's employees are its first customers – if they do everything right, they will take care of external marketplace issues, including the end user.

3M very successfully uses just a few simple metrics, such as the proportion of sales attributable to recent innovations. Many other firms have copied these metrics, but few have succeeded because their leadership styles and cultures are different. The moral is that firms should get away from the detail and first measure these bigger-picture variables. Thus innovation is mostly a question of leadership, and then culture, rather than process. In large companies, much of the formal process gets in the way and should be dismantled.

Some companies, especially consumer service companies, see employees as their first customers. They believe that if management markets to employees correctly, then the front-line employees will take care of the external customers. In this perception, internal marketing becomes, for the board, more important than external marketing and needs its own set of metrics. Some of the most important internal marketing metrics are as follows.

Employee metric	Measured by
Strategy	Awareness of goals (vision)
	Commitment to goals (vision)
	Active innovation support
	Resource adequacy
Culture	Appetite for learning
	Freedom to fail
	Relative employee satisfaction
	Aggregate customer brand empathy (composite index of how well employees see company brands as consumers do)
Outcomes	Number of initiatives in process
	Number of innovations launched
	% revenue due to launches during last three years

Many firms now measure employee indicators but few cross-fertilize employee and customer survey techniques and measures. BP-Amoco is an exception in the way it does this. The oil giant found, unsurprisingly, a good correlation between employee and customer satisfaction.

Source: adapted from Ambler, T. (2000) Marketing metrics. *Business Strategy Review* 11(2), Summer, pp. 59–66; Barwise, P. and Farley, J.U. (2004) Marketing metrics: status of six metrics in five countries. *European Management Journal* 22(3), June, pp. 257–62; Goodwin, K. (2004) Useful e-marketing metrics factor in outcomes. *Marketing News* 38(10), pp. 28–30; McCullough, W.R. (2000) Marketing metrics. *Marketing Management* 9(1), Spring, pp. 64–5

13.4 Controlling the marketing programme

At this point in the marketing planning process, the marketing plan is nearly complete. The final step is to plan how the company will control the plan's implementation. Marketing control keeps both employees and activities on the proper track so the organization continues in the direction outlined in the marketing plan. However, employees in the organization often view 'control' as being negative. If individuals fear that the control process will be used not only to judge their performance but as a basis for punishing them, then it will be feared and reviled.

In preparing a marketing plan, marketers need to plan for three types of marketing control: annual control, profitability control and strategic control.

Annual control

Because marketers generally formulate new marketing plans every year, they need annual plan control to assess the progress of the current year's marketing plan. This covers broad performance measures (e.g. sales results, market share results) to evaluate the company's overall effectiveness. If a company fails to achieve this year's marketing plan objectives, it will have difficulty achieving its longer-term goals and mission. Although 'market share measures', for example, are driven by sales performance, they reflect relative competitive standing. These measures help senior managers gauge their organization's competitive strength and situation over time.

Profitability control

This assesses the organization's progress and performance based on key profitability measures. The exact measures differ from company to company, but they often include ROI, total marketing contribution, contribution margin and net profit margins. Many companies measure the monthly and yearly profit-and-loss results of each product, line and category, as well as each market or segment, and each channel. By comparing profitability results over time, marketers can spot significant strengths and weaknesses, and identify problems and opportunities early. Closely related to profitability control, productivity control measures the efficiency of, say, the sales force, promotions, channels and logistics, and product management. The purpose here is to measure profitability improvements through reduced costs or higher yield. Productivity is so important to the bottom line that some companies appoint marketing controllers to establish marketing productivity standards. Clearly, productivity control is connected not only with profitability but also with customer relationships.

Strategic control

This assesses the organization's effectiveness in managing the marketing function, in managing customer relationships, and in managing social responsibility and ethics issues – three areas of strategic importance. Whereas profitability controls are applied monthly or more often, strategic control may be applied once or twice a year, or as needed to give top management a clearer picture of the organization's performance in these strategic areas.

Summary

Marketing strategies in different international markets directly affect sales revenues per country. The marketing strategies also affect margins, total contribution and marketing costs. These effects, in turn, lead to the total net marketing contribution. Because operating (manufacturing) costs and overhead costs are beyond the control of marketing managers, net marketing contribution plays the most important role for the marketing department, to determine the profit impact of a marketing strategy.

As marketing plans are being implemented, they have to be monitored and controlled.

Control is the process of ensuring that global marketing activities are carried out as intended. It involves monitoring aspects of performance and taking corrective action where necessary. The global marketing control system consists of deciding marketing objectives, setting performance standards, locating responsibility, evaluating performance against standards, and taking corrective or supportive action in each single country and overall.

The most obvious areas of control relate to the control of the annual marketing plan, control of profitability and strategic control. The purpose of the global marketing budget is mainly to allocate marketing resources across countries to maximize worldwide total marketing contribution.

Questions for discussion

1 How would a non-profit organization apply financial budget control to its marketing plan implementation?

2 Given the dynamic and uncertain nature of the business environment, why would marketers bother drafting alternative marketing plans and budgets?

3 What are the main factors that affect marketing control systems?

4 Discuss the problems involved in setting up and implementing a marketing control system.

5 Why is the outcome of one year's marketing control an important input to next year's marketing plan?

6 Comment on the statement: 'Implementors are the most important country organizations in terms of buy-in for effective global marketing strategy implementation.'

7 Why is customer profitability sometimes a better unit of measurement than market profitability?

8 Assess the complexity of developing marketing metrics for a manufacturing company and a financial services company.

9 Which factors can make the interpretation of performance difficult?

10 One of the most efficient means of control is self-control. What type of programme would you prepare for an incoming employee?

References

Abratt, R., Beffon, M. and Ford, J. (1994) Relationship between marketing planning and annual budgeting. *Marketing Intelligence & Planning* 12(1), pp. 22–8.

Grönroos, C. and Ojasalo K. (2004) Service productivity – towards a conceptualization of the transformation of inputs into economic results in services. *Journal of Business Research* 57, pp. 414–23.

Hollensen, S. (2003) *Marketing Management.* London: Financial Times/Prentice Hall, an imprint of Pearson Education.

Johnston, R. and Jones, P. (2004) Service productivity – towards understanding the relationships between operational and customer productivity. *International Journal of Productivity and Performance Management* 53(3), pp. 201–13.

Lenskold, J.D. (2004) Customer-centric marketing ROI. *Havard Business Review*, January/February, pp. 26–31.

Rust, T.M., Ambler, T., Carpenter, G.C., Kumar, V. and Srivastava, R.K. (2004) Measuring marketing productivity: current knowledge and future directions. *Journal of Marketing* 68, October, pp. 76–89.

Stapleton, D., Sanghamitra, P., Beach, E. and Julmanichoti, P. (2004) Activity-based costing for logistics and marketing. *Business Process Management Journal* 10(5), pp. 584–97.

Case 13 Jordan Toothbrushes: developing an international marketing control and budget system

Jordan (www.jordan.no) is a family-owned international manufacturer of mechanical oral hygiene products, household and painting tools, based in Oslo, Norway. It is among the 10 largest manufacturers of toothbrushes in the world, employing 885 people, including 195 in Norway. In 2003 the Jordan Group had net sales of €118 mn, of which 47 per cent originated from toothbrushes. Net profit was €8.8 mn. Jordan-branded toothbrushes can be found in more than 100 countries on all five continents. It is the leading toothbrush manufacturer in more European countries than any other brand.

History

1837: Wilhelm Jordan, a Danish comb maker, moved to Christiania (in Oslo) and opened his workshop in the city centre. Soon after, he discovered that the town needed a brush factory. He hired the best local and foreign craftsmen, and his brushmaking business started to prosper.

1879: His son Fredrik Jordan took over the enterprise. The factory was modernized, and the range of brushes it manufactured became wider and wider.

1911–16: The founder's grandson, Hjalmar Jordan, after taking charge of the company, discovered that corporate changes were required: he bought two local competitors and moved the factory to bigger premises. At that time Jordan's product catalogue contained several thousand articles.

1927: Hjalmar Jordan, during his travels, found a new business opportunity: the toothbrush. Jordan became the first toothbrush manufacturer in Norway, by building a new factory for the sole purpose of toothbrush production. One thing was clear from the very beginning: Jordan's commitment to the highest quality, produced in the most hygienic conditions possible. The toothbrushes were sold under the 'Pronto' brand name.

1937: On its 100th anniversary, the company employed 144 people, produced 225,000 toothbrushes per year and had a turnover of NOK13 mn. Jordan controlled the major part of the Norwegian market.

1940–50: Jordan remained stable after the Second World War, and made further investments in new production technologies.

1958: Jordan entered its first export markets: Denmark, England, West Germany, Sweden and Finland. At the same time, new methods of product presentation were introduced: toothbrushes packed individually in transparent plastic containers.

1960–68: Jordan's product assortment was rationalized, and the focus moved to toothbrushes and oral care products. Manufacturing of dental sticks started. Exports expanded, partnerships were formed, and by the end of the 1960s, Jordan was selling 25 million toothbrushes per year.

1969: Since 1969 Jordan's domestic toothbrushes have, like its export toothbrushes, been sold under the name 'Jordan'. Also in this year, a new production site opened in Flisa, Norway.

1970: Jordan entered the paintbrush market by acquiring ANZA in Sweden. In 1976 its total turnover exceeded NOK100 mn. The company moved to its current location. In 1973 its revolutionary spoon-shaped toothbrush was developed in association with dental experts. This brush (the predecessor of today's Jordan Classic) set the direction for Jordan for coming decades.

1983: The Colgate-Palmolive Company introduced a new type of toothbrush and Jordan was asked to produce it. A long-lasting relationship began, based on this acknowledgement of Jordan's expertise.

1987: Freshly elected as 'Company of the Year 1986' in Norway, Jordan celebrated its 150th anniversary.

1988: Jordan opened its factory in Holland: Sanodent, specializing in private-label products. Peri-dent was created in Scotland as a joint venture and started to produce the total volume of Jordan dental flosses.

1992: Launch of Jordan Magic, the world's first colour-changing toothbrush.

1993: Launch of Jordan ActiveTip.

1995: Launch of Jordan Sport and Jordan Amigo.

1997: Launch of the Philips-Jordan electrical toothbrush.

1998: Jordan acquired Wisdom, England's leading toothbrush manufacturer (total sales in 1997: $16 mn).

2000: Jordan consolidated its Norwegian toothbrush production at Flisa and discontinued production in Oslo.

2003: All toothbrush production moved out of Norway to Wisdom in England.

In addition to the Jordan-owned subsidiaries in Sweden, England, Scotland and Malaysia, Jordan toothbrushes are produced under licence in five countries: India, Nigeria, Syria, Malaysia and Indonesia.

The global toothbrush market

Table 13.2 shows the main world toothbrush market segments.

Table 13.2 **Toothbrush market segments**		
Toothbrush segments in the world market	**Examples of brands**	**Typical retail consumer prices (€)**
1. Manual toothbrushes	Jordan	3
2. Power toothbrush market, which can be divided into two sub-segments:		
(a) Battery-powered toothbrushes	P&G Spinbrush	7–8
(b) Electric toothbrushes (with rechargable batteries)	Braun Oral-B	20

The main impetus to global growth was the phenomenal development of low-priced, mass-market battery-operated toothbrushes, particularly in the USA but also world-wide. This was triggered in the USA by the acquisition of Dr John's Spinbrush by consumer products giant Procter & Gamble in late 2000. The global market for powered toothbrushes (electric and battery-powered) amounted to just 47 million units in 2002, but this was a significant improvement on the level of 12.5 million units recorded in 1998.

The biggest buzz in the oral care category these days has definitely been generated by battery-powered toothbrushes. According to Colgate-Palmolive, battery-powered brushes accounted for just 4 per cent of the toothbrush segment in 1999, yet by the end of 2002 sales of these products accounted for 40 per cent of toothbrush sales in the EU countries. The increasing popularity of powered toothbrushes can also be seen in increasing sales figures for replaceable heads. All this means that manual toothbrushes have experienced a falling market share in the total toothbrush market, whereas powered toothbrushes have increased their market share.

The German toothbrush market

Almost 99 per cent of Germans over 14 years already brush their teeth at least once a day, but there is still scope for growth in toothbrushes. Dentists tend to claim that more people could replace their toothbrush more often, with replacement being rec-ommended at least once every three months.

Table 13.3 shows the general development in the German toothbrush market for manual and powered toothbrushes.

Table 13.3 **German retail sales of toothbrushes by type: value 1998–2003 (as shown, the powered toothbrushes segment is divided into two sub-segments: battery and electric toothbrushes; each of these segments is then further divided into two more segments)**

€ million	1998	1999	2000	2001	2002	2003
Manual toothbrushes	177.5	185.0	199.9	187.5	177.8	175.0
Powered toothbrushes	8.1	20.0	53.1	103.1	120.5	124.5
Battery toothbrushes	–	–	15.7	34.1	43.0	47.0
Battery toothbrush units	–	–	5.4	11.9	15.8	17.2
Battery toothbrush replacement heads	–	–	10.3	22.2	27.2	29.8
Electric toothbrushes	8.1	20.0	37.5	69.0	77.5	77.4
Electric toothbrush units	3.4	9.8	18.1	35.8	41.7	39.5
Electric toothbrush replacement heads	4.7	10.2	19.4	33.2	35.8	37.9
Manual and power toothbrushes	185.6	205.0	253.1	290.6	298.3	299.4

Source: adapted from trade press (*Lebensmittelzeitung, Lebensmittel Report*), company research and reports, trade interviews, Euromonitor estimates

The German market for manual toothbrushes

Private label catches up

Despite a negative attitude towards private-label toothpaste, the share of private-label toothbrushes is relatively high. Private-label brands have adapted to consumer preferences and are now offering products with flexible toothbrush heads, X-shaped bristles or coloured indicators that show when the brush should be replaced. As a result, private-label share has increased from 19 per cent in 2001 to 23 per cent in 2003.

While consumers at the high end of the market are still willing to pay up to €3.79 per brush, users of mid-range-priced brushes are increasingly turning to private-label products. Most of the main mass outlets in Germany, such as Schlecker, Aldi and DM, now include private-label toothbrushes in their product ranges. As a result of growth in private labels and increased competition among brands, the average unit price of manual toothbrushes is stable: €2.30 in 2003.

The size of the market is determined by how often people change their toothbrush. Table 13.4 shows how often they do this.

Table 13.4 **Replacement of manual toothbrushes, 2002 (Germany)**	
% of users changing their manual toothbrush	**2002**
Once a week	1.2
Once a month	27.4
Every three months	48.3
Every six months	16.8
Every six months +	4.4
Never (don't need a manual toothbrush)	1.5
No reply	0.4
Total	**100.0**

Source: adapted from GfK, trade press, Euromonitor estimates

Falling sales of child-specific manual toothbrushes

Value sales of children's toothbrushes have decreased in line with the general decline of manual toothbrushes. Parents hoping to improve their children's dental care are more likely to spend money on powered brushes designed specifically for children, such as Colgate Motion Bzzz. For children, the shape, packaging and marketing of the toothbrushes is more important than the function. Consequently, children's brushes have become very colourful, often in the shape of popular cartoon characters or toys. Manufacturers of manual brushes are trying to attract children and their parents with features such as anti-slip grips or special toothbrushes for the different stages of dental development. This has led to higher average prices for child-specific brushes.

Competition in manual toothbrushes

Together, the four largest companies accounted for 70 per cent of value sales of manual toothbrushes in 2003. GlaxoSmithKline leads the way, with a 32 per cent share, due to the success of its Dr Best brand. Dr Best brushes are associated with a high level of expertise, captured in a wide range of specialized toothbrushes. Oral-B, Procter & Gamble and Gaba follow, with a 14 per cent, 12 per cent and 11 per cent share, respectively, in 2003. Gaba managed to increase its value share between 2001 and 2003, while other company shares remained stable or fell during the same period. Elmex, Aronal and Meridol, the main Gaba brands, have a high level of recognition among German consumers and are known as a forerunners in medical research.

Private-label products are very successful, with a 23 per cent value share in 2003, up by 4.5 percentage points compared to 2001. The success of private-label products in this sub-sector lies in the consumer perception of toothbrushes as secondary to toothpaste in terms of importance. While German consumers are likely to spend money on a 'quality' toothpaste, a private-label toothbrush is perceived to do the same job as a similar branded product. This is especially the case with new private-label brands, which keep up with branded labels in terms of new product developments and innovations.

Powered brushes change oral care

As early as the 1970s, Oral-B produced and sold electrical toothbrushes in Germany and other European countries, but it was not until 1998/1999 that powered brushes really took off. In 2000, the introduction of the first battery-operated toothbrushes gave the market new impetus, and their lower prices made them more affordable.

From 2000 onwards, powered brushes made a real impact on oral hygiene, influencing other sub-sectors such as manual toothbrushes and toothpaste. In 2000, sales of powered brushes and replacement heads amounted to €53.1 mn, which constituted growth of 166 per cent over the previous year. Nevertheless, manual toothbrushes are still the major type, in both value and volume terms.

Some models of battery brushes have to be replaced at regular intervals, while electric brushes merely have to be recharged. This means the number of replacement heads per unit sold is higher for electric brushes as new battery brushes come with a new head.

Switching between models

Consumers are expected to switch between brands and makes. Apart from the regular replacement of disposable battery toothbrushes, consumers are expected to switch from battery brushes to electric brushes. According to industry sources, many consumers use the cheaper battery brushes as an initial 'trial brush' before committing to the price of a more expensive electrical brush that might display additional benefits, such as different speed settings or gum protection (against too much pressure). Likewise, users of electric toothbrushes are likely to upgrade their toothbrushes in line with new product developments.

The task

Until now Jordan's market share in the total toothbrush market has been below 2 per cent. The Jordan management team in Norway is not satisfied with this kind of market share in a non-distant market like Germany. So they contact you ...

Questions

1 Discuss whether it would be a good idea for Jordan to enter the German *powered* toothbrush market with a new product. If yes, how should such a decision be implemented?

2 Outline a marketing plan for Jordan's existing product line (manual toothbrushes) in Germany.

3 Draw up a proposal for Jordan's marketing control and budget system. If possible, outline the specific Jordan marketing budget for the German market. Use the following figures when preparing your marketing budget.

Table 13.5 **Financial calculation for a typical Jordan manual toothbrush**	
	Per unit
Retail price	€4
Ex-works price	€1.5
— Variable costs	€1.0
= Contribution margin	€0.5
Contribution margin	33%

Note: these figures are not official Jordan figures.

Sources: www.jordan.no; *Lebensmittelzeitung, Lebensmittel Report*; company annual reports; Euromonitor estimates

Ethical, social and environmental aspects of marketing planning

Learning Objectives

After studying this chapter you should be able to:

- understand why ethical issues are important for the firm's marketing planning and marketing mix

- explain how ethical marketing is related to relationship building

- define 'social marketing'

- give examples of 'social marketing' campaigns

- explain the role of ethics in marketing planning

- differentiate among various levels of 'green' marketing.

14.1 **Introduction**

Until now we have examined the basic framework for marketing planning. In this last chapter of the book we turn our attention to some important issues that should be considered during the marketing planning process. The relevance of being ethical, social and environmentally responsible has grown considerably over the past few decades, in the light of public demands and changes in national laws. This chapter is divided into three parts:

1 ethical issues in marketing planning (Section 14.2)

2 'social marketing' issues (Section 14.3)

3 environmental/'green' issues (Section 14.4)

14.2 **Ethics**

Marketing ethics refers to morally right and wrong action in marketing. It can be defined in two ways. First, it is a discipline that involves the systematic study of the moral evaluation of marketing decisions, practices and institutions. Second, marketing ethics are the standards, or 'norms', applied in the judgement of marketing activities as morally right and wrong. More simply, marketing ethics is about the moral problems of marketing managers. It includes, for example, the ethical considerations associated with product safety, truth in advertising and fairness in pricing. It is an integral part of decisions regarding marketing planning.

Recent criticism of the ethics of marketing reflects increased societal concern about business practices, and has focused on specific issues, industries and companies. However, there has been a long-standing suspicion of marketing. Many people associate marketing activities, especially selling and advertising, with dishonesty and 'tricks'.

Commentators who suggest that marketing heightens materialism, wastes scarce resources and makes consumption an end in itself, often ignore the role of the consumer in this process and the fact that marketing is a response to consumer preferences. Also frequently overlooked – particularly by critics of marketing's wastefulness – are the intangible benefits that products may provide, including the psychological and social benefits that often accompany marketing activities such as advertising and branding. Hence, an alternative view, often proclaimed by marketing practitioners, is that marketing actually serves society.

These arguments may be sufficient to counter the charge that marketing in general is unethical. However, they require assumptions that do not always hold. First, not all markets are competitive and not all consumers are well informed. Second, the law has limits and shortcomings. Third, marketing practices (such as advertising) are reflective of society.

Ethical issues in the marketing mix

The product

Ethical issues may arise in product policy throughout the product life cycle, from development to elimination. Product safety is often a significant ethical issue in product policy. There is a legal requirement in most countries to provide products worthy of sale and fit for their intended purpose. This requirement encompasses product safety. As well as this 'implied warranty', an absence of 'ordinary care' on the part of sellers (manufacturers, wholesalers and retailers) can give rise to charges of negligence under tort law, with the seller made liable for products proven defective that have caused injury. In addition, sellers must comply with safety regulations established by government agencies. Yet there remain ethical considerations in product safety beyond those established by the law. Marketers have to ask: 'How safe should a product be?' It is not possible to create a risk-free environment, with products incapable of causing harm, largely because product safety is a function of the consumer as well as of the product's design and manufacture.

Pricing

Pricing is the most regulated area of marketing. There are legal prohibitions governing price-fixing, price discrimination, predatory pricing and transfer pricing. In some cases, unethical practices may be possible without actually being illegal.

Distribution

Ethical issues in distribution largely involve conflicts between channel intermediaries, typically reflecting a power imbalance in channel relationships. The size and market power of large retailers, wholesalers or manufacturers may often be open to abuse. The increasing power of the retailer has resulted in demands of suppliers that not all can meet; for instance, listing fees (fees required by retailers for listing a manufacturer's product) have escalated in the grocery trade, with some smaller suppliers crying foul when they are unable to match the fees paid by larger suppliers. Other channel-management issues include grey marketing, where some channel intermediaries have been criticized for free-riding on legitimate channel intermediaries who often face higher costs (e.g. because they have to provide higher levels of customer service).

Communication

The visibility of advertising, coupled with its role as persuasive communication, result in it being one of the most frequently criticized areas of marketing. Truth in advertising has been an ethical issue since the earliest use of advertising. In most countries, advertisers are subject to stringent self-regulation by industry bodies as well as government regulation. Advertisers must be able to substantiate claims about product performance, for example.

Abuses in advertising can range from exaggerated claims and concealed facts to outright lying. Such abuses range from the unethical, which they clearly are, to the illegal, which they may be. The US Federal Trade Commission (FTC) stepped in when KFC promoted the health benefits and low carbohydrate content of its chicken with the slogan, 'If you're watching carbs and going high-protein, go KFC.' Two pieces of fried chicken (skin removed) were being compared to the original Burger King Whopper. Small print at the bottom of the ad noted 'a balanced diet and exercise are necessary for good health' and that 'KFC chicken is not a low fat, low sodium, low cholesterol food'. The FTC required KFC to stop running the advertising, indicating the deceptive nature of the advertisement (Ferrell, 2004).

Sales people are not under direct continuous supervision; rather they are under constant pressure to produce sales and are faced with additional temptations offered by the myriad opportunities for unethical behaviour that the position invites. Some of the more common areas of sales-related misconduct are as follows:

■ overselling

■ promising more than can be delivered

■ lying or making exaggerated claims

■ failing to keep customer confidences by divulging information to competitors

■ offering inappropriate or illegal entertainment.

So, the persuasive purpose of the sales task often creates conflicts for the sales person. These conflicts arise largely within three interfaces: the sales person–customer, the sales person–company and the sales person–competitor.

In the sales person–customer relationship, the best opportunity to maintain ethical standards is through: competent buying and selling, supported by training; insistence on purchase contract performance; acceptance testing; and so on. Most sellers respect the buyer who is thorough and honest in the conduct of the buying office or buying centre, and will usually respond in kind.

The major ethical issues listed under the sales person–competitor interface are largely illegal under laws prohibiting misrepresentation and unfair competition and anti-trust legislation.

Exhibit 14.1 'Natural' cigarette launch causes controversy

Independent tobacco company AE Lloyd is planning to launch a brand of cigarettes that will be positioned as a 'natural' alternative to additive-filled rivals, in a move that has provoked outrage among anti-tobacco campaigners. The cigarette will be advertised as additive-free. The word 'natural' is being considered as part of the brand name, which is yet to be decided. AE Lloyd claims that the cigarette will be better for smokers and the company will try to tap into the more health-conscious side of the smoking population.

The launch comes at a time when the industry has come under attack for lacing its cigarettes with flavourings such as chocolate, cherry and vanilla.

Of course, anti-smoking groups are anxious and say it is worrying that people could be lured into thinking that the product is any healthier or more ethical than 'normal' cigarettes.

Source: Thomas (2004)

Special issues in ethics: ethics in 'global marketing'

More generally, a serious and unresolved situational ethics problem often occurs in global marketing. No international code of business ethics exists because each society's ethics vary – some slightly and others greatly. Fortunately, most of the world's major religions and cultures share common norms and ethics, and would answer the questions in an 'ethical checklist' in a similar way. But in some countries bribes, kickbacks, and dishonesty in advertising, selling and dealing are much more acceptable than in others. How should foreign firms behave in such markets? If they do not tolerate such standard practices, they risk not doing business and may be further hated for arrogantly imposing their values where they are not wanted. For example, should European garment manufacturers be concerned about working conditions in the offshore factories that produce many of their clothing lines?

Bribery

Commercial bribery is ordinarily illegal, but the potential gains from this generally unethical practice are often so great that it can be found in many markets and in all countries. Bribery is defined as 'the offering, promising or giving [of] something in order to influence a public official in the execution of his/her official duties' (Sanyal and Samanta, 2004). Bribes can take the form of money, other pecuniary advantages (such as a scholarship for a child's college education) or non-pecuniary benefits (such as favourable publicity). In the international context, bribery involves a business firm from country A offering financial or non-financial inducements to officials of country B in order to obtain a commercial benefit.

Bribery tends to occur more often in less-developed countries, especially those with a recent colonial past. In these countries the full bureaucratic apparatus of the modern state has been introduced with little regard for the limited capacity of the economy to sustain it. Government officials have heavy responsibilities and much social status but their salaries are often very low in comparison to their social and familial obligations. The need to maintain status, and the heavy burden of traditional obligations encourages corrupt behaviour. Thus, corruption is the result of a

413

combination of opportunity (which comes from the office held) and personal/familial obligations. In addition, the high cost of enforcing rules relative to the available resources, as well as the reluctance of people in power to prosecute corrupt acts (being corrupt themselves), allows such behaviour to persist.

Often it is difficult to distinguish between a bribe, a gift to show appreciation and a reasonable commission for services rendered. Accepting or giving gifts may or may not be ethical, but the practice of gift-giving comes under close scrutiny at many B2B firms. If the giving of a gift is done as a condition of doing business (subtle or otherwise), then clearly the act is immoral and unethical; further, it causes prejudice against those who fail to give a gift. Many firms have stopped the practice of giving holiday gifts to customers, offering instead to contribute to a customer's favourite charity. The problem with this approach, however, is that even those gratuities given to create legitimate goodwill may influence the purchasing decision in some way. Common sense and social intelligence should be good guides in keeping the selling firm within ethical boundaries.

The ethical standards of morality that constrain marketing decision-making should be a product of the combination of personal conscience and the morality of the company as stated in its code of ethics. Ethical behaviour is required to make the market work efficiently and to keep it free and open. Marketing planners must therefore respond to the almost universal ethical codes involved in trading – to be honest and not conspire to cheat and steal – but their decisions as to what to offer the marketplace and how to offer it also have an impact on the prevailing values and ethics of a society. Some products and marketing practices are ethically questionable. This heavy responsibility cannot simply be shrugged off. The enlightened leadership that marketing planners are expected to display is most put to the test when they are faced with ethical dilemmas created by conflicts of interest among customers, employees and owners.

14.3 **Social marketing**

Social marketing can be understood as the application of commercial marketing technologies to the analysis, planning, execution and evaluation of programmes designed to influence the voluntary behaviour of target audiences in order to improve their personal welfare and that of their society.

Social marketing has a clear relationship to commercial marketing. Still, social marketing is distinct from commercial marketing in that it focuses on resolving social problems, whereas commercial marketing focuses on producing various goods or services for a profit. The 'customer' of social marketing is normally not expected 'to pay a price equal to the cost of providing the service', whereas the customer of commercial marketing is expected to do so. Furthermore, social marketing should not be confused with socially responsible marketing, something in which all marketers should be engaged. Socially responsible marketing is commercial marketing that appropriately takes into account its social responsibilities in marketing ordinary products and services.

As such, social marketing focuses on influencing people's behaviour away from ways of acting or lifestyles that are designated as leading or contributing to a social problem, and towards other ways of acting and lifestyles that will improve these people's well-being (or the well-being of others). This attempt to change people's behaviour may also involve modifications in their attitudes, values, norms and ideas. Indeed it may also require behavioural and value changes in the communities or groups of people with whom they live and/or associate.

The well-being of individuals and/or society is not simply subjectively identified by the individuals involved but is subject to determination through processes of social argumentation and justification. This does not mean that everyone will agree with these processes.

Social marketers target people who may not believe, at least at the outset, that they suffer from a problem or any deficiency in their welfare. As such, social problems are identified independently of what any particular person or people may or may not believe. It is compatible with social marketing that the people social marketers address strongly believe that they do not have a problem. These might include teenagers who abuse alcohol or drugs, fathers of Muslim girls in Bangladesh who do not believe their daughters should receive an education, or men in parts of Africa who wish to have their future wives undergo female circumcision.

Exhibit 14.2 **The social marketing of PSI (Population Services International)**

PSI has become the leading social marketing organization in the world, specializing in HIV/AIDS prevention, family planning, and maternal and child health. PSI has almost 65,000 employees in the 70 countries where it operates, of which 98 per cent are citizens of the countries they serve. PSI programmes are funded by foundations and other private donors, and by governmental development assistance and multilateral agencies.

Social marketing, as practised by PSI, combines education to motivate healthy behaviour with the provision of required health products and services to lower-income persons. PSI motivates a wide variety of healthy behaviours, including use of products and services. PSI procures products, establishes an office and distribution system, and sells the products through the wholesale and retail network, primarily to lower-income persons. Products and services are branded, attractively packaged, widely marketed, effectively promoted to the poor and selected target groups, and sold at low prices that are affordable to the poor. Since this retail price is often even lower than the manufacturing cost (so the poor can afford the price), donor contributions are a vital element of the social marketing process.

A key ingredient of successful social marketing is effective communications to encourage the adoption of appropriate health practices (including proper use of the products and services). This is done by brand-specific advertising as well as by generic educational campaigns, using a mix of strategies and channels, including mass media and interpersonal communications, to reach the target audience(s).

PSI markets condoms for AIDS prevention, a wide range of contraceptives for family planning, and a number of health products aimed especially at women and children, such as oral rehydration solutions, mosquito nets, clean water kits, vitamins, antibiotics and iodized salt. Many of these products are donated to PSI by foundations, multilateral international organizations or the overseas development agencies of donor governments. In other instances, donors provide funds to PSI, which procures products at favourable rates on the international market. PSI has also started to socially market health services such as voluntary HIV counselling and testing, and reproductive health services.

Social marketing and relationship building

Social marketing is about changing behaviour: encouraging people to give up smoking, take exercise or visit a sexual health clinic (Andreasen, 1994; Hastings, 2003).

These changes do not, for the most part, occur overnight. They involve a series of steps from initial contemplation through to reinforcement after the fact, a process that is both dynamic and precarious: the individual can regress or have a change of heart at any point.

Social marketing is founded on trust, and therefore it is necessary to start thinking in terms of long-term relationship building. Transactions are shallow and inadequate by comparison. If someone is trying to give up smoking, how much better to interact with them regularly and customize the offering to their needs at any particular stage in the process, rather than fire off ad hoc messages. Add to this the opportunity for cross-selling and up-selling, and the case becomes compelling. A telephone helpline that provides support for those quitting smoking can easily be used to encourage other lifestyle decisions, say about diet or physical activity.

As in commercial marketing, relationship building on this scale will be information technology dependent. Progress down this path has already begun. Database-mining techniques have been used to improve targeting in dietary and mammography interventions.

Databases used to generate bills could be adapted and customized to deliver positive health messages or products. Association with such messages and the health organizations that generate them could help make billing a less negative process and improve the company's corporate image. Moving from transactions to relationships adds the vital dimension of time to the social marketing exchange, which turns trust into commitment and enables long-term, strategic planning.

Figure 14.1 shows that social marketers need to think about building relationships in the same four domains as commercial companies. These are described in more detail below.

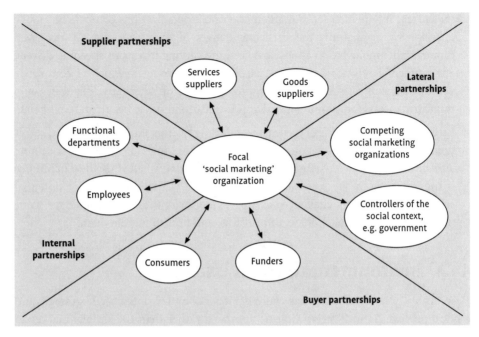

Figure 14.1 Relationships of the focal 'social marketing' organization
Source: adapted from Hastings (2003: 11)

1 **Buyer partnerships:** a distinction is made between the ultimate customer (the beneficiary of the social marketer's endeavours), such as the smoker, and the funder of their activities, such as the government health department (Bagozzi, 1974). With the latter, good relationships can ensure that projects are set realistic objectives and that evaluation feedback will be in a form that helps policy decision-making. The resulting trust and commitment also reduces the tendency to determine renewed funding purely on the basis of bottom-line results. More fundamentally, building relationships with funders enables the social marketer to influence the setting, as well as the implementation, of the policy agenda, which strengthens not just the discipline's effectiveness but also its ethical foundation. Without it, social marketers run the risk of becoming political pawns, who might deliver micro effectiveness but ignore macro issues.

2 **Supplier partnerships:** in the case of suppliers, such as advertising agencies or market research providers, long-term relationships help bridge cultural differences between the private and public sector, and ensure that progress is built on consensus, matched agendas and clearly agreed long-term goals.

3 **Lateral partnerships:** the benefits of working with governments and other controllers of the social context have already been discussed. Strategic alliances with competing social marketers can facilitate efficiency savings and improve competitiveness, just as in commerce. They can also help prioritize issues. This is vital given

417

the current fragmented social marketplace where organizations compete for public attention by highlighting the particular danger of their choosing. At any given moment, the public has to choose between the varying threats of speeding drivers, environmental tobacco smoke and alcohol abuse (none of which is completely within their control). A combined approach, based on long-term alliances, could transform threats into a multifaceted opportunity to improve health and well-being.

4 **Internal partnerships:** as in commerce, fulfilling relationships with external stakeholders depends on the whole organization pulling together. Great data mining and strong interactive communications will be undermined if the dispatch office is unresponsive or the receptionist is obstructive. This multiplicity of potential relationships presents challenges as well as opportunities. Decisions have to be made about which stakeholders to prioritize and how to handle them.

14.4 **Environmental/green issues**

Responsible green marketing has evolved into a complex, integrated, strategic and tactical process. As such, it is a holistic approach rather than the simple 'marketing hype' or tactical opportunism practised by some. It expands on the basic transaction concept by minimizing a transaction's negative impact on the natural environment. Understanding corporate motivations and pressures for 'greening' is essential, because it shapes how green marketing is implemented throughout all organizational activities.

Green, or environmental, marketing is expected to change customers' outlook, provide a new direction for competition and gain market acceptance for innovative environmental solutions. Within the framework of environment-conscious management, green marketing has a duty to ensure that environmental pollution is avoided or reduced at every stage of market-orientated activity (planning, co-ordination, implementation and inspection). The aim is to achieve corporate objectives by permanently satisfying the needs of current or potential clients while exploiting competitive advantages and safeguarding social legitimacy (Meffert and Kirchgeorg, 1998).

In the long run, ecologically and economically ineffective partial solutions could jeopardize the credibility and legitimacy of the enterprise in the market as well as in the community at large. To avoid this, it is essential that marketing management should develop a specific conception of green marketing.

Levels of 'green' marketing

Green marketing activities can occur at three levels in the firm (Polonsky, 2001): strategic, quasi-strategic and tactical.

1 In *strategic greening*, there is a substantial fundamental change in corporate philosophy, such as the Australian firm CarLovers designing its entire carwash process as a closed-loop, recycled-water system (Hollensen, 2004).

2 *Quasi-strategic greening* entails a substantial change in business practices. To reduce water consumption, for example, some hotel chains have begun asking guests to indicate when they want their towels washed by leaving them on the bathroom floor or in the bathtub.

3 With *tactical greening*, there is a shift in functional activities, such as promotion. For instance, in times of drought water authorities might use promotional campaigns to encourage consumers to behave in a more responsible, water-conserving manner.

These three levels can be used to identify the amount of change a firm requires and may reflect the degree of commitment to various environmental objectives. Take the example of a jeans manufacturer who, in the early 1990s, promoted the fact that it would donate a proportion of each sale to be used for planting trees. Such a tactical activity might have been viewed with intense scepticism because there is no apparent logical link between making jeans and planting trees.

Environmental issues in relation to the marketing mix

Product

A product life cycle analysis can provide a sound basis for more eco-friendly solutions to the problems associated with product and packaging policies. In order to resolve product-related environmental problems, it is necessary to analyse the various spheres of responsibility of the supplier, manufacturer, distributor and consumer. From now on, marketing specialists will have to analyse the organization of closed-loop value chains with all of the consequences of this for product design (long-life products, the growing importance of after-sales service, the sale of utility instead of products). Instruments of product policy include product innovation, product variation and product elimination designed to bring programmes into line with ecological requirements. While product variations involve modifying existing products in accordance with ecologically orientated demands, ecologically orientated product innovations entail launching entirely new product concepts on the market.

The introduction of 'takeback' regulations in most European countries obliges both producers and retailers to develop eco-friendly products, packaging and logistic alternatives as part of their product policy. The new regulations are based on the principle of sustainable development and aim to ensure that producers will be forced to play an active part in implementing a circular economy. This new definition of product responsibility can be regarded as a further step in the implementation of the prevention and 'polluter pays' principle, which has guided environmental policy in European countries.

Eco-friendly solutions often require a modification of the logistics and goods representation at the point of sale. The preparation of an ecological balance sheet for packaging materials and packaging systems (e.g. non-returnable and multi-way packaging) will ultimately be the only means of finding out which form of packaging can be considered the most environmentally friendly.

Distribution (place)

Just as producers have traditionally had to choose between various kinds of distribution channel, so they now have to concern themselves increasingly with the task of choosing an appropriate 'retro distribution' channel. The implementation of the closed-loop value chain in green marketing forces us to rethink the distribution mix.

Closed-loop supply chains consist of a *forward supply chain* and a *reverse supply chain*. Loops can be closed in several ways: reusing the product as a whole, reusing the components or reusing the materials. Most closed-loop supply chains will involve a mix of reuse options, where the various returns are processed through the most profitable alternative.

There are five key business processes involved in the reverse chain (Krikke *et al.*, 2004). The importance and sequence of these processes may differ from chain to chain.

1 **Product acquisition:** this concerns retrieving the product from the market (sometimes by active buy-back) as well as physically collecting it. The timing of quality, quantity and composition needs to be managed in close co-operation with the supply chain parties close to the final customer.

2 **Reverse logistics:** this involves the transportation to the location of recovery. An intermediate step for testing and inspection may be needed.

3 **Sorting and disposition:** returns need to be sorted by quality and composition in order to determine the remaining route in the reverse chain. This sorting may depend on the outcome of the testing and inspection process. However, the disposition decision depends not only on product characteristics, but also on market demand.

4 **Recovery:** this is the process of retrieving, reconditioning and regaining products, components and materials. In principle, all recovery options may be applied either in the original supply chain or in some alternative supply chain. As a rule of thumb, the high-level options are mostly applied in the original supply chain and the lower-level options in alternative supply chains. In some areas, the reuse in alternative supply chains is referred to as 'open-loop' applications.

5 **Redistribution and sales:** this process largely coincides with the distribution and sales processed in the forward chain. Additional marketing efforts may be needed to convince the customer of the quality of the product. In alternative chains, separate channels need to be set up and new markets may need to be developed.

The objectives of EU eco regulation are to promote products with a reduced environmental impact throughout their entire life cycle and to provide better information to consumers on the environmental impacts of products. The EU eco-labelling scheme, issued as a regulation, applies directly to all member states and is EU-wide. It is a voluntary scheme and should be self-financing.

Pricing

While green products are often 'priced higher' than traditional goods, this does not always mean they cost more, especially when one considers all associated costs.

Often, green goods have higher initial out-of-pocket expenses but lower long-term costs.

Decisions relating to pricing are mainly determined by the consumer's sensitivity to price, but the need to integrate the cost of legally stimulated pollution control now plays an increasingly important role in this domain.

Pricing strategies should be based on a segmentation of actual and potential target groups classified with the aid of three criteria:

1 ecological awareness

2 personal affectedness

3 willingness to pay a price for pollution control.

Segments displaying varying degrees of price sensitivity constitute the basis for price differentiation strategies.

As a matter of principle, lower introductory prices for eco-friendly products help customers to reorientate their buyer behaviour, thereby facilitating a more rapid diffusion of eco-friendly products. Combined costing at the expense of non-eco-friendly products can ensure a necessary balance here. The return of used packaging and products raises the question of pricing incentives for retro distribution.

Exhibit 14.3 **Marketing planning from an Islamic ethical perspective**

Islam provides a framework that shapes the moral and ethical behaviour of a growing number of Muslim consumers around the globe. These consumers constitute about one-quarter of the total world population and represent a majority in more than 50 countries. In addition, an increasing number of Muslim countries represent some of the most affluent consumers in the world.

There is a growing momentum towards the formation of a Muslim trading bloc. Also the current political mood indicates that there appears to be a definitive push towards greater 'Islamization' of countries where Muslims are in the majority (e.g. Egypt, Algeria, Pakistan, Sudan and Afghanistan to name but a few) in the form of a return to the application of Islamic law (Shari'ah) to all facets of life and thought.

Islamic teachings and religious beliefs are completely incorporated in all economic activities in Muslim countries. It follows that a person's entire life represents a series of activities for which he/she is responsible and will be accountable for to God. Given that commercial transactions are part and parcel of people's daily lives, in Islam undertaking of each and every transaction represents a task that must be executed in accordance with Islamic law and teachings. It is not surprising to learn, therefore, that marketing ethics merit special attention in Islam and constitute a separate discipline underpinned by the documented practices of the Prophet himself.

It follows from the above that any commercial activity, from an Islamic perspective, is governed by two principles: first, submission to the moral order of God and, second, empathy and mercy to God's creations, which implies refraining from doing harm to others and thus preventing the spread of unethical practices.

Islam does not recognize any division between the temporal and the spiritual dimensions. It can appear, at times, to be in conflict with contemporary western marketing practices based primarily on profit maximization. According to the Islamic perspective, such pursuits, based on satisfying material objectives alone, will impede the rational thinking of people and will make them the slaves of marketing firms.

Source: adapted from Al-Buraey, M.A.(2004) Marketing mix management from an Islamic perspective: some insights. *Journal of International Marketing & Marketing Research* 29(3), pp. 139–53; Saeed, M., Ahmed, Z.U. and Mukhtar, S.-M. (2001) International marketing ethics from an Islamic perspective: a value-maximization approach. *Journal of Business Ethics* 32(2), pp. 127–42; Zainul, N., Osman, F. and Mazlan, S.H. (2004) E-commerce from an Islamic perspective. *Electronic Commerce Research & Applications* 3(3), pp. 280–94

Communication

One of the most difficult questions to address is 'What environmental information should be communicated and how should it be communicated?' A primary issue is that there must be something worthwhile to talk about. A good deal of environmental promotion has been labelled 'greenwash' – having little, if any, real ecological meaning. This type of superficial tactical greening is no longer appropriate, and both consumers and regulators are unwilling to accept it. Communicating substantive environmental information is a more appropriate approach to take, but requires real activity changes in order to be meaningful.

Many firms realize that green promotion alone is becoming less effective, so they are shifting to promoting ecological attributes in addition to more traditional ones. It is questionable, for example, whether environmental sponsorships and cause-related marketing programmes will be effective, especially if they are seen as unrelated to a firm's core marketing activities or products. Thus, all green promotional activities need to be evaluated carefully to ensure that the firm is not criticized for greenwashing.

Green promotion needs to communicate substantive environmental information to consumers that has meaningful links to corporate activities. Thus, promoting some real environmental attribute of a product or firm requires a change in the product, process or corporate focus (integration with other activities). Firms should work out holistic, environmentally friendly solutions to their problems before offering information to the public. Yet even when this necessary condition is fulfilled, problems can arise when companies attempt to apply classical advertising techniques (e.g. emotional and empirically orientated sales messages) to the organization of the credible, environmentally orientated marketing messages that can, must or ought to be transmitted. They must also determine to what extent communication in the relevant sector is dominated by environmental arguments.

Summary

Ethics means the standards by which behaviour is judged. Why, though, do we need ethics when we already have the law, which tells us what we can and cannot do? One answer is that the letter of the law is generally considered to be only a minimum ethical standard.

Standards and beliefs about what is right and proper change over time. Thus the question of ethics is becoming more important as our economy becomes more competitive and global, and our technology more complex. Marketing ethics involves moral judgements, standards and rules of conduct relating to marketing decisions and situations.

Bribery distorts the operation of fair bargaining, and sales people should resist any temptation to bribe or accept bribes from those decision-makers who might want to engage in such activity. The use of bribes, although widespread and considered acceptable behaviour within some cultures, should be refused tactfully, allowing sales people to act in the best interests of their employers and in fairness to all customers. Bribery is not only unethical, it can also be illegal.

Social marketing can be defined as the planning and implementation of programmes designed to generate social change (e.g. stop smoking by lifestyle change). Social marketing is a system that can be used to change the way people think or behave. It is still based on concepts of commercial marketing, though. Social marketing, like commercial marketing, utilizes research to tailor messages to a particular target audience. For example, if a company is promoting an issue of major importance to encourage women to take part in annual mammogram testing, the target audience would obviously be women. Consequently, a social marketing campaign would concentrate on adapting commercial techniques to attract and persuade women as necessary.

The goal of social marketing is to get people to think differently about old ideas, and to focus on new concepts that will add values to their lives. Social marketing is especially prevalent among non-profit organizations, government agencies, community-based organizations, private foundations, social/health/ issue coalitions, and indeed any entity that wants to effect social change.

The last decade has seen a paradigm shift in commercial marketing, from transactional to relational thinking, and social marketers need to grasp the opportunity this presents. This has dramatic implications for the discipline, changing it from a branch line of public health to a whole new way of thinking about social problems.

Although environmental issues influence all human activities, few academic disciplines have integrated green issues into their literature. This is especially true of marketing. As society becomes more concerned with the natural environment, businesses have begun to modify their behaviour in an attempt to address society's 'new' concerns. Some businesses have been quick to accept concepts like environmental-management systems and waste minimization, and have integrated environmental issues into all organizational activities.

Green marketing incorporates a broad range of activities, including product modification, changes to the production process and packaging changes, as well as modifying advertising. Yet defining green marketing is not a simple task. Indeed, the terminology used in this area has varied and includes: green marketing, environmental marketing and ecological marketing.

No matter why a firm uses green marketing there are a number of potential problems that must be overcome. One of the main ones is that firms using green marketing must ensure that their activities are not misleading to consumers or industry, and do not breach any of the regulations or laws dealing with environmental marketing.

Another problem firms face is that those who modify their products due to increased consumer concern must contend with the fact that consumers' perceptions are sometimes incorrect. One example of this is that McDonald's is often blamed for polluting the environment because much of its packaging ends up as roadside waste. It must be remembered, however, that it is the uncaring consumer that chooses to dispose of their waste in this inappropriate fashion.

Questions for discussion

1 What conflicts of ethical issues and acceptable corporate behaviour might face a company operating across a spread of international markets?

2 What are the major competing views of corporate responsibility?

3 Why should marketers be concerned with using environmental (green) metrics of performance?

4 How important is the question of bribery in international marketing? What can be done on an international basis to counter it?

5 What role do you think cultural differences play in ethical standards?

6 What are the key elements of a successful corporate ethics programme?

References

Andreasen, A.R. (1994) Social marketing: its definition and domain. *Journal of Public Policy and Marketing* 13(1), pp. 108–14.

Bagozzi, Richard P. (1974) Marketing as an organized behavioral system of exchange. *Journal of Marketing* 38, October, pp. 77–81.

Ferrell, O.C. (2004) Business ethics and customer stakeholders. *Academy of Management Executive* 18(2), pp. 126–9.

Hastings, G. (2003) Relational paradigms in social marketing. *Journal of Macromarketing* 23(1), June, pp. 6–15.

Hollensen, S. (2004) *Global marketing – a decision-orientated approach.* Financial Times/Prentice Hall.

Krikke, H., Blanc, I.L. and Vedde, S. (2004) Product modularity and the design of closed-loop supply chains. *California Management Review* 46(2), Winter, pp. 23–39.

Meffert, H. and Kirchgeorg, M. (1998) *Marktorientiertes Umweltmanagement* (3rd edn). Stuttgart: Schäffer-Poeschel.

Polonsky, M.J. (2001) Revaluating green marketing: a strategic approach. *Business Horizons* 44(5), Sept/Oct, pp. 21–31.

Sanyal, R.N. and Samanta, S.K. (2004) Determinants of bribery in international business. *Thunderbird International Business Review* 46, March–April, pp. 133–48.

Thomas, D. (2004) 'Natural' cigarette launch causes health controversy. *Marketing Week*, 10 May, p. 8.

Case 14 The Body Shop: is it an 'ethical' company?

The Body Shop is a single-brand cosmetics and toiletries producer and retailer, which began as one shop in Brighton, UK, in 1976. Founded by the renowned campaigner Anita Roddick, The Body Shop retains its core values, continuing its campaigning activities and working towards its ultimate goal of being socially, economically and ecologically sustainable. The Body Shop is a globally recognized and respected brand, with an ethical and environmental ethos, as well as the pioneer of natural-ingredient products that are bought on the basis of fair trade.

Today, The Body Shop International plc is a UK-based cosmetics and toiletries firm, with products that are made from natural ingredients, such as its best-selling offerings of Peppermint Foot Lotion, Cocoa Butter Hand and Body Lotion, and Banana Shampoo. The company retails bath and shower products, colour cosmetics, hair, skin and sun care, and men's grooming products. The Body Shop combines social and environmental activism with marketing, and encourages women to focus on self-esteem issues.

Despite relatively strong brand awareness in Europe and North America, the company is ranked only 36th in the industry, with a world share of just 0.4 per cent. The Body Shop's portfolio of products covers most areas of the cosmetics and toiletries market, particularly in colour cosmetics and bath and shower products. There are over 600 products and more than 400 accessories in the company's portfolio, in the mid-priced segment of the cosmetics and toiletries market.

The business's growth has been organic, with a simple formula of franchises coupled with company-owned shops, both in the UK and abroad. In 2003, there were only 14 new store openings, bringing its total to 1968 shops. Of the 1968 stores, there are 1397 franchises and 571 company-owned shops. Organic growth will continue with new store openings as a means of increasing sales in the short term.

Competition from low-cost producers such as pharmacy chains Boots and Superdrug, and multiple retailers Safeway, Tesco and Sainsbury's, as well as strong competition from rivals such Estée Lauder's Aveda range of organic cosmetics and Limited Brand's Bath & Body Works, will intensify. The company is expected to continue to restructure in order to co-ordinate marketing and improve distribution efficiency.

Table 14.1 shows the most important data for financial year 2003/04 by geographic region.

Table 14.1 Body Shop stores by location and revenue, 2003/04

	Number	Revenue (£mn)	Operating profits (£mn)
UK and Ireland	313	130	10.0
Americas	416	126	19.3
Europe and Middle East	754	72	14.2
Asia-Pacific	313	53	18.5
Total	**2007**	**381**	**62.0**

Typically, 70 per cent of revenues are generated in the two months before Christmas.

The 'ethical policy' of The Body Shop is made up of three areas:

1 human and civil rights

2 environmental sustainability

3 animal protection.

The product portfolio of The Body Shop

The Body Shop is uni-brand, which means that all of its products fall under one umbrella brand: The Body Shop. The Body Shop's product portfolio covers most areas of the cosmetics and toiletries market, particularly colour cosmetics and bath and shower products. As mentioned above, there are over 600 products and more than 400 accessories in the company's portfolio, and these fall into the mid-price segment of the cosmetics and toiletries market. The company's products are derived from natural ingredients, and raw materials obtained on the basis of fair trade.

The brand benefits from the ethical and environmental ethos expounded by Body Shop founder, Anita Roddick. The company was the first to denounce the testing of cosmetics products on animals, as well as focus on issues relating to the exploitation of 'third world' resources. The Body Shop is connected to several highly publicized causes, for some of which it partners with Greenpeace and Amnesty International.

The Body Shop world market share

The Body Shop is an unusual player in the global cosmetics and toiletries industry in that its focus lies with its value system and its reliance on natural ingredients that it has sourced itself. A comparison could be made with Molton Brown, the producer of premium cosmetics and toiletries, which has focused on selling its products in premium department and boutique stores as well as in its own shops. Its products are also used by many leading hotels, leisure complexes and spas in their bedrooms and public areas, which is a key element of the company's marketing strategy. Like The Body Shop, Molton Brown uses natural ingredients, although its market position is at the higher end, as it is a brand synonymous with quality.

The Body Shop International plc is ranked only 36th in sales of cosmetics and toiletries with a 0.4 per cent world value share in 2002 (see Table 14.2), despite strong brand awareness in Europe and North America. The company had the highest shares in cosmetics and toiletries in Singapore with 2.5 per cent of sales, followed by a 1.4 per cent share in the UK, compared with only 0.2 per cent in the USA in 2002.

Table 14.2 The Body Shop International plc: world market shares and ranking by sector, 2002

% retail value RSP (retail sales price)	World market share	World market ranking
Bath and shower products	0.7	15
Deodorants	0.1	37
Colour cosmetics	0.9	16
Men's grooming products	0.1	34
Fragrances	0.4	27
Skin care	0.4	28
Sun care	0.2	38
Cosmetics and toiletries	0.4	36

Source: author estimates, adapted from company report, trade sources and Euromonitor

Global share was underpinned by decreased sales in colour cosmetics and fragrances, where it has been hit by strong competition from rivals such as Boots and Estée Lauder's Aveda range of organic cosmetics and fragrances. Recent growth in sales was supported by new product launches, better in-house point-of-sale promotions, and general promotional activity. The company embarked on a major packaging and brand design relaunch in 2002, in order to rejuvenate its ageing image.

Despite the fact that The Body Shop is best known for bath and shower products, the company held only a 0.7 per cent value share and a rank of 15 in bath and shower products in 2002. Sales of such products were particularly strong in the UK, Sweden and Finland. Additional growth in bath and shower products over the next few years is, however, expected to come from the Asia-Pacific region. The company's performance in bath and shower products has been less than robust, and the era has since passed when the company led sales of bath and shower products made from natural ingredients.

In addition to Boots, Safeway and Estée Lauder's Aveda products, The Body Shop faces fierce competition from companies such as British food retailers Tesco plc and J. Sainsbury plc. These firms are attempting to erode share in bath and shower products with innovative product launches. The Body Shop may be able to maintain regional share, particularly in the relatively strong western European region in the short term, if the company's efforts to revamp its products result in more robust sales.

The company had a global colour cosmetics value share of 0.9 per cent in 2002, and a world ranking of 16th. The Body Shop's colour cosmetics share has remained static due to rival offerings.

The Body Shop's share in fragrances was 0.4 per cent in 2002, with a world ranking of 27th. While fragrances are popular in Australasia, particularly in Australia, as well as a relatively strong presence in Africa and the Middle East, specifically in Saudi Arabia, fragrances' presence was weak in western Europe and North America. The company's performance in fragrances is marginal in general, as The Body Shop has yet to produce the sort of brands able to rival high-street shops' own offerings and the plethora of fragrances that can be found in most department stores.

The Body Shop also had a 0.4 per cent value share in skin care in 2002, and a world ranking of only 28th. This was despite the growth potential of skin care, particularly anti-ageing products. The company's skin care range does particularly well in the UK, Sweden and Saudi Arabia, albeit only marginally. The company may be able to maintain its level of regional share in the short term, but will continue to lose share to rival brands in the medium term due to intense competition.

Company market share by geographic region and sector

The Body Shop's cosmetics and toiletries business has been stagnating. In general, weak demand in most product lines has been exacerbated, as already mentioned, by strong competition from rivals such as Boots and Estée Lauder's Aveda range, which has helped stultify the company's share in most regions. In order to attempt to redress this stagnation in consumer demand, the company embarked on a major packaging and brand design and relaunch in 2002. The new packaging will, it is hoped, aid in rejuvenating the brand's ageing image.

The Body Shop had the highest shares in bath and shower products in western Europe (1.3 per cent), with top shares in the UK (3.5 per cent), followed by strong shares in Sweden (3.3 per cent) and Finland with 2.7 per cent. Meanwhile in North America, bath and shower products' value share was 0.9 per cent, with the highest share in the USA (1 per cent).

Despite Asia-Pacific share in bath and shower products being only 0.5 per cent, the largest market share (5.2 per cent) was in Singapore, followed by Hong Kong (0.6 per cent). The Body Shop has not been able to increase its share in this sector and may find it difficult to do so in the short term due to increased competition from rival brands with products made from natural ingredients. However, demand increases could be realized if the company expanded its presence in Asia-Pacific.

The highest share in The Body Shop's colour cosmetics was in western Europe (2.2 per cent), with the highest shares being in the UK (3.1 per cent) and Greece (1.6 per cent). Demand for colour cosmetics had improved only in the UK, remaining at the same levels over the past year in most other markets. The Body Shop's share of colour cosmetics in Africa and the Middle East was 0.8 per cent, with a significant share in Saudi Arabia (1.4 per cent). The Body Shop's colour cosmetics suffer from increased competition from products found in drugstores and department stores, such as Maybelline, Rimmel and Revlon.

The Body Shop's regional fragrances share was highest in Asia-Pacific with a 1.2 per cent share, followed by Africa and the Middle East with 0.6 per cent, and 0.4 per cent in western Europe. Fragrances were particularly strong in Saudi Arabia, where the company held a value share of 1.7 per cent in 2002. The company faces strong competition from direct sales firms, such as Avon and Mary Kay (which are able to continue to launch new products), as well as from private-label products.

The Body Shop's regional share of skin care sales was highest in Africa and the Middle East at 1.4 per cent in 2002. Western Europe's share of 0.6 per cent was a distant second, followed by 0.5 per cent in North America and 0.3 per cent in Asia-Pacific. While The Body Shop's share of skin care was highest in the UK (2.7 per cent) and Sweden (1.8 per cent), the company's skin care share was 1.6 per cent in Saudi Arabia and 1.3 per cent in Hong Kong. The company may be able to maintain its regional shares in the short term, since it has launched a skin care range based on the plant extract kinetin. (The company claims that kinetin contains antioxidants that were originally discovered in green leaves.) Yet future growth will be driven by technological developments in new products, such as anti-wrinkle creams. The Body Shop has an opportunity to fully exploit this sector, since most good anti-ageing products are at present from Shiseido, Estée Lauder and L'Oréal, and are at high price points.

Table 14.3 The Body Shop International plc: regional share by sector, 2002

% retail value RSP Product type	Western Europe	Eastern Europe	North America	Latin America	Asia	Australia/ NZ	Africa/ Middle East
Baby care	–	–	–	–	–	–	–
Bath and shower products	1.3	–	0.9	–	0.5	0.7	0.2
Deodorants	0.3	–	–	–	–	–	–
Hair care	0.1	–	–	–	–	–	–
Colour cosmetics	2.2	–	0.5	–	0.8	–	0.8
Men's grooming products	0.3	–	0.1	–	0.1	–	0.2
Fragrances	0.4	–	0.3	–	1.2	–	0.6
Skin care	0.6	–	0.5	–	0.3	–	1.4
Depilatories	0.2	–	–	–	–	–	–
Sun care	0.2	–	0.1	–	0.5	–	–
Cosmetics and toiletries	0.6	–	0.3	–	0.3	–	0.4

Source: author estimates, adapted from company report, trade sources and Euromonitor

Competitive situation

Despite its recently weak financial performance, The Body Shop International plc is a relatively strong brand and concept, and one that has yet to be replicated fully. While it is true that its products are emulated by rival competitors, no other company appeals to such a wide range of customers, based on an ethical and environmental ethos as a basis for doing business.

Competitors such as Boots' Botanics in the UK, Safeway's Nutri-therapy range and Estée Lauder's Aveda products have recently emerged. In addition, The Body Shop must contend with rivals such as British food retailers Tesco plc and J. Sainsbury plc. Increased competition from low-cost producers such as pharmacy chains Boots and Superdrug, and multiple retailers Safeway, Tesco and Sainsbury's, threaten to make The Body Shop's products seem increasingly expensive. In fact, The Body Shop has been criticized for selling low-end products at a premium price.

In North America, speciality stores in the USA, the Limited Brands' Bath & Body Works, and in Canada, Shoppers Drug Mart Corp., Wal-Mart Canada Corp., Costco Wholesale Canada Ltd and Loblaw Cos Ltd have entered the beauty business with products made from natural ingredients.

These firms are attempting to erode The Body Shop's market share through innovative product launches. The Body Shop may be able to compete somewhat in the short term if the company's efforts to revamp its products stimulate demand. However, price points may be too high to maintain strong demand in the medium term. Still, The Body Shop has attempted to reclaim lost share with new product launches, improved store formats and door-to-door sales.

Increasing market share from multinational players Procter & Gamble and L'Oréal continues to threaten The Body Shop's share across all business segments.

Marketing strategies

The Body Shop was launched on the back of its ethical, socially inclusive, environmentally sustainable stance, and this policy continues to drive its marketing initiatives. The company's campaigning activity centres around five core issues:

1 against animal testing

2 support community trade

3 activate self-esteem

4 defend human rights

5 protect our planet.

Marketing initiatives to date have tended to be predominantly, although not exclusively, campaign-based. This has helped to enforce the notion of the company's products to only a niche segment of the market, and has failed to refresh the company's image, despite it having updated its range in recent years.

Traditionally The Body Shop has spent very little on marketing compared with the industry average, which ranges from 15 to 20 per cent of sales. However, there may soon be a change in this regard (see below).

The company's marketing strategy focuses on sales improvement through new product launches with in-store promotions, including improved visual merchandising. Its most recent campaign, which was rolled out in both the UK and USA during 2003, surrounded the issue of domestic violence. In-store promotions raised around £90,000 for the UK-based domestic violence charity Refuge within six months of the campaign's launch, through a combination of badge sales and the recycling of mobile telephones, and by June 2004 had doubled its target, raising £110,000 in total. In the USA mobile phone recycling activities raised US$80,000 for the National Coalition Against Domestic Violence and the Wireless Foundation. The mobile phone recycling aspect of the campaign has also helped to positively reinforce The Body Shop's environmental values.

Charitable activity through The Body Shop Foundation

Other charitable work is carried out through The Body Shop Foundation, which was established in 1990 to support human rights and environmental protection groups. Included in the work carried out by the Foundation is the Children on the Edge charity, which exists to help the most marginalized children all over the world. The Body Shop Foundation was instrumental in the establishment of the *Big Issue* magazine project for the homeless, and part-funded the launch of the *Big Issue* in Los Angeles in early 1998.

In 1998, The Body Shop launched a joint campaign with Amnesty International to celebrate the 50th anniversary of the Universal Declaration of Human Rights, encouraging customers to 'Make their Mark' for human rights.

Traditional marketing activities also employed

Outside its campaigning issues, the company has also focused on more traditional marketing strategies. In particular, there has been a recent strategy of building its brand through global marketing programmes, following the trend of major companies across the world. These programmes have primarily been created to support new product launches and seasonal events, such as the launch of the new colour cosmetics range. Activities include sampling, gift-with-purchase initiatives and added-value promotions. At present, The Body Shop's advertising has not reached the broadcast media, and its national print advertising is primarily campaign-based.

As part of its £100 million investment programme, announced in 2004, The Body Shop has stated that it is to put greater emphasis on product marketing. This strategy is of vital importance to the company's future success, as although its campaigning stance brings it positive publicity with those who follow the company's established value system, it is vital that it promotes itself more strongly as a global producer of quality cosmetics and toiletries products. If it does not it is likely to remain a niche market within the international industry, no matter how much the company invests in its future.

In April 2002, The Body Shop entered into a joint promotion with *Marie Claire* magazine in order to launch the 'Body Shop Face of 2003' competition. The Body Shop Face of 2003 was a modelling competition open to women regardless of their shape, size, height or age. The competition was featured in the May 2002 edition of *Marie Claire*, and gave entrants the chance to appear in the magazine. The winner of the competition was expected to lead The Body Shop's 2003 marketing campaign, and to appear on all the company's promotional material.

Distribution strategies

The Body Shop International plc distributes its products via retail shops, mail order and direct sales through The Body Shop at Home (see Fig. 14.1).

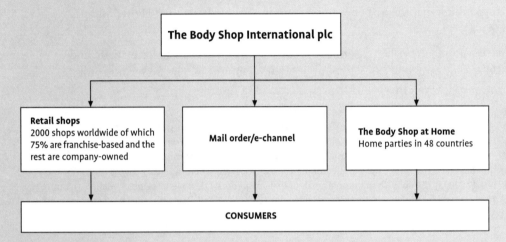

Figure 14.1 The Body Shop's distribution strategy

The company's products are distributed by transportation from the manufacturing plants run by Creative Outsourcing Solutions International (COSI), to The Body Shop's wholly owned distribution centres. However, the UK arm of The Body Shop at Home is not doing as well, and has been integrated into the retail business.

'The Body Shop at Home' is expected to grow

The Body Shop at Home has become a successful distribution channel for the company. The division has increased brand awareness through its direct sales consultants, of which there were 2300 in 2002. The Body Shop at Home is now active in 48 countries, and is performing above company expectations. The Body Shop at Home is the company's direct selling arm, which sees Body Shop products demonstrated and sold in the home environment by a number of trained consultants. This has proved a particularly important channel for the company, and is to be further boosted and expanded as part of its £100 mn investment programme, announced in April 2004.

Further investment in the e-channel

Another focus channel is retail Internet selling, which is also to be upgraded as part of the company's investment programme. In the USA, this is a significant channel, and improvements and enhancements to the company's facilities for dealing with such sales can only boost its position in the market.

Questions

1 Conduct a SWOT analysis for The Body Shop.

2 Do you regard The Body Shop as a 'true' ethical company?

3 Do you think that the £100 mn investment in 'The Body Shop at Home' will pay off? Why/Why not?

4 At the moment, men's grooming products (pre-shave, post-shave, bath and shower, hair care, skin care) account only for 3 per cent of The Body Shop's total turnover. How can this percentage be increased in future?

Source: Briney, C. (2004) Fragrance in Europe: bouncing back? *Global Cosmetic Industry* 10, October, pp. 30–3; Clayton, R. (2003) The Body Shop shapes up to challenge competitors. *Design Week* 18(46), pp. 7–12; Datamonitor (2004) Body Shop International plc SWOT analysis. *Datamonitor*, September; Duber-Smith, D. (2004) Natural color cosmetics enhance personal care opportunities. *Global Cosmetic Industry* 9, September, pp. 44–6; Euromonitor statistics (www.euromonitor.com); MarketWatch (2003) The Body Shop International, *Global Round-up* 2(11), November, pp. 81–90; Research and Markets Ltd (2002) Cosmetics to 2004: global lifestyles and attitudes, M2 PRESSWIRE, 16 December; www.thebodyshopinternational.com, annual results 2003–2004

INDEX